Blueprints

EU Law

Blueprints

Your plan for learning

EU Law

Penelope Kent

PEARSON

Harlow, England • London • New York • Boston • San Francisco • Toronto • Sydney • Auckland • Singapore • Hong Kong
Tokyo • Seoul • Taipei • New Delhi • Cape Town • São Paulo • Mexico City • Madrid • Amsterdam • Munich • Paris • Milan

Pearson Education Limited
Edinburgh Gate
Harlow CM20 2JE
United Kingdom
Tel: +44 (0)1279 623623
Web: www.pearson.com/uk

First published 2014 (print and electronic)

ISBN: 978-1-4082-7902-1 (print)
        978-1-4082-7904-5 (PDF)
        978-1-292-01512-5 (eText)

British Library Cataloguing-in-Publication Data
A catalogue record for the print edition is available from the British Library

Library of Congress Cataloging-in-Publication Data
Kent, Penelope, author.
  EU law / Penelope Kent.
    p. cm.
  Includes index.
  ISBN 978-1-4082-7902-1
  1. Law--European Union countries.   I. Title.   II. Title: European Union law.
  KJE947.K465 2014
  341.242'2--dc23

                                                        2014007327

10 9 8 7 6 5 4 3 2 1
18 17 16 15 14

Cover image © Getty Images

Print edition typeset in 10/12pt Helvetica Neue LT Pro by 35
Print edition printed in Great Britain by Henry Ling Ltd, at the Dorset Press, Dorchester, Dorset

NOTE THAT ANY PAGE CROSS REFERENCES REFER TO THE PRINT EDITION

Brief contents

PART 1

The constitutional law of the European Union and jurisdiction of the EU Courts 2

PART 2

Free movement and the single market 230

Contents

PART 1

The constitutional law of the European Union and jurisdiction of the EU Courts 2

1 The historical background to the European Union 5

2 Decision-making in the EU institutions 27

3 The Court of Justice and the preliminary reference procedure 53

10 Judicial review and damages claims 201

PART 2
Free movement and the single market 230

11 Customs duties, discriminatory taxation and state monopolies 233

12 The free movement of goods 247

13 Union citizenship 273

14 The free movement of workers 303

15 The right of establishment and the freedom to provide services 325

Table of cases and statutes

CASES

STATUTES

European Union secondary legislation

Listed by year and number; short forms follow alphabetically

Regulations

European Union other instruments

National legislation

France

Italy

Poland

Portugal

Spain

United Kingdom

International treaties and resolutions

EUROPEAN UNION TREATY EQUIVALENCES

Italic indicates contributions from/to the specified article(s)

Treaty on the European Union (TEU)

Before Treaty of Lisbon	In Treaty of Lisbon	After Treaty of Lisbon
Title III	Title III	Title III
Article 9 (repealed)	Article 9	Article 13
	Article 9A	Article 14
	Article 9B	Article 15
	Article 9C	Article 16
	Article 9D	Article 17
	Article 9E	Article 18
	Article 9F	Article 19
Title IV	Title IV	Title IV
Article 10 (repealed) (13)	Article 10	Article 20
Articles 27 A to 27 E (replaced)		
Articles 40 to 40 B (replaced)		
Articles 43 to 45 (replaced)		
Title V	Title V	Title V
Article 11	Article 11	Article 24
Article 27A (replaced)	*Article 10*	*Article 20*
Article 27B (replaced)	*Article 10*	*Article 20*
Article 27C (replaced)	*Article 10*	*Article 20*
Article 27D (replaced)	*Article 10*	*Article 20*
Article 27E (replaced)	*Article 10*	*Article 20*
Title VI		
Article 35 (repealed)		
Article 40 (replaced)	*Article 10*	*Article 20*
Article 40A (replaced)	*Article 10*	*Article 20*
Article 40B (replaced)	*Article 10*	*Article 20*
Title VII	Title IV	Title IV
Article 43 (replaced) (24)	*Article 10*	*Article 20*
Article 43A (replaced) (24)	*Article 10*	*Article 20*
Article 43B (replaced) (24)	*Article 10*	*Article 20*
Article 44 (replaced) (24)	*Article 10*	*Article 20*
Article 44A (replaced) (24)	*Article 10*	*Article 20*
Article 45 (replaced) (24)	*Article 10*	*Article 20*
Title VIII	Title VI	Title VI
	Article 46a	Article 47
Article 48	Article 48	Article 48
Article 49	Article 49	Article 49
	Article 49 A	Article 50

Treaty on the Functioning of the European Union (TFEU)

Before Treaty of Lisbon	In Treaty of Lisbon	After Treaty of Lisbon
Part One	Part One	Part One
	Article 2A	Article 2
	Article 2B	Article 3
	Article 2C	Article 4
	Article 2D	Article 5
	Article 2E	Article 6
Article 12 (repealed)	*Article 16D*	*Article 18*
Article 13 (moved)	*Article 16E*	*Article 19*
Article 14 (moved)	*Article 22a*	*Article 26*
Article 255 (moved)	Article 16A	Article 15
Article 286 (moved)	Article 16B	Article 16
	Article 16C	Article 17
Part Two	Part Two	Part Two
Article 12 (moved)	Article 16D	Article 18
Article 13 (moved)	Article 16E	Article 19
Article 17	Article 17	Article 20
Article 18	Article 18	Article 21
Article 19	Article 19	Article 22
Article 20	Article 20	Article 23
Article 21	Article 21	Article 24
Article 22	Article 22	Article 25
Part Three	Part Three	Part Three
Article 14 (moved)	Article 22a	Article 26
Article 23	Article 23	Article 28
Article 25	Article 25	Article 30
Article 26	Article 26	Article 31
Article 28	Article 28	Article 34
Article 29	Article 29	Article 35
Article 30	Article 30	Article 36
Article 31	Article 31	Article 37
Article 34	Article 34	Article 40
Article 37	Article 37	Article 43
Article 39	Article 39	Article 45
Article 40	Article 40	Article 46
Article 41	Article 41	Article 47
Article 42	Article 42	Article 48
Article 43	Article 43	Article 49
Article 44	Article 44	Article 50
Article 45	Article 45	Article 51
Article 46	Article 46	Article 52
Article 47	Article 47	Article 53
Article 48	Article 48	Article 54

Before Treaty of Lisbon	In Treaty of Lisbon	After Treaty of Lisbon
Article 294 (moved)	Article 48a	Article 55
Article 49	Article 49	Article 56
Article 50	Article 50	Article 57
Article 51	Article 51	Article 58
Article 52	Article 52	Article 59
Article 53	Article 53	Article 60
Article 54	Article 54	Article 61
Article 55	Article 55	Article 62
Article 56	Article 56	Article 63
Article 60 (moved)	*Article 61H*	*Article 75*
Title IV	Title V	Title V
Article 61	Article 61	Article 67
	Article 61A	Article 68
	Article 61B	Article 69
	Article 61C	Article 70
	Article 61D	Article 71
Article 64, paragraph 1 (replaced)	Article 61E	Article 72
	Article 61F	Article 73
Article 66 (replaced)	Article 61G	Article 74
Article 60 (moved)	Article 61H	Article 75
	Article 61I	Article 76
Article 62	Article 62	Article 77
Article 63, points 1 and 2, and Article 64, para 2	Article 63	Article 78
Article 63, points 3 and 4	Article 63a	Article 79
	Article 63b	Article 80
Article 64, paragraph 1 (replaced)	*Article 61E*	*Article 72*
Article 65	Article 65	Article 81
Article 66 (replaced)	*Article 61G*	*Article 74*
	Article 69A	Article 82
	Article 69B	Article 83
	Article 69C	Article 84
	Article 69D	Article 85
	Article 69E	Article 86
	Article 69F	Article 87
	Article 69G	Article 88
	Article 69H	Article 89
Article 81	Article 81	Article 101
Article 93	Article 93	Article 113
Article 95 (moved)	Article 94	Article 114
	Article 97a	Article 118
Article 106	Article 106	Article 128
Article 113 (moved)	*Article 245c*	*Article 294*
Article 133 (moved)	*Article 188C*	*Article 207*

Before Treaty of Lisbon	In Treaty of Lisbon	After Treaty of Lisbon
Article 150	Article 150	Article 166
Article 151	Article 151	Article 167
Article 154	Article 154	Article 170
Article 174	Article 174	Article 191
Article 175	Article 175	Article 192
Part Four	Part Four	Part Four
	Part Five	Part Five
Article 133 (moved)	Article 188 C	Article 207
Article 300 (replaced)	Article 188 N	Article 218
Part Five	Part Six	Part Six
Article 190, paras 4 and 5	Article 190	Article 223
Article 191, para 2	Article 191	Article 224
Article 193	Article 193	Article 226
Article 194	Article 194	Article 227
Article 195	Article 195	Article 228
Article 200	Article 200	Article 233
Article 201	Article 201	Article 234
Article 204	Article 204	Article 237
Article 205, paras 1 and 3	Article 205	Article 238
Article 207	Article 207	Article 240
Article 208	Article 208	Article 241
	Article 211a	Article 244
Article 212 (moved)	*Article 218, para 2*	*Article 249, para 2*
Article 213	Article 213	Article 245
Article 215	Article 215	Article 246
Article 216	Article 216	Article 247
Article 218, para 2	Article 218	Article 249
Article 221, paras 2 and 3	Article 221	Article 251
Article 222	Article 222	Article 252
Article 223	Article 223	Article 253
Article 224	Article 224	Article 254
	Article 224a	Article 255
Article 225	Article 225	Article 256
Article 225a	Article 225a	Article 257
Article 226	Article 226	Article 258
Article 227	Article 227	Article 259
Article 228	Article 228	Article 260
Article 230	Article 230	Article 263
Article 231	Article 231	Article 264
Article 232	Article 232	Article 265
Article 233	Article 233	Article 266
Article 234	Article 234	Article 267
Article 236	Article 236	Article 270
Article 239	Article 239	Article 273

Before Treaty of Lisbon	In Treaty of Lisbon	After Treaty of Lisbon
	Article 240a	Article 275
	Article 240b	Article 276
Article 241	Article 241	Article 277
Article 242	Article 242	Article 278
Article 243	Article 243	Article 279
Article 249	Article 249	Article 288
	Article 249A	Article 289
	Article 249B	Article 290
	Article 249C	Article 291
	Article 249D	Article 292
Article 250	Article 250	Article 293
Article 251	Article 251	Article 294
Article 253	Article 253	Article 296
Article 254	Article 254	Article 297
Article 255 (moved)	*Article 16 A*	*Article 15*
	Article 256a	Article 300
Article 259	Article 259	Article 302
Article 262	Article 262	Article 304
Article 263, paras 2–4	Article 263	Article 305
Article 265	Article 265	Article 307
Article 272, paras 2–10	Article 272	Article 314
Part Six	Part Seven	Part Seven
Article 286 (replaced)	*Article 16 B*	*Article 16*
Article 288	Article 288	Article 340
Article 294 (moved)	*Article 48a*	*Article 55*
Article 295	Article 295	Article 345
Article 300 (replaced)	*Article 188 N*	*Article 218*
Article 308	Article 308	Article 352
	Article 308a	Article 353

Acknowledgments

A number of people have played an important part in the preparation and production of this book. I am particularly grateful to my editors at Pearson Education, Josie O'Donoghue who oversaw the first half of the book, and Stuart Hay, who covered the second half. Both provided invaluable comments on draft chapters. Christine Statham, formerly Associate Editor for Law at Pearson, provided strategic direction for the series as a whole. Their expertise, patience and encouragement were greatly appreciated, as we explored the best way to present material within the new series. I would also like to thank the tabler, Gary Birch, for his care in checking the citations.

All the chapters in the book have been reviewed by four academic readers. While their comments were made anonymously, all four have agreed to waive their anonymity so I can now thank them publicly for their very thoughtful and constructive comments. They are Dr Theodore Konstanides, Senior Lecturer of the University of Surrey, Dr Jessica Guth, Lecturer at the University of Bradford, Dewi Williams, Senior Lecturer at Staffordshire University and Sarah Willis, Senior Lecturer at the University of Northampton. It has also been helpful to receive anonymous student feedback from a focus group arranged by Pearson. Needless to say, any errors are my own responsibility.

The many students of EU law I have taught over the years at Middlesex University also deserve recognition for their contribution to the development of my own ideas about the subject. Finally, my husband David has played a key part in supporting me over the two and a half years it has taken to write this book.

The law is as stated on 30 November 2013 although a few later points are included.

Penny Kent
November 2013

How to use this guide

Blueprints was created for students searching for a smarter introductory guide to their legal studies

This guide will serve as a primer for deeper study of the law – enabling you to get the most out of your lectures and studies by giving you a way in to the subject which is more substantial than a revision guide, but more succinct than your course textbook. The series is designed to give you an overview of the law, so you can see the structure of the subject and understand how the topics you will study throughout your course fit together in the big picture. It will help you keep your bearings as you move through your course study.

Blueprints recognises that students want to succeed in their course modules

This requires more than a basic grasp of key legislation; you will need knowledge of the historical and social context of the law, recognition of the key debates, an ability to think critically and to draw connections among topics.

Blueprints addresses the various aspects of legal study, using assorted text features and visual tools

Each Blueprints guide begins with an **Introduction**, outlining the parameters of the subject and the challenges you might face in your studies. This includes a **map** of the subject highlighting the major areas of study.

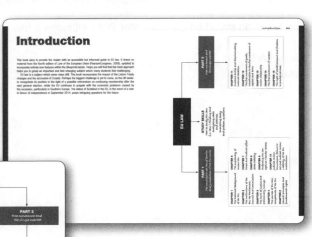

Each **Part** of the guide also begins with a map of the main topics you need to grasp and how they fit together.

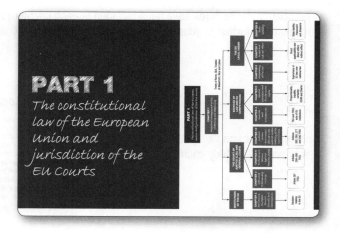

Each guide includes advice on the specific **study skills** you will need to do well in the subject.

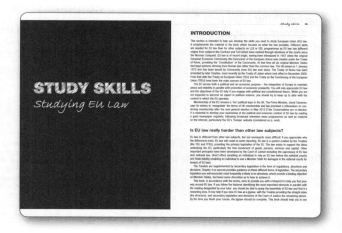

Each chapter starts with a **Blueprint** of the topic area to provide a visual overview of the fundamental buildings blocks of each topic, and the academic questions and the various outside influences that converge in the study of law.

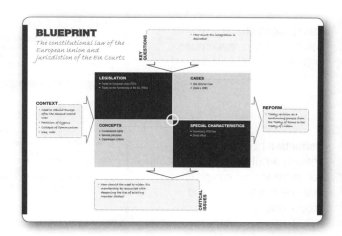

A number of text features have been included in each chapter to help you better understand the law and push you further in your appreciation of the subtleties and debates:

Setting the scene illustrates why it is important to study each topic.

Setting the scene

Imagine that Europe has been affected by a sudden increase in global warming leading to a severe and prolonged water shortage which could destroy crops, cause famine and threaten the economies of the Member States. How might such a problem be addressed within the EU? At a political level the European Council (a summit meeting of heads of state) would determine strategies and set priorities. The Council of the EU (a different body comprising ministers from Member States) would meet to address the problems posed by the shortage – in this case the ministers for agriculture, as well as ministers for environment and finance. The European Commission would monitor the position. The European Parliament would debate the water shortage. If the crisis persisted it may be necessary to adopt legislation, in which case a regulation or directive requiring water conservation measures would be drafted by the Commission for adoption by the Parliament and Council.

Cornerstone highlights the fundamental building blocks of the law.

CORNERSTONE

Conditions for direct effect

A Treaty provision which is intended to benefit individuals is directly effective when it is sufficiently clear, precise and unconditional (*Van Gend en Loos*, as amended by later decisions).

Application shows how the law applies in the real world.

APPLICATION

Imagine there is a serious problem of pollution in the River Rhine, which flows through several Member States before reaching the sea. Legislation is needed to address the problem. Who should legislate – the EU or the Member States? The environment is an area of shared competence under Article 4 TFEU. Applying the principle of subsidiarity, action should be taken by the Member States unless it can better be achieved by the EU. As action is likely to be more effective at EU level, an act (probably a directive) may be adopted by the EU. It should not impose any more restrictions than necessary, to accord with the principle of proportionality.

Intersection shows you connections and relationships with other areas of the law.

INTERSECTION

The problems posed by supremacy may sometimes be avoided by recourse to the principle of *indirect effect*, requiring national courts to interpret national legislation to comply with EU obligations, passed before *or* after the relevant EU law (Case C-106/89 *Marleasing*). (Indirect effect is considered further in Chapter 7.)

Reflection helps you think critically about the law, introducing you to the various complexities that give rise to debate and controversy.

REFLECTION

The Scottish government can charge students from England and Wales to attend university in Scotland as this is an internal situation in EU law, provided Scotland remains part of the UK, but not students from other Member States which would discriminate against them relative to students from Scotland paying no fees. This anomaly raises the question as to whether students from Northern Ireland entitled to apply for an Irish passport would have to pay fees as they would hold the nationality of another Member State.

Context fills in some of the historical and cultural background knowledge that will help you understand and appreciate the legal issues of today.

> Treaty reform reflects changes in the EU and varying levels of enthusiasm for European integration at different periods. The Single European Act, signed in 1986 when enthusiasm for integration was low, effectively 'relaunched' the Community. The Maastricht Treaty was adopted in 1992 during a period of greater support for integration led by France and Germany. The Constitutional Treaty failed due to lack of political support, and had to be followed by the less aspirational Treaty of Lisbon which was needed to address the challenges posed by enlargement.
>
> **CONTEXT**

Take note offers advice that can save you time and trouble in your studies.

> **Take note**
>
> The combination of direct effect, indirect effect and State liability is intended to provide a complete set of remedies under EU law in the national courts. These concepts are at the heart of the EU legal order and are essential for students to grasp.

This chapter examines the rules on *direct effect*, as well a those on *indirect effect* where the requirements for direct effe are not satisfied. The Court of Justice has also developed a thir type of remedy known as *State liability* where Member States ar in breach of EU law in certain circumstances (covered in Chapter 8

DIRECT APPLICABILITY AND DIRECT EFFECT

The terms 'direct applicability' and 'direct effect' are not define in the Treaties. In the early years of the Community the Court

Key points lists the main things to know about each topic.

KEY POINTS

- The EU has operated as a customs union since 1968.
- Customs duties are financial charges payable when goods cross a border. They are illegal when goods move between Member States, as are charges equivalent to customs duties.
- Member States may administer their own system of taxation provided it does not discriminate against goods from other Member States.

Core cases and statutes summarises the major case law and legislation in the topic.

CORE CASES AND STATUTES

Case	About	Importance
Case 166/73 *Rheinmühlen v. Einfuhr- und Vorratsstelle Getreide*	Referral by German court to clarify law on refusal of export licence.	Established that preliminary reference procedure provides uniform interpretation throughout EU.
Case 104/79 and Case 244/80 *Foglia and Novello (No. 1 & No. 2)*	Two wine merchants agreed to sell wine to third, provided one seller should not be liable for charges contrary to EU law.	CJEU refused to answer questions as they were 'artificial', having arisen from 'dispute' found to have been concocted to obtain ruling on

Further reading directs you to select primary and secondary sources as a springboard to further studies.

FURTHER READING

Craig, P. 'The legal effect of directives: policy, rules and exceptions' (2009) 34 *European Law Review* 349
Reconsiders the legal effect of directives in EU law, critically examining the policy underlying denial of horizontal effect.

Curtin, D. 'The province of government: Delimiting the direct effect of directives in the common

Laenaerts, K. and Gutiérez-Fons, J. A. 'The constitutional allocation of powers and general principles of EU law' (2010) 47 *Common Market Law Review* 1629
Examines the role of general principles in filling the gaps left by the Treaties and secondary legislation.

Pescatore, P. 'The doctrine of direct effect: an infant disease of

A **glossary** provides helpful definitions of key terms.

Accession The act of a new Member State joining the EU.

Acte clair Where the meaning is clear, national courts need not refer a question for interpretation to Court of Justice (CJEU) under Article 267 TFEU.

Acte éclairé When CJEU has already pronounced on a materially identical point, there is no need to refer under Article 267 TFEU.

Acts of the EU institutions Acts adopted under Article 288(1) TFEU to exercise the

Charge having equivalent effect (CEE) Pecuniary charge imposed on domestic or foreign goods crossing a frontier and which is not a customs duty in the strict sense. CEEs are prohibited under Article 30 TFEU.

Charter of Fundamental Rights Annexed to Treaty of Nice as Declaration but given same legal value as Treaties by Treaty of Lisbon, so it can be invoked before national courts.

Comitology Process of delegation of legislative powers to committees, reformed by Treaty of Lisbon which introduced new

What is a Blueprint?

Blueprints provide a unique plan for studying the law, giving you a visual overview of the fundamental buildings blocks of each topic, and the academic questions and the various outside influences that converge in the study of law.

At the centre are the 'black-letter' elements, the fundamental building blocks that make up what the law says and how it works.

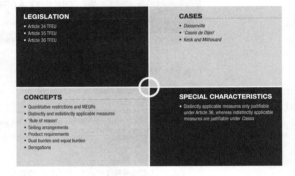

As a law student you will need to learn what questions or problems the law attempts to address, and what sort of issues arise from the way it does this that require critical reflection.

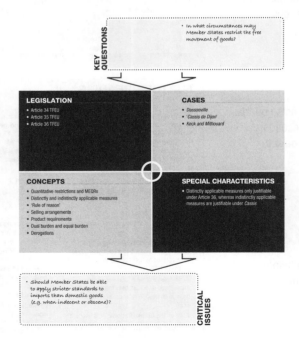

To gain a more complete understanding of the role of law in society you will need to know what influencing factors have shaped the law in the past, and how the law may develop in the near future.

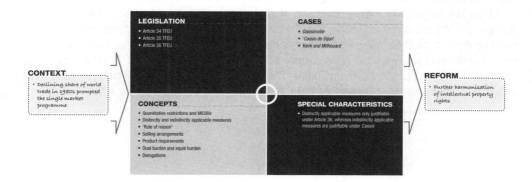

You can use the Blueprint for each topic as a framework for building your knowledge in the subject.

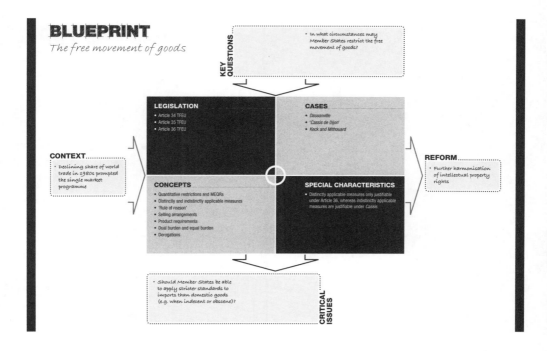

Introduction

This book aims to provide the reader with an accessible but informed guide to EU law. It draws on material from the fourth edition of *Law of the European Union* (Pearson/Longman, 2008), updated to incorporate entirely new features within the *Blueprints* series. I hope you will find that this fresh approach helps you to grasp an important and fast-changing subject which many students find challenging.

EU law is a subject which never stays still. This book incorporates the impact of the Lisbon Treaty changes and the accession of Croatia. Perhaps the biggest challenge is yet to come, as the UK seeks to renegotiate its position in the light of a possible referendum on continuing membership after the next general election, while the EU continues to grapple with the economic problems caused by the recession, particularly in Southern Europe. The status of Scotland in the EU, in the event of a vote in favour of independence in September 2014, poses intriguing questions for the future.

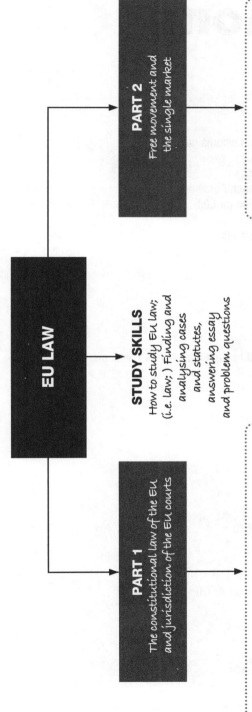

EU LAW

STUDY SKILLS

How to study EU law
(i.e. law;) Finding and
analysing cases
and statutes,
answering essay
and problem questions

PART 1

The constitutional law of the EU
and jurisdiction of the EU courts

CHAPTER 1
The historical background
of the EU

CHAPTER 2
The institutions of the
EU: the Parliament,
Council and Commission

CHAPTER 3
The Court of Justice and
preliminary rulings

CHAPTER 4
The sources of EU law;
competences of the EU

CHAPTER 5
General principles and
fundamental rights

CHAPTER 6
The supremacy of
Union law

CHAPTER 7
Direct and indirect effect

CHAPTER 8
State liability

CHAPTER 9
Enforcing EU law
against Member States

CHAPTER 10
Judicial review:
annulment, failure to
act and indirect review;
Liability of the EU
institutions

PART 2

Free movement and
the single market

CHAPTER 11
Customs duties and discriminatory
internal taxation

CHAPTER 12
The free movement of goods;
Introduction to the free movement of
capital and EMU

CHAPTER 13
Union citizenship

CHAPTER 14
The free movement of workers

CHAPTER 15
The right of establishment and freedom
to provide services

Abbreviations

AFSJ	Area of freedom, security and justice
CAP	Common Agricultural Policy
CCT	common customs tariff
CEE	charge having equivalent effect (to a customs duty)
CFI	Court of First Instance
CFSP	Common Foreign and Security Policy
CISA	Convention Implementing the Schengen Agreement
CJEU	Court of Justice of the European Union (or ECJ)
CoR	Committee of the Regions
COREPER	Committee of Permanent Representatives
CT	Constitutional Treaty
DG	Directorate General
EAT	Employment Appeals Tribunal
EAW	European Arrest Warrant
EC	European Community/Communities
ECA	European Communities Act (1972)
ECB	European Central Bank
ECHR	European Convention on Human Rights and Fundamental Freedoms
ECtHR	European Court of Human Rights
ECOFIN	Economic and Financial Affairs
ECR	European Court Reports
ECSC	European Coal and Steel Community
ECU	European currency unit
EEA	European Economic Area
EEC	European Economic Community
EFTA	European Free Trade Association
EMI	European Monetary Institute
EMS	European Monetary System
EMU	Economic and Monetary Union
EP	European Parliament
EPO	European Patent Office
EPU	Economic and Political Union
ERTA	European Road Transport Agreement (or AETR)
ESC	Economic and Social Committee
EU	European Union
EUA	European Union Act 2011
EURATOM	European Atomic Energy Community
GATT	General Agreement on Tariffs and Trade
GDP	gross domestic product
HL	House of Lords

IGC	intergovernmental conference
IIA	inter-institutional agreement
MAFF	Ministry of Agriculture, Fisheries and Food
MEP	Member of the European Parliament
MEQR	measure having equivalent effect
NCA	national competition authorities
PJCC	Police and Judicial Cooperation in Criminal Matters
PR	proportional representation
QBD	Queen's Bench Division
QMV	qualified majority voting
SEA	Single European Act
SIS	Schengen Information System
TEC	Treaty establishing the European Community
TEU	Treaty on European Union
TFEU	Treaty on the Functioning of the European Union
ToA	Treaty of Amsterdam
ToL	Treaty of Lisbon
ToN	Treaty of Nice
TRIPS	Trade-Related Aspects of Intellectual Property Rights
WTO	World Trade Organization

STUDY SKILLS

Studying EU Law

INTRODUCTION

This section is intended to help you develop the skills you need to study European Union (EU) law. It complements the material in the book which focuses on what the law provides. Different skills are needed for EU law than for other subjects on LLB or GDL programmes as EU law has different origins from subjects like Contract and Tort which have evolved through decisions of the courts since the Norman Conquest. EU law is of recent origin, having been introduced in 1957 when the original European Economic Community (the forerunner of the European Union) was created under the Treaty of Rome, providing the 'Constitution' of the Community. At that time all six original Member States had legal systems deriving from Roman law rather than the common law. The UK joined on 1 January 1973 and has been bound by Community (now EU) law ever since. The Treaty of Rome has been amended by later Treaties, most recently by the Treaty of Lisbon which took effect in December 2009. From that date the Treaty on European Union (TEU) and the Treaty on the Functioning of the European Union (TFEU) have been the main sources of EU law.

The EU serves both a political and an economic purpose – the integration of Europe to maintain peace and stability in parallel with promotion of economic prosperity. You will only appreciate EU law and the objectives of the EU fully if you engage with political and constitutional theory. While you are not expected to become an expert in political science, you should try to keep up to date with the context in which the EU operates.

Membership of the EU remains a 'hot' political topic in the UK. The Prime Minister, David Cameron, says he wishes to 'renegotiate' the terms of UK membership and has promised a referendum on continuing membership after the next general election in May 2015 if the Conservatives are re-elected. It is essential to develop your awareness of the political and economic context of EU law by reading a good newspaper regularly, following broadcast television news programmes as well as material on the internet, particularly the EU's 'Europa' website (considered on p. lvii).

Is EU law really harder than other law subjects?

EU law is *different* from other law subjects, but *not necessarily more difficult*. If you appreciate why the differences exist, EU law will cease to seem daunting. EU law is a *system* created by the Treaties (the TEU and TFEU), providing the primary legislation of the EU. The law exists to support the ideas underlying the EU, particularly the free movement of goods, persons, services and capital. Other important principles have been developed by the Court of Justice including the supremacy of EU law over national law, direct effect (enabling an individual to rely on EU law before the national courts) and State liability (enabling an individual to sue a Member State for damages in the national courts for breach of EU law).

The Treaties are supplemented by secondary legislation in the form of regulations, directives and decisions. Chapter 4 on sources provides guidance on these different forms of legislation. The secondary legislation you will encounter most frequently is likely to be directives, which provide a binding objective on Member States, but leave some discretion as to how to achieve it.

This book, in accordance with the series, aims to provide you with a blueprint to help you find your way around EU law. If you follow the features identifying the most important elements in parallel with the reading designated by your tutor, you should be able to grasp the essentials of EU law and find it a rewarding area. It may help if you view EU law as a jigsaw, with the Treaties providing the straight sides (the structure), and secondary legislation and decisions of the Court of Justice the remaining pieces. By the time you finish your course, the jigsaw should be complete. This book should help you to see

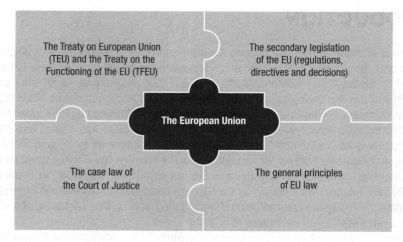

Figure 1 The jigsaw of the EU

how the pieces fit together and appreciate how EU law operates as an integrated system supporting the political and economic purpose of the EU.

How does the study of EU law differ from English law?

It may take you several weeks to become used to the way EU laws are set out. Treaties and EU secondary legislation are divided into 'Articles' and 'paragraphs' rather than 'sections' and 'subsections'. Directives, for example, are normally preceded by a preamble which will help you understand the purpose of the legislation. The Court of Justice seeks to give effect to the purpose of EU law when faced with a question of interpretation, by adopting what is known as a 'purposive' rather than a literal approach (see Chapter 7).

Example

The Preamble to Directive 2004/38 Citizens' free movement rights (see Chapter 13) states in paragraph 17 that:

> Enjoyment of permanent residence rights by Union citizens who have chosen to settle long term in the host Member State would strengthen the feeling of Union citizenship and is a key element in promoting social cohesion . . . one of the fundamental objectives of the Union.

Article 28 of the directive gives effect to this aim, providing:

> Before taking an expulsion decision on grounds of public policy or public security, the host Member State shall take account of considerations such as how long the individual concerned has resided on its territory, his/her age, state of health and economic situation, social and cultural integration into the host Member State and the extent of his/her links with the country of origin.

Unlike English statutes which usually contain a definition section, terms are rarely defined in the Treaties, but may be clarified by secondary legislation and decisions of the Court of Justice.

The procedure and approach of the Court of Justice, deriving from the continental tradition may initially seem unfamiliar. The judges of the Court of Justice and General Court act as a *college*, issuing a single judgment with any differences of opinion resolved behind closed doors. This means that you do not have to wrestle with nuances of differing and sometimes dissenting judgments as in English law. There is no doctrine of binding precedent in the Court, although it usually follows its previous decisions and signals clearly when it intends to depart from earlier case law.

In complex or significant cases the judgment may be preceded by the Opinion of the Advocate-General, an officer of the Court whose submissions may assist it in reaching judgment. The Opinion is longer and more fully reasoned than the judgment, and may help you to understand the issues under consideration. However, you must be careful to compare the wording of the final submissions of the Advocate-General with the judgment itself, as there is no obligation for the Court to follow the submissions or even to consider all its analysis. Once you have read a few judgments, the approach should become as familiar as English reports. Another difference between EU and English law is that EU law operates as a coherent system with internal rules supported by underlying fundamental principles such as free movement, whereas English law is made up of a more disparate collection of laws serving a range of purposes.

The preliminary reference procedure in the Court of Justice

The procedure you will meet most often is the preliminary reference procedure under Article 267 TFEU (examined in Chapter 3). You will see that a national court faced with interpreting EU law where the meaning is unclear or needing confirmation of its validity may ask the Court of Justice for guidance. The national court suspends proceedings until it receives an interpretation from the Court which it applies to the facts of the case. Initially you may find the Court of Justice's preliminary rulings 'different' as they focus on interpreting the law without applying it to the facts, which is the responsibility of the national court.

Many requests for rulings by national courts indirectly try to establish whether national law is compatible with EU law. The Court of Justice cannot interpret national law under Article 267 and so tends to rule that EU law *precludes* a particular practice (meaning that it is incompatible with EU law) or *does not preclude* it (so it is compatible). The more reports or transcripts you read, the more confident you will become in handling this procedure.

Bear in mind that decisions of the Court of Justice under the preliminary reference procedure may originate in *any* of the Member States, but bind all States equally. You should not be deterred by unfamiliar-sounding case names. With twenty-eight Member States and twenty-four official and working languages, the parties' names may seem unfamiliar, although some significant cases are given nicknames like '*Cassis de Dijon*' (see Chapter 12).

READING ABOUT EU LAW

Annotated reading lists at the end of each chapter directing you to journal articles should enable you to examine material in more depth. Extracts from journals may be found in collections such as the highly regarded Craig and De Burca, *EU Law: Text, Cases and Materials* (5th edition, Oxford University Press: Oxford, 2011) or Chalmers, Davies and Monti, *European Union Law: Text and Materials* (2nd edition, Cambridge University Press: Cambridge, 2010). However, there is no substitute for reading journal articles in their entirety. Electronic databases to which your university may subscribe such as 'Westlaw' are also invaluable, enabling you to search for journal articles through terms, authors and titles.

Various journals provide interesting and authoritative analysis of EU law. Specialist journals with wide-ranging coverage of EU law (constitutional law, single market law and competition law) include:

- *European Law Review* (EL Rev)
- *Common Market Law Review* (CMLRev)
- *Maastricht Journal* (MJ)
- *European Law Journal* (ELJ).

Journals focusing on European integration include:

- *Journal of Common Market Studies* (JCMS)
- *Legal Issues of European Integration* (LIEI).

Journals of general academic interest with occasional articles on EU law include:

- *International and Comparative Law Quarterly* (ICLQ)
- *Law Quarterly Review* (LQR)
- *Modern Law Review* (MLR)

Only by reading widely, particularly journal articles, will you develop the critical awareness necessary to underpin analysis, particularly in essay writing. The level of analysis is what distinguishes a first-rate essay from one which merely achieves a pass, so if you aim to achieve the best results in EU law you must read critically throughout.

Keeping up to date

EU law changes rapidly, so it is never enough to learn about the law from textbooks. Reading newspapers regularly is important. There is excellent coverage of EU affairs in the *Guardian* (with free online access) and *The Times*. You must be able to access information online, particularly through the official EU website known as 'Europa', available at http://europa.eu, with which you should familiarise yourself from the start of your course. The website provides a gateway to information on EU activities, laws and policies, as well as links to sites of the EU institutions such as the Court of Justice. The homepage lists headings including 'How the EU works' (with links to the EU institutions), 'Your life in the EU', 'EU law' (with links to finding legislation) and 'EU by topic', from which you can follow hyperlinks to key sites, documentation, summaries of legislation and legal texts.

'Live' links such as 'Highlights of current activities' on the Council website (available on http://www.consilium.europa.eu) enable you to follow EU law as it is decided, making the subject more interesting and relevant, such as the agreement reached in the Council on 21 June 2013 on revision of tobacco rules, with links to a press release, public debate, a press conference webcast and a press release from the Irish Presidency. Staying alert to developments and following them up will help you to develop your research skills when writing essays.

Example

On 29 June 2013 the BBC News website carried an item entitled 'Irish turf cutters stage protest over EU bog law' http://www.bbc.co.uk/news/world-europe-23112105 following the end of a ten-year exemption for Ireland on an EU prohibition on turf cutting had ended. The Commission website includes a Press Release from 2011 (reference IP/11/70) 'Environment: Commission urges Ireland to act swiftly to improve protection of peat bogs' http://europa.eu/rapid/press-release_IP-11–730_en.htm in which it announces the Commission's action against Ireland for breaches of the Habitats Directive 92/43 and Environmental Impact Assessment (EIA) Directive 85/337, and that there have been earlier proceedings in the Court of Justice. These may be traced through the Court's 'Curia' website – Case C-392/96 *Commission* v. *Ireland* (decision of 21 September 1999) resulting in a declaration that Ireland was in breach of Directive 85/337 by failing to transpose (implement) into national law the obligation to carry out EIAs in relation to projects including turf cutting.

These proceedings illustrate the use of the enforcement procedure (see Chapter 9).

Useful websites

'Europa' is the EU's official website with links to EU institutions, activities, policies and legislation.	http://europa.eu/
The European Parliament's website. The Press Office link provides information on current issues.	http://www.europarl.europa.eu/portal/en
'Curia' is the website for the Court of Justice and the General Court, with access to transcripts of decisions on the day of the judgment. You can search by case name or number, names of parties, subject matter, etc. Press reports summarise decisions of particular interest.	http://curia.europa.eu
'Consilium' is the Council's website, with links to its policies, documents, reports and proceedings. You will also find highlights of current activities.	http://www.consilium.europa.eu
The Commission's website, providing information on EU policies, laws and recent activities.	http://ec.europa.eu/index_en.htm
'EUR-Lex' is the website for the official database in EU law, with full text of preparatory documents, case law and consolidated versions of EU legislation.	http://eur-lex.europa.eu/en/index.htm
A new version of EUR-Lex was launched in 2013, with three levels of search and a personal space (my EUR-Lex). It is the single point of access to the authentic electronic version of the Official Journal (OJ) in which all EU laws are published.	http://new.eur-lex.europa.eu/homepage.html
'Eurostat' provides official EU statistics.	http://europa.eu/publications/statistics/index_en.htm

Useful websites	
Provides links to 'easy to read' guides on the history and operation of the EU.	http://europa.eu/about-eu/index_en.htm
European Documentation Centres (EDCs) Are major collections of EU documentation, mainly in university libraries.	http://europa.eu/europedirect/meet_us/#documentation_centres
Prepared by the European Commission's Directorate General Communications for journalists, with links to useful websites and a guide to finding and tracking legislation.	http://www.eu4journalists.eu
A very comprehensive gateway to EU law prepared by the Commission for its delegation to the US.	http://www.eurunion.org/infores
UK government website with information on EU law in the UK.	https://www.gov.uk/
BBC News website covering European news.	http://www.bbc.co.uk/news/world/europe
The Guardian's website has a free online section on law, with good coverage of European affairs.	http://www.guardian.co.uk

Tying recent developments in with your studies

Two examples of political developments which may affect the development of EU law are shown below. The first concerns EU enlargement.

Example

The first chapter of this book introduces you to the context of the EU including enlargement. Turkey has long sought to join the EU but has not yet satisfied the 'Copenhagen criteria' (which includes a satisfactory human rights record). On 14 June 2013 Alexander Christie-Miller reported in *The Times* on the European Parliament's resolution 'deploring' the Turkish response to anti-government protests. Ian Trayner commented in the *Guardian* on 21 June 2013 that Turkey is unlikely to be able to relaunch its bid for EU membership after its government's 'ruthless response' to street protests in Istanbul and worsening relations with Germany (http://www.guardian.co.uk/world/2013/jun/21/turkey-eu-membership-falters-row-germany). On a more positive note, you may also access an EU news report welcoming Croatia to membership of the EU on 1 July 2013 on http://europa.eu/newsroom/highlights/croatia-joins-eu/. The EU maintains its own web page on enlargement on http://europa.eu/pol/enlarg/index_en.htm.

This example is relevant to:

- Chapter 1 (The historical background to the European Union)
- Chapter 5 (General principles and fundamental rights).

The second example concerns the attitude of the UK to the EU following the results in the UK local elections in 2013.

Example

The BBC News website is a useful way to access political developments online. You can read comments on 3 May 2013 from Prime Minister David Cameron and the BBC Political Editor, Nick Robinson, on the success of the UK Independence Party (which is highly 'Eurosceptic') in local elections on http://www.bbc.co.uk/news/uk-politics-22382098. Lord Lawson, former Chancellor of the Exchequer, called for the UK to withdraw from the EU, reported in Roland Watson's article in *The Times* of the same date ('Lord Lawson: It's time to quit the EU'). There is further discussion of the UK position in the EU in relation to a referendum on continuing membership on the BBC News website on 14 May 2013 ('UK and the EU; Better off out or in?', compiled by Brian Wheeler and Laurence Peter, available at http://www.bbc.co.uk/news/uk-politics-20448450).

This example is relevant to:

- Chapter 1 (The historical background to the European Union)
- Chapter 6 (The supremacy of EU law).

STUDY SKILLS FOR EU LAW

Reading a law report or transcript of a decision of the Court of Justice

You will be required to read reports of decisions of the Court of Justice, available in hard copy in the official European Court Reports (ECR) or electronically in transcripts, available on the 'Curia' website on http://curia.europa.eu/.

Example

Case C-348/09 *P.I.* v. *Oberbürgermesterin der Stadt Remscheid* (decision of 22 May 2012) provides an example of a decision under the preliminary reference procedure. You should read the Opinion of Advocate-General Bot (delivered on 6 March 2012) with care, as it differs from the final judgment of the Court. Both Opinion and Judgment state the facts, which concern an appeal by Mr I., an Italian national, against deportation from Germany to Italy after his conviction and imprisonment for serious sexual offences of a minor over an eleven-year period. As Mr I. had lived in Germany for over ten years he could only be deported on 'imperative grounds of public security' under Article 28(3) of Directive 2004/38. The German court hearing the appeal made a preliminary reference to the Court of Justice to clarify whether 'imperative grounds' covered only threats posed to the internal and external security of the State in terms of its continued existence. The Advocate-General submitted that Article 28(3) did not apply as the offence did not threaten public security, unlike Case C-145/09 *Tsakourides* [2010] ECR I-0000 where organised dealing in narcotics was seen as a direct threat. He considered that the enhanced protection from deportation under Article 28(3) could not arise from criminal activity. The Court in its judgment, however, approached Article 28(3) differently, leaving it to the Member States to decide what sort of criminal offences might pose a threat to the calm and physical security of the population. It held that expulsion was conditional on establishing that the individual's personal conduct represented a present threat to one of the fundamental interests of society (i.e. whether the individual is likely to act in the same way in future). Before taking a decision on expulsion, the host State must take into account all the factors in Article 28(1) of Directive 2004/38, such as length of residence.

Points to note from this example include:

- The national court made the referral because it was uncertain of the meaning and scope of 'imperative grounds of public security' under Article 28(3) of Directive 2004/38.
- The Advocate-General submitted that this phrase did not apply to serious sexual offences against a minor.
- The Court of Justice did *not* follow the Advocate-General's approach but left it to the national courts to determine whether such criminal offences could amount to a threat covered by 'imperative grounds of public security'.
- Following the Court's interpretation, it was the responsibility of the national court to apply the law to the facts of the case.

This example is relevant to:

- Chapter 3 (Preliminary references)
- Chapter 13 (Union citizenship).

Example

A more straightforward case may be found in Case C-428/11 *Purely Creative Ltd and Others* v. *Office of Fair Trading*, a UK case arising from a dispute between the Office of Fair Trading (OFT) and traders distributing promotional mailings. The OFT brought proceedings in the High Court to stop traders distributing promotions which the OFT considered were 'aggressive commercial practices' (e.g. scratch cards and promised prizes, using premium rate telephone lines) contrary to UK regulations implementing the Unfair Commercial Practices Directive 2005/29. The High Court referred to the Court of Justice to clarify whether the words 'false impression' in the directive prohibited imposition of a cost on consumers told they had won a prize.

The Court of Justice adopted a purposive approach, referring to the objective in Article 1, namely 'To contribute to the proper functioning of the internal market and achieve a high level of consumer protection', as well as to paragraph 31 of Annex 1 of the directive prohibiting imposition of any cost on the consumer. It interpreted the directive as prohibiting aggressive practices such as giving consumers the false impression they had already won a prize, while taking further action requiring the consumer to pay money.

Points to note include:

- There were no submissions by an Advocate-General.
- The Court expressed its interpretation of the law by reference to the facts of the case as an example. This demonstrates how the Court manages to give a general ruling on the law nevertheless expressed in a fairly narrow context.
- While it remains the national court's task to apply the law to the facts, it has limited discretion on how to do so, in this case by assessing the information provided to consumers to see whether it is clear and understandable.

This example is relevant to:

- Chapter 5 (General principles and fundamental rights – legal certainty)
- Chapter 3 (Preliminary rulings)
- Chapter 7 (Direct and indirect effect – methods of interpretation).

Developing good study techniques

Let's say you have started to read around the topic of direct effect, but you're not sure where to start. There are many different ways to approach studying law. You may be a visual learner who finds diagrams helpful. There are chapter grids at the start of each chapter providing an overview, followed by diagrams such as the flow chart in Figure 2, to help you to develop such an approach. Other students prefer to make notes of key points. Whichever approach you choose, you should normally start by defining a key concept before moving on to consider the case law of the Court of Justice and academic theories.

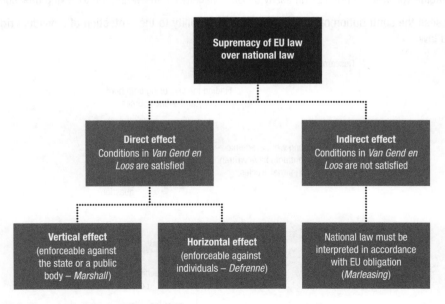

Figure 2 Flow chart of the 'new legal order'

Example

Take supremacy and direct effect as examples. In Chapters 6 and 7 we look at their meaning and development, as well as their part in the EU legal order. You will see that there is no provision in the Treaties for either principle. However, the Court of Justice recognised at an early stage (1963) in *Van Gend en Loos* that it was essential to make it clear that the EU (then known as the EEC) represents a 'new legal order' in national and international law characterised by the supremacy of EU law over national law and the principle of direct effect. By creating your own flow chart or alternative diagram you can focus on the central elements when undertaking background reading. This should help you prepare for seminars and consolidate your material for revision.

Key study skills

The assessment of EU law usually involves essays and examination questions, although the weighting attached to each will vary between universities.

Study skill: When it comes to writing an essay on EU law

Essays tend to be set in parts of the syllabus lending themselves to a discursive treatment, such as the changes to the EU institutions under various Treaty reforms or the development of fundamental rights, with problem questions in areas of substantive law like free movement. You will find it useful to obtain copies of past exam papers from your university's online learning environment to see how EU law has been examined in the past.

Imagine you want to practise an essay on State liability by answering the following question:

Assess the contribution of the concept of State liability to the protection of individual rights in EU law.

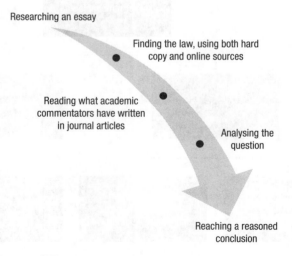

Researching an essay

Finding the law, using both hard copy and online sources

Reading what academic commentators have written in journal articles

Analysing the question

Reaching a reasoned conclusion

Figure 3 Writing an essay on EU law

You should think carefully about what the question asks before beginning to write. As you would do in an exam, it helps to write a brief outline breaking down the question using bullet points, encouraging you to be analytical rather than descriptive. Writing an answer which is little more than a set of notes will not impress the examiner! You must resist the temptation to write 'all you know' about State liability. The issues the question raises are more subtle and complex than the rather straightforwardly worded question suggests.

- The question is about state liability, but raises other areas as well, which may not be immediately obvious.

- In order to 'assess' the contribution of state liability to the protection of rights in EU law, you will need to examine why this concept was introduced by the Court of Justice in *Francovich*.

- This means examining the limitations of concepts providing rights for individuals, namely direct and indirect effect, particularly the problems resulting from the lack of horizontal direct effect for directives (*Marshall*). Indirect effect can only provide the basis for a remedy where the Member State has legislation which can be interpreted in accordance with the EU legislation (*Von Colson*), but this obligation to interpret national law only applies as far as it's possible to do so (*Marleasing*), so there is no remedy where national law cannot be given such an interpretation.

- The Court was concerned in *Francovich* that Member States should not ignore their obligations by failing to implement a directive, depriving individuals of rights. Member States are obliged to observe EU law by (what is now) Article 4 TEU. This obligation underlay the Court's approach to the introduction of State liability, as it wanted to 'plug the gap' left by direct effect and indirect effect.

- You should also examine how the Court developed state liability, extending it to cover infringements of EU law generally, broadening the scope of individual protection. It did this in *Brasserie/Factortame* by applying the conditions developed in relation to liability of the EU institutions under (what is now) Article 340 TFEU, particularly the requirement for the breach to be 'sufficiently serious', which is examined by the court in relation to the discretion enjoyed by the Member State. This condition is hard to establish, which may deprive individuals of a possible remedy.

- Your answer should show awareness of the views of academic commentators on State liability such as Tridimas and Dougan (introduced in the 'Reflections' in Chapter 8) as to whether the introduction of State liability has completed the package of remedies which include direct and indirect effect.

- Finally, you should reach a conclusion reflecting your analysis of the subject matter of the question.

Study skill: Improving your essay-writing

It is essential when writing essays to acknowledge your sources fully. Most universities use anti-plagiarism software which may enable you to check your work for plagiarism before submission. You should ensure that you leave enough time to respond to the electronic report before the deadline. A finding of plagiarism or any form of cheating in a law subject would have a disastrous effect on your record, and may prevent future progression into the legal profession.

Successful essay writing in EU law requires preparation, planning, time management and focus on the question. If you want to learn more about improving your essay-writing skills, you may wish to read, Foster, S. *How to Write Better Law Essays* (Pearson: Harlow, 2009) or McBride, N. J. *Letters to a Law Student: a guide to studying law at university* (Pearson: Harlow, 2007) ('Letter 16 – Writing Essays').

STUDY SKILLS FEATURE: WHEN IT COMES TO ANSWERING PROBLEM QUESTIONS IN EU LAW

Assessment in EU law almost always involves an element of written examination, with seen or (more often) unseen questions or a combination of both. Seen questions provide you with time to prepare. This means that the examiner will expect you to have done so effectively so that you can produce your arguments confidently in the exam, and will be less tolerant of half-remembered or misspelt case names.

Problem questions tend to be set in areas of substantive law like free movement of goods or persons. As with essay questions, it makes sense to write a plan using bullet points before you begin your answer. Figure 4 provides an outline of an approach you may find helpful.

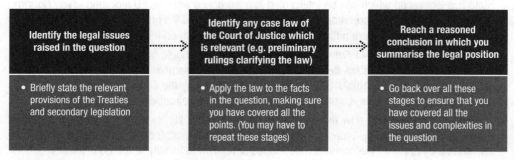

Figure 4 Answering problem questions in EU law

You will see from Figure 4 that to answer problem questions, you need to be aware of the Treaties, relevant secondary legislation and the case law of the Court of Justice. The Treaties state the law on broad terms which can only be understood by reference to later case law or secondary legislation. Article 34 TFEU, for example, comprises a single sentence: 'Quantitative restrictions on imports and all measures having equivalent effect shall be prohibited between Member States.' The brevity of this provision belies its fundamental importance to the free movement of goods. If you try to represent the main provisions on free movement of goods schematically, it may help you to examine how the law applies to a factual scenario.

For example:

Following discovery of a new disease in pigs which may have an adverse effect on the health of consumers, the UK government has imposed a licensing system on pork importers. Michael, an importer, complains that the requirements are so strict that they are impossible to satisfy. Advise Michael.

The law to consider in relation to this problem may be summarised as in Figure 5.

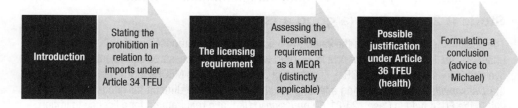

Figure 5 Summary of the law to answer the question

Student 1's answer (a poor answer)

Michael should be advised that the UK often responds to apparent threats to health which may originate in goods from other Member States by imposing a restriction on imports. The *French Turkeys* case shows just how protectionist the UK government can be when faced with such a threat and sets out some rules for invoking restrictions which the UK government does not seem to have followed here. This is against the provisions of EU law which treat the free movement of goods as very important. Michael should reapply for a licence in the knowledge that the UK restrictions cannot be enforced against him.

Student 1's answer is very basic, showing little knowledge of the law on the free movement of goods (below pass standard at degree level). It demonstrates basic errors which might have been avoided by following an approach closer to that in Figure 5, supported by a greater knowledge of the law.

- It starts with the conclusion – the advice to Michael – instead of an introduction identifying the problem and the relevant law.

- It fails to state the central legal principle – prohibition of quantitative restrictions and MEQRs on imports under Article 34 TFEU.

- It fails to examine the legal status of the restriction – the requirement for a licence – which should have been assessed as a MEQR. The requirement is distinctly applicable as it applies only to imports, so can only be justified under Article 36 TFEU (see Chapter 12).

- The reference to the *French Turkeys* case is vague and fails to state the conditions on which a Member State may rely on the public health derogation in Article 36 TFEU.

- Statements are badly written and based on personal prejudice rather than knowledge and analysis of the law.

- The final statement that 'Michael should reapply for a licence . . .' is speculative. It is not a reasoned conclusion.

Student 2's answer (a good answer)

The question is concerned with the validity of a licensing system imposed by the UK government under EU law, in particular under Article 34 TFEU which prohibits measures equivalent to quantitative restrictions on imports (MEQRs). The Court of Justice has given MEQRs a wide definition under the *Dassonville* formula, covering anything which makes it more difficult for goods to circulate within the EU. It held in Case 124/81 *Commission* v. *UK* that a requirement for a licence to import goods is a MEQR. As the measure has only been imposed in relation to imports, it is a distinctly applicable measure under Directive 70/50, and so may only be justified under Article 36 TFEU – in this case if it satisfies the public health derogation. It cannot be justified as a mandatory requirement under *Cassis de Dijon* which only applies to indistinctly applicable measures.

The question provides little information about the nature of the threat apparently posed by discovery of the disease in pigs other than it is 'new'. If there has been no EU harmonisation, it is open to the UK to apply the precautionary principle where scientific opinion is divided as to the nature of the threat (Case 174/82 *Sandoz*). Under this principle it would be open to the UK to license pork imports provided any restrictions are proportionate. On the facts there may be some scope for claiming, as Michael does here, that the UK action in imposing a licensing system is disproportionate.

Where scientific opinion is not divided, the UK would have to satisfy the requirements imposed by the Court of Justice in Case 40/82 *Commission* v. *UK* (the '*French Turkeys*' case) (there must be a real not a slight risk to health, the measure must be part of a seriously considered health policy, and it must not operate as a disguised restriction on trade between Member States). It must also be proportionate. In Case 124/81 *Commission* v. *UK* the requirement for a licence for imported UHT milk was found to be unjustified, whereas in Case 74/82 *Commission* v. *Ireland* it was justified as poultry from the UK did not reach the standards of Irish poultry.

Michael should be advised that a measure of this type is a MEQR, which is illegal under Article 34 unless it can be justified on public health grounds under Article 36. Whether the measure is justified or proportionate depends on the circumstances outlined above.

Student 2's answer is well-written, demonstrating sound knowledge of the law on the free movement of goods. It is well structured, setting out the nature of the problem, stating the law and applying it before reaching a conclusion in terms of advice to Michael at the end. He or she correctly identifies the public health derogation which may provide a justification for the UK's action and is aware of the relevance of the precautionary principle in this context. The student is not afraid to identify gaps in the factual scenario (often a factor in problem questions) and avoids making assumptions about such missing information. Relevant authorities (decisions of the Court of Justice) are correctly cited.

STUDY SKILLS FEATURE: WHEN IT COMES TO USING STATUTES IN ASSESSMENTS

Most universities allow students to bring statute books into the examination. This is only useful if you are extremely familiar with the layout of the book so you do not waste time in the exam trying to find the relevant material. The most significant statutory material is likely to be the Treaties, as any discussion in either an essay or problem question should start with the appropriate primary legislation.

If we look at Article 45 TFEU we can see that it provides as follows:

1. Freedom of movement for workers shall be secured within the Union.
2. Such freedom of movement shall entail the abolition of any discrimination based on nationality . . .
3. It shall entail the right, subject to limitations justified on grounds of public policy, public security or public health:
   (a) to accept offers of employment actually made;
   (b) to move freely within the territory of a Member State for this purpose;
   (c) to stay in a Member State for the purpose of employment . . .

How would you use Article 45 in an assessment? Let's say you are faced with a question about whether John, a UK national working in France, may be deported back to the UK when the French government discovers he has been convicted two years ago of possession of cannabis. For a start, you should appreciate that Article 45 has been subject to secondary legislation (Directive 2004/38, consolidating earlier secondary legislation and decisions of the Court). Case law and the directive will help you to understand who is a 'worker' and what their rights are. You would see that Article 27 of Directive 2004/38 provides the principle under which the movement of a Union citizen may be restricted, consolidating decisions such as Case 30/77 *Bouchereau*. This means that Union citizens (including workers) may not be restricted in their movements unless they pose a 'sufficiently serious threat to one of the fundamental interests of society'. We will consider how permanent residence rights provide extended protection under Article 28 of Directive 2004/38 (see p. 294).

You would need to address the following points in your answer:

- John's status as both a worker under Article 45 TFEU and Union citizen under Directive 2004/38.
- Whether his residence in France may be restricted as a result of his conviction under Article 45(3) TFEU and Article 27 of Directive 2004/38.
- This involves assessing whether his personal conduct poses a threat to one of the fundamental interests of society – unlikely as Article 27(2) explicitly provides that convictions do not in themselves constitute grounds for taking such action.

STUDY SKILLS FEATURE: WHEN IT COMES TO RESEARCHING A TOPIC FOR AN ASSESSMENT

Let's say you have been asked to write an essay on the current significance of the Charter of Fundamental Rights, requiring research to support your arguments. You may start by using this or another textbook or casebook to ensure you understand the basic role of the Charter. You could follow up end-of-chapter references to articles such as the *European Law Review* or the *Common Market Law Review* in hard copy form in your university library or electronically through 'Westlaw'. A significant advantage of using electronic sources is that you can search for key terms such as 'Charter of Fundamental Rights' which should yield a number of journal articles on the subject. It is very important to obtain material from authoritative sources such as peer-reviewed journals and not from 'Wikipedia' which may contain inaccurate information.

You will see from textbooks that the Charter was given the same legal status as the Treaties by the Treaty of Lisbon, enabling the Court of Justice to refer to it in its judgments. You should also look for evidence of citation of the Charter in the decisions of the Court since the Treaty came into effect in December 2009. The form on the Court's 'Curia' website enables you to search for key words in the judgment or Advocate-General's submissions. Finally, you should assemble your material so that you engage with the question you have been set and produce reasoned arguments and a conclusion.

SUMMARY

- EU law can be mastered and enjoyed if you read widely and complete the tasks your tutor has set.
- You must appreciate the nature and purpose of EU law in order to do well.
- It is essential that you develop the key skills necessary to write both essays and answers to problem questions in EU law.
- It is very important to understand the central provisions of the Treaties, as well as relevant secondary legislation and to be able to use these materials confidently in the exam.
- You must be able to conduct independent research in EU law to complete assignments, using materials selectively to develop your argument and reach a logical conclusion.

PART 1

The constitutional law of the European Union and jurisdiction of the EU Courts

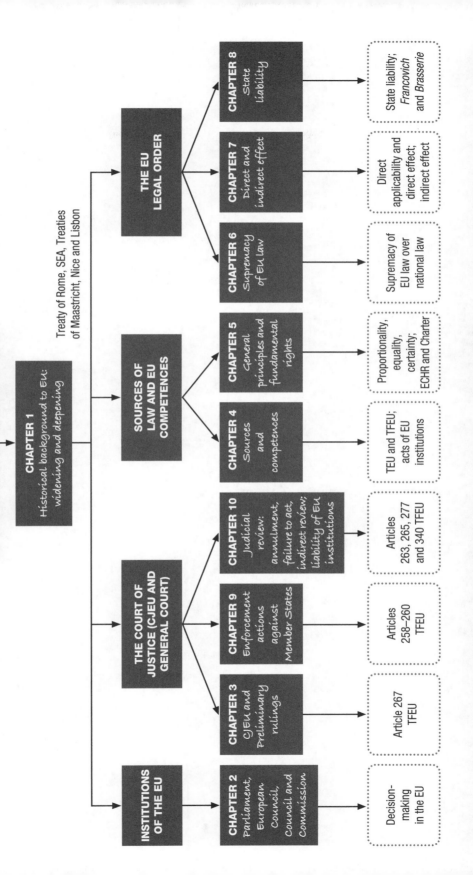

CHAPTER 1

The historical background to the European Union

BLUEPRINT

The constitutional law of the European Union and jurisdiction of the EU Courts

KEY QUESTIONS

LEGISLATION

- Treaty on European Union (TEU)
- Treaty on the Functioning of the EU (TFEU)

CONTEXT

- Need to rebuild Europe after the Second World War
- Partition of Cyprus
- Collapse of Communism
- Iraq War

CONCEPTS

- Fundamental rights
- General principles
- Copenhagen criteria

- How should the need to widen EU membership be reconciled with deepening the ties of existing Member States?

- How much EU integration is desirable?

CASES

- *Van Gend en Loos*
- *Costa* v. *ENEL*

SPECIAL CHARACTERISTICS

- Supremacy of EU law
- Direct effect

REFORM

- Treaty revision as a continuing process from the Treaty of Rome to the Treaty of Lisbon.

CRITICAL ISSUES

Setting the scene

The European Union (EU) evokes strong feelings from passionate enthusiasm to hostility and mistrust, sentiments which continue to affect political and legal development. EU law today may only be understood by placing it in the context of European integration in the twentieth century. Grand designs to unite Europe have a long history. While military leaders from Julius Caesar to Adolf Hitler have asserted their territorial claims through force, a more idealistic basis for cooperation between nation states through a 'social contract' may be traced through the writings of the Swiss philosopher Rousseau in the late eighteenth and early nineteenth centuries. Political leaders strongly favoured cooperation in rebuilding Europe after the Second World War to avoid repeating the failure to find a permanent solution after the First World War.

The inspiration for the three institutions which evolved to become the European Union came from the plan devised in 1950 by Robert Schuman, the French Foreign Minister, and Jean Monnet, who was responsible for overseeing France's economic recovery after the war.

At the time, Europe was reliant on US-provided aid and needed to become self-sufficient. The *Schuman Plan* involved France and Germany pooling production of coal and steel. Monnet and Schuman believed that Germany should be helped to rebuild, but only if bound politically and economically within an organisation of European states as a step towards prosperity and a deterrent to future military conflict. Over sixty years have passed since Monnet and Schuman's original plan, a period of relative peace and prosperity between the Member States. The Union now has twenty-eight Member States, with further candidates waiting in the wings.

CONTEXT

THE CREATION OF THE ECSC, EEC AND EURATOM

The **Treaty** of Paris was signed in 1951 by France, Germany, Italy, Belgium, the Netherlands and Luxembourg, establishing the European Coal and Steel Community (ECSC). Its objective was to create a common market in coal and steel, the raw materials of military weapons and civilian heavy industry. The UK was invited to participate, but did not do so for reasons including concern over the nature and powers of the institutions.

The ECSC proved to be a successful model for further integration. In 1955 the foreign ministers of the six ECSC states met at Messina to discuss the creation of a more wide-ranging common market. The meeting led to production of the Spaak Report in 1956 recommending creation of two new communities. In 1957 the same six states signed two further treaties in Rome creating the European Economic Community (EEC) and the European Atomic Energy Community (Euratom), together known as 'the Communities'. Like the ECSC, Euratom was limited to a single sector, atomic energy, whereas the EEC was a more ambitious enterprise, intended to evolve towards 'ever closer union among the peoples of Europe' (Preamble to the EEC Treaty). Initially the ECSC, EEC and Euratom shared only two institutions, the Assembly (or Parliament) and the Court. This was an inefficient arrangement and in 1965 the Merger Treaty led to the formation of a single Council and a Commission. After the merger the three communities functioned separately but with common institutions.

Integration under the Treaty of Rome

The states forming the European Economic Community (EEC), forerunner of the EU, sought integration in 1957 under the Treaty of Rome (the EEC Treaty) by merging their separate interests into a **common market** where goods, persons, services and capital could circulate freely.

The original Treaty of Rome has been amended a number of times, but remains the basis of primary law of the European Union in its amended form. Today the main legal obligations of the EU may be found in two Treaties consolidating earlier amending Treaties: the Treaty on European Union (TEU) and the Treaty on the Functioning of the European Union (TFEU).

INTERSECTION

The sources of EU law including the TEU and the TFEU are considered in more detail in Chapter 4. Other sources include the **acts of the EU institutions** (secondary legislation in the form of **regulations**, **directives** and **decisions**) and the case law of the Court of Justice (CJEU).

The creation of the European Community in 1957 required a pooling of sovereignty in the areas covered by the Treaty of Rome, which at that time were mostly economic – including free movement of goods, persons and services. The Community reflected an ideal reminiscent of Churchill's vision of a 'United States of Europe' (from his 1946 'Speech to the academic youth' at Zurich University), operating not as a single territory under a federal authority but as a supranational organisation, above the Member States and capable of making binding policies and rules. The founder members of the EEC, particularly France and Germany, the driving force in European integration for many years, saw the gain in peace, stability and economic development as outweighing the inevitable loss of sovereignty.

Take note

As you begin to study EU law you will encounter economic terminology which may at first seem unfamiliar, such as the distinction between a customs union and a common market.

A **customs union** involves removal of customs duties between participating states, and the creation of a common external tariff on goods entering the customs union from outside the area (i.e. the payment of a fixed rate of duty on goods from outside the customs union). Thus if a customs union comprises states A, B, and C, any goods produced in A may move to B or C without incurring any **customs duty** at the border. Goods produced in non-Member State X will incur the same rate of duty regardless as to where the goods enter the customs union.

In a common market, participating states agree that goods, persons, services and capital may circulate freely, without any barriers. It follows that in a common market consisting of states D, E and F, a worker moving from D to F will not need a work permit.

Evolving aims: from European Economic Community to the European Union

The European Economic Community (EEC) had ambitious aims under the Treaty of Rome to improve the lives of its citizens through economic cooperation, particularly by creating a common market. The Maastricht Treaty 1992 (in force from 1993) amended these aims to reflect the commitment to political and monetary union, along with strengthening social cohesion.

CORNERSTONE

The current aims of the Union are set out in Article 3 (ex 2 TEC). They include the promotion of 'peace, its values and the well-being of its peoples', creation of an area of freedom, security and justice without internal frontiers and establishment of an **internal market**.

The pursuit of such ambitious aims has not been straightforward, as the Union has evolved from a largely economic community (the EEC) to a more complex, current model (the EU). It has required a balancing of conflicting tensions between the parallel themes of widening (broadening the base of the EU to admit more members) and deepening (developing closer ties of integration with the existing members).

Position of the United Kingdom

When the Treaty of Rome was signed in 1957 the UK was unwilling to sacrifice national sovereignty to join the Communities (the EEC, ECSC and Euratom), preferring to retain its 'special relationship' with the USA and trade links with the Commonwealth. Instead the UK proposed a **free trade area** in Europe. In 1959 the European Free Trade Association (EFTA) was founded by the UK, Norway, Denmark, Sweden, Austria and Portugal, later drawing in states such as Ireland and Finland.

A free trade area is a less demanding form of integration than a customs union or common market. In a free trade area, tariff barriers such as customs duties are removed on goods moving between Member States, leaving members free to impose tariffs on goods entering from outside the area, whereas goods entering a customs union from outside meet a standardised tariff wherever they enter.

APPLICATION

A, B and C are independent, sovereign states wishing to strengthen their trade links without losing sovereignty. They could enter into a free trade area, requiring removal of tariff barriers between themselves, while retaining their sovereignty. If they find cooperation successful and wish to strengthen their ties, they may enter into a customs union. This would involve some loss of sovereignty, as A, B and C would no longer be free to fix the rates of duty on goods entering their country from outside the customs union, but would have to operate a common external tariff. If A, B and C wished to integrate further, they could form a common market, with free movement of goods, persons, services and capital between the territories of the Member States. However, the formation of a common market would necessitate its own system of law and institutions, with some loss of sovereignty.

The UK became aware of its growing economic isolation and applied for full membership of the Communities in 1961. The application was initially unsuccessful due to French opposition led by President de Gaulle, but a later application in 1967 was accepted in 1972.

WIDENING THE TIES: ENLARGEMENT

First three rounds of enlargement 1973–1986

The UK's 1967 reapplication was followed by Denmark, Norway and Ireland, leading to the signing of the Treaty of Accession with all four states in 1972. While the UK, Ireland and Denmark joined the Communities on 1 January 1973, Norway decided against membership after a referendum in 1972, with a second negative referendum in 1994. Greenland (then an autonomous territory within Denmark) withdrew in 1985 following a similar 'no' vote. It is now an overseas territory in association with the EU.

Greece joined the Community in 1981 after its return to democracy, followed by Spain and Portugal in 1986. The reunification of Germany in 1989 led to the incorporation of the former East Germany into the Communities in 1990 without formal enlargement.

Three of the former EFTA states, Austria, Sweden and Finland, signed the European Economic Area (EEA) Agreement (in force 1 January 1994) extending the application of the single market to the territory of the signatory states. The EEA Agreement set up its own institutions and as a prelude to full membership of the European Union which had been created under the Maastricht Treaty in 1993. The EU was enlarged on 1 January 1995 by a further Act of Accession by which Austria, Finland and Sweden became full members. Unlike previous enlargements which had involved extensive transitional arrangements the three EEA states acceded to the EU *acquis* with limited temporary exceptions. Only Switzerland, Norway, Iceland and Liechtenstein remain members of EFTA, although they retain close ties with the EU.

> **Take note**
> The EU acquis is the full body of EU law and obligations binding the Member States. Any new Member State has to agree to be bound by the acquis on joining the EU.

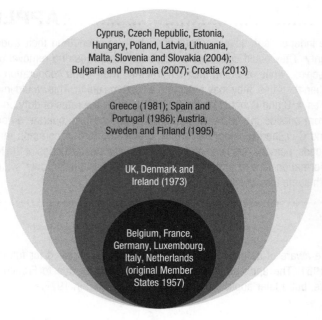

Cyprus, Czech Republic, Estonia,
Hungary, Poland, Latvia, Lithuania,
Malta, Slovenia and Slovakia (2004);
Bulgaria and Romania (2007); Croatia (2013)

Greece (1981); Spain and
Portugal (1986); Austria,
Sweden and Finland (1995)

UK, Denmark and
Ireland (1973)

Belgium, France,
Germany, Luxembourg,
Italy, Netherlands
(original Member
States 1957)

Figure 1.1 Enlargement of the EU

Enlargement 2004–2013

The EU enlarged dramatically on 1 May 2004 when ten new Member States joined the EU. The catalyst for change was the collapse of Communism, a process symbolised by the fall of the Berlin Wall in 1989 after a decade of political upheaval in Eastern Europe. Many of the states previously under Soviet domination looked to the West to provide the way forward, with membership of the EU recognising their new identity. The Copenhagen Summit of 1993 paved the way for **Europe Agreements** signed with a number of East European states to promote convergence, integration and regional cooperation, and providing for a structured relationship with the EU once economic and political conditions were satisfied.

CORNERSTONE

The Copenhagen criteria

Candidate countries for membership of the EU must demonstrate that they have:

- stable institutions which guarantee democracy, the rule of law, human rights, and respect for and protection of minorities;

- a functioning market economy, with capacity to cope with competitive pressures and forces within the Union;

- the ability to take on the obligations of membership, including the EU *acquis* and political, economic and monetary union.

Negotiations opened in 1998 for Cyprus, the Czech Republic, Estonia, Hungary, Poland and Slovenia. Six further countries were added by the Helsinki Summit in December 1999: Bulgaria, Latvia, Lithuania, Malta, Romania and the Slovak Republic. The **European Council** meeting at Laeken in December 2001 agreed that accession treaties setting out the terms for membership would be drafted in 2002, with negotiations concluded by the end of the year. Bulgaria and Romania were considered not 'ready' but were encouraged to persevere with negotiations. On 16 April 2003 the Treaty of Accession was signed, coming into effect on 1 May 2004. As a result, the EU gained ten new Member States: Cyprus, the Czech Republic, Estonia, Hungary, Latvia, Lithuania, Malta, Poland, Slovakia and Slovenia. Bulgaria and Romania joined the EU on 1 January 2007. A similar accession process was followed for Croatia which joined the EU on 1 July 2013.

Future enlargement

Entry negotiations with Turkey began in October 2005, and a new Accession Partnership adopted by the Council of the EU in 2008, but no date for accession has been agreed. The **Copenhagen criteria** are not yet satisfied, with continuing concern over Turkey's human rights record, including treatment of demonstrators in 2013, and lack of resolution of the 'Cyprus problem'.

Cyprus is effectively partitioned. The Republic of Cyprus under Greek Cypriot control in the south is recognised in international law as having legal authority over the island of Cyprus apart from UK military bases. However, it is not recognised by the Turkish Republic of Northern Cyprus which has occupied and controlled most of Northern Cyprus since 1974 when Greek Cypriots sought union with Greece.

CONTEXT

Iceland applied to join the EU in 2009, but its economy remains weak after the 2008 financial crisis. The former Yugoslav Republic of Macedonia, as well as Montenegro and Serbia have applied for membership. Bosnia and Herzegovina, and Albania have been identified as potential candidate states.

DEEPENING THE TIES: FURTHER INTEGRATION

Treaty reform

The obligations of the Member States are contained in the Treaties. Amending the Treaties requires unanimous agreement of Member States with some exceptions (considered in Chapter 2). It is usually preceded by an **intergovernmental conference** (IGC), sometimes lasting several years when the issues under consideration are controversial. Treaties only come into effect when ratified by all the Member States.

After amendment by the Treaty of Lisbon there are two main treaties:

- the Treaty on the Functioning of the EU (TFEU)
- the Treaty on European Union (TEU).

The TFEU is a consolidated version of the Treaty establishing the European Community (TEC), amended by later treaties including acts of accession and the treaties shown in the box:

Treaty	Date in force
Single European Act	1 July 1987
Treaty on European Union (Maastricht Treaty)	1 November 1993
Treaty of Amsterdam	1 May 1999
Treaty of Nice	1 February 2003
Treaty of Lisbon	1 December 2009

Background to the Single European Act

During the 1970s and early 1980s progress towards integration stagnated as Member States focused on national self-interest. The rationale for the Single European Act emerged through a 1985 White Paper on Completion of the Internal Market issued by the Commission under its President, Jacques Delors, showing that obstacles to trade between Member States damaged the Community's global trading position. The single market initiative was supported by all Member States. The emphasis of the White Paper was on *mutual recognition* by which each Member State accepts the standards of others, rather than *harmonisation* through specific directives, a process seen as too slow.

INTERSECTION ....

Mutual recognition has been an invaluable tool in completing the internal market. It is considered further in relation to goods in Chapter 12 and recognition of qualifications in Chapter 15.

The Single European Act (SEA), signed and effective from 1986, represented the first major revision to the EEC Treaty. It was a highly significant development, reflecting a shared commitment from all Member States to eliminate obstructions to free movement. The Commission took the lead role, influenced as Armstrong and Bulmer (1998) point out, by contributions of Member States and the European Council. The objective of the SEA was to remove all remaining barriers to free movement, whether physical, technical or fiscal. The previous requirement for unanimity in the Council was dropped in favour of qualified majority voting (QMV), a system of weighted voting (considered in Chapter 2). This meant that a single state could no longer halt progress. The single market programme of 282 directives was adopted, requiring removal of the barriers to free movement by the end of 1992. The programme was a great success, rekindling Member States' enthusiasm for integration.

CORNERSTONE

Article 26(1) TFEU (ex 14 TEC) provides that the Union 'shall adopt measures with the aim of establishing or ensuring the functioning of the internal market, in accordance with the relevant provisions of these Treaties.'

The internal market is defined by Article 26 TFEU (ex 14 TEC) as 'an area without internal frontiers in which goods, persons, services and capital is ensured in accordance with the provisions of the Treaties'. The legal obligation to achieve a common market in the original Treaty of Rome may not seem fundamentally different from the internal market under the SEA. The single market programme fostered a spirit of goodwill, hitherto lacking, to promote integration and a timetable for its achievement. By December 1992 the single (or internal) market was largely complete. A single market 'scoreboard' listing barriers removed and those remaining began to be published on Europa (the EU website) and regularly updated. Member States defaulting on implementation could be subject to action in the Court of Justice, reinforced (after the Maastricht Treaty) by financial penalties under Article 260 TFEU (ex 228 TEC).

THE EUROPEAN UNION AND THE MAASTRICHT TREATY

No intergovernmental conferences (IGCs) were held until 1985 when the integration process prompted by the SEA initiated an almost continuous process of Treaty review. Two IGCs were convened in 1990, one to consider **economic and monetary union (EMU)** and the other, **political union (EPU)**. France and Germany were seen as providing the 'motor' for European integration during negotiations over the Maastricht Treaty (1990–1991), with the political leaders of both countries firmly committed to both EMU and EPU. Other states such as the UK and Denmark were opposed to deeper integration, fearing a further loss of sovereignty. Such differing views could not be fully resolved in the body of a single Treaty.

When the Maastricht Treaty was signed in December 1991 it provided for both political and economic union. The UK and Denmark, however, 'opted out' of the commitment to EMU in a Protocol. The UK further opted out of the 'Social Chapter' (or the Social Policy Agreement), providing a limited legal basis for employment protection measures to which the Conservative government under John Major objected. From the compromises needed to ensure passage of the TEU there emerged what the legal academic Curtin (1993) termed 'a Europe of bits and pieces'. While purists might decry the resulting legal complexities, it could be argued that such 'flexibility' was essential to achieve European Union in terms of widening and deepening. It facilitated the admission of new Member States with varying levels of integration into the activities of the EU, and allowed existing states to advance at different speeds. The Treaty also introduced the concept of 'subsidiarity' to determine whether action should be taken by the EU or Member States (see 'Take Note' box).

The Maastricht Treaty embodied a far-reaching commitment towards European Union in which all Member States agreed to move to political union, although some states did not participate in

Take note

Subsidiarity is an important term which you will often meet in your studies of EU law. It governs the allocation of **competences** (capabilities) in areas where the EU shares the role with the Member States.

Subsidiarity was introduced by the Maastricht Treaty and is set out in Article 5(3) TEU. This Article provides that in areas where the EU does not have exclusive competence (i.e. where competence is shared with Member States) the Union shall act 'only if and so far as the objectives of the proposed action cannot be sufficiently achieved by the Member States, either at central level or at regional level, but can rather, by reason of scale or effects of the proposed action, be better achieved at Union level'. Subsidiarity is considered further in Chapter 4.

EMU. It introduced a two-Treaty system, with strategic obligations in the Treaty on European Union (TEU) while the main legal provisions for the EU institutions and single market were provided in the Treaty establishing the European Community (TEC). The two-Treaty approach was retained under the Treaty of Lisbon, with the TEU and the Treaty on the Functioning of the EU (TFEU) replacing the TEC.

Ratification of the Maastricht Treaty

Ratification of the Maastricht Treaty was fraught and slow. There was considerable UK opposition before it was accepted by Parliament. The Danish people rejected the Treaty in a referendum, only accepting it in a second referendum after concerns about key policies such as **subsidiarity** and **Union citizenship** were allayed. The Treaty came into force on 1 November 1993 when all Member States had ratified.

The Three Pillars under the Maastricht Treaty

Under the Maastricht Treaty, EPU was to be achieved through a new structure comprising **three pillars**, later collapsed into a single pillar, the European Union, under the Treaty of Lisbon. At the time of the Maastricht Treaty the areas within the second and third pillars were administered through intergovernmental cooperation as they were not considered suitable for regulation by law. The three pillars were:

- *Pillar One*, comprising the three previous Communities: the ECSC, Euratom and the EC (as the EEC had been renamed), governed by law under the Treaty establishing the EC (TEC).
- *Pillar Two, the Common Foreign and Security Policy (CFSP)*, covering joint foreign action and security, regulated through intergovernmental cooperation. The policy covered aspects of the EU's external relations (i.e. relations with non-Member States) including diplomatic contacts and peacekeeping, but not economic activities such as trade or aid agreements. A unanimous vote in the Council was required. After amendment by the Treaty of Lisbon, the CFSP continues to be covered by intergovernmental cooperation under the EU.
- *Pillar Three, Police and Judicial Cooperation in Criminal Matters (PJCCM)*, covering some aspects of regulation of external borders and free movement of persons, such as asylum and immigration policies, as well as cooperation between judicial, police and customs authorities.

Figure 1.2 The three pillars

The difficulties in seeking unanimity in such a sensitive area as the CFSP are demonstrated by the differing responses of Member States to US military intervention in Iraq in 2003 when the UK supported the US action despite strong opposition from France and Germany.

CONTEXT

Other changes introduced by the Maastricht Treaty

Important institutional changes were introduced by the Maastricht Treaty, notably:

- Introduction of the *co-decision procedure* (renamed the ordinary procedure by the Treaty of Lisbon) strengthening the role of the European Parliament without giving it power to adopt laws on its own. This procedure, now the main legislative mechanism of the EU, involves adoption of legislation jointly by the Council and European Parliament. It is considered further in Chapter 2.
- The European Council, comprising heads of state or government and the President of the Commission, meets at least twice a year under Article 15 TEU (replacing Article 4 TEU in substance), providing the Union with 'the necessary impetus for its development'.
- *Citizenship of the Union* for EU nationals under Article 20 TFEU (ex 17 TEC). Union citizenship is not merely symbolic but provides for residence rights for Union nationals throughout the EU, as well as democratic rights including the right to stand and to vote in European Parliamentary elections.

INTERSECTION

The rights of Union citizens are considered in Chapter 13. They have developed through the case law of the Court of Justice and enable individuals with the nationality of a Member State to establish residence rights without necessarily falling into an economic category such as 'worker'.

The EU declared its allegiance to fundamental human rights in Articles 6 and 7 of the TEU, although the provisions could not be enforced in the courts until the Treaty of Lisbon gave the TEU legal force.

INTERSECTION

Fundamental rights are the rights guaranteed by the **European Convention on Human Rights and Fundamental Freedoms (ECHR)** and those resulting from the constitutional traditions common to the Member States. Fundamental rights are considered further in Chapter 5.

Titles and terminology under the Maastricht Treaty

Following ratification of the Maastricht Treaty in 1993, the European Union (EU) was established as an over-arching entity covering the EC, ECSC and Euratom. These three communities, acting under the first pillar, became known as the **European Community (EC)**, the word 'Economic' having been dropped from the title 'European Economic Community' to signify the evolution from a mainly

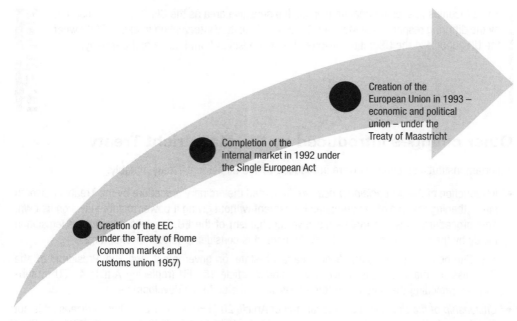

Figure 1.3 Development of the European Union – from EEC to EU

economic community to the Union, with its wide-ranging interests. The expression 'EC law' rather than 'EU law' was used to cover the legal regulation of first pillar activities until December 2009 when the Treaty of Lisbon amalgamated the three-pillar structure into a single European Union.

There is a considerable body of academic literature on European integration and the process of Treaty reform, much of it focusing on the conflict between the desire of Member States to retain sovereignty and pressure for deeper EU integration, seen by some as promoting a **federal** European state. Mancini (1998, p.31), a former judge of the Court of Justice is firmly of the view that the Maastricht Treaty has not led to the creation of a federal state. Indeed he considers that '[T]he closer the Union moves towards statehood, the greater the resistance to the attainment of this goal becomes.' However, if Member States seek to exert tighter control over the legislative process, it would undermine the advances of European integration. Mancini's preferred alternative would be for the Union to evolve into a democratic, stateless entity.

Weiler (1991), a leading legal theorist on European integration, sees the single market programme as representing both a 'unity' vision in which the Community operated as a political union of federal governance and an 'ideal type' based on 'uneasy co-existence' of the Community and the Member States (1991, p.2479). He warns of the dangers of transferring power from Member States to the Community, while remaining optimistic of the relevance of the Community model for other regimes. Weiler (2001, p.12) sees further dangers in adopting a European constitution in response to EU enlargement, preferring to leave development of the EU to its 'own brand of constitutional federalism' based on what he called the 'principle of tolerance'.

REFLECTION

THE TREATY OF AMSTERDAM 1997

An intergovernmental conference (IGC) was held between 1996 and 1997 to review the operation of the Maastricht amendments in the light of the challenge posed by further EU enlargement. The Treaty was signed in October 1997 and took effect in May 1999, renumbering the TEC as part of the process of simplification and consolidation. The Social Chapter was incorporated into the Treaty after Tony Blair and the 'New Labour' government came to power in 1997. Many commentators considered that the Treaty of Amsterdam was a missed opportunity as it failed to reform the institutions, making modest alterations to the decision-making structure, while simplifying and extending the co-decision procedure.

> The Berlin Wall had fallen in 1989. The newly democratic countries in Eastern Europe sought freedom to join the EU as a badge of their political status and to provide funds to develop their economic base. Clearly an EU of twenty-five or more states could not function in the same way as one of fifteen. However, existing Member States were reluctant to yield power and influence in the institutions at Amsterdam, for example, by agreeing to reduce the number of Commissioners.

CONTEXT

The Treaty of Amsterdam retained the three-pillar approach, but moved activities from the third pillar to the first pillar, bringing them within the jurisdiction of the Court of Justice. The *Schengen Agreement* providing for gradual relaxation of border controls on the movement of persons between participating states was moved to the first pillar in a Protocol. The UK and Ireland did not sign the Agreement or Protocol owing to concern over immigration, terrorism and drug trafficking, but reserved the right to participate in matters of national interest. Some aspects of immigration policy were also moved to the first pillar, with the UK and Ireland again opting out. Under the second pillar (CFSP) Member States were required to ensure that their national policies complied with the EU model in areas such as the common defence policy and peace keeping. The third pillar was renamed 'Police and Judicial Co-operation in Criminal Matters' to reflect the intention to provide citizens with a high level of safety within an area of freedom, security and justice. Rules were to be drawn up on common action on asylum, visas, immigration and controls at external borders.

Policies and tasks under the Treaty of Amsterdam

The Treaty of Amsterdam introduced new tasks reflected in amendments to the Treaty in areas including:

- promotion of equality between men and women;
- a high level of protection and improvement of the quality of the environment;
- promotion of a high degree of competitiveness;
- economic development which must be 'sustainable' as well as 'balanced and harmonious'.

Articles 43–45 TEU (now Article 20 TEU) enabled Member States to use the institutional framework to establish closer cooperation between themselves, recognising the desire for certain states to move faster than others towards European integration. Economic and Monetary Union (EMU) involving those Member States satisfying economic criteria and wishing to participate is a form of flexibility (known as 'enhanced cooperation' under the Treaty of Lisbon). EMU involves the use of a common currency, the euro, and acceptance of the authority of the **European Central Bank (ECB)**.

THE TREATY OF NICE

The next IGC was convened at the Cologne Summit in June 1999 to address issues left unresolved by the Treaty of Amsterdam, particularly institutional reform prior to enlargement. The Treaty of Nice was signed in February 2001 despite the dissatisfaction of many citizens who felt isolated from the EU institutions and the integration process. A Protocol to the Treaty provided methods to introduce changes to the institutions (considered in Chapter 2).

The Treaty extended the application of the co-decision procedure and reformed the judicial system. It provided more detailed procedures on the use of Article 7 TEU, with suspension of voting rights in the Council for a serious and persistent breach of human rights. Changes were made to the second pillar, the CFSP, particularly to the security and defence policy. New provision was made for 'enhanced cooperation', where a minimum of nine Member States agree to participate, subject to a list of conditions including the need to respect the EU *acquis*, continued under the Treaty of Lisbon in Article 20 TEU. Although ratification proceeded fairly smoothly in fourteen of the fifteen Member States, the Irish people rejected the Treaty in a referendum in June 2001. A second referendum in Ireland in October 2002 secured the requisite majority, and the Treaty came into force on 1 February 2003, just over a year before enlargement of the Union to twenty-five Member States on 1 May 2004.

The Charter of Fundamental Rights

The Charter in December 2000 was signed by the fifteen Member States at the European Council meeting at Nice and annexed to the Treaty of Nice as a *declaration*, which meant that it did not *at that time* have legally binding status.

The non-binding status of the Charter resulted from the differing positions of the Member States, with the UK arguing in negotiations that the Charter was unnecessary, while most other Member States supported it as a formal element within the Treaty. The Treaty of Lisbon gave the Charter the *same status as the Treaties* in Article 6 TEU, which means that has been a legally binding source of law since December 2009 when the Treaty of Lisbon took effect. (The Charter as a source of law is considered further in Chapter 2.) The Charter incorporates rights from international sources, particularly the European Convention on Human Rights. It recognises rights under six headings: dignity, freedom, equality, solidarity, citizens' rights and justice. The UK position is now covered by a Protocol under the Treaty of Lisbon.

THE FAILED CONSTITUTIONAL TREATY

The Convention on the Future of Europe was set up after the Laeken Summit of the European Council in December 2001 to explore areas identified by the Nice IGC as requiring further action – subsidiarity, the status of the Charter of Fundamental Rights, simplification of the Treaties and the role of national and regional parliaments to the EU. Under the Chairmanship of Valéry Giscard d'Estaing, former President of France, the Convention drew up the Treaty establishing a **Constitution for Europe (CT)** in July 2003. Although signed by all Member States in June 2004, popular unease and frustration over the role and functions of the EU led to resounding 'no' votes in referenda in France and the Netherlands in 2005. Ratification stalled and the CT was abandoned.

THE TREATY OF LISBON

Despite the failure of the CT it was clear that a new Treaty was essential to the future effectiveness of the Union. The Member States convened an IGC in 2007 which identified the need for greater efficiency in decision-making, increased democracy through a greater role for the European Parliament and national parliaments, and a clearer presence outside the EU. The Reform Treaty (Treaty of Lisbon) was signed in December 2007. Ratification was difficult, particularly in Ireland where the Irish people rejected ratification in a referendum in June 2008. A second referendum in October 2009 resulted in a positive vote after Ireland was given guarantees that the Treaty would not affect significant areas of its sovereignty including military neutrality, taxation and abortion.

Key changes under the Treaty of Lisbon

The Treaty of Lisbon simplified the structure and organisation of the EU. It amended the Treaty on European Union (TEU) and the Treaty establishing the European Community (EC), renamed the Treaty on the Functioning of the Union (TFEU) by Article 1(3) TEU. The European Community ceased to exist, having been subsumed into the European Union. References to the internal market replaced the term common market in the Treaties. Article 1(1) TEU provides for the establishment of the Union, and Article 1(3) for both Treaties to have the same legal value – an important change as the TEU previously lacked legal force. The three-pillar structure was merged into a single pillar, 'the Union', although special procedures were retained in foreign policy, security and defence. Before the Treaty of Rome no mechanism existed for a Member State to leave the EU. Article 50(1) TEU now provides a procedure enabling a Member State to withdraw from the Union 'in accordance with its own constitutional requirements'.

The Treaties do not provide for the **primacy** of Union law over national law. However, a Declaration annexed to the Treaties recalls that in accordance with 'well-settled case law of the Court of Justice', the Treaties and secondary legislation 'shall have primacy over the law of Member States' under the conditions laid down by the Court. Supremacy is considered further in Chapter 6.

The Treaty of Lisbon introduced changes to the institutional framework to make the enlarged Union more workable. One of the most significant was the extension of **qualified majority voting (QMV)** in the Council to new areas, with a new definition of what constitutes a qualified majority in Article 238 TFEU (with effect from 2014). The position of the European Council was strengthened by its recognition as an institution under Article 13 TEU, with an elected President instead of the previous rotating presidency (Article 15(5) TEU). The first holder of this title is Hermann van Rompuy, a former Prime Minister of Belgium. The institutions are considered in Chapter 2.

The profile of the Union in the world was raised by creation of a new post of High Representative of the Union for Foreign Affairs and Security Policy under Article 18(1) appointed by the

> **Take note**
>
> Treaties are divided into Titles, Chapters and Articles. As part of the simplification process under the Treaty of Lisbon, Treaty Articles were renumbered for the second time, the first being under the Treaty of Amsterdam. Treaty Articles in both TEU and TFEU are cited by reference firstly to the new, post-Lisbon numbering and secondly (in brackets) to the pre-Lisbon system. Thus, for example, the prohibition on discrimination on grounds of nationality is cited as Article 18 TFEU (ex 12 TEC). In this book references to Treaty Articles are to the current, post-Lisbon numbering unless it is necessary to use the earlier version to avoid confusion or because the wording has changed significantly.

European Council, a position currently occupied by Baroness Ashton, previously the UK member of the Commission. A new Title V TFEU on the Area of Freedom, Security and Justice, covering border checks, asylum and immigration replaced the previous Title IV TEU on Visas, Asylum and Immigration.

Fundamental rights under the Treaty of Lisbon

Before amendment by the Treaty of Lisbon, the Union lacked legal personality, preventing it from acceding to international treaties such as the European Convention on Human Rights (ECHR). This gap was rectified by Article 47 TEU, which states that 'The Union shall have legal personality'. Article 6(1) TEU provides for recognition of the rights, freedoms and principles in the Charter of Fundamental Rights, which is stated to have the same legal value as the Treaties, making it legally enforceable. However, the new status of the Charter does not create additional competences (capabilities) for the EU, as Article 6(1) TEU states that the provisions of the Charter 'shall not extend in any way the competences of the Union as defined in the Treaties'.

A Protocol annexed to the Treaty limits the application of the Charter. It provides that the Charter does not extend the ability of the Court of Justice or any court or tribunal of the UK or Poland to find that the laws, regulations or administrative provisions are inconsistent with the fundamental rights and principles in the Charter. This is considered further in Chapter 5.

A new set of aims

CORNERSTONE

Article 2 TEU provides for the Union to be founded on the values of 'respect for human dignity, freedom, democracy, equality, the rule of law and respect for human rights'.

These values are to be achieved through a new set of aims in Article 3 TEU including:

- promotion of peace, its values and the well-being of its peoples;
- an area of freedom, security and justice without internal frontiers, in conjunction with external border controls;
- establishment of an internal market: the Union is required to work for the sustainable development of Europe, combat social discrimination and exclusion, promote social justice and equality and respect cultural and linguistic diversity;
- establishment of economic and monetary union;
- pursuit of its objectives by appropriate means commensurate with its competences conferred on it by the Treaties.

The Union is required to develop a 'special relationship with neighbouring countries' founded on the values of the Union and 'characterised by close and peaceful relations based on cooperation' (Article 8 TEU).

The Treaty of Lisbon introduced a new Title II on democratic principles, entitling every citizen to participate in the democratic life of the Union (Article 10(3) TEU). A million or more citizens may submit a proposal for action to the Commission where they consider that a legal act is necessary (Article 11(4) TEU). National parliaments are given a new role in the legislative process by scrutinising draft legislation to see whether it accords with the principle of subsidiarity (Article 12(a) TEU) (i.e. whether the action could be more effectively undertaken by the Member States).

The distribution of competences between the EU and the Member States

The Treaty of Lisbon clarified the distribution of competences between the EU and the Member States.

Article 5(2) TEU provides that the limits of Union competences are governed by the principle of conferral. Competences may be 'exclusive' (conferred on the Union alone) or 'concurrent' (shared with Member States). Only the Union may act where it has exclusive competence unless a Member State is empowered to act by the Union. Where competence is shared, both Union and the Member States may act, subject to the principles of subsidiarity and **proportionality** (considered in Chapter 5).

> **Take note**
> 'Competence' is capacity to act. The EU has capacity to act only where the Treaties confer it (the principle of 'conferral') to attain the objectives of the Treaties.

ECONOMIC AND MONETARY UNION

Economic and monetary union (EMU) was introduced in 1999 following the Treaty of Maastricht. Article 3(3) TEU (ex 2 TEU) requires the EU to establish an economic and monetary union whose currency is the euro. The idea behind a single currency was to provide greater currency stability for participating states under the control of the European Central Bank in Frankfurt. Seventeen 'Eurozone' states adopted the euro, having satisfied the economic criteria for membership. The UK and Denmark secured 'opt outs' during the Maastricht negotiations. EMU has come under great strain since the financial crisis in 2008 and its future is uncertain.

The financial crisis in the Eurozone states has been particularly severe in Greece but has also affected Spain, Italy and Ireland. Measures to 'bail out' the affected economies were taken in 2011, followed by the Fiscal Compact in 2012, a form of Treaty adopted under enhanced cooperation enabling participating states to cooperate more closely to prevent excessive budget deficits. All the EU Member States were invited to sign although not all participate in EMU. Two prime ministers refused – the Czech Prime Minister, Peter Nečas, and David Cameron, the UK Prime Minster, who saw the Compact as a threat to the independence of financial institutions in the City of London.

CONTEXT

THE EU TODAY

The EU has evolved from an economic community of six States to a complex political union of twenty-eight. Today it faces great political and economic challenges following the Eurozone crisis and global recession. The Coalition government in the UK is committed to renegotiating some provisions of the Treaties and seeks to 'repatriate' powers from the EU back to the Westminster Parliament, with a referendum on continuing EU membership after the next general election. The Union will continue to develop in the future, though its exact political form and membership remain subject to negotiation.

KEY POINTS

- EU law can only be understood in its historical and economic context, including its origins in the need for stability in Europe after the Second World War.
- The EU has evolved from a community of six Member States to a Union of twenty-eight Member States with common policies and complex institutions.
- The EU has responded to major political change in Eastern Europe by admitting many new Member States.
- The priorities of the Union have been affected at different times by the need for widening (enlargement) and deepening (increased integration between existing Member States).

CORE STATUTES

Statute	About	Importance
Article 3(2) TEU (ex 2(2) TEC)	Provides for EU to be an **Area of freedom, security and justice (AFSJ)** without internal frontiers, ensuring free movement of persons.	The AFSJ was covered by former third pillar under Maastricht Treaty and brought within the single pillar by Treaty of Lisbon.
Article 3(3) TEU (ex 2(3) TEC)	Provides for EU to establish internal market, working for sustainable development.	Economic objectives are supplemented by far-reaching social and cultural objectives.
Article 4(2) TEU	EU is required to respect equality of Member States before the Treaties, national identities, and essential state functions.	Introduced by Treaty of Lisbon, demonstrating respect for constitutional position of Member States.
Article 4(3) TEU	Sets out principle of sincere cooperation, by which EU and Member States respect and assist each other to carry out tasks under the Treaties.	Lies at heart of Member States' duty to observe EU law and carry out their duties under the Treaties.

FURTHER READING

Armstrong, K.A. and Bulmer, S.J. *The Governance of the Single European Market* (Manchester University Press: Manchester, 1998).
Analyses the origins, development and dynamics of the single market.

Cecchini, P. *The European Challenge: the Benefits of a Single Market ('The Cecchini Report')* (Wildwood House: Kentucky, 1988)
Compares the costs of keeping and abolishing barriers to free movement between Member States.

Curtin, D. 'The Constitutional Structure of the Union: A Europe of Bits and Pieces' (1993) 30(1) *Common Market Law Review* 17
Assesses the scope for flexibility in European integration.

Dell, E. *The Schuman Plan and the British Abdication of Leadership in Europe* (Clarendon: Oxford, 1995)
Examines why the UK did not join the ECSC, EEC and Euratom at the outset.

Majone, G. 'Unity in Diversity: European Integration and the Enlargement Process' (2008) 33(4) *European Law Review* 457
Discusses widening and deepening, particularly the role played by multi-speed integration.

Mancini, G. 'Europe: The Case for Statehood' (1998) 4(1) *European Law Journal* 29
The author, a former judge of the Court of Justice, examines EU development up to the Treaty of Amsterdam and considers whether the EU can become democratic without being a federal state.

Weatherill S. 'Why Harmonise?' in T. Tridimas and P. Nebbia (eds) *European Union Law for the Twenty First Century* (Hart Publishing: Oxford, 2004)
A thoughtful analysis of the rationale for harmonisation in the single market.

Weiler, J.H.H, 'Federalism without constitutionalism: Europe's Sonderweg' in Nicolaidis, K. and Howse, R. (eds), *The Federal Vision: Legitimacy and Levels of Governance in the US and EU* (Oxford University Press: Oxford, 2001)
The author, a leading political and legal theorist, examines what he calls the 'Principle of Tolerance' in the development of the EU.

Weiler, J. 'The Transformation of Europe' (1991) 100 *Yale Law Journal* 2405
Traces the evolution of the division of competences between the EU and Member States after completion of the single market.

CHAPTER 2

Decision-making in the EU institutions

BLUEPRINT

Decision-making in the EU institutions

KEY QUESTIONS

LEGISLATION

- Article 16(1) TEU
- Article 17(1) TEU

CONTEXT

- The EU has nearly doubled in size since 2003, but existing Member States have been reluctant to agree changes to the institutions
- Political groups in the European Parliament
- Population and weighting of votes

CONCEPTS

- European Parliament
- European Council
- Council of the EU
- European Commission
- Democratic deficit

- Is decision-making in the EU sufficiently democratic?

- Are the institutions 'fit' for an enlarged EU?
- How can the EU be brought closer to the citizen?

CASES

REFORM

- The Treaty of Lisbon introduced long-overdue reforms to the EU institutions, some in 2009 and others only in 2014
- Further reform may be needed if the EU continues to enlarge

SPECIAL CHARACTERISTICS

- The European Parliament is the only democratically elected EU institution.
- Most laws are adopted jointly by Parliament and the Council.
- The Council wields political power and tends to reflect interests of Member States.
- The Commission has both executive and limited legislative functions.

CRITICAL
ISSUES

Setting the scene

Imagine that Europe has been affected by a sudden increase in global warming leading to a severe and prolonged water shortage which could destroy crops, cause famine and threaten the economies of the Member States. How might such a problem be addressed within the EU? At a political level the European Council (a summit meeting of heads of state) would determine strategies and set priorities. The Council of the EU (a different body comprising ministers from Member States) would meet to address the problems posed by the shortage – in this case the ministers for agriculture, as well as ministers for environment and finance. The European Commission would monitor the position. The European Parliament would debate the water shortage. If the crisis persisted it may be necessary to adopt legislation, in which case a regulation or directive requiring water conservation measures would be drafted by the Commission for adoption by the Parliament and Council.

OVERVIEW OF THE EU INSTITUTIONS

Take note

As the EU institutions are unique, it is best to approach studying them with no preconceptions based on national law about their roles.

The EU institutions can only act under powers agreed by Member States in the Treaties (the TEU and TFEU). Apart from the Court of Justice which exercises a judicial function, the EU does not operate under a classic separation of powers into legislative, executive and judiciary as the roles of the institutions overlap. The Commission proposes legislation but also has a limited legislative function. The Parliament and the Council adopt most of the laws, but Parliament is the only elected body.

Article 13 TEU

Article 13 of the Treaty on European Union provides that

> The Union shall have an institutional framework which shall aim to promote its values, advance its objectives, serve its interests, those of its citizens and those of the Member States, and to ensure the consistency, effectiveness and continuity of its policies and actions.

The institutions are listed in Article 13 as the:

- European Council
- European Parliament
- Council
- European Commission (known as 'the Commission')
- Court of Justice of the European Union
- European Central Bank
- Court of Auditors.

The functions of the institutions other than the Court of Justice (discussed in Chapter 3) are considered below. A brief outline of their roles may be helpful. The European Council establishes the EU's strategic direction. The Commission proposes policy and legislation, operating as the EU's executive arm.

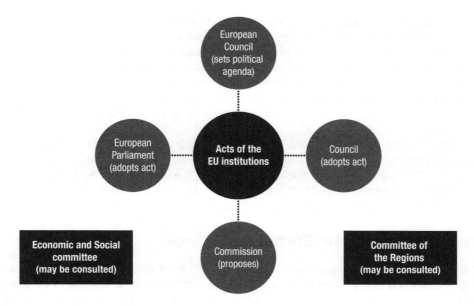

Figure 2.1 Acts of the EU institutions

The Council, made up of ministers of the Member States, adopts legislation jointly with the European Parliament. Successive Treaty revisions have altered the institutions' composition and powers, particularly over the weighting of votes in the Council and the number of MEPs and Commissioners.

THE EUROPEAN COUNCIL

CORNERSTONE

Article 15(1) TEU states that 'The European Council shall provide the Union with the necessary impetus for its development and shall define the general political directions and priorities.'

The European Council is a regular summit meeting of Heads of State, Foreign Ministers, the President of the European Council, President of the Commission and High Representative of the Union for Foreign Affairs. It must meet at least twice every six months under Article 15 TEU to enable European political leaders to agree the EU's strategic agenda for action by the Council.

The Treaty of Lisbon introduced two new roles to raise the international profile of the EU. The President of the European Council represents the EU to the world, particularly over the

> **Take note**
>
> It is important not to confuse the European Council attended by heads of state with the Council of the EU attended by ministers of Member States.

Common Foreign and Security Policy, in conjunction with the High Representative who also acts as the Vice-President of the Commission. Their roles are considered below.

The European Council process may be seen in the Copenhagen Council of 1992 when the main concern was the response to the challenge posed by emerging new democracies in central and Eastern Europe after the collapse of Communism. The European Council laid down the conditions for applicant states to join the EU. These terms (often called 'the Copenhagen criteria') formed the basis for the 2003, 2005, 2009 and 2013 *accession agreements* by which thirteen new Member States joined the EU.

European Council meetings to discuss Treaty reform are followed by intergovernmental conferences (IGCs), a continuing dialogue between officials from the Member States preparing a draft Treaty for discussion. The European Council also meets to discuss the budget, as it did in February 2013 when the UK Prime Minister, David Cameron, obtained a reduction in the UK's contribution to the EU budget in view of the economic crisis. The overall EU budget was substantially reduced.

The President of the European Council

It became clear in discussions before the Lisbon Treaty that no single individual represented the foreign and security policy of the EU internationally. To rectify this gap a new role of President of the European Council was introduced, in conjunction with that of High Representative of the Union for Foreign Affairs and Security Policy under Article 15(6) TEU. While the purpose of the role of President of the European Council was to raise the awareness of EU foreign policy, the appointment in 2009 of Hermann van Rompuy, former Prime Minister of Belgium, may indicate that the role is closer to that of a chief executive than high-profile international statesman.

The maximum term of office for the President is five years (two and a half years, renewable once). Article 15(6) TEU provides that the President shall:

- chair the European Council and drive it forward;
- ensure the preparation and continuity of the European Council's work in cooperation with the President of the Commission and on the basis of the General Affairs Council;
- endeavour to facilitate cohesion and consensus within the European Council;
- report to the Parliament after each European Council meeting.

The High Representative of the Union for Foreign Affairs and Security Policy

The role of High Representative of the Union for Foreign Affairs and Security was introduced under the Treaty of Lisbon to conduct the EU's Foreign and Security Policy. Article 18(1) TEU provides for appointment of the High Representative by the European Council by qualified majority voting (QMV) with approval of the President of the Commission. The first office-holder is Catherine Ashton, a UK national and former EU Trade Commissioner. The High Representative has a dual role under Article 18(2–4) TEU in relation to the Council and Commission, with responsibility for conducting the foreign and security policy of the Union, chairing the Foreign Affairs Council while also serving as Vice-President of the Commission.

THE EUROPEAN PARLIAMENT

The European Parliament (EP) provides a forum to consider legislation and review the activities of other institutions including the Commission. Its stature and influence have increased steadily since direct elections were introduced in 1979.

The Parliament is based in Strasbourg, with some sessions held in Brussels where committee meetings also take place. Members (MEPs) are elected for five years. Before the Maastricht Treaty, Parliament had only an indirect role in the legislative process as EU laws (regulations, directives and decisions) were adopted by the (unelected) Council, sometimes after consultation with Parliament. The powers of Parliament were greatly enhanced by the Maastricht Treaty which introduced a new procedure enabling the Council and Parliament to adopt laws jointly under what is now Article 289(1) TFEU. The 'co-decision procedure' (as it was originally known) was renamed the *ordinary legislative procedure* by the Treaty of Lisbon.

> **Take note**
>
> It is important to appreciate that the role of the European Parliament differs from a national parliament as it can only adopt laws jointly with the Council, the principal source of political power in the EU.

Composition of the Parliament

Agreement on Parliamentary reform proved elusive before the Lisbon Treaty. Article 14(2) TEU requires the European Council, acting unanimously, to adopt a new system to establish the total number of MEPs and the allocation of seats based on *degressive proportionality*, by which the higher the population of a Member State, the more MEPs. Article 14(2) TEU provides that no single Member State may have more than ninety-six or fewer than six MEPs. Table 2.1 shows the composition of the Parliament after Croatia joined the EU in July 2013.

Seats in Parliament have not been distributed evenly according to population. Citizens in smaller Member States are better represented than those in larger ones, with Luxembourg enjoying representation of one MEP for about 65,550 citizens, compared with Germany, where the ratio is one MEP for about 400,000 citizens. The 2013 redistribution made some changes, although the number of MEPs for Germany and Luxembourg have not altered. While common electoral procedures based on proportional representation (PR) have been used in Parliamentary elections since 2002, Member States have discretion in the choice of PR system and size of constituencies, contributing to this disproportionate result.

Political groupings and parties

Most MEPs sit in one of eight *cross-national political groupings*, reflecting traditional ideological divisions, but vote on an individual and personal basis. Groupings include the European People's Party (centre-right, the largest party), the Group of the Progressive Alliance of Socialists and Democrats, the Group of Alliance of Liberals and Democrats for Europe, and the European Conservative and Reformists Group (a new centre-right group including UK Conservative MEPs).

Table 2.1 Allocation of seats in the European Parliament until 2014

Member State	Number of MEPs
Germany	99
France	74
Italy and the UK	73
Spain	54
Poland	51
Romania	32
Netherlands	26
Belgium, the Czech Republic, Greece, Hungary and Portugal	22
Sweden	20
Austria	19
Bulgaria	18
Denmark, Finland, Slovakia	13
Croatia, Ireland	12
Latvia and Lithuania	9
Slovenia	8
Cyprus, Estonia, Luxembourg, Malta	6
TOTAL	766

Recognition as a group requires strong political affinity between members, achieved when the European Conservative and Reformists Group was formed in 2009 by an alliance of MEPs from seven Member States. This action reflected the stated intention of David Cameron (then in Opposition as leader of the UK Conservative Party) and Mirek Topolanek (Prime Minister of the Czech Republic and leader of the Civic Democratic Party) for the Conservatives and Civic Democratic Party to leave the federalist European People's Party for a more Eurosceptic, centre-right group.

European political parties contribute to 'forming a European awareness and to expressing the political will of the citizens of the Union' under Article 224 TFEU (ex 191 TEC). However, they have done little to awaken the interest of voters in European issues. While Union citizenship carries the right to vote in Parliamentary and local elections, Union citizens tend to identify themselves as nationals of their own Member State rather than as part of a European people or *demos* (the Greek word for a 'people' from which the expression 'democracy' originates). As the political theorist Joseph Weiler (2003) observes:

[E]urope's political architecture has never been validated by a process of constitutional adoption by a European constitutional *demos* and, hence . . . does not enjoy the same kind of authority [as] that . . . in federal states where their federalism is rooted in a classic constitutional order.

Functions of the Parliament

The Parliament has important functions, including:

- supervision of the Commission;
- adoption of legislation (jointly with the Council);
- amendment and delay over adoption of the budget.

Supervision of the Commission

Parliament supervises the Commission through an annual report of its activities debated in open session under Article 233 TFEU (ex 200 TEC). Parliament may pass a censure motion on the Commission under Article 234 TFEU (ex 201 TEC), enabling it to dismiss *all* its members, but it cannot dismiss individual Commissioners. The Council may apply to the Court of Justice under Article 247 TFEU (ex 216 TEC) for a Commissioner's compulsory retirement where he is guilty of serious misconduct or cannot carry out his duties.

The censure motion is a cumbersome mechanism requiring a two-thirds majority of votes cast. It has been threatened eight times, but never pursued to a conclusion. A censure motion was tabled in 1999 after publication of a highly critical report by a Committee of Experts into allegations of fraud and mismanagement by the Commission. In March 1999, the day before the vote, all members of the Commission including President Santer resigned and the motion was dropped. Even where a censure motion is passed and the Commission required to resign, Article 246 TFEU (ex 215 TEC) provides for the Commission to remain in place until a new Commission is appointed. A new President, Romano Prodi, was introduced in September 1999 with a 'new' Commission which included some members who had previously resigned.

Approval of the Commission and nomination of its President

Parliament is consulted on appointment of the President of the Commission under Article 17(6) TEU and on final approval of the Commission as a whole. In 2004 Parliament came close to rejecting the Commission proposed by José Barroso, its President, objecting to views expressed by Rocco Buttiglione, nominee for the Justice, Freedom and Security portfolio which included anti-discrimination policy. The problem was resolved without rejection of the Commission following a compromise involving replacement of two Commissioners.

Parliament's role in the legislative process

The Parliament is the only *elected* body in the Union. Political union was the centrepiece of the Maastricht Treaty creating the European Union, with a commitment to a European ideal of deeper integration bringing the EU closer to the citizen. The introduction of co-decision acknowledged that the Parliament should share equal legislative responsibility with the Council, an *unelected* body drawn from the ministers of the Member States. Progressive Treaty reforms have continued to develop Parliament's role to the point where the ordinary legislative procedure under Article 294 TFEU (ex 218 TEC) has become the norm for legislation. A special legislative procedure replacing the old consultation procedure enables the Council to adopt legislation after consultation with Parliament in a few areas where the Treaties provide, such as competition law.

Is there a 'democratic deficit' in the EU?

Despite Treaty reforms, academic scholars have long commented on the democratic deficit at the heart of the EU, as the European Parliament, the only democratically elected institution, cannot legislate alone. Progress has been made following the introduction of co-decision and its extension to most areas of the EU's activities. As a result, Parliament's influence on decision-making has been greatly enhanced. Nevertheless it is unrealistic to expect Member States to give Parliament sole legislative power, as it would mean relinquishing political influence on legislation through the Council with a significant loss of sovereignty. The compromise represented by the ordinary legislative procedure with its joint legislative role for the Council and Parliament is likely to remain for the foreseeable future. The efforts to bring the EU closer to the citizen and reduce the democratic deficit are discussed below.

REFLECTION

There is an extensive body of commentary on the question of the democratic deficit. The following brief account of a dialogue between three legal academics provides a taste of some differing perspectives. Majone (2005) claims that the criticism that the EU is subject to a democratic deficit is misplaced. In his view most EU policies are 'regulatory' (administrative) and driven by 'efficiency' (results) which can be judged in terms of accountability, rather than by the intention to redistribute resources which would require legitimation by a democratic process. This point has validity as direct taxation (e.g. income tax) is administered by Member States to fund national expenditure agreed through representative parliamentary democracies. However, Snell (2008) criticises Majone, arguing that policies geared towards efficiencies may significantly contribute to redistributing resources, and rejects the claim that the EU's limited competences justify a narrow role for democracy. Dougan (2006) also disagrees with Majone's approach which he considers undervalues the extent to which legitimacy derives from the citizen's participation in decision-making, particularly through the directly elected European Parliament. Majone (2007) responds to Dougan's criticisms, arguing that the EU needs radical reform to face the demands of an enlarged EU, given the failure of the existing system to produce the competitive economy which its citizens expect from integration. This debate will continue as the EU expands and the Parliament seeks more power.

The ordinary legislative procedure

The ordinary legislative procedure under Article 294 TFEU (ex 251 TEC) recognises the joint involvement of Parliament and the Council in law-making. Each Treaty revision since Maastricht has increased Parliament's involvement in the legislative process by extending the scope of co-decision. The Treaty of Lisbon added the area of freedom, security and justice, as well as international trade, agriculture and fisheries.

In 1999 the institutions adopted the Joint Declaration on practical arrangements to make co-decision operate smoothly by encouraging the institutions to reconcile their positions to enable *acts* (i.e. laws) to be adopted at first reading. The Declaration led to the introduction of *trilogues*, preparatory meetings during the legislative process, usually between a Council representative, a senior Commission official and several MEPs. While trilogies have been criticised for lacking formality and transparency, they may have facilitated agreement during the first reading stage when the proposal is considered by Parliament and the Council. Parliament's statistics for 2009–2011 for the first half of the seventh legislative term reveal that 78% of proposals were agreed at first reading, 18% at second

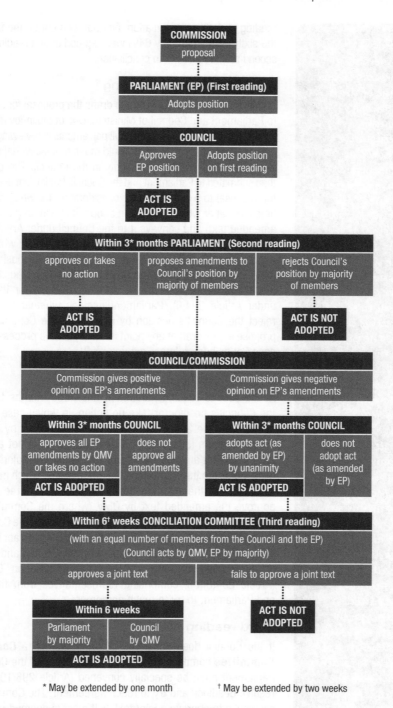

COMMISSION
proposal

PARLIAMENT (EP) (First reading)
Adopts position

COUNCIL

| Approves EP position | Adopts position on first reading |

ACT IS ADOPTED

Within 3* months PARLIAMENT (Second reading)

| approves or takes no action | proposes amendments to Council's position by majority of members | rejects Council's position by majority of members |

ACT IS ADOPTED

ACT IS NOT ADOPTED

COUNCIL/COMMISSION

| Commission gives positive opinion on EP's amendments | Commission gives negative opinion on EP's amendments |

Within 3* months COUNCIL

| approves all EP amendments by QMV or takes no action | does not approve all amendments |

ACT IS ADOPTED

Within 3* months COUNCIL

| adopts act (as amended by EP) by unanimity | does not adopt act (as amended by EP) |

ACT IS ADOPTED

Within 6† weeks CONCILIATION COMMITTEE (Third reading)

(with an equal number of members from the Council and the EP)
(Council acts by QMV, EP by majority)

| approves a joint text | fails to approve a joint text |

Within 6 weeks

| Parliament by majority | Council by QMV |

ACT IS ADOPTED

ACT IS NOT ADOPTED

* May be extended by one month   † May be extended by two weeks

Figure 2.2 The ordinary procedure under Article 294 TFEU

Take note

It is easier to understand the legislative process if you follow the passage of draft legislation on 'Europa', for example through Parliament's Legislative Observatory (known as 'Oeil', available at http://www.europarl.europa.eu/oeil/) tracking the progress of legislation. Taking as an example the revision of the Tobacco Products Directive, a measure to deter young people from smoking, you would see that the Commission adopted a proposal to revise the previous directive in December 2012. The Council agreed to revise the rules in June 2013. In July 2013 the draft was amended by the Public Health Committee of MEPs to require health warnings on all sides of cigarette packages, with a ban on slim cigarettes and attractive packaging. In December 2013 Member States and the Parliament supported strengthening the rules on tobacco and related products. The Parliament formally approved the revised directive on 26 February 2014, with the Council adopting it on 14 March 2014. The new directive will enter into force when it has been signed by the Presidents of the Parliament and the Council, and published in the Official Journal. Member States will have two years to transpose it into national law.

reading and 4% in conciliation, an improvement on the first half of the sixth term when only 64% were agreed at first reading, 29% at second reading and 7% in conciliation.

Proposal and first reading

Under Article 294 the Commission drafts the proposal for submission to Parliament and Council of Ministers. One of the innovations of the Lisbon Treaty was to involve national parliaments in reviewing the draft. Failure to obtain their consent would make it unlikely that a proposal would gain the necessary majority in the Council. The proposal is then submitted to Parliament and the Council. Parliament usually sends the proposal to a committee for consideration for which there is no time limit, after which Parliament adopts its position (i.e. agrees an amended text) and conveys it to the Council under Article 294(3).

The Council may approve the position by QMV, in which case it adopts the act in accordance with Parliament's position under Article 294(4). Otherwise the Council must adopt a position which it conveys to the Parliament, with full reasons for its decision under Article 294(6). Parliament decides whether to amend or reject the Council's position by unanimity. The Commission may propose a new draft at any point in the legislative process, in which case Council amendment requires QMV.

Second reading

At the second reading Parliament has three months to approve the Council's position or take no action, in which case the act is adopted (Article 294(7)(a)). If it rejects the position by a majority of its members (384 of its 766 MEPs), the act is not adopted. If the Parliament amends the Council's position by majority, it must send the text to the Council and the Commission, which must deliver an opinion on the amendments. The Council has three months to approve the amended text by QMV (where the Commission has approved the amendments) or by unanimity (where the Commission has rejected the amendments). Approval means the act is deemed to be adopted. If not, the President of the Council and President of the Parliament must convene the Conciliation Committee (Article 294(8)(b)), comprising representatives from the Council and Parliament to try to reach agreement.

Third reading

If the Council does not agree all amendments, a **Conciliation Committee** composed of equal representation of the Council and Parliament must be specially convened (Article 296(10) TFEU) to resolve deadlock and try to reach agreement. The Committee has six weeks to approve a joint text or the act is deemed not to have been adopted (Article 296(12)). Failure to agree in the Committee is unusual, but occurred with the proposed amendment in 2011 to Regulation 258/97 to simplify the procedure authorising the sale of 'novel foods' (including foods from genetically modified organisms) despite many trilogues and meetings of the Conciliation Committee. If the Committee agrees a joint text, Parliament (by simple majority) and Council (by QMV) have six more weeks to adopt the text, after which it will be adopted by a joint act of the Parliament and Council and signed by the President of each institution.

Recent examples of successful use of conciliation may be found in the Activity Report 2009–11 of the Conciliation Committee, including the conciliation on telecoms (2009). After the Council had rejected a Parliamentary amendment, the Committee produced a new wording guaranteeing the rights of internet users whose access may only be restricted where 'appropriate, proportionate and necessary within a democratic society'.

Special legislative procedure

While most legislation is adopted under the ordinary legislative procedure, the Treaty of Lisbon retained the old 'consultation' procedure (by which the Council adopted an act after consultation with Parliament) as a **special legislative procedure** where the Treaties specifically provide for its use under Article 289(2) TFEU. While the exact nature of a special procedure is not stated, most provisions require the Council to act after consultation with the Parliament. Such procedures tend to apply in areas of particular national sensitivity including harmonisation of indirect taxation under Article 113 TFEU (ex 93 TEC) where the Council must consult both Parliament and the Economic and Social Committee and action to combat discrimination under Article 19(1) TFEU (ex 13 TEC) where the Council acts unanimously after consulting Parliament.

Article 223(2) TFEU (ex 190(5) TEC) provides a rare basis for *Parliament* to adopt a law under a special legislative procedure, in this case to regulate MEPs' performance and duties, after seeking the Commission's opinion and with approval of the Council.

Consent procedure

Parliament retains the power of veto where its consent is required under the Treaties before an act may be adopted by the Council under Article 218 TFEU. The consent (previously 'assent') procedure is a form of special legislative procedure best suited to issues not requiring complex interaction between the institutions such as:

(a) accession of new Member States (Article 49 TEU);

(b) association agreements between the EU and non-Member States (Article 218 TFEU), such as the original Association Agreement providing for a customs union between the EEC and Turkey;

(c) accession of the EU to the European Convention on Human Rights (ECHR) under Article 6(2) TEU (considered in Chapter 5);

(d) sanctions over persistent and serious breach of human rights (Article 7 TEU);

(e) action to attain one of the objectives of the Treaties where the Treaties have not provided the necessary powers (Article 352 TFEU (ex 308 TEC)). While Article 352 appears to provide a wide-ranging legislative power, a Declaration annexed to the Treaty of Lisbon states that it may be invoked in the context of the objectives of the EU in Article 3 TEU, but cannot extend the Union's powers beyond the general framework of the Treaties. Article 352(3) prohibits measures involving harmonisation excluded by the Treaties and Article 352(4) forbids their use for the CFSP.

INTERSECTION

The objectives of the EU in Article 3 TEU are considered in Chapter 1 of this book. They include promotion of peace, the area of freedom, security and justice and establishment of the internal market.

Parliament and the budget

The Parliament has significant powers to amend the budget under Article 314 TFEU (ex 272 TEC). The budgetary procedure resembles the ordinary legislative procedure except that the budget is adopted by Parliament when its President makes a declaration under Article 314(9) TFEU whereas legislation is normally adopted jointly by the Parliament and Council.

Bringing the Union closer to the citizen

The EU has long been criticised for its remoteness. Since the Maastricht Treaty the EU has tried to bring the Union closer to the citizen, providing new routes for individuals to make their views known. Article 226 TFEU (ex 193 TEC) enables Parliament to set up temporary Committees of Inquiry to invest-igate alleged contraventions or maladministration in implementation of EU law. Under Article 227 TFEU (ex 194 TEC) any EU citizen or resident may petition Parliament on any Union matter affecting him or her directly. Article 228 TFEU (ex 195 TEC) enables Parliament to appoint an *Ombudsman* to receive complaints about maladministration by the institutions other than the Court of Justice but with no powers of enforcement.

Provisions on democratic principles

The Treaty of Lisbon introduced new provisions on democratic principles in Title II TEU, declaring that 'The functioning of the Union shall be founded on representative democracy' (Article 10 (1) TEU), followed by statements on the direct representation of citizens in Parliament and Union citizens' right to participate in the democratic life of the Union, with decisions taken 'as openly and as closely as possible to the citizen' (Article 10(3) TEU). Article 11(1) TEU requires the institutions to enable citizens to 'make known and publicly exchange their views in all areas of Union action'. This provision empowers citizens to petition the Commission to propose legislation to implement the Treaties provided they are supported by at least one million citizens from a significant number of Member States. The procedure to implement this right is not yet determined.

Role of national parliaments

Another change under the Lisbon Treaty was to give national parliaments a direct role in the legislative process. Under Article 12 TEU they are entitled to receive the draft legislative acts of the Union in accordance with a Protocol on the role of national parliaments in the EU to ensure that they comply with the principle of subsidiarity (i.e. to confirm that action is needed at EU rather than national level).

INTERSECTION...

You can find out more about the principle of subsidiarity as a general principle of law and in relation to the role of national parliaments in Chapter 5.

Article 12(c) TEU enables national parliaments to assess mechanisms implementing policies in the area of freedom, security and justice (e.g. on asylum or immigration) in accordance with Article 70 TFEU. National parliaments can also participate in the *ordinary revision procedure* under Article 48(1) TEU, a 'fast-track' method of Treaty reform enabling the government of any Member State, the Parliament or

Commission to submit proposals to the Council to amend the Treaties. If the European Council decides by simple majority to examine the proposals, the President of the European Council will convene a convention to adopt a recommendation to a conference of representatives of governments, which will determine by common accord the amendments to be made to the Treaties, for ratification in the normal way.

Simplified Treaty revision procedure

Article 48(6) TEU provides a *simplified revision procedure*, enabling governments of Member States, Parliament or Commission to submit proposals to the European Council on internal policies and actions of the Union. Acting unanimously after consulting the Parliament and Commission, the European Council may adopt a decision adopting all or part of the provisions of Part Three of the TFEU. The European Council must inform national parliaments which have six months to object. If any objection is made, the decision is not adopted.

THE COUNCIL OF THE EUROPEAN UNION

CORNERSTONE

Role of the Council

The Council is made up of *ministers* from Member States, meeting to take decisions and participate in the legislative process. The Council exercises joint legislative and budgetary functions with the Parliament under Article 16(1) TEU and undertakes policy-making and coordinating functions under the Treaties.

Composition and functions

The Council is the powerhouse of the EU, providing a forum for political decision-making. It tends to be dominated by the interests of Member States and the office of the President of the Council is held by each state in turn for six months. The Council is composed of ministers from the Member States, with a variable membership depending on the subject under consideration. The Council meets in recognised formations such as Economic and Financial Affairs (ECOFIN) (finance ministers) dealing with economic policy coordination, or the General Affairs and External Relations Council (foreign ministers) handling issues transcending policy boundaries such as enlargement. The General Affairs Council also has responsibility for preparing and following up meetings of the Heads of Government in the European Council. There are also seven specialised formations with the following responsibilities:

1. Justice and Home Affairs
2. Agricultural and Fisheries
3. Environment
4. Competitiveness (including the internal market)
5. Employment, Social Policy and Consumer Affairs

6. Transport, Telecommunications and Industry

7. Education, Youth and Culture.

Only one voting delegate per Member State is allowed, with meetings in private unless the Council unanimously decides otherwise. The Council is assisted by a General Secretariat under a Secretary-General whose office is combined with that of 'High Representative of the CFSP' (Article 18 TEU). Decisions taken under the ordinary legislative procedure are adopted jointly by the Parliament and Council. Parliamentary objections may be overcome only where there is unanimity in the Council.

Voting procedures

Under Article 238 TFEU (ex 205 TEC) voting may be by:

- Simple majority
- Qualified majority
- Unanimity.

Simple majority

Article 238 TFEU defines a simple majority as 'the majority of the component members of the Council'. This method is used rarely, mainly in procedural areas.

Qualified majority

Qualified majority voting (QMV) is based on a system of weighted voting. This has become the usual method of voting after Treaty revisions extended its application to cover most areas. The arrangements for QMV have been subject to intense negotiation, particularly in the context of recent enlargements as Member States sought to ensure that their interests were represented.

> One of the most controversial issues surrounding weighting of votes has been its relationship with the population. Before the 2004 enlargement small states had greater weighting relative to their populations than larger states such as Germany, which feared further dilution of influence with the influx of the (mostly small) 2004 accession states. This fear was understandable as the weighting of votes under the Treaty of Nice was a compromise, with a final decision on weighting deferred to a later date which has not yet been reached.

CONTEXT

To avoid unfairness, a *verification procedure* was introduced under the Treaty of Nice, enabling a Member of the Council to request verification that the Member States constituting the qualified majority represent at least 62 per cent of the total population of the Union.

Unanimity

Unanimous voting enables a single state to veto proposals. It is rarely invoked following the Treaty of Lisbon as most areas have moved to QMV.

Under the original version of the Treaty of Rome, many important areas required a unanimous vote. The intention of the Treaty-drafters was to move swiftly towards voting by qualified majority as unanimity enabled a single Member State to block progress.

The Luxembourg Accords were drawn up in 1966 and have never been revoked, after a political crisis caused by a French boycott of Council meetings after negotiations on the Common Agricultural Policy (CAP) broke down. Under the Accords, which do not have the force of law, Member States may insist on a unanimous vote where vital national interests are at stake. The Accords have rarely been formally invoked, and have fallen into disuse since the 1980s.

Each Treaty revision has reduced the number of areas requiring unanimity, which is still required to amend a Commission proposal under Article 293 TFEU (ex Article 250 TEC). Other areas such as action to achieve one of the objectives of the EU under the general legislative power under Article 352 TFEU (ex 308 TEC) are now regulated by a special legislative procedure requiring unanimity in the Council after obtaining Parliament's consent.

Weighting of votes in the Council

Following enlargement to twenty-eight Member States, voting in the Council has been weighted for the purpose of QMV as shown in Table 2.2.

The Treaty of Nice and later accession treaties introduced a new requirement for a qualified majority threshold under (old) Article 205 TEC, which applies until November 2014, namely 260 votes in favour, cast by a majority of Member States where a proposal from the Commission is required, as is usual. In other cases the 260 votes must come from at least two-thirds of the members (i.e. nineteen Member States).

From November 2014 Article 238(3)(a) TFEU (ex 205 TEC) redefines a qualified majority as at least 55% of members of the Council, comprising at least fifteen of them, and representing at least 65% of the Union's population. A *blocking majority* would require at least the minimum number of Council members representing more than 35% of the population of participating states, plus one member, failing which the qualified majority will be deemed to have been reached. Article 238 allows for *derogations*

Table 2.2 Qualified majority voting in the Council

Member State	Weighting of votes
Germany, France, Italy and the UK	29
Spain and Poland	27
Romania	14
Netherlands	13
Belgium, Czech Republic, Greece, Hungary and Portugal	12
Austria, Bulgaria, Sweden	10
Croatia, Denmark, Finland, Ireland, Lithuania, Slovakia	7
Cyprus, Estonia, Latvia, Luxembourg	4
Malta	3

from 2014 where the Council does not act on a proposal from the Commission or High Representative for Foreign Affairs. In that case, a blocking majority is defined as 72 per cent of the members of the Council representing participating states, comprising at least 72 per cent of their population.

COREPER

Since Council membership varies and is combined with full-time responsibilities in the home state, the **Committee of Permanent Representatives (COREPER)** undertakes much of the work. COREPER's function under Article 240(1) TFEU (ex 207(1) TEC) is to examine and sift Commission proposals before a final decision is made by the Council. It is responsible for preparing the agenda, dividing the list into uncontroversial 'A Points' for adoption without discussion (e.g. amending a directive in July 2013 to provide a quick reaction mechanism to VAT fraud) and 'B Points' requiring discussion (e.g. support for long-term development in Afghanistan in June 2013).

THE EUROPEAN COMMISSION

The Commission is an appointed body consisting of the President and High Representative/Vice-President of the Commission, twenty-eight Commissioners nominated by Member States, and about 32,666 staff employed by the Commission (as at July 2013), mostly based in Brussels. It is responsible for drafting and overseeing EU policies and legislation, giving it a wider function than that of a traditional national civil service.

CORNERSTONE

Role of the Commission

The Commission's role is to 'promote the general interest of the Union and take appropriate measures to that end' (Article 17(1) TEU)).

Article 17(1) requires members of the Commission to be accountable to the EU rather than Member States, while Article 17(3) TEU provides that they must be 'completely independent', prohibiting them from taking instructions from Member States or other bodies such as lobbying organisations.

Composition of the Commission

Article 17(4) TEU temporarily provides for the Commission, including the President and the High Representative of the Union for Foreign Affairs and Security Policy, to consist of one national from each Member State until 31 October 2014. From 1 November 2014, Commission members will be chosen on a *rota system* (Article 17(5) TEU and 244 TFEU) whereby Member States are treated on a 'strictly equal footing', subject to which each successive Commission will be composed 'to reflect satisfactorily the demographic and geographical range of all the Member States' under a scheme to be established unanimously by the European Council. The number of members of the Commission will be limited to *two-thirds of the number of Member States* unless the European Council unanimously agrees to alter this number.

Before the 2004 enlargement each Member State had a single Commissioner and five States had two. While Member States accepted in principle the need to reduce the number of Commissioners as the EU prepared to enlarge, they were reluctant to give up their individual Commissioners and could not agree on institutional reform. A Protocol on Enlargement annexed to the Treaty of Nice enabled the number of Commissioners to be specified in the Treaty of Accession. The 2003 Accession Treaty provides for a national from each new Member State to be appointed to the Commission from the date of accession. Numbers were reduced to one Commissioner per Member State in 2004. The present Commission's term of office expires in October 2014, after which the new system of rotation will begin.

> While reform in the early years was largely driven by an alliance of the Commission and the Parliament, the dynamics of the EU today are more complex. The legal academic Christiansen (2012) highlights the complexities of shifting relationships: '[T]he traditional balance between the Commission and the Parliament on the one side, and the Council and the rotating Presidency [of the Council] on the other side, has been replaced by a more complex arrangement with a heightened demand for negotiation and coordination across various institutional boundaries', rendering the search for institutional balance 'increasingly elusive'. It remains to be seen whether the post-Lisbon arrangements meet the needs of a greatly enlarged EU.

REFLECTION

How does the Commission work?

The Commission operates on the principle of *collegiality*, with the College of Commissioners taking collective responsibility for all decisions. Its term of office is five years under Article 17(3) TEU. The Commission meets weekly in private, taking decisions by simple majority. Commissioners are assisted by their own *Cabinets* – officials responsible to them. The Commission is divided into Directorates General (DGs) covering matters such as external relations, competition and the internal market. There are also various specialised services such as the Legal Service advising all the DGs and representing the Commission in legal proceedings.

Article 245 TFEU (ex 213 TEC) provides that members of the Commission 'shall refrain from any action incompatible with their duties'. They cannot engage in any other paid or unpaid occupation during their term in office and must undertake to respect their duties, behaving 'with integrity and discretion' in terms of accepting appointments or benefits after their term in office. Breach of this duty entitles the Council or Commission to apply to the Court of Justice under Article 247 TFEU to have a member compulsorily retired or deprived of their pension.

Replacement of Commissioners and the High Representative

Article 246 TFEU (ex 215 TEC) provides for appointment of Commissioners, the President and High Representative in the event of resignation or retirement. Vacancies should be filled by a new member of the same nationality, appointed by the Council with the Commission after consultation with the Parliament. Article 246 also provides that if the *entire* Commission resigns, members will remain in office until replaced. This happened in 1999 when the Santer Commission resigned en masse but most members continued on a temporary basis.

The President of the Commission

Article 17(7) TEU provides for the appointment of the President of the Commission. The European Council proposes a suitable candidate by qualified majority, taking into account the views of the

Parliament which is empowered to elect the President by a majority of its component members. In the absence of majority approval, the European Council should propose an alternative candidate within one month. The current President, José Manuel Barroso, was re-elected to a second term until 2014. Like many of his predecessors, President Barroso was a politician in his home state (as Prime Minister of Portugal). The role of President is significant, with responsibility for the Commission's political direction and priorities during his or her term of office. Following confirmation of the President's appointment, which requires approval of the Member States and Parliament, the President chooses his or her Commission, subject to the approval of Parliament (under Article 17) TEU.

Functions of the Commission

The Commission is required under Article 17(1) TEU to:

- promote the general interest of the Union and measures adopted by the institutions;
- supervise the application of EU law;
- represent the EU externally, apart from foreign and security policy;
- initiate programmes to achieve inter-institutional agreements (i.e. agreements between institutions to facilitate their activities);
- participate in decision-making under the Treaties.

These duties fall into three broad categories typifying the Commission's role: as initiator, guardian of the Treaties and as the executive of the EU.

The Commission as initiator

The Commission initiates EU legislation and policy in accordance with Article 17(2) TEU which provides that Union legislative acts (i.e. laws) may only be adopted on the basis of a Commission proposal unless the Treaties provide otherwise. 'Other acts' (non-legislative measures) may also be adopted on a Commission proposal in accordance with the Treaties. This enables the Commission to draft proposals on any matter within the scope of the Treaties, either where power is specifically provided, such as Article 19 TFEU (ex 13 TEC) empowering the Council with Parliament's consent to take action to combat discrimination or under the general power in Article 352 TFEU (ex 308 TEC) where action is necessary to achieve one of the objectives of the EU but has not been provided in the Treaties. The Commission's priorities may be found in their annual work programmes (available on the 'Europa' website).

The Commission proposes draft legislation under the ordinary legislative procedure in Article 251 TFEU. Most Union legislation is made following a Commission proposal, although some measures may be adopted under a special legislative procedure where the Treaties specify. The special power under Article 241 TFEU enables the Council to request the Commission to undertake studies and make an appropriate proposal to achieve the common objectives of the Treaties. The Treaty of Lisbon introduced a 'citizens' initiative' under Article 11(4) TEU enabling not less than one million citizens who are the nationals of a 'significant number' of Member States to invite the Commission to propose a legal act where they consider it necessary to achieve the objectives of the Treaties.

The Commission as guardian of the Treaties

Under Article 4(3) TEU, Member States must take 'any appropriate measure, general or particular, to ensure fulfilment of the obligations imposed by the Treaties or resulting from the acts of the institutions of the Union'. The Commission has a duty to investigate and end infringements of EU law, and may bring an action against a Member State under Article 258 TFEU (ex 226 TEC). It has an administrative and enforcement role in competition policy although this has largely been devolved to national competition authorities.

The Commission as the executive of the Union

The Commission acts as the executive of the EU, implementing policies decided on by the Council. This often involves drawing up detailed legislation which may require a final decision by the Council. Decisions may only be delegated under strict limits. Failure to observe these rules may result in annulment by the Court, as in Case C-137/92P *Commission* v. *BASF AG (PVC)*, in which the Court of Justice upheld a CFI decision to annul a Commission decision where the Commission had failed to adopt an authenticated version of the text.

Other Commission functions

The Commission exercises various representative and financial functions. In external relations it negotiates treaties which are concluded by the Council after consultation with Parliament under Article 218 TFEU (ex 300 TEC). The Commission drafts the preliminary budget for adoption by the Council and Parliament under a special legislative procedure in Article 314 TFEU (ex 272 TEC).

Delegated legislation

Both the Commission and Council have for many years exercised delegated powers to make laws through a process subject to control by committees known as *Comitology*, a process criticised as undemocratic, particularly by Parliament which objects to its lack of involvement in the process which lacks the detailed scrutiny of the ordinary legislative process. The Treaty of Lisbon reformed the basis for delegation to both the Commission and Member States.

INTERSECTION

The introduction of legislative and non-legislative acts under the Treaty of Lisbon is considered in more detail in Chapter 4, as well as the distinction between delegated and implementing acts, significant in the context of judicial review. *Delegated acts* not requiring implementing measures are more widely open to challenge in the General Court by non-privileged applicants (individuals) under Article 263 TFEU.

Article 290 TFEU provides for a *legislative act* (i.e. regulation or directive adopted under the ordinary legislative procedure or a special procedure) to delegate to the Commission the power to adopt *non-legislative acts of general application* to supplement or amend legislative acts, enabling the Commission to provide more detailed measures or amend laws. Article 291(1) TFEU provides for Member States to adopt *implementing measures* ('measures of national law to implement legally binding Union acts'). Article 291(2) enables the Commission and Council to adopt implementing measures where uniform conditions to implement legally binding Union acts are required. However, it is unlikely the problems of comitology have been resolved in the post-Lisbon system of delegation, with uncertainty, for example, over the distinction between delegated and implementing acts, as the academic commentator, Craig (2011) observes.

APPLICATION

Imagine that the Council and the Parliament adopt a directive promoting cultural diversity under Article 167(5) TFEU (ex 151(5) TEC) under the ordinary procedure. Its stated objective is to facilitate exchange of cultural objects and works of art, with EU funding through a scheme administered by the Commission. The directive empowers the Commission to adopt further measures to clarify how the funding should be distributed. The Commission adopts a decision providing information on eligibility for funding. The directive is a legislative act whereas the Commission decision is a delegated, non-legislative act under Article 290. If the directive had alternatively provided for Member States to administer the funding, leading to a measure by the UK setting up the terms of a scheme, the UK measure would be an implementing act under Article 291(1). If the scheme had to be applied uniformly by the Commission which adopted a decision to achieve this, the decision would be an EU implementing act under Article 291(2).

The Union's advisory bodies

Article 300 TFEU provides for the Parliament, Council and Commission to be assisted by two advisory bodies, each with up to 350 members – the **Economic and Social Committee (ESC)** and the **Committee of the Regions (COR)**. As consultation with either body is an essential procedural requirement where the Treaties provide, failure to consult is a ground for annulment. Where the ESC is consulted, the COR must be informed, and vice versa.

The Economic and Social Committee

The Economic and Social Committee (ESC) supports the EU institutions in decision-making, providing non-binding advice reflecting the impact of proposals where it is consulted. Article 302 TFEU (ex 259 TEC) provides for the Council, acting unanimously on a proposal from the Member States, to adopt a list of members after consulting the Commission. Members are appointed for up to five years and normally include farmers, trade unionists, producers and the general public. The ESC may be consulted by the Council and Commission wherever they consider it appropriate. It may advise the Council and Commission on its own initiative under Article 304 TFEU (ex 262 TEC).

The Committee of the Regions

The Committee of the Regions (COR) operates as an advisory committee providing an opinion in matters of local or regional interest within the EU such as the provision of funding for different regions. Article 263(1) provides for the Council, acting unanimously on a Commission proposal, to adopt a decision determining the Committee's composition. The appointment procedure follows a similar pattern to the ESC, with members appointed by the Council for up to five years in accordance with proposals from Member States (Article 305 TFEU (ex 263 TEC)). Its members are usually individuals elected to local and regional authorities or politically accountable to a democratically elected assembly. Article 307 TFEU (ex 265 TEC) requires the Parliament, Council and Commission to consult the COR where the Treaties provide (such as education, culture and environmental policy) and in other cases where one of the institutions considers it appropriate.

The Court of Auditors

The Court of Auditors was established in 1975 under the Budgetary Powers Treaty to control and supervise implementation of the budget and to audit the accounts of the institutions.

The European Central Bank

The European Central Bank (ECB) in Frankfurt acts as the central bank for states participating in Economic and Monetary Union within the European System of Central Banks and is responsible for monetary policy. It conducts foreign exchange operations, holds and manages the official reserves of the Member States, and promotes the smooth operation of the payments systems. The ECB is the only body entitled to issue euro banknotes under Article 128 TFEU (ex 106 TEC). It may adopt regulations on monetary policy, take decisions, make recommendations and deliver opinions.

KEY POINTS

- The European Parliament is the sole elected EU institution but can only adopt legislation jointly with the Council, leading to criticism that there is a 'democratic deficit' at the heart of the EU.
- The Council, which tends to reflect the national interests of Member States, is the most politically powerful of the EU institutions.
- Most legislation is adopted jointly by the Parliament and the Council under the ordinary legislative procedure.
- The Commission initiates policy and legislative proposals in the EU, as well as ensuring that Member States observe EU law.
- The EU has sought to address the need for institutional balance through the process of treaty reform, most recently under the Treaty of Lisbon.

CORE STATUTES

Statute	About	Importance
TEU, Title II Articles 9–12	Democratic principles.	New Title under Treaty of Lisbon to strengthen EU commitment to democratic principles.
Article 11(4) TEU	Empowers one million Union citizens to invite Commission to submit a proposal for draft law.	Intended to bring EU closer to citizen.
Article 12 TEU	Provides for draft legislative acts to be sent to national parliaments for compliance with subsidiarity.	Gives national parliaments direct input to legislative process.
Title III TEU (Articles 13–19 TEU)	Provisions on EU institutions.	Sets out basis for EU institutional framework, with more detailed provision in TFEU.

Statute	About	Importance
Article 15 TEU	Declares that European Council will provide Union with necessary strategic lead and define its political direction and priorities.	Enables heads of state with President of Commission and High Representative to set EU agenda.
Article 16 TEU and Article 237 TFEU (ex 204 TEC)	Provides for EP and Council to exercise legislative and budgetary functions.	Article 237 TFEU amplifies rules in Article 16 TEU, including provision for QMV.
Article 218 TFEU (ex 300 TEC)	Council may adopt measures with consent of EP under special legislative procedure.	Enables EP to veto measure. Used in areas including accession to EU of new Member States.
Article 238 TFEU (ex 205 TEC)	Defines QMV in Council, with effect from November 2014.	Introduces greater fairness into Council voting by redefining qualified majority in terms of Council membership and population.
Article 293 TFEU (ex 250 TEC)	Provides for unanimous vote in Council in certain circumstances.	Enables single Member State to veto proposal.

FURTHER READING

Biondi, A., Eeckhout, P. and Ripley, S. (eds) *EU Law after Lisbon* (Oxford University Press: Oxford, 2012)
Collection of essays by leading academics, with contributions on the EU institutions.

Christiansen, T. 'The European Union after the Lisbon Treaty: an elusive "institutional balance"' in Biondi, A., Eeckhout, P. and Ripley, S. (eds), above.

Craig, P. 'The Treaty of Lisbon: process, architecture and substance' (2007) 33 *European Law Review* 137
Examines Treaty reform leading to the Treaty of Lisbon and the changes under it.

Craig, P. 'Delegated acts, implementing acts and the new Comitology Regulation' (2011) 36 *European Law Review* 671
Critical examination of the hierarchy of norms under the Treaty of Lisbon, particularly the distinction between delegated and implementing acts.

Dougan, M. ' "And some fell on stony ground" – a review article of Giandomenico Majone's *Dilemmas of European Integration*' (2006) 31 *European Law Review* 865
Succinct analysis of perceived strengths and weaknesses of Majone's monograph.

European Parliament, Activity Report 14 July 2009–31 December 2011, available at http://www.europarl.europa.eu/code/information/activity_reports/activity_report_2009_2011_en.pdf
The most recent annual report, with analysis of Parliament's participation in the legislative process.

Majone, G. *Dilemmas of European Integration: The Ambiguities and Pitfalls of Integration by Stealth* (Oxford University Press: Oxford, 2005)
Worth reading for its refreshing approach to political theory prompting a debate with leading academic scholars about the approach to European integration underpinning EU governance.

Majone, G. 'Legitimacy and effectiveness: a response to Professor Michael Dougan's review article on *Dilemmas of European Integration*' (2007) 32 *European Law Review* 70
Robust response to criticisms in review article.

Snell, J. '"European constitutional settlement", an ever closer union and the Treaty of Lisbon: democracy or relevance?' (2008) 33 *European Law Review* 619
Challenges the view of Majone and others that the EU does not suffer from a democratic deficit.

Weiler, J. 'A constitution for Europe? Some hard choices?' in J. Weiler, I. Beggand and J. Peterson (eds) *Integration in an Expanding Europe* (Blackwell Publishing: Oxford, 2003)
Joseph Weiler, a leading constitutional theorist, has written extensively on the EU. This collection reflects on problems associated with the (failed) Constitutional Treaty.

CHAPTER 3

The Court of Justice and the preliminary reference procedure

BLUEPRINT

*The Court of Justice
and the preliminary
reference procedure*

LEGISLATION

- Article 267 TFEU

CONTEXT

- Need for an independent Court to develop EU law

CONCEPTS

- New legal order
- Direct actions
- Preliminary rulings
- Court or tribunal
- Discretionary and mandatory references
- Abstract or concrete theory
- Validity

- Is the Court of Justice too 'activist' in its use of Article 267 to develop the law?

- How is the Court of Justice to remain effective and authoritative with an increased workload in an enlarged EU?

CASES

- *Dorsch Consult*
- *CILFIT*

SPECIAL CHARACTERISTICS

- No formal doctrine of precedent
- Independence of judges
- Single judgment
- Role of Advocates-General

REFORM

- General Court may give preliminary rulings
- Procedures for simplified, expedited and urgent cases introduced
- Possible need for more judges

CRITICAL ISSUES

Setting the scene

The Court of Justice has breathed life into the structure created by the Treaties through its case law, promoting European integration in bold decisions such as Case 26/62 *Van Gend en Loos*, in which it declared that the Community [EU] created 'a new legal order in international law'. This order was based on two central ideas, neither of which was explicit in the Treaties – the *supremacy* of EU law over national law and *direct effect*, by which EU law may be relied on directly by individuals in the national courts. The creativity of the Court was made possible by the *preliminary reference procedure* under Article 267 TFEU (ex 234 TEC) enabling national courts to seek guidance from the Court on the meaning or validity of EU law. These rulings bind all Member States, ensuring the uniform interpretation of EU law.

THE COURT OF JUSTICE

The Court of Justice of the EU (CJEU or ECJ) is the highest authority on EU law. While no provision in the TEU or TFEU makes this exact statement, it may be inferred from Article 19(1) TEU which declares that the Court 'shall ensure that the interpretation and application of the Treaties is ensured'. Article 19(1) also provides that the Court of Justice consists of the *General Court* (previously known as the Court of First Instance or CFI) and the *specialised courts* such as the Civil Service Tribunal.

> It was essential when the Community was created in 1957 that Member States and the international community had confidence in the Court of Justice as an independent authority uninfluenced by individual Member States or other EU institutions. Nevertheless the Court sometimes takes account of political or economic considerations when reaching its decisions, such as the need not to expose employers to the economic uncertainty of backdated equal pay claims from women employees in Case 43/75 *Defrenne* v. *Sabena*.

CONTEXT

Take note

It is important to distinguish the Court of Justice of the EU in Luxembourg from the European Court of Human Rights (ECtHR) in Strasbourg. While the Court of Justice derives its authority from the TEU and TFEU, the European Court of Human Rights derives it from the European Convention on Human Rights (ECHR).

The Court of Justice is governed by the Treaties (TEU and TFEU) and the Statute of the Court annexed to the Treaties. Specialised courts (previously known as judicial panels) cover areas such as disputes involving staff of the EU institutions. The Court of Auditors exercises specific functions of financial control over the institutions. This chapter provides an overview of the composition, functions and procedures of the Court of Justice and General Court, particularly the preliminary reference procedure. The Court's jurisdiction in areas such as enforcement and judicial review (known as *direct actions*) is examined in Chapters 9 and 10 (see Figure 3.1).

Functions of the Court of Justice

The main functions of the Court of Justice are to:

(a) provide a uniform interpretation of EU law throughout Member States and ensure that EU law is observed (Article 19 TEU);

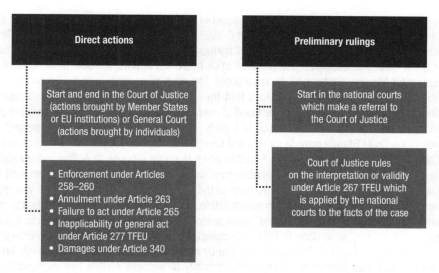

Figure 3.1 Actions in the Court of Justice and General Court

(b) provide a forum to resolve disputes between Member States and the EU institutions (e.g. under the enforcement mechanism in Article 258 TFEU (ex 226 TEC)) as well as between the institutions;

(c) review acts of the EU institutions (e.g. under Article 263 TFEU (ex 230 TEC));

(d) protect individual rights (e.g. through the preliminary reference procedure in Article 267 TFEU (ex 234 TEC)).

Composition

Article 19 TEU (ex 221 TEC) states that the Court of Justice consists of one judge from each Member State (i.e. twenty-eight judges). It is assisted by eight *Advocates-General* under Article 252 TFEU providing the Court with non-binding submissions on the law but assigned only to complex or significant cases. Both judges and Advocates-General must be 'persons whose independence is beyond doubt' (Article 253 (ex 223 TEC)) as judges or academics in their own country.

Judges are appointed by 'common accord' of the Member States' governments for staggered terms of six years after consultation with the new *panel on suitability* under Article 255 TFEU, acting on the initiative of the President of the Court. It comprises seven members drawn from former members of the Court of Justice and the General Court, members of national supreme courts and lawyers of recognised competence, one of whom will be proposed by Parliament. The judges appoint a President for three years from among their own ranks (Article 253 TFEU).

A judge may only be removed under the Statute of the Court of Justice if all the other judges and Advocates-General agree that he or she is no longer qualified or fit to hold office. This has never happened. Judges must not be influenced by their national origins but must strive for a Union approach in reaching a decision.

Full Court, Grand Chamber and Chamber

One of the consequences of enlargement has been that it is no longer practical for all cases to be heard by a *full court* of twenty-eight judges. Recourse to a full court is now unusual but is required to remove the members of the Commission, the Court of Auditors and the Ombudsman. It may also be used in cases of particular importance such as C-406/01 *Germany* v. *EP and Council* where Germany unsuccessfully sought to annul Directive 2001/37 harmonising the sale and advertising of tobacco outside the EU. If the Court had allowed the application to be heard out of time, it would have had significant implications for Member States and the legal order. The application was declared inadmissible.

Article 251 TFEU (ex 221 TEC) provides that the Court of Justice may sit as a full court or in chambers under rules in the Statute of the Court of Justice. It sits as a *Grand Chamber* when requested by a Member State or EU institution which is a party, or in particularly complex or important cases. The rules in the Court Statute provide for a Grand Chamber of thirteen judges with a minimum of nine, as in Case C-364/10 *Hungary* v. *Slovak Republic* when Hungary brought an action under Article 259 TFEU (ex 227 TEC) against the Slovak Republic over exclusion of its President from a planned visit to a Slovak town on the anniversary of the invasion of the Czech Republic by soldiers from Warsaw Pact countries. The Court declared the action inadmissible, holding that the movement of heads of state was governed by international, not EU law. More straightforward actions may be heard in a *chamber* of three or five judges, as in Case C-75/11 *Commission* v. *Austria*, enforcement proceedings under Article 258 TFEU (ex 226 TEC). The Court held that by restricting reduced fares for students on public transport to those with parents receiving Austrian family allowances Austria had infringed Directive 2004/38 on citizens' rights.

Advocates-General

The Advocate-General is a neutral officer of the Court of Justice who presents an *Opinion* based on reasoned submissions on the law and recommendations for a decision. The Advocate-General's submissions do not bind the Court. They are more fully reasoned than the judgment but do not represent the views of either party. Many cases are now decided without an Opinion where the Court considers that the case raises no new points of law under the amended Statute of the Court.

INTERSECTION ....

Advocate-General Jacobs (now retired from the Court of Justice) gave many controversial and influential opinions such as that in Case C-50/00P *UPA* v. *Council*. Although the Opinion was not followed in the judgment, it raised important points about access (or 'standing') of individuals to challenge acts of the EU institutions which are examined in Chapter 10.

Judicial style and procedures

Procedures in the Court of Justice derive from the continental tradition with its origins in Roman law. They are mainly *inquisitorial* (enquiry into truth), with the emphasis on written pleadings, rather than *adversarial* as in the courts of England and Wales. The Court's approach to statutory interpretation is also of continental origin, with strong emphasis on the *purposive* (or *teleological*) (rather than literal) approach by which legislation is interpreted in accordance with the purpose and context in which it was adopted. (The purpose is often set out in a preamble preceding the legislation.) Sometimes the Court adopts a *historical* approach, examining preparatory documents to determine the intention of the legislators (similar to the 'mischief' rule in English law by which the court seeks to find the 'mischief' addressed by the law).

Case C-64/09 *Commission* v. *France* over a directive on disposal of vehicles provides an example of the use of a purposive approach. The directive was adopted to encourage recycling vehicles for scrap in 'authorised treatment centres', an expression interpreted purposively in view of the objective in the directive to enable the last user to deliver vehicles for disposal free of charge. The Court found France in breach of the directive by excluding car shredders from an obligation to accept such vehicles.

How does the Court of Justice work?

The Court of Justice is the highest authority on EU law, hearing appeals from the General Court as well as direct actions and requests for preliminary rulings. The judges work as a judicial college to produce a single judgment, formally and relatively briefly expressed, with no dissenting judgment.

INTERSECTION ....

More examples of the Court's approach to statutory interpretation may be found in the section on Skills in Studying EU law and in Chapter 7 in relation to indirect effect.

ROLE OF THE COURT OF JUSTICE IN DEVELOPING EU LAW

The Court of Justice has played an enormously important role in developing EU law, particularly through the use of the preliminary reference procedure.

The Court of Justice has been criticised as being 'activist', that is, acting for political rather than purely legal purposes. This may be unfair, as it fails to take account of the unique nature of the Court. Tridimas (1996), a legal academic, argues that the underlying rationale of its contribution has been to build a 'constitutional order of States' (in other words, to develop the 'new legal order' identified in *Van Gend en Loos*). In his view the Court has achieved such development in three areas: promotion of economic integration through the establishment of the internal market, protection of individual rights and extension of Community (EU) competences. He notes that the judges do not necessarily share pro-federalist ideas, nor favour the Community at the expense of Member States. The Court's purposive approach, he argues, is well suited to Community law, as the goal of European integration is inherent in the Treaties. This means there is an underlying *purpose* to the EU itself supporting European integration. The EU is a single market based on free movement with no discrimination on nationality, as well as a political union with common policies. The Court interprets the law by reference to these underlying ideas.

REFLECTION

Precedent and the Court of Justice

Although the Court of Justice does not operate a formal doctrine of precedent, it normally follows its own previous decisions. Where it intends to depart from an earlier judgment, it usually makes the position very clear.

A good example of such a departure is provided by Cases C-267 and 268/91 *Criminal Proceedings against Keck and Mithouard* in which the Court introduced a new approach to *selling arrangements* (rules on how goods are sold in Member States such as a ban on evening opening). The Court in *Keck* declared it was necessary to re-examine its approach to the use of (what is now) Article 34 TFEU to challenge national rules on how goods are sold. It signalled its change of direction with the words, 'Contrary to what has previously been decided . . .', ruling that Member States can adopt their own rules on selling goods provided they do not contravene Community [EU] law (see Chapter 12 on the free movement of goods).

Language in the Court of Justice

Cases in the Court of Justice and General Court may be conducted in any of the twenty-four official languages, as well as in Irish. French continues to be the working language, a legacy of the early years when continental procedures predominated. After translation into the 'authentic' language, usually that of the applicant, the judgment will be translated into the remaining official languages before publication in the European Court Reports (ECR).

The Court has taken a firm view on the publication requirement for secondary legislation in the official languages. In Case C-161/06 *Skoma-Lux sro* v. *Celni ředitelství Oloumouc* it held that a regulation not published in the Official Journal in all the official languages of a Member State cannot be enforced against individuals in that State, even where they could have discovered the legislation by other means. Different language versions of a text are often examined in the Court in order to determine meaning.

THE GENERAL COURT

The General Court was established as the Court of First Instance (CFI) in 1989 to ease the workload of the Court of Justice and was renamed the General Court by the Treaty of Lisbon. It has jurisdiction under Article 256 TFEU to hear first instance actions brought by individuals (natural and legal persons) under Article 263, 265 and 277 TFEU (judicial review) and damages actions under Article 340 TFEU, but not cases assigned to a specialised court under Article 257 TFEU or otherwise reserved for the Court of Justice.

The General Court also hears appeals from decisions of the specialised courts, at present, only the Civil Service Tribunal (see p. 61) under Article 270 TFEU, which may be reviewed by the Court of Justice where there is a serious risk affecting the unity or consistency of EU law. There is a right of appeal from decisions of the General Court to the Court of Justice which may give the final judgment itself or send the case back to the General Court.

Unlike the Court of Justice, which is limited to one judge per Member State, the number of judges in the General Court is determined by the Statute of the Court, which may also provide for appointment of Advocates-General (Article 254 TFEU (ex 224 TEC)), although none have been appointed so far. Provision for appointment of judges to the General Court mirrors that of the Court of Justice, being by 'common accord' of the Member States after consultation with a suitability panel under Article 255 TFEU. Both institutions require the same qualities of independence and ability for appointment to high judicial office. Judges are appointed for six years, with partial renewal of overall membership every three years. The judges elect a president for a term of three years. The General Court may sit in plenary session, in chambers of three or five judges or as a single judge where no difficult questions of law or fact are raised.

The General Court was empowered from 2003 to hear preliminary rulings in areas provided by the Statute of the Court. Where the General Court considers that the case involves the unity or consistency of EU law, it may refer it to the Court of Justice for a ruling under Article 256(3) TFEU (ex 225(3) TEC). The Court of Justice may also hear appeals from preliminary rulings of the General Court where there is a serious risk to the unity or consistency of EU law. Nevertheless the General Court has made *no* preliminary rulings so far, demonstrating the continuing reliance placed on the authoritative nature of rulings by the Court of Justice under Article 267.

SPECIALISED COURTS

The Civil Service Tribunal

Article 257 TFEU (ex 225A TEC) provides that Parliament and the Council may establish specialised courts (previously known as judicial panels) attached to the General Court to hear certain cases at first instance. There is a right of appeal on points of law to the General Court. The first of these panels, the EU Civil Service Tribunal, was established in 2004 to handle the large volume of staff cases (employment disputes involving staff employed by the EU institutions).

Direct actions in the Court of Justice

The procedures under Articles 258 TFEU (ex 226) and 263 TFEU (ex 230 TEC) are particularly important. They are examples of *direct actions* where the procedure begins and ends in the Court (unlike the preliminary reference procedure under Article 267 which begins in the national courts).

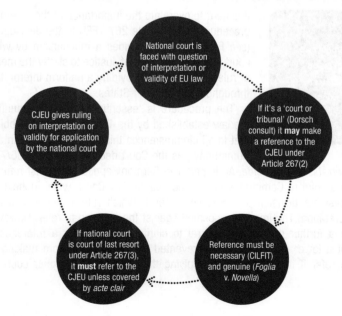

Figure 3.2 The preliminary reference procedure under Article 267 TFEU

Under Article 258 TFEU enforcement proceedings may be brought by the Commission against a Member State in breach of its obligations under the Treaties. The Court may impose penalties (lump sum or daily penalties) under Article 260 TFEU (ex 228 TEC) if the Member State does not comply with a judgment. Article 263 provides another type of direct action, to review the legality of acts of the Council and the Commission (i.e. to challenge a regulation, directive or decision). The Court can also rule on failure to act under Article 265 TFEU (ex 232 TEC) and the inapplicability of an act of general application under Article 277 TFEU (ex 241 TEC), as well as to award compensation under Article 340 TFEU (ex 288 TEC) for loss caused by the EU institutions.

APPLICATION

Imagine that the Council and Parliament have adopted a directive requiring Member States to develop a 'green' transport policy to deal with carbon emissions. The UK wants to challenge the directive as it considers that transport policy should be left to the Member States. It could bring an action against the Council and Parliament in the Court of Justice under Article 263 TFEU, seeking to have the directive annulled. Spain has ignored the directive. The Commission could bring enforcement proceedings under Article 258 TFEU.

PRELIMINARY RULINGS AND THE DEVELOPMENT OF EU LAW

Take note

From a student perspective, the preliminary reference procedure is the procedure you will encounter most often when studying EU law.

It is hard to overstate the importance of the preliminary reference procedure under Article 267 TFEU in the development of EU law (see Figure 3.2). It provides a mechanism by which a national court may ask the Court of Justice to clarify the meaning of EU law or rule on its validity, providing a uniform interpretation of EU law throughout the Member States.

The procedure is 'essential for the Community character of the law established by the Treaty and has the object of ensuring that in all circumstances this law is the same in all states in the Community', as the Court declared in Case 166/73 *Rheinmühlen v. Einfuhr-und Vorratsstelle Getreide*. An importer in Germany appealed against refusal of an export rebate based on a point of Community law to the Federal Tax Court, which upheld his appeal and sent back the case for decision to the regional court, which referred questions to the Court of Justice for interpretation. The importer appealed against the decision to refer. However, the Federal Tax Court made a further preliminary referral to clarify the scope for a reference. The Court of Justice held that a lower court cannot be prevented by national law from making a referral, but must be free to refer if it considers that applying the decision of a higher court would infringe EU law.

Once a reference has been made to the Court of Justice, proceedings in the national court are suspended until the Court has ruled. It is the function of the national court, with the benefit of the ruling from the Court of Justice, to apply the law and reach a decision on the facts.

Article 267 has played a key role in developing the constitutional principles of EU law, particularly direct effect, indirect effect and *State liability*. The Court of Justice has used requests for preliminary rulings to declare its views on the EU legal order in seminal cases such as Case 26/62 *Van Gend en Loos*, Case 6/64 *Costa* v. *ENEL*, and Case C-6/90 *Francovich*, filling the gaps left by the Treaties. These cases are considered in Chapters 7 and 8.

> ## Take note
> It is important to remember that the Court of Justice does not act as an appellate court under Article 267 but supports national courts which make the final decision to apply the law. As its jurisdiction under Article 267 is restricted to EU law, the Court cannot interpret domestic law or rule on its validity under EU law.

PRELIMINARY RULINGS UNDER ARTICLE 267 TFEU

CORNERSTONE

Article 267(1)

Article 267(1) empowers '*any court or tribunal of a Member State*' to make a reference to the Court of Justice to clarify the meaning or validity of EU law.

It does not matter what the body making the reference is called. The criteria to establish whether a body is a 'court or tribunal' under Article 267 were established in Case C-54/96 *Dorsch Consult* (referral from the Federal Supervisory Board in Germany seeking clarification of a procedure for awarding public service contracts under a directive).

CORNERSTONE

A body is a 'court or tribunal' if it:

(a) is permanent;

(b) is independent;

(c) has compulsory jurisdiction;

(d) applies legal rules;

(e) hears cases between parties (Case C-54/96 *Dorsch Consult*).

Bodies found to be a 'court or tribunal' under Article 267

Case	About	Importance
Case 246/80 *Broekmeulen*	Dutch appeal committee refused the applicant's registration as a GP.	Found to be a 'court or tribunal' under Article 267(2) as it made final decisions by an adversarial procedure subject to appeal to the courts.
Case 14/86 *Pretore di Salò* v. *Persons Unknown*	A magistrate acting as both prosecutor and investigating judge.	Although some of magistrate's functions were not judicial, he was regarded as a 'court or tribunal' as his decisions were legally binding and he was exercising a public function.
Case C-210/06 *Cartesio Oktató és Szolgáltató bt*	Cartesio, a limited partnership, appealed to an appellate court in Hungary against refusal of registration of the transfer of its company seat to Italy.	An appellate court hearing an appeal from a lower court responsible for maintaining a commercial register was regarded as a court or tribunal under Article 267 as it was exercising a judicial function adversely affecting the applicant, but was not covered by the obligation to refer under Article 267(3).

It is essential to apply the *Dorsch Consult* criteria, particularly whether a body is *exercising a judicial function*, to decide whether it is a court or tribunal. If the lower court in *Cartesio* had been taking a purely administrative decision on company registration, it would not have been a court under Article 267. Article 267(3) did not apply although there was limited scope for appeal under national law and the decision appealed was not suspended. A key factor is the element of *public control or participation*, found to be lacking in the following, held *not* to constitute a court or tribunal:

- The Council of the Paris Bar (arising from a request for a declaration that a member of the Paris Bar denied access to a court in Germany was entitled to provide legal services under EU law (Case 138/80 *Borker*)).
- An arbitrator appointed under a private contract (Case 102/81 (*Nordsee Deutsche Hochseefischerei GmbH*)). The Court of Justice found that the parties had removed their dispute from the court structure by opting for resolution through an arbitration clause. The arbitrator could not therefore be regarded as a court or tribunal.

Discretionary referrals under Article 267(2)

Any court or tribunal not covered by the obligation to refer has discretion to refer to the Court under Article 267(2) when it considers that a reference is *necessary*.

In Case 283/81 *CILFIT* a group of textile firms brought an action in the Italian courts arising from their refusal to pay a government levy on wool from outside the EU. The central question was whether wool should be regarded as an animal product as such products were outside the scope of the Regulation applying the levy. The Italian Ministry of Health argued that there was no need to refer to the Court as it was obvious that wool was an animal product. The Italian Supreme Court nevertheless decided to make a referral to the Court which provided guidance on the need to refer.

CORNERSTONE

Case 283/81 *CILFIT*

A referral is *not* necessary when the:

- question of EU law is irrelevant to the decision;
- question has already been decided by the Court of Justice;
- correct interpretation is so obvious as to leave no room for doubt (*acte clair*).

While the *CILFIT* guidelines were drawn up in relation to the mandatory jurisdiction under Article 267(3) they also apply to discretionary jurisdiction under Article 267(2). It is clear from the decision that preliminary references must be considered in relation to the special features of EU law, particularly the need for a uniform interpretation despite the existence of texts in different languages and use of concepts and terminology unlike national legislation.

Some commentators including the legal academic Rasmussen (1989) have argued that the *CILFIT* criteria are almost meaningless. What matters is how national courts are encouraged to reach their own decisions on matters of EU law. In practice many national courts have exercised their independence by failing to refer questions that were necessary to resolve a dispute. The statistics accompanying the 2010 Report of the Court of Justice on references from 1952–2010 show that only Malta, Slovakia and Slovenia made *no* referrals from their highest courts. In the UK the House of Lords made 44 references.

REFLECTION

Recent referrals from UK courts to the Court of Justice

The UK courts are now more willing to refer to the Court of Justice than in the early years when they were dissuaded by Lord Denning's guidance in *Bulmer* v. *Bollinger* (overruled by *CILFIT*). For example, in Case C-206/01 *Arsenal Football Club* v. *Matthew Read* the Chancery Division of the High Court asked the Court of Justice to interpret Directive 89/104 in a dispute between Arsenal Football Club and an unauthorised merchandise seller to establish whether the use of the cannon and shield emblems on shirts infringed Arsenal's exclusive trademark. The Court found that a proprietor could rely on the directive to prevent unauthorised use of a sign identical to a validly registered trademark.

The Chancery Division again referred to the Court in Case C-324/09 *L'Oreal* v. *eBay International AG* over L'Oreal's dissatisfaction with counterfeit products sold through eBay. After writing to eBay to express its concerns, L'Oreal brought proceedings in Member States including the UK, alleging trademark infringement. The Court of Justice (Grand Chamber) interpreted Directive 2004/48 which it found required Member States to ensure that national courts dealing with intellectual property rights could order online sellers to end infringements.

There must be a genuine question of EU law

The Court of Justice held it will not rule on an artificially fabricated question (Case 104/79 *Foglia* v. *Novello (No. 1)* and Case 244/80 *(No. 2)*). *Foglia and Novello (No. 1)* arose from a contract between two Italian wine merchants to sell wine to a third party in France subject to a condition that one (Foglia) should not be liable for charges contrary to EU law. When the French authorities imposed a tax on the wine entering the country, it was paid by Foglia who tried to recover the cost from Novello. The Italian court referred questions for a ruling but the Court refused to answer on the basis that they were 'concocted' to obtain a ruling on national law (validity of the French tax). Undeterred, the Italian court made a further reference in *Foglia* v. *Novello (No. 2)*. The Court of Justice again declined to rule, holding it was entitled to confirm its own jurisdiction and must ensure that the preliminary reference procedure is 'not employed for purposes . . . not intended by the Treaty'. The Court stated that its function under Article 267 was to assist in administration of justice in the Member States, not to give advisory opinions on general or hypothetical questions.

> The refusal to rule in *Foglia* v. *Novello* was hard for the parties, as there may have been a genuine dispute between them. The Court used the second *Foglia* reference to assert its authority over national courts, reminding them of the division of responsibilities. The decision was criticised by academics such as Bebr (1980) who asks whether we can be sure of distinguishing a test case and a fabrication, but supported by Wyatt (1982) who argues that the Court must be free to determine its own jurisdiction.

REFLECTION

The Court refused to rule in Case C-83/91 *Meilicke* v. *Meyer* because it considered the question to be artificially constructed to test an academic lawyer's theories of company law. It also refuses to rule where the question appears 'manifestly irrelevant' to the decision. In Case C-343/90 *Dias* v. *Director da Alfandego do Porto* on interpretation of EU law on a tax on motor vehicles which did not apply to light commercial vehicles, the Court refused to rule whether the tax applied to vintage cars, deeming it irrelevant.

The Court summed up its position in Case C-130/95 *Giloy*, stating that it will only reject a request for a reference 'if it appears that the procedure laid down in Article [267] has been misused and a ruling elicited from the Court by means of a contrived dispute, or it is obvious that EU law cannot apply'. In practice it also refuses to hear cases where the national court fails to provide enough information on the background, as in Case 157/92 *Pretore di Genova* v. *Banchero* where the Court rejected a request from an Italian court as it had not been sufficiently informed about the Italian tobacco monopoly forming the context of the case.

The 2012 Recommendation to national courts and tribunals on initiation of preliminary reference proceedings makes the following observation about the position of the national court with discretion to refer:

> [A] national court or tribunal may, in particular, when it considers that sufficient guidance is given by the case law of the Court of Justice, itself decide on the correct interpretation of European Union law and its application to the factual situation before it. However, a reference for a preliminary ruling may prove particularly useful when there is a new question of general interest for the uniform application of European Union law, or when the existing case law does not appear to be applicable to a new set of facts.

Mandatory referrals under Article 267(3)

While any court or tribunal *may* make a reference to the Court of Justice, under Article 267(2), courts of last resort do not have such discretion, but are *obliged* to refer. Article 267(3) provides that, where a question of interpretation is raised before any court or tribunal of a Member State against whose decisions there is no judicial remedy under national law, that court or tribunal *shall* bring the matter before the Court of Justice. Identification of courts covered by the obligation to refer has not been straightforward and has led to differing approaches in the Member States.

Given the mandatory nature of the referral, the principle of *acte clair* is particularly important for courts of last resort as it provides an escape route from the obligation to refer where the meaning of the provision is clear. However, it should be noted that the interpretation must be equally obvious to the courts of the other Member States (Case C-495/03 *Intermodal Transports*).

The Court of Justice gave limited endorsement to the principles of *acte clair* and *acte eclairé* in *CILFIT*, holding that courts of last resort were not obliged to refer where there was a ruling on the point of law already or where the answer to the question could not affect the outcome of the case. Such courts could, however, refer where they considered it necessary to do so.

Abstract or concrete theory?

The scope of Article 267(3) has led to controversy. According to the 'abstract' or 'narrow' view, only courts of final resort such as the Supreme Court in the UK and the Conseil d'Etat in France are covered by the obligation to refer. However, in many circumstances there may be no right of appeal from a lower court (e.g. the Court of Appeal in the UK when leave to appeal to the Supreme Court is refused). The UK courts initially favoured the abstract view, with the result that referrals sometimes did not take place until the appeal reached the House of Lords (before creation of the Supreme Court).

> **Take note**
>
> You will meet various French terms in the context of procedure and approaches in the Court of Justice:
>
> - *Acte clair* derives from French administrative law according to which no question of interpretation is taken to arise from a provision whose meaning is clear. National courts need not refer a question for interpretation to the Court in these circumstances.
>
> - *Acte éclairé* refers to the entitlement of national courts not to refer when the Court has already pronounced on a materially identical point.

INTERSECTION

An example of UK courts' early unwillingness to refer before a case reached the highest court may be seen in Case 34/79 *R* v. *Henn and Darby* in which the House of Lords referred questions over the public morality exception to the free movement of goods (considered further in Chapter 12).

The Court of Justice has long followed the 'concrete' or 'wide' view as to which courts are obliged to refer, as shown by Case 6/64 *Costa* v. *ENEL*, a referral from an Italian small claims court from which there was no right of appeal due to the low sum claimed. The Court of Justice treated the court as one against whose decision there is no judicial remedy. The present position is summarised in the 2011 Information Note which provides as follows:

[C]ourts or Tribunals against whose decision there is no judicial remedy must, as a rule, refer such a question to the Court, unless the Court has already ruled on the point (and there is no new context that raises any serious doubt as to whether that case-law may be applied), or unless the correct interpretation of the rule of law in question is obvious.

Courts covered by the obligation to refer

Until Case C-99/00 *Kenny Roland Lyckeskog*, the Court of Justice had not ruled on the position of a national court where appeal requires leave (i.e. subject to a declaration of admissibility). Lyckeskog was convicted by a district court in Sweden of attempting to smuggle 500kg of rice from Norway into Sweden. The court found that the quantity of rice showed he was a commercial importer as the permissible level for importation was only 20kg. Lyckeskog appealed to the Court of Appeal for Western Sweden from which an appeal lay to the Supreme Court with leave. The Appeal Court decided to refer to the Court of Justice to clarify whether a court in its position was obliged to refer under Article 267(3).

The Court of Justice held that decisions of a national appellate court which may be challenged before a supreme court are *not* covered by the duty to refer under Article 267(3), even where leave to appeal is required. It found there are two points when a supreme court may make a reference on interpretation or validity – either when it hears the application for leave to appeal or when it hears the case itself.

.... APPLICATION

Imagine a UK case has reached the Court of Appeal which has not made a referral to the Court of Justice although the EU law point is unclear. Applying *Lyckeskog*, the Court of Appeal is not obliged to refer under Article 267(3). The Supreme Court must refer, either when considering an application for leave to appeal or when hearing the appeal itself. In other circumstances the Supreme Court may not be the only court in the UK covered by the obligation to refer. It is always necessary to consider whether an appeal lies to a higher court and whether leave to appeal is required.

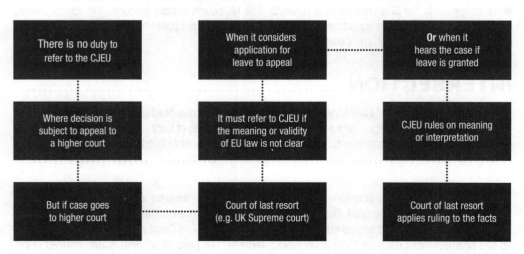

Figure 3.3 Courts covered by the duty to refer under Article 267(3) applying the *Lyckeskog* decision

In Case C-210/06 *Cartesio Oktató és Szolgáltató bt* the Court of Justice held that a court such as the referring court (in this case an appeal court in Hungary hearing an appeal from a lower court responsible for maintaining a commercial register) was not a court of last resort under Article 267(3). The Court's reasoning was based on the scope for appeal to a higher court on a point of law, even though the appeal was restricted under national law and the decision appealed was not suspended.

It should be remembered that *acte clair* and *acte éclairé* apply to Article 267(3). A national court of last resort need refer under Article 267(3) where one of the three criteria in *CILFIT* is satisfied.

National courts wrongly refusing to refer cases to the Court under Article 267 may be accountable for State liability following Case C-224/01 *Köbler* v. *Austria*. The Court of Justice held that damages may be available where it was manifestly apparent that a court had failed to observe its duties under Article 267 where neither *acte clair* nor *acte éclairé* applied. In this case the Court did not find Austria liable, as it wrongly but in good faith considered the matter covered by a previous ruling.

Rulings on validity

The Court may rule on the validity of secondary legislation under Article 267. In Case 314/85 *Foto-Frost* v. *Hauptzollamt Lübeck-Ost* it held that national courts cannot declare the acts of the EU institutions invalid. Only the Court of Justice may do so, as its 2011 Information Note states:

> Although national courts may reject pleas before them challenging the validity of acts of an institution . . . of the Union, the Court of Justice has exclusive jurisdiction to declare such an act invalid. All national courts must therefore refer a question to the Court when they have doubts about the validity of such an act.

The likelihood of obtaining a declaration of invalidity under Article 267 is low. As Tridimas and Gari (2010) note in their study of judicial review from 2001 to 2005, a declaration was made in only six cases (13.6% of referrals), compared with a success rate of 31.8% in actions before the CFI for annulment by individuals and 30.7% in actions brought by privileged applicants. The low success rate in obtaining invalidity is a matter of concern, given the difficulty for individuals in establishing standing to bring an action for annulment under Article 263 TFEU (ex 230 TEC).

REFLECTION

The Court of Justice indicated in *Foto-Frost* that there may be scope for a national court to grant an interim injunction, although it did not rule on this point. *Interim remedies* are important as a ruling under Article 267 from the Court of Justice may take up to two years. The question of an interim injunction arose in Joined Cases C-143/88 & C-92/89 *Zuckerfabrik Suderdithmarschen AG* v. *Hauptzollamt Itzehoe*. Zuckerfabrik, a sugar producer in Germany, refused to pay a levy based on an EU regulation which he claimed was invalid. The German court referred questions to the Court of Justice to clarify whether it was possible to suspend the national measure based on the regulation. The Court held that the power of national courts to suspend an administrative act of a national authority based on an EU measure where validity is in doubt was equivalent to the power of the Court of Justice to suspend a contested act under Article 278 (ex 242 TEC) TFEU in interim proceedings. A national court may thus suspend a national measure implementing an EU regulation where:

(a) it has serious doubts about validity of the EU measure and refers validity question to the Court of Justice;

(b) there is an urgent need for a remedy, and irreparable damage to the applicant;

(c) due care is taken of the EU interest.

Effect of an Article 267 ruling

An Article 267 ruling by the Court of Justice binds the national court making the reference and any other national court considering the same point of EU law (Case 29/68 *Milch, Fett- und Eierkontor* v. *HZA Saarbrücken*). It is open to another national court to request a fresh interpretation (Joined Cases 28–30/62 *Da Costa*), although not on a question of validity (Case 66/80 *ICI* v. *Italian Financial Administration*).

TRANSITIONAL ARRANGEMENTS AND THE FORMER THIRD PILLAR

Before amendment by the Treaty of Lisbon, restrictions applied to the availability of preliminary rulings in relation to the Area of freedom, security and justice (AFSA) and to other measures such as those relating to asylum, immigration and action to combat crime between states. As the AFSA and related areas are now covered by the TFEU, these restrictions no longer apply, except under transitional arrangements until December 2013 under old Article 35 TEU. This Article empowered the Court to give preliminary rulings on framework decisions (used to harmonise the law under the old third pillar but now within the AFSA) where the Member State had accepted the Court of Justice's jurisdiction in a declaration, as Italy had done. This provision is retained under transitional arrangements until December 2013 or a third pillar measure is amended.

Case C-105/03 *Pupino* provides an example in which a nursery school teacher in Italy was accused of having mistreated children in her care. The Italian Public Prosecutor sought to take evidence from the children at the first stage of criminal proceedings contrary to normal practice under Italian law. It requested guidance from the Court on the status of a Council *framework decision* on the standing of victims. The framework decision was interpreted as meaning that young children should be able to give evidence with appropriate levels of protection.

A more recent example of a ruling on a framework decision is shown in Case C-168/13 *Jeremy F* v. *Premier Ministre* over use of a *European Arrest Warrant (EAW)* under the urgent procedure, with the ruling given only five weeks after the application. The case involved the flight of a teacher and abduction of an under-age school girl from the UK into France. Proceedings were brought by Mr F against the French court which had consented to his surrender under a European Arrest Warrant issued by the UK authorities who then stated that they wanted to prosecute Mr F for offences *not* in the original warrant. The French Cour de Cassation sought guidance from the Court of Justice which ruled that the Framework Decision 2002/584 'did not preclude' Member States from providing for an appeal suspending execution of a decision in such circumstances (i.e. such national action did not infringe the framework decision).

European Arrest Warrants (EAWs) enable a Member State to pursue a suspect who has left the country and moved into another Member State. 'Surrender' replaced extradition as a mechanism to retrieve suspects. EAWs are politically controversial in the UK where the Conservative Party wishes to see cooperation withdrawn or reduced as part of the 'repatriation' of powers from the EU to the UK.

CONTEXT

Reforming the preliminary reference procedure

The workload of the Court has increased greatly with enlargement, leading to a backlog of cases. The average time taken to obtain a ruling under Article 267 in 2010 was 16.1 months (Annual report of the Court of Justice 2010). Various solutions have been proposed such as encouraging national courts to filter references more effectively. Some changes have been made including permitting the General Court to hear preliminary rulings in areas prescribed by the Statute of the Court, but no cases have yet been assigned under Article 256(3). However, streamlined procedures have helped to reduce the backlog.

SIMPLIFIED, EXPEDITED AND URGENT PROCEDURES

The Court of Justice may make preliminary rulings *without* an opinion from the Advocate-General where no new point of law is raised (Article 20 of the Statute of the Court). About half its judgments in 2010 were delivered without an opinion, according to the Annual Report of the Court for that year. Various procedural instruments have been introduced to speed up the process of referral, including the urgent preliminary reference procedure for cases within the area of freedom, security and justice (Article 62a, Rules of Procedure of the Court of Justice).

A swift ruling may also be obtained where the question is identical to one referred earlier, where the answer may clearly be deduced from case law or where the answer admits of no reasonable doubt (Article 104, Rules of Procedure). The reference is concluded by a reasoned order after national courts have been informed and interested parties heard without oral arguments or Advocate-General's submissions. However, as Koutrakos (2008) points out, it is important to strike a balance between the need for speed and time for reflection. The Court of Justice continues to hold a pivotal role in the development of EU law, particularly through the preliminary reference procedure. Future reforms will have to safeguard the Court's pre-eminence in providing legal certainty while ensuring that it is not overwhelmed.

KEY POINTS

- The Court of Justice is the ultimate authority on EU law.
- It has played a central role in the development of EU law, making particular use of the preliminary reference procedure under Article 267 TFEU to provide for uniformity of interpretation of EU law.
- The preliminary reference procedure links the Court of Justice and the national courts and fosters cooperation.
- It enables the national courts to obtain a ruling as to the validity of EU secondary legislation.
- Article 267(2) TFEU enables any court of tribunal of a Member State to make a referral to the Court provided the reference is necessary, according to the criteria in *CILFIT* and there is a genuine question of EU law.
- Article 267(3) TFEU requires courts of last resort to make a referral to the Court of Justice where a question of interpretation of EU law has been raised, subject to the principle of *acte clair*.
- Rulings under Article 267 bind the national courts of all Member States, regardless as to which national court made the referral.

CORE CASES AND STATUTES

Case	About	Importance
Case 166/73 *Rheinmühlen v. Einfuhr- und Vorratsstelle Getreide*	Referral by German court to clarify law on refusal of export licence.	Established that preliminary reference procedure provides uniform interpretation throughout EU.
Case 104/79 and Case 244/80 *Foglia and Novello (No. 1 & No. 2)*	Two wine merchants agreed to sell wine to third, provided one seller should not be liable for charges contrary to EU law. Seller then sought to recover charge in Italian courts, which made two referrals to CJEU.	CJEU refused to answer questions as they were 'artificial', having arisen from 'dispute' found to have been concocted to obtain ruling on national law.
Case 283/81 *CILFIT Srl*	Textile importers in Italy refused to pay levy on wool from outside EU under regulation applying to animal products. Liability depended on whether or not wool was animal product. Supreme Court referred to CJEU.	CJEU found it is not necessary to refer under Article 267(2) where: – question of EU law is irrelevant – question has already been decided by CJEU – correct interpretation is so obvious as to leave no scope for doubt.
Cases C-143/88 & C-92/89 *Zuckerfabrik Süderdithmarschen*	Zuckerfabrik refused to pay levy based on EU regulation which he claimed was invalid. National court referred to CJEU to clarify whether it could suspend national measure based on the regulation.	National court may suspend national measure implementing EU regulation where certain conditions are satisfied and EU interest is protected.

Case	About	Importance
Case C-54/96 *Dorsch Consult*	Referral from Federal Supervisory Board in Germany to clarify procedure for awarding public service contracts under directive.	Establishes that body is a 'court or tribunal' if it is permanent, independent, has compulsory jurisdiction, applies legal rules and hears cases between parties.
Case C-99/00 *Kenny Roland Lyckeskog*	Lyckeskog was convicted of smuggling rice from Norway into Sweden. He appealed to the Court of Appeal for Western Sweden from which it was possible to appeal to Supreme Court with leave. Court of Appeal referred to CJEU.	Courts whose decisions could be appealed with leave are not covered by duty to refer in Article 267(3). There are two points when supreme court may satisfy duty to refer – when it hears application for leave to appeal or when it hears case itself.
Case C-224/01 *Köbler* v. *Austria*	Professor brought State liability action over refusal of Austrian university to pay salary increments recognising time working in universities in other Member States.	State liability result for breach of EU law by court such as supreme court where conditions for liability are fulfilled.

Statute	About	Importance
Article 267(1) TFEU (ex 234 TEC)	CJEU can rule on interpretation of Treaties and validity and interpretation of acts of EU institutions.	Empowers CJEU to rule on meaning of EU law or on validity of secondary legislation.
Article 267(2) TFEU	Where question is raised before any court or tribunal of Member State, that court or tribunal may, if it considers that decision on question is necessary to enable it to give judgment, request Court to give ruling on it.	Article 267(2) applies to any court or tribunal in Member States with discretion to request a ruling. It is important to distinguish between courts with discretion to refer under Article 267(2) and those obliged to refer under 267(3).
Article 267(3)	Where question is raised in case pending before court or tribunal of Member State against whose decisions there is no judicial remedy under national law, that court or tribunal shall bring the matter before the Court.	Article 267(3) applies to courts of last resort, with duty to refer.

FURTHER READING

Annual Report of the Court of Justice 2010, available at http://curia.europa.eu/jcms/jcms/Jo2_7000/ Annual Report.

Bebr, G. 'The existence of a genuine dispute: an indispensable precondition for the jurisdiction of the Court under Article 177 EEC Treaty' (1980) 17 *Common Market Law Review* 525
Critical examination of *Foglia*.

Komárak, J. 'In the court we trust? On the need for hierarchy and differentiation in the preliminary ruling procedure' (2007) 32 *European Law Review* 467
Advocates limiting power of national courts to make preliminary references, while differentiating the procedure.

Koutrakos, P. 'Speeding up the preliminary reference procedure – fast but not too fast' (2008) 33 *European Law Review* 617
Strikes a note of caution over balancing urgency and time for reflection in the urgent reference procedure.

Rasmussen, H. 'The European Court's *acte clair* strategy in *CILFIT*' (1989) 9 *European Law Review* 242
Provides insight into the relationship between the Court of Justice and the national courts after *CILFIT*.

Recommendation 2012/C 338/01 to national courts and tribunals in relation to the initiation of preliminary reference proceedings, available at http://eur-lex.europa.eu/LexUriServ/LexUriServ.do?uri=OJ:C:2012:338:0001:0006:EN:PDF
The Recommendation provides guidance to national courts seeking a preliminary ruling from the Court of Justice.

Report of the European Union Committee of the House of Lords of April 2011, available at http://www.publications.parliament.uk/pa/ld201011/ldselect/ldeucom/128/12802.htm
Critical assessment of workload problems of the Court of Justice and General Court.

Tridimas, T. 'The Court of Justice and judicial activism' (1986) 21 *European Law Review* 199
Analysis of the Court's role in developing the law under the preliminary reference procedure.

Tridimas, T. and Gari, G. 'Winners and losers in Luxembourg: Statistical analysis of judicial review before the Court of Justice and CFI (2001–2005)' (2010) 35 *European Law Review* 131
Mainly a statistical analysis of judicial review, but includes interesting material on preliminary references.

Wyatt, D. 'Foglia (No. 2): the Court denies it has jurisdiction to give advisory opinions' (1982) 7 *European Law Review* 186
A positive view of *CILFIT* as affirmation of the Court's right to decide its own jurisdiction.

CHAPTER 4

The sources of EU law and competences of the EU

BLUEPRINT

The sources of EU law and competences of the EU

KEY QUESTIONS

LEGISLATION

- Article 4 TEU
- Article 5(2) and (3) TEU
- Article 47 TEU
- Article 288 TFEU
- Article 290(1) TFEU

CONTEXT

- The need for continuing Treaty revision
- Failure of the Constitutional Treaty after referenda in France and the Netherlands

CONCEPTS

- Treaties
- Ratification
- Regulations
- Directives and decisions
- Legislative and non-legislative acts
- Delegated and implementing legislation
- Exclusive and concurrent jurisdiction
- Subsidiarity
- Proportionality

- Areas of debate, moral and philosophical reflection, what do you think?
- Should the EU be competent to act where the Treaties have not provided it with express powers?

- How should the Member States empower the Union to act?

CASES

- *International Fruit*
- *ERTA*
- *Inuit*
- EEA Opinion

SPECIAL CHARACTERISTICS

- TEU and TFEU as framework
- Binding nature of secondary legislation
- EU may only act where power has been conferred by the Member States
- Express and implied powers

REFORM

- Need to monitor changes under Treaty of Lisbon including operation of conferred powers

CRITICAL ISSUES

Setting the scene

The six Member States signing the Treaty of Rome in 1957 embarked on an ambitious experiment in European integration. The Treaties established three original Communities – the EEC under the Treaty of Rome 1957, Euratom under the European Atomic Energy Authority Treaty 1957 and the European Coal and Steel Community (ECSC) under the Treaty of Paris 1951 (wound up in 2002). The Treaty of Lisbon merged the communities into one, the European Union, under the Treaty of European Union (TEU) and the Treaty on the Functioning of the European Union (TFEU). The legal regime under the Treaties is thus of recent origin, unlike with the national systems of the Member States and should be understood in the context of its origins.

The legal systems of the six original signatory States derive from Roman law, with the basic legal principles provided in codes such as the Code Napoléon in France. The Treaty of Rome followed a similar 'continental' approach as the UK did not join until 1973. The 'code' in EU law is found in the Treaties (the TEU and TFEU) providing the primary sources of EU law, a framework filled out by secondary legislation (the acts of the institutions) and decisions of the Court of Justice. This chapter examines the sources of EU law, as well as the powers and competences of the EU conferred in the Treaties.

> ## Take note
>
> Before the Treaty of Lisbon took effect on 1 December 2009, the system of law was known as Community law, as it was adopted under the legal regime of the Treaty establishing the European Community (TEC). The Treaty of Lisbon replaced the Community (EC) with the Union (EU). As a result the law is now known as Union (or EU) law.

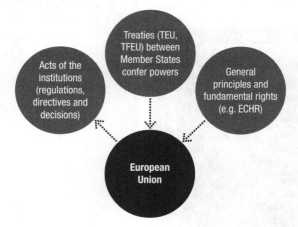

Figure 4.1 Sources of EU law

THE FOUNDING TREATIES

Treaties creating the institutions

The two principal founding treaties are:

1. The Treaty on European Union (TEU)
2. The Treaty on the Functioning of the Union (TFEU).

Treaty reform reflects changes in the EU and varying levels of enthusiasm for European integration at different periods. The Single European Act, signed in 1986 when enthusiasm for integration was low, effectively 'relaunched' the Community. The Maastricht Treaty was adopted in 1992 during a period of greater support for integration led by France and Germany. The Constitutional Treaty failed due to lack of political support, and had to be followed by the less aspirational Treaty of Lisbon which was needed to address the challenges posed by enlargement.

The current version of the founding treaties, TEU and TFEU, provides the framework of EU law, taking precedence over conflicting obligations in subsidiary treaties or secondary legislation. The TEU and TFEU incorporate amendments from earlier treaties up to and including the Treaty of Lisbon and various Acts of Accession by which new Member States joined the EU.

The status of the Treaties

The TEU and the TFEU were agreed through treaty reform requiring agreement of *all* the Member States. The Treaty of Lisbon does *not* set out to be a constitutional document (unlike the failed Constitutional Treaty) but operates as an amending treaty. The law thus represents the original Treaty of Rome (or EEC Treaty), as amended by later Treaties up to and including the Treaty of Lisbon and the Act of Accession with Croatia.

Tables 4.1 and 4.2 provide an overview of the most significant amending Treaties. Table 4.1 covers Acts of Accession (i.e. Treaties signed by new Member States joining the EU) and Table 4.2 covers Treaties deepening integration.

Take note

Treaties are international agreements between sovereign states, taking effect when ratified by the Member States. Ratification is the national procedure to incorporate treaties – normally by national parliaments or referendum. The UK ratified the 1972 Act of Accession in the European Communities Act 1972.

Table 4.1 Amending Treaties – Acts of Accession

Acts of Accession	Purpose	Signed	In force
Denmark, Ireland and UK	To join EC	1972	1 January 1973
Greece	To join EC	1979	1 January 1981
Portugal and Spain	To join EC	1985	1 January 1986
Austria, Finland and Sweden	To join EC	1994	1 January 1995
Cyprus, Czech Republic, Estonia, Hungary, Latvia, Lithuania, Malta, Poland, Slovakia and Slovenia	To join EU	2003	1 January 2004
Bulgaria and Romania	To join EU	2005	1 January 2007
Croatia	To join EU	2011	1 July 2013

Table 4.2 Amending treaties – deepening integration

Treaty	Purpose	Signed	In force
Single European Act (SEA)	Completion of internal market. Introduced cooperation procedure, completion of the single market. Spurred relaunch of EC.	1986	1 July 1987
Treaty of Maastricht (Treaty on European Union or TEU).	Introduced new entity, the EU, providing for political union supported by 'three pillar system': 1. EC (governed by TEC) 2. Common Foreign and Security Policy (CFSP, under governmental cooperation) 3. Police and Judicial Cooperation in Criminal Matters (under intergovernmental cooperation) and EMU for participating states.	1992	1 January 1993
Treaty of Amsterdam (ToA)	Moved some areas from Third Pillar to First Pillar. Provided for 'closer cooperation' to enable participating states to proceed more rapidly towards integration. Renumbered TEC and TEU.	1997	1 May 1999
The Treaty of Nice (ToN)	Addressed important issues left unresolved by ToA, particularly size and composition of Commission and weighting of QMV in Council. Established template for future enlargement. Changes to EU institutions are set out in Accession Treaties of 2003, 2005 and 2011.	2001	1 February 2003
The Treaty of Lisbon	Amended and renumbered TEU and TEC, which was renamed Treaty on Functioning of European Union (TFEU). Provides for enlarged EU while increasing democratic involvement of citizens and allowing for greater transparency.	2007	1 December 2009

INTERSECTION

You may find it helpful to read the section on Study skills in EU law which provides guidance on reading and understanding EU legislation and the decisions of the Court of Justice.

The current version of the Treaties – TEU and TFEU

The TEU contains the strategic principles underpinning the EU. Article 1 TEU provides for both the TEU and TFEU to have 'the same legal value', giving rise to enforceable rights on the same basis as the TFEU. Nevertheless many areas in the TEU are still governed by intergovernmental cooperation rather than law, reflecting the earlier, pre-Lisbon approach to the Second and Third Pillars which covered the Common Foreign and Security Policy (CFSP) and Cooperation in Justice and Home Affairs. Under the Treaty of Lisbon the three-pillar structure disappeared and was replaced by a single body, the European Union, although some separate procedures continue for the CFSP under the TEU.

INTERSECTION

When the Maastricht Treaty was negotiated, intergovernmental cooperation was considered more suitable than legal regulation for sensitive areas like foreign policy where Member States wished to preserve their autonomy. The three-pillar structure, introduced under the Treaty of Maastricht, is considered in Chapter 1.

Whereas the TEU expresses broad principles (e.g. Article 2 TEU, 'The Union is founded on respect for human dignity'), the TFEU makes more specific and clear-cut statements such as 'Freedom of movement for workers shall be secured within the Union' (Article 45 TFEU).

International treaties

CORNERSTONE

Article 47 TEU provides for the Union to have legal personality, enabling it to enter into international treaties on behalf of the Member States.

International treaties form 'an integral part of Community [Union] law' (Case 181/73 *Haegeman* v. *Belgium*) in which the Association Agreement between Greece and the Community before Greece joined the EC was found to be subject to interpretation by the Court of Justice under the preliminary reference procedure.

Before amendment by the Treaty of Lisbon, the EU lacked legal personality, preventing it from acceding to the European Convention on Human Rights (ECHR), as the Court of Justice ruled in Opinion 2/94. After the Lisbon amendments, the Union not only has international legal capacity but is *obliged* by Article 6(2) TEU to accede to the ECHR.

INTERSECTION

The Court of Justice has recognised various Articles of the ECHR as a source of EU law on a case-by-case basis under the preliminary reference procedure. The Court's role in developing fundamental rights, as well as the current status of the Charter and the European Convention on Human Rights (ECHR) are examined in more detail in Chapter 5.

The adoption of international treaties by the EU

Treaties may be adopted in the following ways:

(a) By the EU exclusively under powers conferred by the Treaties. Where the Treaty provides for the EU to exercise exclusive powers, Member States no longer have power to act, and must leave all action to the EU as with commercial agreements under Article 207 TFEU (ex 133).

(b) By the EU on succession to an earlier agreement. The most significant example remains the General Agreement on Tariffs and Trade (GATT) 1947, an international agreement providing for multilateral trade negotiation ('rounds') with participating states to reduce trade barriers. The Final Act embodying the results of the Uruguay Round 1994 included a new agreement setting up the World Trade Organization (WTO) with effect from 1995. The WTO continues to work to reduce trade barriers and provides a forum to resolve disputes.

In Cases 21–24/72 *International Fruit* the Court held that the Community took over the powers of the Member States in relation to GATT 1947. The Court accepted in Case C-69/89 *Nakajima* that where the Community adopted legislation to comply with an international obligation such as GATT 1947, any inconsistent provisions will be regarded as in breach of the Treaties or rule relating to its application, providing grounds for judicial review under Article 263 TFEU. WTO Agreements, with a different mechanism for dispute resolution from the GATT, are not subject to judicial review before the Court of Justice (Case C-149/96 *Portugal* v. *Council*).

Acts of the institutions

The Treaties – the TEU and TFEU – provide the primary law within which EU law may operate. The detail is supplied by the institutions in 'acts' – regulations, directives and decisions – which constitute the secondary legislation of the EU as provided by Article 288(1) TFEU (ex 249(1) TEC) which states that, 'To exercise the Union's competences, the institutions shall adopt regulations, directives, decisions, recommendations and opinions'. Each 'act' is considered individually below.

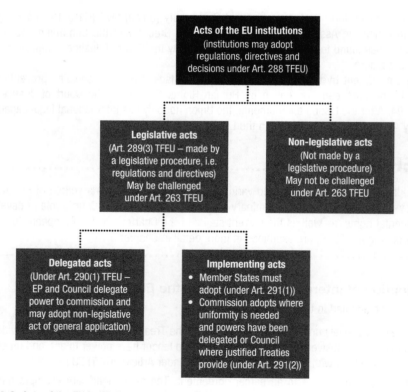

Figure 4.2 Acts of the EU institutions

CORNERSTONE

'To exercise the Union's competences, the institutions shall adopt regulations, directives and decisions, recommendations and opinions' (Article 288 TFEU).

Acts of the institutions are normally adopted by the Council and the European Parliament under the ordinary legislative process in Article 294 TFEU (ex 251). Where the Treaties provide, Article 289(2) TFEU enables the adoption of legislation under a special legislative procedure. (The legislative process is considered in Chapter 2.)

Regulations

Article 288(2) TFEU states that a regulation has 'general application', and is 'binding in its entirety and directly applicable in all Member States'. This means that regulations set out rules applying to all Member States, taking effect without the need for implementing legislation. The Court of Justice has found that they are also 'directly effective' and so may be relied upon by individuals before the national courts (discussed in Chapter 7). Regulations are usually adopted when detailed rules are needed for uniform application across the EU such as Regulation 492/2011 on freedom of movement for workers, with Article 9(2) providing for a worker to put his name down on the housing list in the region where he is employed.

Directives

Article 288(3) states that a directive is 'binding, as to the result to be achieved, upon each Member State to which it is addressed', but leaves to the national authorities 'the choice of form and methods'. Directives are more flexible than regulations, as they state the objective, but leave the Member States to decide how to achieve it. Implementation may be by legislation or administrative action.

The Product Liability Directive 85/374 exemplifies a typical directive, imposing a requirement on Member States to introduce strict liability for defective products. Article 1 provides: 'The producer shall be liable for damage caused by a defect in his product.' The UK implemented the directive in the Consumer Protection Act 1987. The flexibility of directives is attractive to EU institutions not wanting to prescribe detailed rules. Directives are normally addressed to *all* Member States, with a deadline for *transposition* (implementation), although they may be addressed to a limited number of Member States, such as the measures adopted under the Social Chapter (not applied to the UK).

The Social Chapter was not supported by the Conservative UK government at the time, with the UK remaining outside the arrangements. Acts such as Directive 94/95 establishing a European Works Council were addressed to all Member States *other than* the UK. The Chapter was incorporated in the TEC by the Treaty of Amsterdam (effective 1997) after the Labour Party came to power.

CONTEXT

Directives are seen as the best way to advance integration without unnecessarily detailed EU legislation. They were used to complete the internal market in 1992. The process of adopting common standards through directives is known as *harmonisation* or *approximation*.

Decisions

Article 288(4) TFEU provides that: 'A decision shall be binding in its entirety. A decision which specifies those to whom it is addressed shall be binding only on them.' Decisions are made by the Council or Commission. As they are addressed to specific persons (states or individuals) they do not apply across the EU. No further implementation is required. A typical Commission decision in competition would be addressed to an undertaking to cease an anti-competitive practice such as a cartel, possibly imposing a fine.

Framework decisions

Framework decisions are designed to harmonise the law across the EU. For example, Framework Decision 2002/584/JHA on the European Arrest Warrant and surrender procedures between Member States is based on the principle of mutual recognition. This framework decision enables national courts to issue a European Arrest Warrant (EAW) to conduct criminal prosecution, execute a custodial sentence or detention order for a named individual. The use of EAWs has been controversial, with criticism over possible human rights abuses, and calls in 2013 from UK Conservative MPs to withdraw from the system.

Binding nature of secondary legislation

Regulations, directives and decisions are legally binding. Article 296(3) TFEU (ex 253(3)) requires these acts to 'state the reasons on which they are based'. They must also 'refer to any proposals or opinions . . . required to be obtained pursuant to this Treaty'. These procedural requirements are regarded as essential. Failure to comply may lead to annulment under Article 263 TFEU.

The Charter of Fundamental Rights

Before amendment by the Treaty of Lisbon, the Charter of Fundamental Rights lacked legal force as it was only a declaration, although it was cited in the Court of Justice to clarify fundamental rights. In Case C-540/03 *European Parliament* v. *Council of the EU*, for example, Directive 2003/86 on conditions for family reunification by third-country nationals residing lawfully in the Member States was considered in the light of the Charter. After amendment by the Treaty of Lisbon, the Charter was given the same legal force as the Treaties by Article 6(1) TEU, enabling individuals to invoke it in the national courts where the conditions for direct effect are satisfied (clear, unconditional, requiring no further action).

Soft law

Article 288(5) (ex 249(5) TEC) provides that: 'Recommendations and opinions shall have no binding force.' The use of non-binding instruments (collectively referred to as 'soft law') such as guidance and codes of conduct has grown since the Lisbon European Council in 2000 where ambitious goals were set to achieve economic growth with greater cohesion by 2010. Soft law has some advantages over traditional law-making (flexibility and scope for diversity), but disadvantages as it may be unclear or ineffective.

National courts should not ignore soft law which may be used as an aid to statutory interpretation. In Case C-322/88 *Grimaldi* v. *Fonds des Maladies Professionelles* the Court of Justice stated that national judges must consider relevant **recommendations** in dealing with cases before them, particularly where they clarify the interpretation of other provisions of national or EU law.

Legislative acts may also be adopted under Article 289(4) TFEU where provided by the Treaties on the initiative of a group of Member States or the European Parliament.

Classification of secondary legislation

The formal designation of an act as regulation, directive or decision under Article 288 TFEU should not be taken at face value as the Court considers that the substance of the act rather than its form determines its nature. In Cases 16 & 17/62 *Confédération Nationale des Productions de Fruits et Légumes* v. *Council*, the Court held that where a regulation 'fails to lay down general rules', it may be relabelled a 'disguised decision'. This meant that the act could be challenged by an individual under old Article 230(4) TEC (now Article 263(4) TFEU). Before amendment by the Treaty of Lisbon, the distinction between Regulations and decisions was particularly significant in the context of judicial review, as individuals could only challenge a measure under 230(4) TEC if it was a decision addressed to them or a measure equivalent to a decision and in which they were directly and individually concerned. After amendment by the Treaty of Lisbon, Article 263(4) TFEU widened the categories of reviewable measures, empowering individuals to challenge an *act* addressed to that person or which is of direct and individual concern to them.

INTERSECTION

It is difficult for individuals to establish 'individual concern' under Article 263(4) as the test for *standing* is very rigorous. Reviewable acts and standing are discussed further in Chapter 10.

Classifications of acts under the Treaty of Lisbon

Legislative and non-legislative acts

The Treaty of Lisbon introduced a new type of measure known as a *legislative act*, defined under Article 289(3) TFEU as a legal act 'adopted by legislative procedure', that is, under the ordinary procedure in Article 289(1) TFEU or a special procedure (Article 289(4)) where the Treaties provide.

Acts outside the definition in Article 289(3) are *non-legislative acts* laying down general, legally binding rules, but not considered to be legislative acts.

Delegated and implementing acts

Acts in the form of regulations and directives often require further measures to complete the provision. The Treaty of Lisbon introduced two new categories of act: delegated acts and *implementing acts*. *Delegated acts* are acts of general application, amending or supplementing a legislative act. *Implementing acts* give effect to a legislative act without amending or supplementing it.

Before the Treaty of Lisbon, delegated acts were adopted through the *Comitology* process. The Council devolved powers to the Commission to adopt measures jointly with national officials through advisory, management and regulatory committees. Parliament disliked the process as it had only a limited role, whereas the Council could veto the decisions of management and regulatory committees.

After the Treaty of Lisbon, Comitology is only used for delegated acts adopted by advisory committees, although a modified form of the process continues to apply to implementing acts under Article 290 TFEU. Comitology is considered further in relation to decision-making in the EU institutions in Chapter 2.

CORNERSTONE

Article 290(1) TFEU

Article 290(1) TFEU enables the Council and Parliament to delegate power to the Commission under a legislative act to adopt 'non-legislative acts of general application'.

The purpose of the delegation is to enable the Commission to supplement or amend 'non-essential elements' of a legislative act, for example by providing further information. Under Article 290(2) TFEU the legislative act must define the scope and conditions of the delegation. Either the Parliament or the Council may decide to revoke the delegation under Article 290(2)(a). A delegated act will enter into force only if the Council or Parliament does not object within the time stated in the legislative act under Article 290(2)(b). The word 'delegated' must appear in the title of the legislation (Article 290(3)). Member States must adopt measures of national law necessary to implement legally binding acts (Article 291).

Implementing acts

Implementation of legally binding acts may be undertaken by Member States under Article 290(1) or the Commission (or occasionally, Council) where uniform conditions for implementation are required (Article 291(2). The word 'implementing' must be inserted in the title of implementing acts (Article 291(4)).

The classification of acts is important as it determines how far they can be challenged by individuals under Article 263(4) TFEU. The creation of a new category of acts known as *regulatory acts not requiring implementing measures* under Article 263(4) has made it easier for individuals to challenge without demonstrating 'individual concern'.

Judicial clarification or regulatory act

While the term *regulatory act* does not appear in Articles 288–292 TFEU, it was considered by the General Court in Case T-18/10 *Inuit Tapiriit Kanatami and others* v. *Parliament and Council*. In this case (upheld by the Court of Justice in Case C-583/11P), seal traders and others sought to challenge a regulation harmonising the seal trade. The General Court held that regulatory acts are 'acts of general application apart from a legislative act'. As the measure had been adopted under the co-decision procedure, it was a legislative not a regulatory act, requiring both direct and individual concern to challenge.

The General Court followed a similar approach in Case T-262/10 *Microban International Ltd* v. *Commission*, but found that the measure (decision prohibiting marketing of materials containing substance used by the applicants to make plastics) was a regulatory not a legislative act. The Court held that the prohibition did not require implementation as no discretion was left to Member States. Since Microban was directly concerned, there was no need to establish individual concern to challenge under Article 263(4).

REFLECTION

The introduction of two new categories of measure, delegated and implementing acts, represents a controversial change under the Treaty of Lisbon. Craig (2011) argues that the new regime will increase institutional complexity, encourage EU institutions to categorise acts to maximise their own control and possibly undermine the rationale for the distinction between the categories. So far it's too early to reach an assessment.

The meaning and scope of 'regulatory acts not requiring implementing measures' has been criticised. Balthasar (2010) argues for a liberal interpretation, but the General Court in *Inuit* (upheld by the Court of Justice on appeal) and *Microban* followed a strict approach, defining regulatory acts as those adopted by a legislative procedure.

Thus while the Treaty of Lisbon has introduced new categories of act into the legislative repertoire, it has not (greatly) increased the extent to which they may be reviewed.

THE COMPETENCE OF THE UNION

Express and implied powers

Under Article 5(2) TEU (ex 5 TEC) the Union is empowered to act within the limits of the powers conferred on it by the Treaties within the objectives assigned to it. This is called the *principle of conferral* (see Chapter 1) and refers to the powers expressly given to the Union under the Treaties. However, Treaties cannot provide for every eventuality. The theory of implied powers may provide support for action in other areas. The theory may take either a narrow or wide form. In its *narrow* form, an *express power* implies the existence of any other power reasonably necessary to exercise the express power. Cases 281 etc./85 *Germany* v. *Commission* concerned Article 137 TEC (now 253 TFEU) which required the Commission to promote cooperation in the social field without providing the necessary powers. A Commission decision on social cooperation was challenged by Germany. The Court held that the provision must be regarded as implicitly conferring on the Commission the powers 'indispensible in order to carry out that task'. In its *wide* form, an *express function* implies the existence of a power necessary to achieve it. This is supported by the general power in Article 353(1) TFEU (ex 308) to adopt 'appropriate measures'.

The theory of implied powers was recognised in Case 22/70 *Commission* v. *Council (Re European Road Transport Agreement)*. Five of the six Member States signed the first European Road Transport Agreement (AETR) in 1962 with other European states. As it was not ratified the Member States began negotiations to conclude a second AETR. Meanwhile the Council issued a regulation deriving from its *internal* power in the same areas. The Commission objected to the decision to allow continuing negotiations sought to annul the Council proceedings leading to conclusion of the AETR. The second AETR was nevertheless concluded in 1970. The Court held that the Community (now EU) had authority to enter into such an agreement. Authority may arise not only out of express provision in the Treaty but also from other Treaty provisions and secondary legislation. When the Community adopted common rules to implement a transport policy in 1960, Member States lost their competence to conclude international agreements in this area.

General powers under Article 352 TFEU

The Community (now Union) possesses wide-ranging treaty-making powers. After the *ERTA* decision particular use has been made of the so-called general powers under Article 352 TFEU (ex 308 TEC). This provides for the Council to take the necessary measures to attain one of the objectives of the Union where the Treaties have not provided the necessary powers, acting unanimously on a Commission proposal after consulting Parliament.

Article 352 has provided a useful base for legislation in areas such as environmental protection before Treaty amendment made this unnecessary. As the Court usually adopts a *purposive* approach to interpretation (i.e. according to the spirit or purpose of the Treaties), the wording of the Article has not proved particularly limiting. However in Opinion 2/94 on Accession of the Community to the ECHR, the Court of Justice held that Article 308 TEC (now Article 352 TFEU) could not extend the Community powers beyond the framework under the TEC as a whole as such usage would circumvent the normal Treaty amendment process.

The Court's main objection to Article 352 as a legal base has been that it reduces the role of the Parliament in the legislative process. Thus Article 352 should only be used where there is no other legal base. The Court has ruled that it will examine closely the use of Article 352 when an alternative legal base is available providing greater involvement of the Parliament. In Case C-350/92 *Spain* v. *Council* Spain unsuccessfully challenged adoption of a regulation on medicinal products under Article 100 A EEC (now Article 114 TFEU), claiming it should have been adopted under (what is now) Article 352 TFEU, requiring unanimity.

Union competences under the Treaty of Lisbon

Conferral, subsidiarity and proportionality

The Treaty of Lisbon provides for the principle of conferral in new Article 4 TEU under which competences (powers or authority) not conferred on the Union in the Treaties remain with Member States. Where the Treaties provide that the EU has exclusive competence, Member States lose the power to act (Article 2 TFEU). Where competence is shared Member States may act where the Union has not acted or has ceased to act.

Article 5(2) TEU provides that under the principle of conferral, the Union shall act only within the limits of the competences conferred on it by Member States in the treaties to attain the Union's objectives. Competences not conferred on the Union remain with the Member States.

Article 5(3) adds a new requirement that *national parliaments* shall 'ensure compliance with the principle of subsidiarity' in accordance with the procedure set out in the Protocol on Subsidiarity.

The principle of subsidiarity

The principle of subsidiarity was introduced by the Maastricht Treaty to govern the *allocation of competences* where responsibility is shared between the Union and Member States. It was seen by the treaty-drafters as offsetting the tendency for 'competence creep' (the gradual increase in the number and range of areas within the EU's exclusive competence).

CORNERSTONE

Under Article 5(3) TEU (ex 5(1) TEC), in areas of shared competence, the Union may act under the principle of *subsidiarity*

only if and so far as the objectives of the proposed action cannot be sufficiently achieved by the Member States, either at central level or at regional or local level, but can rather, by reason of the scale or effects of the proposed action, be better achieved by the Union.

Article 5(3) creates a rebuttable presumption in favour of action by Member States in areas of shared competence, where the EU has not already acted.

INTERSECTION

The principles of subsidiarity and proportionality are considered in the context of general principles of EU law (Chapter 5).

Article 5(4) TEU provides that 'the content and form of Union action' should 'not exceed what is necessary to achieve the objective in question' under the principle of *proportionality*. This is an important principle often invoked as a ground for annulment under Article 263 TFEU.

APPLICATION

Imagine there is a serious problem of pollution in the River Rhine, which flows through several Member States before reaching the sea. Legislation is needed to address the problem. Who should legislate – the EU or the Member States? The environment is an area of shared competence under Article 4 TFEU. Applying the principle of subsidiarity, action should be taken by the Member States unless it can better be achieved by the EU. As action is likely to be more effective at EU level, an act (probably a directive) may be adopted by the EU. It should not impose any more restrictions than necessary, to accord with the principle of proportionality.

The inter-relationship of principles in this area may seem confusing. Article 5 TEU distinguishes between the *limits* of Union competences, governed by the principle of conferral (i.e. the EU can only act within the powers conferred by the Member States), and their *use* (i.e. how the powers are exercised), governed by the principles of subsidiarity and proportionality.

Exclusive competences under the Treaty of Lisbon

After amendment by the Treaty of Lisbon, the areas in which the EU has exclusive competences are listed under Article 3 TFEU as follows:

(a) the customs union;

(b) establishment of competition rules necessary for internal market;

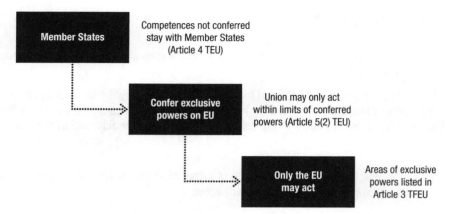

Figure 4.3 Exclusive powers of the Union

(c) monetary policy for Member States whose currency is the euro;

(d) conservation of marine biological resources under the common fisheries policy;

(e) the common commercial policy.

Article 3(2) TFEU also gives the Union exclusive competence to conclude an international agreement where:

• provided for in a legislative act, or

• necessary to enable the Union to exercise its internal competence, or

• its conclusion may affect common rules or alter their scope.

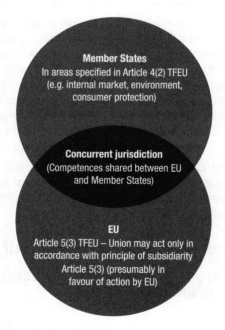

Figure 4.4 Shared powers of EU and Member States

Shared competences under the Treaty of Lisbon

Article 4 TFEU provides for the Union to share competence with Member States where the treaties confer on it a competence not relating to the areas in Articles 3 and 6 TFEU. Article 6 TFEU gives the Union competence to support, coordinate or supplement Member State action in protection and improvement of human health, industry, culture, tourism, education, vocational training and sport, civil protection and administrative cooperation.

Under Article 4 TFEU the areas of shared competence are listed as:

- the internal market
- social policy where defined in the Treaties
- economic, territorial and social cohesion
- environment
- consumer protection
- transport
- trans-European networks
- energy
- area of freedom, security and justice
- common safety concerns in public health matters, where defined in the TFEU.

Complementary competences under the Treaty of Lisbon

The Treaty of Lisbon does not refer to 'complementary competences' but as Schutze (2008) notes, it is useful to identify competences which are neither exclusive nor shared. Article 2(5) TFEU empowers the Union to undertake actions to 'support, coordinate or supplement the actions of the Member States' without superseding their competence. Legally binding acts in these areas will not harmonise national law. Seven areas are listed in Article 6 TFEU:

1. protection and improvement of human health
2. industry
3. culture
4. tourism
5. education, vocational training, youth and sport
6. civil protection
7. administrative cooperation.

It is unclear whether Article 6 TFEU provides an exhaustive list. Schutze (2008) claims that these are really shared competences subject to the principle of subsidiarity. While the Lisbon Treaty appears to have clarified what constitutes exclusive and shared competences by listing them in the Treaties, he argues that the classification represents a 'serious step backward' by providing three 'official' and several unofficial types of competence, which are difficult to distinguish.

REFLECTION

Decisions of the Union courts

Decisions of the Union courts are an important source of EU law, binding on all the Member States.

The Court of Justice has played a central role in developing the EU legal order, making particular use of the preliminary reference procedure under Article 267 TFEU (ex 234), starting with Case 26/62 *Van Gend en Loos*. The Court has also used the procedure to recognise the *general principles* of law as a source of EU law. These principles derive from international law such as the European Convention on Human Rights and Fundamental Freedoms (ECHR) and from the laws of the Member States. Examples include the principles of equality (or non-discrimination) and legal certainty.

INTERSECTION

The central role of the Court of Justice is considered in Chapter 3, development of fundamental rights (Chapter 5), supremacy (Chapter 6), direct and indirect effect (Chapter 7) and State liability (Chapter 8).

KEY POINTS

- The Treaties, particularly the TEU and the TFEU, provide the primary sources of EU law.
- It is important to distinguish between different types of EU secondary legislation (regulations, directives and decisions) to appreciate their purpose and legal status.
- The Treaty of Lisbon introduced new categories of measures (legislative and non-legislative acts) and made explicit the scope for Member States and EU institutions to adopt delegated and implementing acts.
- The principle of conferral recognises powers expressly granted under the Treaties to enable the EU institutions to carry out their tasks.
- The principle of conferral determines the allocation of competences between the EU and Member States, whereas subsidiarity and proportionality determine the legality of their exercise.

CORE CASES AND STATUTES

Case	About	Importance
Case T-18/10 *Inuit Tapiriit Kanatami and others* v. *Parliament and Council* (upheld in Case C-583/11P)	Meaning of 'regulatory act' in context of seal traders' attempt to challenge regulation harmonising trade in seal products.	Defined regulatory acts as 'all acts of general application other than legislative acts'.
Case T-262/10 *Microban International Ltd, Microban (Europe) Ltd* v. *Commission*	Meaning of 'regulatory act not requiring implementing measures' under Article 263(4) TFEU.	Measure was found to be regulatory act, applying *Inuit* definition. Action was admissible without individual concern as implementation was not required.
Case 22/70 *Commission* v. *Council (Re European Road Transport Agreement)*	Five of six EC Member States signed agreement on road transport (ERTA) with other states in Europe. When not ratified, Member States negotiated another ERTA, while Council adopted regulation on road transport challenged by Commission.	EC had implied authority to enter into such agreement as result of other Treaty provisions and secondary legislation. Once EC had acted, Member States lost authority to act.

Statute	About	Importance
Article 4 TEU	Provides for principle of conferral.	Competences not conferred on Union stay with Member States.
Article 5(1) TEU	Limits of Union competences are covered by principle of conferral, whereas use is covered by subsidiarity and proportionality.	Member States have agreed limits of competences under Treaties. Subsidiarity and proportionality provide check on exercise of competence.
Article 5(2) TEU	Union can only act within powers conferred by Treaties and their objectives.	Defines principle of conferral.
Article 6(1) TEU	Gives Charter of Fundamental Rights same force as Treaties.	Enables individuals to rely on Charter before national courts.
Article 2 TFEU	Where Treaties confer exclusive competence on Union, only Union may act.	Member States may not act unless power has been delegated to them or to implement Union acts.

→

Statute	About	Importance
Article 5(3) TFEU	In areas of shared competence, Union may act only where action can be better achieved by Union than by Member States.	The principle of subsidiarity creates presumption in favour of action by Member States.
Article 5(4) TFEU	Content and form of EU action should not exceed what is necessary to achieve objectives in question.	The principle of proportionality.
Article 288(3) TFEU	Defines directives as 'binding as to result to be achieved but leaving Member States the choice of form and method'.	Directives are flexible measures giving Member States discretion on achieving objective.
Article 288(4) TFEU	Defines decisions as binding in their entirety.	Addressed to specific persons, so not binding across EU.
Article 289(3) TFEU	Defines legislative act as act adopted 'by a legislative procedure'.	Only covers acts adopted under ordinary or special legislative procedure.

FURTHER READING

The following journal articles focus on new categories of legislation under the Treaty of Lisbon which have generated particular academic interest.

Balthasar, S. 'Locus standi rules for challenges to regulatory acts by private applicants: the new Article 263(4) TFEU' (2010) 35 *European Law Review* 542
Written before *Inuit* and *Microban*, but worth reading on regulatory acts.

Craig, P. 'Delegated acts, implementing acts and the new comitology regulation' (2011) 36 *European Law Review* 671
Examines the hierarchy of norms under the Lisbon Treaty, particularly the distinction between delegated and implementing acts.

Kral, R. 'National, normative implementation of EC regulations. An exceptional or rather common matter?' (2008) 33 *European Law Review* 243
Compares national legislative implementation of regulations and directives, written before the Lisbon reforms.

Peers, S. and Costa, M. 'Judicial review of EU acts after the Treaty of Lisbon' (2012) 8 *European Constitutional Law Review* 82
Case note on *Inuit* and *Microban* with analysis of what constitutes a regulatory act.

Schutze, R. 'Lisbon and the federal order of competences: A prospective analysis' (2008) *33 European Law Review* 709
Assesses whether listing exclusive and shared competences in the Lisbon Treaty has clarified the Union's order of competences.

CHAPTER 5
General principles and fundamental rights

BLUEPRINT

*General principles and
fundamental rights*

LEGISLATION

- Article 5 TEU
- Article 18 TFEU
- Article 40 TFEU
- Article 157 TFEU

CONTEXT

- Protection of
  fundamental rights
  in post-war German
  Constitution

CONCEPTS

- Fundamental rights
- Proportionality
- Equality
- Legal certainty
- Subsidiarity
- Transparency

- What will be the relationship
  between the CJEU and the ECHR
  in the future?

- Will accession of the EU to the European Convention on Human Rights (ECHR) enhance protection of fundamental rights in EU law?

CASES

- *Stauder*
- *Kirk*

SPECIAL CHARACTERISTICS

- General principles may derive from domestic law of Member States or from international law
- Importance of ECHR
- Role of Charter of Fundamental Rights

REFORM

- Obligation under Article 6(2) TEU for EU to accede to ECHR
- Charter given same force as Treaties

CRITICAL ISSUES

Setting the scene

Imagine the EU adopts a directive requiring Member States to harmonise train timetables immediately to facilitate free movement. The UK could challenge such a measure in the Court of Justice as it infringes the principle of legitimate expectations by requiring an unexpected change with no period of notice. The incorporation of general principles such as legitimate expectations is a distinguishing feature of EU law. The Court of Justice has played a unique role in developing general principles and fundamental rights, recognising principles such as legal certainty (including legitimate expectations) which are accepted in the Member States or in international treaties, particularly the European Convention on Human Rights. Protection of fundamental rights has shifted from the Court to the Treaties, a transformation symbolised by the obligation on the EU under Article 6 TEU to join the Convention.

GENERAL PRINCIPLES

Article 6 TEU identifies the sources of 'rights, freedoms and principles' as:

- The Charter of Fundamental Rights of the EU, which has 'the same legal force as the Treaties' after the Treaty of Lisbon. The Charter was first annexed to the TEC as a declaration in 2000.
- Fundamental rights under the European Convention for the Protection of Human Rights and Fundamental Freedoms (ECHR) and resulting from the constitutional traditions common to the Member States, which 'shall constitute general principles of the Union's law' (Article 6(3) TEU). Fundamental rights originating in the traditions of Member States are considered below. They include generally recognised principles such as legal certainty.

The European Convention on Human Rights

The European Convention on Human Rights and Fundamental Freedoms (ECHR) is a Treaty agreed by states through the Council of Europe, a body established after the Second World War. The UK played a leading role in drafting the Convention which sets minimum standards to protect individual human rights such as the right to liberty (Article 5), procedural fairness (Article 6) and freedom of expression (Article 10). It was signed in 1950 and came into force in 1953. The European Court of Human Rights (ECtHR) hears cases against states which have first been sifted by the Commission of Human Rights. Adherence to the Convention is a prerequisite for membership of the EU. The UK made rights under the Convention enforceable under the Human Rights Act 1998 which requires UK law to be interpreted as far as possible in accordance with the Convention.

General principles in the legal systems of the Member States

General principles are considered below. They include:

- Fundamental rights
- Proportionality
- Equality

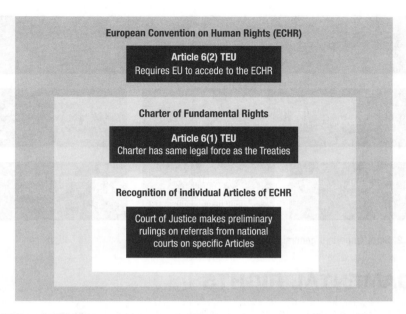

Figure 5.1 Sources of fundamental rights in EU law

- Legal certainty
- Procedural rights.

The expression 'general principles' is likely to be more familiar to lawyers in continental legal systems. Concepts like *proportionality* (a measure should be no more restrictive than necessary to achieve its objectives) are recognised in both French and German law, and now also in the UK.

Sources of general principles

General principles of law are found in international law, particularly in the ECHR and domestic legal systems of Member States, as expressed in the decisions of the Court of Justice. These sources are not mutually exclusive. To be accepted by the Court of Justice the principle need not be common to *all* the Member States, provided it is accepted by most. As Advocate-General Lagrange stated in Case 14/61 *Hoogovens* v. *High Authority*: 'The Court . . . chooses from each of the Member States those solutions which, having regard to the objects of the Treaty, appear to be the best or . . . most progressive.'

Role of general principles in EU law

The general principles of law are an independent source of law which may be invoked to interpret EU law but cannot prevail over express provisions of the Treaties (Case 40/64 *Sgarlata*, on common organisation of the citrus fruit market where the restrictive wording of Article 173 EEC (now 263 TFEU) in an annulment application took precedence over an alleged infringement of fundamental rights).

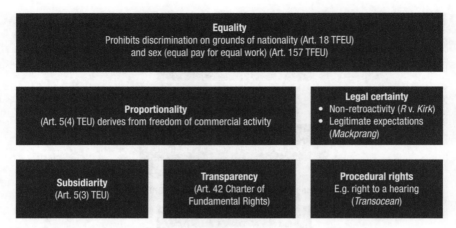

Figure 5.2 Some important general principles

FUNDAMENTAL RIGHTS

As the Court declared in Case C-540/03 *European Parliament* v. *Council*, 'Fundamental rights form an integral part of the general principles of law, the observance of which the Court ensures.' Parliament failed in an annulment action against the Council based on a claim that Directive 2003/86 on family reunification infringed Article 8 of the ECHR and Article 7 of the Charter.

Before the Treaty of Lisbon

In the absence of specific Treaty provision in the Community's early years, the Court of Justice identified fundamental rights through references from the national courts, often on a case-by-case recognition of individual Articles of the ECHR. Protection shifted to the Treaties when the EU adopted the Charter of Fundamental Rights as a Declaration to the Treaty of Nice. However, the Charter could not be relied upon before the national courts until it was given legal force under the Treaty of Lisbon in December 2009.

The protection of fundamental rights in the Court of Justice

The protection of fundamental rights in post-war Europe has raised difficult questions, requiring the Court of Justice to tread a delicate path between maintenance of the EU legal order and the sensitivities of Member States.

The development of fundamental rights in EU law had been particularly influenced by rights entrenched in the *German constitution* after the Second World War, empowering the Federal Constitutional Court to invalidate conflicting national law. The constitution thus prevents individuals claiming they were obeying lawful orders, as some Nazi leaders claimed when tried for war crimes before the International Court of Justice at Nuremburg. German litigants have argued that EU law should comply with fundamental rights provisions of the German constitution, a claim underlying some of the cases considered below. However, to make EU law subject to German law would conflict with the doctrine of supremacy of EU law.

CONTEXT

As a response to the German constitutional arguments the Court of Justice formulated its own doctrine of fundamental rights, declaring it would annul any provision of EU law which contravened human rights.

CORNERSTONE

Stauder

Any provision of EU law which conflicts which fundamental rights may be annulled (Case 29/69 *Stauder* v. *City of Ulm*).

Stauder arose from a Community scheme to provide cheap butter for welfare benefit recipients. The applicant objected to the requirement to divulge his name and address on a coupon (sensitive in wartime) and challenged the law as a violation of human rights in the German courts. The Court of Justice found that the scheme did not require the applicant's name and the scheme did not prejudice fundamental human rights enshrined in the general principles of Community law.

Should EU law be assessed by national or EU standards?

Case 11/70 *International Handelsgesellschaft* arose from a dispute under the Common Agricultural Policy (CAP). The applicants objected to forfeiting their deposit for failing to export agricultural products within the term of the licence, claiming it was contrary to the German constitution, particularly the principle of proportionality. The Court of Justice found that such a scheme did *not* infringe fundamental rights, holding that Community measures may be judged only according to *Community* criteria and not by *national* standards, even those relating to fundamental human rights. *Handelsgesellschaft* provided an opportunity for the Court to affirm the importance of fundamental rights, declaring that:

> Respect for fundamental rights forms an integral part of the general principles of law protected by the Court of Justice. The protection of such rights, whilst inspired by the constitutional traditions common to the Member States, must be ensured within the framework of the structure and objectives of the Community.

Importance of national traditions

The scope of fundamental rights was extended in Case 4/73 *J. Nold* v. *Commission*. The applicant, a German coal wholesaler, challenged a Commission decision under the ECSC Treaty on the ground that it violated the company's fundamental human rights (right to free pursuit of economic activity and property rights). While the Court of Justice considered there was no breach of fundamental rights, it repeated that fundamental principles form an integral part of the general principles of law, declaring:

> In safeguarding these rights, the Court is bound to draw inspiration from constitutional traditions common to the Member States, and it cannot therefore uphold measures . . . incompatible with fundamental rights recognised and protected by the constitutions of those states.

Stauder, *Handelsgesellschaft* and *Nold* were important decisions enabling the Court of Justice to emphasise the Community's (now EU's) commitment to fundamental rights while reminding Member States that Community law may only be assessed under Community standards.

The ECHR and the Court of Justice

The Court of Justice has acknowledged the significance of the Convention as a source of EU law since Case 36/75 *Rutili* (concerning restrictions on movement of an Italian trade unionist in France). The Court has recognised various specific rights under the ECHR as directly enforceable.

Examples of ECHR Articles recognised by the Court of Justice

Case	ECHR Article	Background and principle
Case 44/79 *Hauer* v. *Rheinland-Pfalz*	First Protocol – right to property	EC prohibition on planting vines found to be proportionate and pursuant to general interests of the Community, so not in breach of the right to property.
Case 63/83 *R* v. *Kirk*	Article 7 – right to non-retroactivity of penal provisions	Arose from prosecution of a Danish fisherman who had fished within UK's twelve-mile coastal fishing zone after date when it could be enforced by the UK. The EC later adopted a backdated regulation allowing the UK to retain exclusion for ten more years. The CJEU held that the non-retroactivity of penal provisions was a general principle of Community law.
Case C-60/00 *Mary Carpenter*	Article 8 – right to family life, home and correspondence	Deportation of a third-country national married to a UK national offering services across Member States. The Treaty provision on services was held to be subject to Article 8 of the ECHR, so that any decision to deport was contrary to EU law.
Case 136/79 *National Panasonic*	Article 8 – right to family life, etc.	The Commission investigated alleged anti-competitive practices including a search of the applicant's home without notice. The right to family life in Article 8(1) was found to be subject to considerations of national security in Article 8(2) ECHR.
Case 130/75 *Prais* v. *Council*	Article 9 – right to freedom of religion	Ruling in context of competition for a Commission post held on Jewish holiday. Article 9 ECHR was recognised by the CJEU, but not infringed where applicant had not mentioned religion.
Case C-112/00 *Schmidberger* v. *Austria*	Article 10 and Article 11 – right to freedom of assembly	Arose from German decision not to ban demonstration resulting in temporary closure of Brenner motorway. The CJEU found decision legitimate in view of protection of fundamental rights. Freedom of expression was recognised, subject to public interest limitations.

Case	ECHR Article	Background and principle
Case 222/84 *Johnston* v. *Chief Constable of the RUC*	Article 6 – right of access to the courts; Article 13 – right to effective judicial remedy before national courts	Ruling in context of decision not to arm women members of RUC without allowing individuals access to courts to assert their rights.
Case 117/01 *KB* v. *NHS Pensions Agency and Secretary of State for Pensions*	Article 12 – right to marry; Article 8 – right to family life	Denial of new birth certificate under UK law to trans-sexual (KB) after gender reassignment surgery, preventing KB from marrying post-operative man, with loss of pension rights on partner's death. CJEU held that Article 141 TEC (now 157 TFEU) on equal pay for men and women precluded legislation denying such individuals right to marry, contrary to ECHR. Decision followed *ECtHR ruling* in *Goodwin* v. *UK* (2002) that UK had infringed Articles 8 and 12 ECHR by refusing to register change of gender of trans-sexuals.

ACCESSION TO THE EUROPEAN CONVENTION ON HUMAN RIGHTS

The *ad hoc* recognition by the Court of Justice of individual ECHR Articles led to calls for the Convention to be formally incorporated into EU law. Before amendment by the Treaty of Lisbon, accession to the ECHR was ruled out by the Court of Justice in Opinion 2/94 where it held that the Community lacked the necessary competence to accede to the Convention.

The Treaty of Lisbon remedied the lack of competence, providing for the Union to have legal personality under Article 47 TEU and requiring it to accede to the ECHR under Article 6(2) TEU. The obligation to accede requires preparatory action by the European Council, but no date for accession has been agreed. Article 6(2) also states that accession will not affect the Union's competences. Article 6(3) TEU provides for fundamental rights to constitute general principles of Union law, as guaranteed by the ECHR and resulting from the constitutional traditions common to the Member States. Article 6(1) TEU further strengthened EU commitment to fundamental rights by giving the Charter of Fundamental Rights 'the same legal values as the Treaties'.

Breach of human rights by the Member States

Article 2 TEU declares that: 'The Union is founded on the values of respect for human dignity, the rule of law and respect for human rights, including the right of persons belonging to minorities.' Article 7(1) TEU empowers the Council to determine a 'clear risk of a serious breach by a Member State of the values in Article 2'. Where such a breach continues, the European Council acting unanimously on a proposal by one-third of Member States or by the Commission after obtaining Parliament's consent, may determine the existence of a 'persistent and serious breach', after which it may suspend rights including voting rights in the Council, by QMV (Article 7(3) TEU). So far the procedure has not been invoked.

···**APPLICATION**

Imagine that Italy bans public demonstrations after an extreme 'right wing' political party wins a general election. Such a prohibition would infringe Article 10 of the Charter of Fundamental Rights, as well as Articles 10 (freedom of expression) and 11 (freedom of assembly) ECHR. Under Article 6 TEU an individual prevented from participating in demonstrations in Italy could rely on Article 10 of the Charter in the national courts. Both Articles 10 and 11 ECHR were recognised by the Court of Justice as a source of EU law in Case C-112/00 *Schmidberger* v. *Austria*. The Council could identify the ban to be a serious breach of values in Article 2 TEU, enabling the European Council to determine the existence of a 'persistent and serious' breach by unanimity. Italy would risk suspension of voting rights in the Council under Article 7(3) TEU if it failed to allow public demonstrations.

Relationship between the European Court of Human Rights and EU law

The relationship between the Court of Justice and the European Court of Human Rights (ECtHR), the primary protector of Convention rights for over sixty years, could become problematic if the ECtHR rules EU action unlawful. The ECtHR has been willing to review protection of rights by the EU when strictly necessary, as its decisions on the voting rights of Gibraltar residents and on seizure of an aircraft pursuant to international law demonstrate (see below).

> The constitutional status of Gibraltar is a sensitive political issue as Spain does not accept UK sovereignty there. Gibraltar was ceded to the British Crown by Treaty in 1713 and is classed as a British Overseas Territory with the Queen as constitutional head. EU law applies in Gibraltar which joined the Community with the UK in 1973. Continuing tension leads to sporadic closure of the Gibraltar/Spain border.

CONTEXT

The tensions between the UK and Gibraltar were revealed in *Matthews* v. *UK* (App. No. 24833/94). The applicant, a Gibraltar resident, brought an action in the ECtHR relying on Article 3 of Protocol 1 of the ECHR (right of free election) when denied the right to vote in European Parliamentary elections. The ECtHR upheld her claim that the UK was in breach. The UK adopted the European Parliament (Representation) Act in 2003 to rectify the situation. Spain brought proceedings under Article 227 TEC (now 259 TFEU) against the UK in the Court of Justice in Case C-145/04 *Spain* v. *UK*, alleging that the 2003 Act infringed the Treaties including Article 17 TEC (now 20 TFEU) on citizenship. The Court of Justice found against Spain, holding that the UK could not be penalised for compliance with ECtHR case law.

The *Bosphorus* case also involved decisions of both the Court of Justice and the ECtHR. Ireland had seized an aircraft leased by Bosphorus Airways under EU Regulation 990/03, adopted following UN Resolution 820 (1983) to impose sanctions against the Federal Republic of Yugoslavia. Bosphorus challenged the seizure, claiming that the Regulation did not apply to aircraft. The Supreme Court of Ireland referred to the Court of Justice to clarify the Regulation. In Case C-84/95 *Bosphorus* v. *Minister for Transport, Energy and Communications* the Court of Justice found the seizure justified by the general interest. In parallel proceedings (*Bosphorus* v. *Ireland* (App. No. 45036/98)) the ECtHR held that the Irish government had not infringed Article 1 of Protocol 1 of the ECHR (peaceful enjoyment of possessions).

Both cases demonstrate acknowledgement by the ECtHR that protection of fundamental human rights under EU law was adequate. However, the ECtHR may reach a different decision in future if EU law fails to reach the standard of Convention rights.

There remains a danger of inconsistency between protection of fundamental human rights by the ECtHR and the Court of Justice. Parga (2006) considers that *Bosphorus* clarifies the conditions under which Member States may be held responsible for breaches of human rights under EU law or national implementation. In her view the decision demonstrates that the ECtHR remains the guardian of fundamental rights in Europe, only willing to interfere with the EU legal system when 'strictly necessary'. This could arise when EU law measures are at stake (*Matthews*) or in relation to implementation of EU law where national authorities have no discretion (*Bosphorus*). While there is no indication at present of conflict between the ECtHR and Court of Justice, future cases will continue to raise questions and the need for dialogue between the two courts.

REFLECTION

THE CHARTER OF FUNDAMENTAL RIGHTS

The development of fundamental rights in EU law has been piecemeal, with initial responsibility for identifying and clarifying fundamental rights left to the Court of Justice. While successive Treaty amendments referred to strengthening fundamental rights, the Cologne Council decided in 1999 that these rights should be consolidated in a single instrument. The Charter of Fundamental Rights was drafted under the 'Convention' process (like the failed Constitutional Treaty), with membership drawn from Heads of State, the Commission, the Parliament and national parliaments. The Convention proposed a draft Charter of Fundamental Rights in 2000 which was approved by the European Council in October 2000. As agreement could not be reached to include the Charter in the Treaty, it was annexed to the Treaty of Nice as a Declaration in December 2000. This meant that the Charter was unenforceable in the courts until the Treaty of Lisbon gave it legal force under Article 6 TEU.

Protection of fundamental rights under the Charter

The rights under the Charter are inspired by the ECHR, but in a form reflecting the EU legal order and changes in society since the Convention was signed in 1950, such as protection of personal data (Article 8) and integration of persons with disabilities (Article 26). The Charter is arranged under six chapters: Dignity, Freedoms, Equality, Solidarity, Citizens' rights and Justice.

While Article 51(2) states that the Charter does not create new rights, the reference in Article 51(1) to the need to 'promote' the application of the Charter may imply that it is more than a declaration of existing rights. Article 52 enables Member States to depart from rights under the Charter subject to the principle of proportionality, if necessary to meet objectives of general interest recognised by the Union or to protect the rights and freedoms of others. Article 53 provides for the Charter to be interpreted so as to avoid restricting or adversely affecting human rights and fundamental freedoms under EU or international law.

Reliance on the Charter after the Treaty of Lisbon

Following amendment by the Treaty of Lisbon the Charter was given 'the same legal effect as the Treaties' in a new Article 6(1) TEU and can be invoked before the national courts and Court of Justice. The UK and Poland sought to limit application of the Charter in Protocol 30 to the Treaty of Lisbon.

The UK/Poland Protocol has been described as an 'opt out', although this description may be misleading. Tony Blair, then UK Prime Minster, was anxious to reassure industry that the Charter posed no threat or cost, declaring to the House of Commons European Security Committee on 18 June 2007 that the Charter would not change UK law 'in any way' and that there would be no UK loss of control over the common law or judicial and police system.

CONTEXT

Article 1 of Protocol 30 declares that the Charter does not extend the ability of the Court of Justice or any court or tribunal of these Member States to find that laws or administrative provisions are inconsistent with the fundamental rights under the Charter. Article 2 provides that references in the Charter to national law only apply to the UK as far as they are recognised in UK law or practice.

APPLICATION

Imagine the EU adopts a directive requiring Member States to provide equality of access to a full range of medical services. The UK and Denmark adopt laws permitting euthanasia in defined circumstances. Legal challenges to both laws are made in the national courts. The UK law could not be invalidated on the basis of possible conflict with Article 2 of the Charter (right to life), whereas there may be scope for such a ruling in Denmark provided Danish law allows for such a possibility. However, the ruling in *NS* indicates that it would be necessary to interpret UK law in line with EU law including the right to life in Article 2.

The UK and the Charter after Lisbon

Protocol 30 is *not* an 'opt out' of the Charter for the UK or Poland. Both countries must apply the Charter and interpret it in their courts. The status of the Charter was clarified by the Court of Justice sitting as a Grand Chamber in a reference from the Court of Appeal in Case C-411/10 *NS* (joined with Case C-493/10 *ME and others*). NS, an Afghan national, had come to the UK after travelling through Greece where he was arrested and ordered to leave. He said he was expelled to Turkey and detained for two months in terrible conditions before travelling to the UK and applying for asylum. NS claimed his fundamental human rights would be jeopardised if he returned to Greece, a claim resisted by the UK Home Secretary who ordered his removal in 2009. The Court of Justice held that the Common European Asylum System was adopted on the basis that *all* participating States observe fundamental rights and that treatment of asylum seekers complies with the Charter, the Geneva Convention (a UN instrument) and the ECHR. It found that under Article 4 of the Charter, Member States may not transfer asylum seekers to another Member State where they were aware of serious deficiencies in procedure and conditions. The Court found that Protocol 30 'does not call into question the applicability of the Charter in the UK or Poland', whose courts must apply and interpret the Charter strictly in accordance with the explanations at the end of the Protocol. However, the note on Article 51 makes it clear that the Charter may not extend competences and tasks which the Treaties confer on the Union, a particular concern of the UK when the Charter was negotiated.

> The legal academic, Barnard (2010) comments that the UK saw economic and social rights as *principles* which were not directly effective and would have preferred them to have been separated from civil and political rights which may not have economic consequences. Nevertheless, in her view both Article 28 on collective agreements and Article 30 on unfair dismissal were drafted in terms of rights, making them 'potentially justiciable' before the courts. Later developments such as Case C-411/10 *NS* support Barnard's view.

REFLECTION

The Charter was considered by the UK High Court in *The Queen (on the application of the United Road Transport Union)* v. *Secretary of State for Transport* (2012) in relation to the Road Transport Working Time Directive. The Court found that the Directive was 'not written in the language of workers' rights' and rejected the application. Article 31 of the Charter recognising worker's rights to limitation of working time was viewed as merely requiring Member States to take measures to ensure workers were entitled to adequate rest. No mention was made of Protocol 30 in the judgment, implying that the Court assumed the Charter applied to the UK.

Other decisions after Lisbon

After the Treaty of Lisbon the Charter has frequently been cited in the Court of Justice, although its application has mostly been limited to established principles in the Treaties. In Case C-7/11 *Fabio Caronna* the Court held (in a referral on distribution of medical products) that the obligation to interpret national law in criminal matters is subject to the principles of legal certainty and non-retroactivity under the Charter. A more assertive reference to the Charter was made in Case C-614/10 *Commission* v. *Austria* where Austria's failure to provide sufficient protection to individuals under a directive in processing and free movement of personal data was found to infringe EU primary law, including Article 8(3) of the Charter (protection of personal data) and of Article 16(2) TFEU (providing for the Parliament and Council to provide rules on the processing of personal data).

Several cases have arisen in relation to the European Arrest Warrant (EAW) and surrender procedures under Framework Decision 2002/584. Case C-396/11 *Radu* arose from proceedings to execute four EAWs by the German authorities against a Romanian national, over prosecutions for armed robbery. Although Radu had not been heard in the German proceedings, the Court found no infringement of fundamental rights, including right to a fair trial under Article 47 or defence under Article 48 of the Charter. It made a similar ruling in Case C-399/11 *Melloni* v. *Ministerio Fiscal* over an EAW issued by the Italian authorities to execute a prison sentence pronounced in the applicant's absence.

PROPORTIONALITY

CORNERSTONE

Article 5(4) TEU

Article 5(4) TEU provides:

> Under the principle of proportionality, the content and form of Union action shall not exceed what is necessary to achieve the objectives of the Treaties. The institutions of the Union shall apply the principle of proportionality as laid down in the Protocol on the principles of subsidiarity and proportionality.

Proportionality derives from German law where it is regarded as one of the rights underlying the constitution. It has been applied to constrain public authorities in Member States which can only impose obligations which are appropriate and necessary to achieve the objective of the measure. Proportionality implies a relationship between the means and the ends of legislation – the means must be reasonably likely to achieve the objective, and the advantage to the public must be greater than the disadvantage.

APPLICATION

Imagine the EU adopts a directive to improve young people's rights at work. Its stated objective is to prevent exploitation of school-leavers and graduates under unpaid internships. The UK adopts the Internships Act 2013 prohibiting *all* forms of unpaid internships and work experience. School students can no longer undertake any form of unpaid work experience. The 2013 Act is disproportionate as the prohibition goes further than the objective of the Directive which was stated to apply to school-leavers and graduates. The objective could have been achieved by limiting the prohibition.

Proportionality has frequently been invoked before the Court of Justice, particularly in actions for annulment under Article 263 TFEU (ex 230 TEC), as Case 181/84 *R* v. *Intervention Board for Agricultural Produce, ex parte Man (Sugar)* illustrates. An export company paid the Intervention Board for Agricultural Produce (an EC body under the Common Agricultural Policy) a deposit of £1,670,000 to support its application for an export licence. When the application was submitted four hours late, the Commission ruled that the entire deposit was forfeit. The Court ruled that forfeiture of the entire deposit for a trivial breach was disproportionate.

Proportionality was unsuccessfully invoked in Case T-246/08 and T-332/08 *Melli Bank* v. *Council* (upheld by a Grand Chamber of the Court of Justice in Case C-380/09P).The CFI held that freezing the funds of organisations engaged in nuclear proliferation does not infringe the principle of proportionality where appropriate and necessary to maintain international peace and security, an objective justifying restrictions on Melli Bank's right to property and conducting economic activity.

Proportionality and the internal market

Proportionality has also been applied to limitations on free movement of goods and of persons.

INTERSECTION ....

Restrictions on free movement of Union citizens are considered in Chapter 13. Article 27(2) of Directive 2004/38 provides that measures taken on grounds of public policy or public security must comply with the principle of proportionality. It would be disproportionate to expel a Union citizen from another Member State merely because his or her passport had expired.

Proportionality was invoked in Case 145/88 *Torfaen Borough Council* v. *B&Q* over a UK prohibition on selling goods on a Sunday. The Court of Justice held that national measures banning Sunday trading must not exceed what was necessary to achieve the objectives in question (religious observance, cultural and social tradition). In Case 120/78 *Rewe-Zentrale* (**Cassis de Dijon**) the Court laid down mandatory restrictions which Member States may impose on free movement of goods, provided they are not disproportionate.

APPLICATION

The UK adopts a law prohibiting the sale of peanuts in supermarkets, after publication of research showing that individuals with a peanut allergy may suffer from toxic shock. This impacts badly on peanut growers in other Member States. While free movement of goods may be restricted in some circumstances (see Chapter 12), any restriction must be proportionate and non-discriminatory after *Cassis*. The Court of Justice would probably regard the peanut ban as excessive, as consumers could be protected by a notice that goods may contain peanuts.

Relationship between proportionality and the exercise of Union competence

Article 5(1) TEU provides for the *limits* of Union competences to be governed by the principles of conferral, and their *use* by subsidiarity and proportionality. This means that the allocation of competence is governed by conferral, while decisions about its exercise are governed by proportionality and subsidiarity. The relationship between proportionality and Union competences was made explicit under the Treaty of Lisbon which introduced the principle of conferral.

Freedom of commercial activity

Proportionality reflects a broader concept, freedom of commercial activity, a wide-ranging freedom deriving from German law where it is protected under the constitution. Freedom of commercial activity includes the principle of proportionality, freedom to pursue a trade or profession, freedom from unfair competition and a general freedom to act where no legal prohibition applies. All four principles were unsuccessfully invoked in Cases 133 etc/85 *Walter Rau* v. *BALM* and Case 249/85 *Albako* v. *BALM*. The dispute arose from a Commission scheme in 1985 by which residents of West Berlin were offered two blocks of butter for the price of one to increase butter consumption. Rau, an aggrieved margarine manufacturer, challenged the decision in the Court of Justice, which held that none of the principles had been infringed.

EQUALITY

CORNERSTONE

Equality

The principle of equality implies that persons in similar situations should be treated in the same way unless there is objective justification for different treatment.

The Treaties explicitly prohibit discrimination in certain circumstances:

- on grounds of nationality (Article 18 TFEU (ex 12 TEC));
- on grounds of sex, in the context of equal pay for men and women (Article 157 TFEU (ex 141 TEC));
- against producers or consumers under the CAP (Article 40(2) TFEU (ex 34(2) TEC)).

Discrimination on grounds of nationality

The principle has provided the basis for a remedy in the absence of secondary legislation. Case C-164/07 *James Wood* v. *Fonds de garantie des victims des actes de terrorisme et d'autres infractions* arose from a claim before the Compensation Board in France after the applicant's daughter died in an accident in Australia. The applicant had lived and worked in France for over twenty years with his partner, a French national, and had brought up their three children there. The Board agreed to compensate all family members except the applicant for the daughter's death as he was a British national. The Court ruled it was illegal for a Member State to exclude nationals of other Member States living and working there from compensation for offences committed outside its territory solely on grounds of nationality.

Discrimination on grounds of sex and other areas

Non-discrimination (equal treatment) has been particularly important in employment. The drafters of the Treaty of Rome saw non-discrimination on grounds of sex in economic terms, reflecting the Community's original emphasis. Article 157 TFEU (ex 141 TEC) provides for equal pay for men and women. Equal treatment in employment has been covered by a series of directives. Directive 2006/54 currently provides for equal opportunities and equal treatment of men and women in employment.

The EU gradually developed a *social dimension* to law and policy, a change of emphasis reflected by the introduction (under the Treaty of Amsterdam) of a legal base under Article 19 TFEU (ex 13 TEC) for action to combat discrimination on grounds of sex, racial or ethnic origin, religion or belief, disability, age or sexual orientation. This was a radical innovation as discrimination had previously only been prohibited in relation to employment. Three directives were introduced under Article 19:

1. Directive 2000/43 implementing the principle of equal treatment irrespective of racial or ethnic origin.
2. Directive 2000/78 establishing a general framework for equal treatment and occupation.
3. Directive 2004/113 equal treatment between men and women in access and supply of goods and services, introduced mainly to apply the same rules on insurance to men and women. In Case C-236/09 *Association belge des Consommateurs Test-Achats* v. *Conseil de ministres* the Court held that the same premiums and benefits must apply to men and women under Article 5 of the directive. This has meant that actuarial factors resulting in lower premiums for women in motor insurance due to their lower risk of accident cannot be applied.

Directives 2000/43 and 2000/78 have opened up a new range of areas to legal protection. In the UK, legislation was introduced to prohibit age discrimination, making it illegal to discriminate against young people by paying them less or older workers by making them retire at a specific age.

Discrimination under the CAP

The Common Agricultural Policy (CAP) provides another area in which discrimination is forbidden. Article 40(3) TFEU prohibits discrimination between producers or consumers. In Cases 103 & 145/77 *Royal Scholten-Honig* the Court held that the production levy system for isoglucose (high-fructose corn syrup) under the CAP infringed 'the general principle of equality' expressed specifically in (what is now) Article 40(2) TFEU by discriminating against producers of isoglucose compared with sugar producers.

A general principle of equality

It is clear from the case law of the Court of Justice that EU law recognises a general principle of equality or non-discrimination. In Case C-13/94 *P.* v. *S.* the Court found it unlawful to dismiss a trans-sexual employee after gender reassignment surgery. It held that the Equal Treatment Directive simply expressed the 'principle of equality which is one of the fundamental principles' of EU law, which should be 'liberally interpreted and not limited to discrimination on grounds of gender'.

The Court took a more conservative line in Case C-249/96 *Grant* v. *S. W. Trains*, refusing to extend equal treatment to sexual orientation in a claim for same-sex partners to benefit from travel facilities for spouses. Such discrimination would now infringe Article 21 of the Charter of Fundamental Rights (not then in force).

The principle of non-discrimination on grounds of age was confirmed by the Court in Case C-144/04 *Mangold* v. *Helms* (over fixed-term contracts for older workers under German law) as a general principle of EU law. The Court based its judgment on the general principles of EU law rather than Directive 2000/78 (the General Directive). There is a growing body of case law on age discrimination in the Court despite initial uncertainty when it failed to refer to *Mangold* in several cases on age discrimination. The Court reaffirmed age discrimination as a general principle in Case C-555/07 *Kücükdeveci*, confirming that age discrimination covers both young and older people.

INTERSECTION

Kücükdeveci is an important decision, enabling individual applicants to rely on the principle directly 'horizontally' in the national courts against private bodies, whereas rights derived from directives are only enforceable 'vertically' against public bodies. *Kücükdeveci* is considered in Chapter 7 in relation to the direct effect of general principles.

Other examples of decisions on equality

The Court of Justice has developed an extensive body of case law on equality. In Case 20/71 *Sabbatini* v. *European Parliament* a female official at the Parliament was denied an allowance because she was not the 'head of the family'. (Under Community law at the time a woman could only be defined as a 'head of the family' in exceptional circumstances.) The Court found the provision discriminatory.

Case 21/74 *Airola* v. *Commission* involved a claim by a female Community employee who lost her expatriation allowance on marriage to an Italian national. (Foreign women marrying Italian men automatically acquired Italian nationality on marriage but foreign men marrying Italian women did not.) The Court held that Community law cannot take account of nationality involuntarily acquired under a discriminatory national law.

In Case 130/75 *Prais* v. *Council* a Jewish woman applicant sought annulment of a Council decision to hold a competitive examination for a post as an EC official on a Jewish festival. The applicant had not mentioned her religion on the application form and there was no specific evidence of religious discrimination. The Court held that the appointing authority was *not* obliged to avoid holding the examination on a religious holiday since it had not been informed of the fact in advance although it should try to avoid such dates where advance information was given.

LEGAL CERTAINTY

Legal certainty is an important principle underpinning EU law and most national legal systems. It can be subdivided into non-retroactivity and legitimate expectations.

CORNERSTONE

Non-retroactivity

EU legislation is presumed not to be retroactive unless there is clear evidence to the contrary (Case 63/83 *R* v. *Kirk*).

In *R* v. *Kirk* the captain of a Danish fishing vessel was charged with fishing within the UK's twelve-mile coastal fishing zone. While the UK was entitled to exclude non-UK vessels until 31 December 1982 under the Act of Accession, Kirk had fished in January 1983. The EC later adopted a regulation allowing the UK to retain the exclusion for ten more years, backdated to January 1983. The Court held that the non-retroactivity of penal provisions was a general principle of Community law. A later regulation could not retrospectively validate national but otherwise invalid penal provisions.

The principle of non-retroactivity prevents EU secondary legislation from taking effect before publication in the *Official Journal*. In Case 88/76 *Société pour l'Exportation des Sucres* v. *Commission* the Commission adopted a regulation on 30 June 1976 removing exporters' right to cancel their licences. The regulation was dated 1 July, the expected date of publication of the *Official Journal (OJ)*, but the *OJ* did not appear until 2 July due to a strike. The applicant applied for cancellation on 1 July but was refused. The Court ruled that the regulation did not come into force until 2 July, the actual date of publication.

Retroactivity is prohibited unless the measure may not otherwise be achieved and the principle of legitimate expectations is respected. In Case 88/76 *Société pour l'Exportation des Sucres* v. *Commission* a regulation establishing a system of levies and quotas for production of isoglucose had been annulled for non-consultation with Parliament. Another regulation was issued retrospectively under the correct procedure. The Court upheld the regulation on the basis that isoglucose producers should reasonably have expected it.

The Court has occasionally limited the *temporal effect* of its rulings (i.e. when the judgment takes effect). In Case 43/75 *Defrenne* v. *Sabena* (No. 2) it held that considerations of legal certainty required that claims for equal pay under Article 157 TFEU (then 119 EEC) could only be brought from the date of the judgment unless proceedings had already commenced. The *Defrenne* approach was reserved for exceptional cases where the Court introduced a new principle or the judgment might cause serious difficulties such as substantial claims for back pay, as in Case C-262/88 *Barber* v. *Guardian Royal Exchange* where occupational pensions were held to be pay.

Legitimate expectations

EU measures must not violate legitimate expectations unless there is overriding public interest. An expectation will only be legitimate if it is reasonable, that is, within the contemplation of a prudent person acting within the course of business (Case 2/75 *EVGF* v. *Mackprang*). The applicant was a German grain dealer prevented by a Commission decision from taking advantage of a fall in the value of the French franc, which had made it profitable to buy grain in France and resell it to EVGF (the German grain intervention agency). He brought proceedings against EVGF in the German courts, claiming he had a legitimate expectation of selling the grain to the agency. The Court ruled that the decision did not infringe the principle of legitimate expectations but was a justified precaution against speculation (i.e. profiting from currency fluctuations).

The principle may be invoked as a rule of interpretation (Case 78/74 *Deuka* v. *EVGE*), in an action for damages (Case 74/74 *CNTA* v. *Commission*, involving the ending of compensation schemes under the CAP without warning) and as a ground for annulment. However, few cases claiming legitimate expectations have succeeded in the Court as findings against the EU institutions disturb the legal order. Thus a legitimate expectation was found *not* to have arisen in the following three circumstances:

1. Commission failure to create an authenticated version of a measure in contravention of its own procedural rules (Case C-137/92P *Commission* v. *BASF AG*, upholding the CFI refusal of annulment).
2. Incorrect acceptance by an official of a defective document (Joined Cases 98&230/83 *Van Gend en Loos NV and Expeditiebedrijf Wim Bosman BV* v. *Commission*).
3. Incorrect calculation by a Union institution of a trader's previous profit (Case 112/77 *Töpfer* v. *Commission*).

APPLICATION

Imagine a farmer has received subsidies paid under the CAP for years. The rules suddenly change without notice. He is informed by the Commission that his subsidy is withdrawn with immediate effect. There may be scope to claim damages against the Commission based on infringement of his legitimate expectation of a notice period before changing the basis for subsidy. Another farmer receives a subsidy under the CAP but he is told that it will be subject to review in six months if the price of grain changes. When the price increases six months later, the subsidy is withdrawn, leaving the farmer worse off. In this case (applying *Mackprang*), the second farmer would not be entitled to compensation as he should have foreseen that prices might rise.

PROCEDURAL RIGHTS

Procedural rights in EU law are usually provided in secondary legislation. Where they are not, the person affected may rely on general principles in areas such as the right to a hearing, the duty to give reasons and the right to an effective judicial remedy. Most rights are now covered by the Charter of Fundamental Rights.

The right to a hearing

The right to a hearing derives from the English principle of natural justice. It was first raised in the Court of Justice in Case 17/74 *Transocean Marine Paint Association* v. *Commission*, a competition case under Article 101 TFEU (ex 81 TEC). The Commission had addressed a decision to the applicants without referring to a condition which was applied later. The applicants sought annulment of the decision in relation to this condition. The Court held there is a general principle of Community law that a person whose interests are perceptibly affected by a decision taken by a public authority must be given the opportunity to make his views known. The condition was annulled. The decision was followed in Case C-49/88 *Al-Jubail Fertilizer* v. *Council* where the Court annulled a regulation imposing anti-dumping duty on products from Libya and Saudi Arabia after the applicants complained they had been denied a fair hearing.

The duty to give reasons

The duty to give reasons was established in Case 222/86 *Union Nationale des Entraîneurs et Cadres Techniques Professionels du Football (UNECTEF)* v. *Heylens*. Heylens was a Belgian national with a Belgian football trainers' diploma. His application to the French authorities to recognise the diploma was refused without any reason. Heylens was charged with practising in France as a football trainer without the necessary French diploma. The Court held that the right of free movement under Article 45 TFEU (then 39 TEC) requires there to be legal redress from a decision affecting access to employment and that reasons for the decision should be given.

The right to an effective judicial remedy

The right to an effective judicial remedy in the national courts was upheld in Case 222/84 *Johnston* v. *Chief Constable of the Royal Ulster Constabulary*, arising from the RUC's refusal to renew contracts of women members of the RUC Reserve. Following a decision that full-time Reserve members were to be fully armed. Women, however, were not issued with firearms or trained to use them. Mrs Johnston, a full-time member, claimed the measure contravened Directive 76/207 (equal treatment for men and women in employment). The Secretary of State for Northern Ireland certified that the purpose of the refusal was to safeguard national security and public order, 'conclusive evidence' of purpose. The Court held that Article 6 of Directive 76/207 requiring Member States to pursue their claims by judicial process after recourse to the competent authorities reflected a general principle under Articles 6 and 13 ECHR. Member States must ensure effective judicial control of directly applicable Community law and national implementing legislation. The Court further held that national legislation stating that a compliance certificate was conclusive deprived the individual of access to the courts to assert his or her rights under EU law, contrary to Article 6 of the Directive.

OTHER GENERAL PRINCIPLES

Other general principles that have been identified by the Court of Justice include the right to be assisted by counsel (Case 115/80 *Demont*), confidentiality of communication between lawyer and client (Case 155/79 *AM&S*) and the right to exercise a profession (Case 234/85 *Keller*).

Subsidiarity

The principle of subsidiarity is concerned with the allocation of competences (who does what) between the EU and Member States.

CORNERSTONE

Under Article 5(3) TEU (ex 5 TEU) where responsibility is shared between the EU and Member States, the EU may only act where the objectives of the proposed action cannot be better achieved by the Member States and can be better achieved at EU level by reason of 'scale or effect'.

Subsidiarity was inserted into the Treaties by the Treaty of Maastricht.

When the Treaty of Maastricht was under negotiation, the EU was criticised for extending its competences too far. The principle of subsidiarity was introduced, partly due to pressure from the UK, to redress the balance by providing a presumption in favour of action by Member States where competences were shared between the EU and the Member States.

CONTEXT

Article 5(4) TEU states that: 'The content and form of Union action shall not go beyond what is necessary to achieve the objectives of the objective in question.'

INTERSECTION

While subsidiarity is a general principle of EU law, it is essentially concerned with the allocation of competences (examined in Chapter 2).

Subsidiarity and national parliaments

The Treaty of Lisbon has enhanced the role of national parliaments by providing in Article 12(a) for draft legislative acts to be forwarded to them under the Protocol on the role of National Parliaments and in Article 12(b) for respect for the principle of subsidiarity in accordance with the Protocol on Subsidiarity. The Protocol on Subsidiarity and Proportionality provides for the Commission to forward its proposals to national parliaments at the same time as the Union legislator. If by a majority of 55 per cent of Council members or a majority of votes cast in the Parliament, the legislator is of the opinion that the proposal is incompatible with the principle of subsidiarity (i.e. that action should be taken at Member State level), the proposal will be given no further consideration (the *red card procedure*).

Subsidiarity before the Court of Justice

When subsidiarity has been raised in annulment actions, it has usually failed. Cases C-504 & 505/09P *Poland* v. *Commission* and *Estonia* v. *Commission* provide a rare example of successful invocation of the principle as a ground for annulment. The cases arose over Directive 2003/87, adopted to promote reductions in greenhouse gases by establishing an EU scheme for trading emission allowances, environmental protection being a shared competence subject to subsidiarity under Article 5 TEU (then 5 TEC). Article 9(1) of the Directive permitted Member States to develop a national allocation plan (NAP) to show intended emission allowances during the relevant period, subject to Commission verification. The Commission found in both cases that the NAPs did not satisfy the criteria and reduced their emission allowances. Poland and Estonia successfully sought annulment in the CFI (upheld by the Court of Justice) which found that the Commission had exceeded its powers as the method of calculating allowances should have been left to Member States.

Usually, however, the Court has found no breach of subsidiarity, as in Case C-84/94 *UK* v. *Council* (UK challenge by to the 'Working Time' Directive) and Case C-377/98 *Netherlands* v. *EP and Council* (Netherlands challenge to Directive 98/44 on legal protection of biotechnological inventions).

Transparency

The principle of transparency was introduced into the TEU by the Treaty of Amsterdam and is now also recognised by Article 42 of the Charter of Fundamental Rights. The Treaty of Lisbon further strengthened the principle by introducing new Article 10(3) TEU providing for decisions to be taken as closely as possible to the citizen, as well as Articles 11 and 15 TEU.

Under Article 11(1) TEU institutions must give citizens and representative associations 'the opportunity to make known and publicly exchange their views in all areas of Union action' and 'maintain an open, transparent and regular dialogue with representative associations and civil society' (Article 11(2)). The Commission must carry out 'broad consultations' with parties concerned to ensure that the Union's actions are coherent and transparent (Article 11(3)). Article 11(4) provides for a *citizens' initiative*, an innovation under the Lisbon Treaty whereby one million citizens may petition the Commission to submit a proposal for new legislation (discussed in Chapter 2).

Article 15(3) TFEU (ex 255(1) TEC) gives Union citizens and businesses with registered offices in a Member State right of access to Parliament, Council and Commission documents. The Council adopted Regulation 1049/2001 providing for Union citizens and residents to have access to documents subject to exceptions where disclosure would undermine the protection of court proceedings and legal advice unless there is an overwhelming public interest in disclosure.

Most cases in the General Court involve assessing the balance between the citizen's desire for information against institutional need for confidentiality, as in Case T-194/94 *Carvel* in which a journalist was denied access to information relating to the Social Affairs and Justice Council in 1993 and the Agriculture Council in 1994. The CFI held that by automatically refusing access the Council Secretariat had infringed Decision 93/731 (in force at the time) requiring a balancing of the applicant's interest with the Council's wish for confidentiality. *Carvel* led to release of further information about the Council's activities, including broadcasting of debates on matters of public interest. Joined Cases C-39/05P & 52/05P *Sweden and Turco* v. *Council* arose from the Council's refusal to provide access to documents on the agenda of the Justice and Home Affairs meeting. The Court of Justice overturned the decision on appeal, ruling that disclosure of legal advice does not undermine the validity of a legislative act but 'contributes to greater legitimacy and confidence in the eyes of European citizens'.

The establishment of the 'Europa' official website of the EU (available on http://europa.eu) represents a significant commitment to transparency.

INTERSECTION

> The Study skills section at the beginning of the book provides guidance on the 'Europa' website, with links to the EU institutions, EU legislation, transcripts of decisions in the Court of Justice, and access to information on the Union's activities and policies.

Transparency and the processing of personal data

Advances in technology bring new challenges in balancing transparency and individual right to privacy. In Case C-73/07 *Tietosuojavaltuutettu* v. *Satakunnan Markkinapörssi Oy* the Court considered Directive 95/46 on processing personal data. The case arose over collection of personal information on higher-income tax-payers in Finland. Markkinapörssi obtained data annually from the tax authorities, publishing extracts identifying individuals in regional newspapers and passing the data to a media company owned by the same shareholders. The information was disseminated by text messaging to mobile phone users. The Court found that activities involving collection and dissemination of information in such circumstances amounted to 'processing of personal data' which Member States must ensure flows freely, while reconciling protection of privacy and freedom of expression. Any departure must be interpreted strictly and made solely for journalistic purposes or for artistic or literary expression.

KEY POINTS

- General principles are an important source of EU law found in the Charter of Fundamental Rights, international law (especially the ECHR) and the constitutional traditions common to the Member States.
- Respect for fundamental rights is an integral part of the general principles of EU law.
- EU action should not exceed what is necessary to achieve the objective in question under the principle of proportionality.
- The principle of equality requires persons in similar situations to be treated in the same way unless there is objective justification for differentiation.
- Under the principle of legal certainty legislation should not be retroactive or violate the legitimate expectations of those concerned unless there is overriding public interest.
- Where competence is shared between the EU and Member States, the Union should act in accordance with the principle of subsidiarity (Article 5(3) TEU).

CORE CASES AND STATUTES

Case	About	Importance
Case 11/70 *Internationale Handelsgesellschaft*	Forfeiture of deposit for failure to carry out export within licence period held not to infringe fundamental rights, and must be judged by Community criteria.	CJEU declared that respect for fundamental rights forms integral part of general principles of Community (EU) law.
Case 4/73 *Nold* v. *Commission*	Wholesale coal company challenged Commission decision within ECSC on basis that it infringed company's right to pursue economic activity and its property rights. CJEU found no breach of fundamental rights.	CJEU repeated declaration on integral nature of fundamental rights, stating it could not uphold measures incompatible with fundamental rights recognised by Member States or under international treaties to protect human rights signed by Member States.
Case 63/83 *R* v. *Kent Kirk*	Danish fisherman was prosecuted for fishing within a coastal fishing zone claimed by UK. EU *later* adopted regulation extending UK's exclusive rights to the zone.	Non-retroactivity of penal provisions is general principle of EU law.
Case C-60/00 *Mary Carpenter*	Third-country national (TCN) married and cared for children of UK national who offered services across borders.	Provisions on services in the Treaties were subject to Article 8 ECHR (right to family life).
Case 84/95 *Bosphorus* v. *Minister for Transport*; *Bosphorus* v. *Ireland* (App. No. 45036/98)	Proceedings in CJEU and ECtHR after seizure of aircraft in Ireland under EU regulation pursuant to UN resolution imposing sanctions against Federal Republic of Yugoslavia.	CJEU held that such interference with property rights was justified by general interest. ECtHR found no breach of right to property under ECHR by Irish government and that EU law provided equivalent protection to ECHR.
Case 181/84 *R* v. *Interventions Board for Agricultural Products, ex p. Man (Sugar)*	Commission ruled that entire deposit should be forfeited when application for export licence was submitted four hours late.	CJEU considered it disproportionate to forfeit whole deposit for trivial breach.
Case C-504 & 5/09 *Poland* v. *Commission* and *Estonia* v. *Commission*	Successful challenges by Poland and Estonia to Commission decisions refusing to verify national allocation plans showing intended emissions.	Provide rare examples of successful invocation of subsidiarity as ground for annulment.

Statute	About	Importance
Article 2 TEU	EU values e.g. respect human dignity, freedom, democracy.	Introduced under Treaty of Lisbon.
Article 5(1) TEU	Provides for principle of conferral (Union may only act within limits of powers conferred by Member States under Article 5(2) TEU).	Governs limits of Union competences.
Article 5(3) TEU	Provides for principle of subsidiarity. Union may act only where objectives of proposed action cannot be better achieved by the Member States.	Only applies to areas of shared competence.
Article 5(4) TEU	Provides for principle of proportionality.	Content and form of Union action should not exceed what is necessary to achieve objectives of Treaties.
Article 6(1) TEU	Charter of Fundamental Rights is given same legal force as Treaties.	Protocol 30 limits application of Charter for UK and Poland.
Article 6(2) TEU	Union must accede to the ECHR.	Union is given legal capacity by Article 47 TEU for this purpose.
Article 18 TFEU	Prohibits discrimination on grounds of nationality.	Provision at the heart of single market, frequently invoked in absence of specific rights.
Articles 6–12 ECHR	Provides for access to courts (Art. 6), non-retroactivity of penal provisions (Art. 7), right to family life (Art. 8), freedom of religion (Art. 9), freedom of expression (Art. 10) and freedom of assembly (Art. 11).	Rights have been individually recognised by CJEU through preliminary reference procedure.
Charter of Fundamental Rights	Arranged under six chapters: dignity, freedoms, equality, solidarity, citizens' rights, justice.	Declared at Nice and appended to the Treaties. Given same force as Treaties by Lisbon Treaty. UK and Poland have limited 'opt out'.

FURTHER READING

Barnard, C. '"The opt-out" for the UK and Poland from the Charter of Fundamental Rights: triumph of rhetoric over reality' (2010) available at http://www.law.cam.ac.uk/faculty-resources/summary/barnard-uk-opt-out-and-the-charter-of-fundamental-rights/7309
Assesses of impact of Protocol for UK and Poland.

Butler, I. de J. 'Ensuring compliance with the Charter of Fundamental Rights in legislative drafting: the practice of the European Commission' (2012) 37 *European Law Review* 397
Examines Commission initiatives for compliance with the Charter.

Marguery, T.P. 'The protection of fundamental human rights in European criminal law after Lisbon:
what role for the Charter of Fundamental Rights?' (2012) 37 *European Law Review* 444
Assessed relevance of the Charter for the Area of freedom, security and justice.

Morano-Foadi, S. and Andredakis, S. 'Reflections on the judicial architecture of the EU after the Treaty of Lisbon: the European judicial approach to fundamental rights' (2011) 17 *European Law Journal* 595
Analyses CJEU practice and impact of the Charter in view of interviews with judges and Advocates-General in the CJEU.

Parga, A.H. (2006) '*Bosphorus* v. *Ireland* and the protection of fundamental rights in Europe' (2006) 31 *European Law Review* 251
Case note on *Bosphorus* and relationship between CJEU and ECtHR.

CHAPTER 6

The supremacy of
EU law

BLUEPRINT

The supremacy of EU law

LEGISLATION

- Article 4 TEU
- Article 267 TFEU
- European Community Act 1972 s. 2
- European Union Act 2011, ss. 2, 3, 6, 18

CONTEXT

- Senstivity in Member States, over sovereignty and rights entrenched in national constitutions

CONCEPTS

- 'New legal order'
- Supremacy
- Direct effect
- State liability
- Referendum
- 'Passerelle' clause
- 'Emergency brake'

- Should EU law be given precedence over fundamental rights entrenched in a national constitution?

- How is the supremacy of EU law to be maintained if national constitutional courts regard EU law as subject to national constitutions?

CASES

- *Van Gend en Loos*
- *Costa* v. *ENEL*
- *Handelsgesellschaft*
- *Simmenthal*
- *Factortame Nos. 2 and 3*
- *Melki* and *Abdeli*

SPECIAL CHARACTERISTICS

- Interplay between national courts and CJEU over interim remedies and conflict with national constitutions

REFORM

- No immediate proposals for reform

CRITICAL ISSUES

Setting the scene

Imagine the UK adopts a law requiring jobs to be offered to UK nationals before Union citizens may be considered. Such a law infringes Article 45 TFEU on the free movement of workers which takes precedence over any conflicting national law. The supremacy of Union law over national law is central to the EU legal order. Controversy over supremacy has continued for over fifty years as the Community of six states developed to a Union of twenty-eight. The Treaties do not provide explicitly for supremacy, although Article 4 TEU (ex 10 TEC) imposes a duty on Member States to cooperate to fulfil their obligations. It was left to the Court of Justice to fill the gap, starting with its seminal judgment in Case 26/62 *Van Gend en Loos* that the Community represents a 'new legal order' in national and international law, based on the concepts of supremacy and direct effect.

INTRODUCTION

The constitutional principles underpinning the EU legal order – direct effect, indirect effect and State liability – are connected by the principle of supremacy. This chapter examines the supremacy (or primacy) of EU law over national law and its application in the Member States.

INTERSECTION

A directly effective provision creates rights on which individuals may rely before the national courts. Direct effect is considered in Chapter 7, as well as indirect effect (the duty to interpret national law in accord with EU law). State liability for breach of EU law is examined in Chapter 8.

While the doomed Constitutional Treaty (CT) would have provided for supremacy in the body of the Treaty, the Treaty of Lisbon merely recalls in a Declaration that the Treaties and law adopted under them have primacy over laws of the Member States 'in accordance with well settled case law of the Court of Justice'. The move to a declaration makes no real legal difference but was a response to popular suspicion of constitutionalism which found its voice in 2005 when the peoples of France and the Netherlands rejected the CT in referenda.

SUPREMACY, THE TREATIES AND INTERNATIONAL LAW

The TFEU and the TEU are international agreements entered into by sovereign states. The treaties recognise the primacy of international law, particularly the Charter of the United Nations, as Joined Cases C-402/05 P and C-415/05 P *Yassin Abdullah Kadi and Al Barakaat International Foundation* v. *Council and Commission* illustrate. The UN Security Council was required under a resolution to maintain a list of individuals and bodies associated with Osama bin Laden to prevent funds being used to benefit the Taliban. The EU implemented the resolution in a Council regulation identifying the applicants, effectively freezing their assets. The CFI dismissed the action, holding it could not review the

Figure 6.1 Methods of incorporation of EU law

regulation. The Court of Justice overruled the decision, ruling that the Community [EU] must be able to review all its acts in view of fundamental rights, including measures adopted to implement Security Council resolutions, although it was not competent to review the lawfulness of the resolutions themselves. It follows from *Kadi* that EU law recognises the primacy of international law under the UN Charter. There is no conflict between international law and EU law provided the UN acts consistently with protection of fundamental rights in the EU.

Incorporation of treaties

The original Treaty of Rome required *incorporation* into the domestic legal systems of Member States before taking effect as an international agreement. The same is true of later treaties including the Treaty of Lisbon.

Member States operate two main approaches to incorporation (see Figure 6.1):

- *the monist approach*: the Treaty takes effect in the domestic legal system as soon as the Treaty is ratified, as in France and the Netherlands;

- *the dualist approach*: the Treaty takes effect only when incorporated into the domestic legal system by statute, as in Germany, Italy and the UK which adopted the European Communities Act 1972 to implement its obligations under the Treaty of Rome.

Member States with a written constitution may also refer to it and to the practice of the courts to establish the status of the TEU and TFEU in domestic law.

ROLE OF THE COURT OF JUSTICE

Need for a uniform approach

To avoid disparities between national approaches and to ensure uniformity of application, the Court of Justice developed its own

> *Take note*
>
> The preliminary reference procedure enables the Court to rule on the meaning and validity of Union law, binding all Member States (see Chapter 3). It is important to understand the procedure which has provided the basis for the Court's rulings on supremacy and direct effect.

jurisprudence on the supremacy of EU law, mainly through the preliminary reference procedure under Article 267 TFEU.

A new legal order

The Court used the request for a preliminary reference from a Netherlands court in *Van Gend en Loos* to make an important ruling on the nature of Community law.

CORNERSTONE

'The Community [EU] constitutes a new legal order in international law, for whose benefits the States have limited their sovereign rights, albeit within limited fields' (*Van Gend en Loos*).

The case arose from a clash between old Article 12 of the EEC Treaty (now 30 TFEU) prohibiting new customs duties between Member States and a Dutch law imposing a new duty. The Court held that Article 12 was *directly effective*, taking precedence over national law and enabling individuals to rely on it directly in the national courts. The conditions for direct effect in *Van Gend en Loos* (the measure must be clear, unconditional and requiring no further action by the EU or Member States) are examined in Chapter 7. The Court held that the Community was a 'new legal order' in both international law and national law as the EEC Treaty (now TFEU) created rights and duties which could be enforced in the national courts.

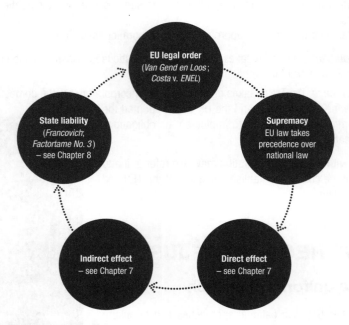

Figure 6.2 The legal order of the Union

CORNERSTONE

Costa v. ENEL

Member States have limited their sovereign rights in the areas within the Treaties (Case 6/64 *Costa v. ENEL*).

The Court developed its approach to the legal order in *Costa* v. *ENEL*. Costa was a shareholder in an Italian electricity company nationalised by a statute *after* the Ratification Act incorporating the EEC Treaty into Italian law. He refused to pay his electricity bill, claiming the nationalisation statute contravened the Treaty. The Italian court referred to the Court of Justice which held that the reception of Community law into the Member States' legal system prevents states from giving a later national measure priority over Community law. Its reasoning was based on Article 189 EEC (now 288 TFEU) that regulations have 'general application', are binding in their entirety and directly applicable in all Member States. The Court found that this provision would be 'meaningless if a state could unilaterally nullify its effects by . . . a legislative measure which could prevail over Community law'. It declared that:

> The transfer, by Member States . . . in favour of the Community order of the rights and obligations arising from the Treaty, carries with it a clear limitation of their sovereign right upon which a subsequent unilateral law, incompatible with the aims of the Community, cannot prevail.

EU law may not be invalidated by national law

In Case 11/70 *Internationale Handelsgesellschaft* v. *EVGF* the Court confirmed that Community law may only be assessed under Community standards. This case arose from an apparent clash between a requirement for an export licence under the CAP and German fundamental rights. The applicant sought to annul the regulation in the German courts, claiming that the German constitution enshrining

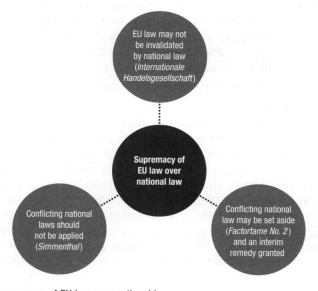

Figure 6.3 The supremacy of EU law over national law

fundamental rights took precedence over Community law. The Court of Justice rejected this claim, declaring that:

> Recourse to the legal rules or concepts of national law . . . to judge the validity of measures adopted by the institutions . . . would have an adverse effect on the uniformity and efficacy of Community law. The validity of such measures can only be judged in the light of Community law.

Conflicting national legislation should not be applied

CORNERSTONE

Member States must not apply legislation which conflicts with EU law, even where it is adopted *after* the relevant EU law (Case 106/77 *Simmenthal SpA (No. 2)*).

Simmenthal arose from conflict between an Italian statute passed after the Ratification Act and Article 30 EEC (now 34 TFEU) on the free movement of goods. The Italian judge referred to the Court of Justice to clarify whether he should wait for the national court to declare the measure void (as it had declared it would do if the Italian law conflicted with Community law) or give immediate priority to Community law. The Court of Justice replied that a national court must not apply conflicting national legislation even if adopted subsequently and should not wait for the decision of a higher court.

The Court reconsidered *Simmenthal* in Joined Case C-10–22/97 *Ministero delle Finanze* v. *In.Co.Ge.'90*, holding that a national law (here, a tax law) conflicting with an earlier Community law was not invalidated (or *non-existent*). The national court should disapply the conflicting national rule and reclassify it.

APPLICATION

Assume that the UK, after lobbying by employers complaining of the effect of the recession, adopts the Small Businesses Act 2013 permitting employers of twenty or fewer employees to set 'independent' pay rates for men and women. The effect is that women are paid less than men for the same work. Such a law would infringe Article 157 TFEU providing for equal pay for equal work for men and women. Following *Simmenthal* and *In.Co.Ge.'90*, the UK courts should not apply the conflicting UK statute which should be repealed.

A qualification of this approach in *final* decisions may be seen in Case C-234/04 *Kapferer* v. *Schlank & Schick* on the principle of cooperation in Article 10 TEC (now Article 4 TEU). The referral arose from a refusal by a German mail order company to pay prize money to an Austrian national resident in Austria who had been told that she had won a prize. The applicant returned the notification form to the defendants but did not place an order (one of the conditions for obtaining a prize), later bringing proceedings in the Austrian courts for damages. The defendants initially claimed the court had no jurisdiction as there was no contract. When the District Court dismissed the claim on the merits, the applicant appealed to the Landesgericht Innsbruck which doubted whether the lower court could hear the case. It sought guidance from the Court of Justice as to whether the principle of co-operation under Article 5 TEC obliged it to review and set aside a final judgment conflicting with Community law. The Court of Justice held that a national court was not required to disapply its inter-nal rules of procedure to set aside a *final* decision conflicting with Union law. (It would disturb the national legal order to overturn final decisions retrospectively.)

INTERSECTION

The problems posed by supremacy may sometimes be avoided by recourse to the principle of *indirect effect*, requiring national courts to interpret national legislation to comply with EU obligations, passed before *or* after the relevant EU law (Case C-106/89 *Marleasing*). (Indirect effect is considered further in Chapter 7.)

The *Factortame* decisions

The *Factortame* series of decisions clearly confirms the *supremacy of EU law* over national law, with important rulings on the need for an *interim remedy* at national level where there may be a clash between EU law and national law, as well as guidance on the meaning of *State liability*.

CORNERSTONE

National law should be set aside where it prevents granting interim relief in a dispute under EU law (Case C-213/89 *R* v. *Secretary of State for Transport, ex p. Factortame (Factortame No. 2)*).

The dispute in *Factortame No. 2* arose from the introduction under the Merchant Shipping Act 1988 of strict rules against fishing in UK waters by vessels not registered as British. Under the Act many Spanish vessels previously registered as British failed to qualify for registration and could not share the UK 'catch quota' (i.e. amount of permissible catch under the Common Fisheries Policy). The Queen's Bench Divisional Court referred to the Court of Justice and temporarily suspended the controversial provisions until the ruling. After the Court of Appeal quashed the suspension order an appeal was made to the House of Lords which referred further questions to the Court of Justice.

The Court of Justice held that a national law should be set aside where it prevents the granting of interim relief in a dispute governed by Community law. This means that an individual whose rights under EU law appear to be at risk from national legislation is entitled to an interim injunction setting the offending statute aside until the position is clear, usually after a ruling of the Court.

APPLICATION

Imagine the EU adopts a directive in 2012 requiring Member States to obtain sixty per cent of their energy requirements from renewable sources. France adopts a statute in 2013 providing that 'renewable sources' include nuclear power when used in conjunction with solar or wind energy. A protest group entitled 'Les Champs Verts' challenges the statute in the French courts but is refused an interim order as French law prohibits individual remedies in relation to energy supply. A reference is made to the Court of Justice to clarify the directive. There is a strong case that France is in breach of EU law by adopting a statute which does not fully implement the directive. Following *Factortame (No. 2)*, the rights of Les Champs Verts have been jeopardised by denial of an interim order. The French courts should therefore make such an order pending the Court of Justice's decision.

English law did not previously recognise the possibility of an injunction against the Crown which would have infringed the principle of Parliamentary sovereignty. *Factortame (No. 2)* proved to be of great constitutional significance in the UK as it overturned the previous bar on an interim injunction where English law appeared to conflict with EU law. Lord Bridge in the House of Lords applied the Court of Justice ruling in *Factortame (No. 2)*, stating that under the terms of the ECA 1972:

> It has always been clear that it was the duty of a United Kingdom court, when delivering final judgment, to override any rule of national law found to be in conflict with any directly enforceable rule of Community law. [*R* v. ***Secretary of State for Transport, ex p. Factortame*** (1990)]

Enforcement decision and ruling on substantive issues

By the time the Court of Justice ruling in *Factortame (No.2)* was received, the offending parts of the Merchant Shipping Act had been suspended following parallel enforcement proceedings brought by the Commission in Case 246/89R *Commission* v. *UK Re Merchant Shipping Rules*. The Court of Justice ruled on the substantive issue (establishment) in Case C-221/89 *R* v. *Secretary of State for Transport ex p. Factortame*, holding that the requirement for owners of vessels to be UK nationals to register infringed the *right of establishment*.

Ruling on State liability

The Spanish fishermen sued the UK government for losses from the UK's breach of EU law in Case 48/93 *R* v. *Secretary of State for Transport, ex p. Factortame* [*Factortame (No. 3)*]. The Court of Justice clarified the requirements for State liability, extending it to all 'sufficiently serious' breaches of EU law, not just losses arising relating to directives. It provided guidance on what constitutes a sufficiently serious breach, including consideration as to whether a Member State had deliberately infringed EU law, as the UK had done by adopting the Merchant Shipping Act.

INTERSECTION ....

The Court of Justice had previously recognised that a Member State may be liable for damages from failure to implement a directive in Cases 6 & 9/90 *Francovich* v. *Bonifaci*. It extended liability in *Factortame (No. 3)* to *any* sufficiently serious breach of EU law causing loss to individuals. The conditions for State liability are considered in more detail in Chapter 8.

State liability is an application of the supremacy of EU law over national law. The Court of Justice's decision in *Factortame (No. 3)* reminds Member States of the financial implications of infringing their obligations under EU law. The House of Lords (1999) found that the UK's deliberate adoption of legislation contrary to the Treaty *was* a sufficiently serious breach for which the UK government was liable in damages.

EU LAW IN THE UK

The European Communities Act 1972 (ECA) was enacted to implement UK obligations under the EEC Treaty. Later Treaties have been ratified by Acts amending the ECA. The most recent UK constitutional statute is the European Union Act 2011 introducing a requirement for a referendum when events occur such as an EU proposal to create a new EU competence or extend an existing one (i.e. to enlarge the powers of the EU).

Direct applicability, direct effect and indirect effect

Section 2(1) of the European Communities Act (ECA) provides for the **direct applicability** and direct effect of Community (now EU) law in the UK:

> All such rights, powers, liabilities, obligations and restrictions from time to time created or arising by or under the Treaties, as in accordance with the Treaties, are without further enactment to be given legal effect . . . and shall be recognised and available in law, and be enforced, allowed and followed accordingly, and the expression 'enforceable Community right' and similar expressions shall be read as referring to one to which this subsection applies.

Put simply, an 'enforceable Community [EU] right' is a directly effective right which may be enforced in the UK courts without further legislation.

Section 2(2) ECA provides for implementation of Community (now EU) obligations which are not directly applicable by means of secondary legislation. Section 2(4) ECA deals with the relationship between Community [EU] law and national law without making express provision for supremacy, stating that 'Any enactment passed or to be passed . . . shall be construed and have effect subject to the foregoing provisions of this section'. Section 3(1) ECA provides for the meaning and effect of the Treaties to be treated as a question of law for the UK courts, whether or not a referral is made to the Court of Justice, ensuring that any decisions of the Court of Justice on meaning and effect of EU law are authoritative and bind the UK courts.

Approach of the UK courts

The UK courts approached some early cases where there appeared to be a clash between EC law and UK law by adopting a 'rule of construction approach' to section 2(4) so that English law was interpreted to comply with the relevant EC obligation. *Garland* v. *British Rail Engineering Ltd* (1979) provides an example, in a clash between the Equal Pay Act 1970 and Article 119 (now Article 157 TFEU) over exemption of death and retirement from the equal pay provision under section 6(4) of the Act. The House of Lords held that section 6(4) must be construed to conform with Article 119 EEC. In *Pickstone* v. *Freemans plc* (1988), the House of Lords went further, interpreting the regulations amending the Equal Pay Act 1970 *against* their literal meaning in order to comply with Community law. Such an approach is in keeping with a *purposive* interpretation whereby national law is interpreted in compliance with the spirit and purpose of the relevant Union law, as the House of Lords indicated in *Litster* v. *Forth Dry Dock Engineering Co. Ltd* (1989) (in which UK regulations on the transfer of undertakings were interpreted purposively in accordance with the relevant directive).

As Hoffman J. declared in the Chancery Division (1990), the EC Treaty is 'the supreme law of our country, taking precedence over Acts of Parliament. Our entry into the Community meant that Parliament had surrendered its sovereign rights to legislate contrary to the provisions of the Treaty on matters of social and economic policy which it regulated' (*Stoke-on-Trent* v. *B&Q plc*, on the compatibility of a UK prohibition on Sunday trading with the free movement of goods in EC law, considered in Chapter 12).

EU law and 'implied repeal'

The special constitutional status of EU law in the UK, particularly the European Communities Act 1972, was confirmed in *Thoburn* v. *Sunderland County Council* (the 'Metric Martyrs' case) (High Court, 2002) where the applicant unsuccessfully challenged a UK requirement that produce not already packaged must be sold in metric rather than imperial measures. Without referring to the Court of Justice the court dismissed the application, rejecting a claim that the Weights and Measures Act 1985 had by implication repealed the ECA 1972. It found that the ECA has a 'constitutional quality' and was not subject to implied repeal. It could only be repealed expressly and unambiguously by Act of Parliament, not by implication within another statute.

> The use of imperial measures in the UK has long been associated with national identity. Following advice from the EU Commission, the UK government issued guidance in 2007 that imperial measures may still be used in beer sold by the pint in public houses and milk in returnable pint containers, although pounds and ounces may not be used for goods such as fruit and vegetables sold loose.

CONTEXT

The European Union Act 2011

The European Union Act 2011 (EUA) (effective September 2011) was introduced to increase participation of the British people in decision-making at national level on EU matters.

Transfer of powers from UK to EU

Where certain powers or policies are to move from the UK to EU control, a *referendum* and an *Act of Parliament* will be required (European Union Act 2011 (EUA) ss. 2, 3 and 6). The EUA also provides that an Act of Parliament will be needed to give effect to all types of Treaty change (not previously the case). It also gives Parliamentary approval to a Transitional Protocol on MEPs, increasing the number of MEPs once the Protocol has been ratified by the other Member States. The Act provides for increased control over *passerelle (or 'ratchet') clauses* in the Treaties.

> The EUA originated in political problems from the abortive Constitutional Treaty. The Prime Minister at the time, Tony Blair, promised to hold a referendum on the Treaty. This proved unnecessary after the Treaty was rejected by France and the Netherlands in referenda. David Cameron, in Opposition as leader of the Conservative Party, stated that if elected he would introduce a *referendum lock* on transfer of future powers from the UK to the EU, requiring the consent of the UK people in a referendum before power could be transferred to the EU. Powers would be 'repatriated' (handed back) from the EU to the UK in areas such as social policy. The subsequent Coalition government considered it was released from the requirement to hold a referendum on the Lisbon Treaty after securing changes recognising the UK position on areas such as the Charter of Fundamental Rights. The Lisbon Treaty was ratified by Act of Parliament in 2009, but popular demand for a referendum on Treaty changes remained. The EUA is a compromise seeking to reconcile 'Eurosceptic' Conservative Party tendencies with the 'Europhile' Liberal Democratic approach.

CONTEXT

Sovereignty and section 18 of the EUA

Section 18 of the EUA provides that:

> Directly applicable or directly effective EU law (i.e. the rights, powers, liabilities, obligations, restrictions, remedies and procedures referred to in s. 2(1) of the ECA) falls to be recognised and available in law in the UK only by virtue of that Act or where it is required to be recognised and available in law by virtue of any other Act.

Although section 18 was seen as controversial, it adds nothing to the House of Lords' decision in *Factortame (No. 2)* that the supremacy of EU law over UK law derives from an Act of Parliament, which could presumably be repealed.

The system of control under the EUA

Three main types of measure will require both a national referendum and an Act of Parliament under sections 2, 3 and 6 of the Act. These are shown in Figure 6.4.

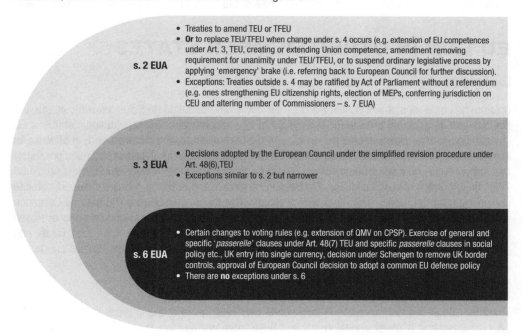

s. 2 EUA
- Treaties to amend TEU or TFEU
- **Or** to replace TEU/TFEU when change under s. 4 occurs (e.g. extension of EU competences under Art. 3, TEU, creating or extending Union competence, amendment removing requirement for unanimity under TEU/TFEU, or to suspend ordinary legislative process by applying 'emergency' brake (i.e. referring back to European Council for further discussion).
- Exceptions: Treaties outside s. 4 may be ratified by Act of Parliament without a referendum (e.g. ones strengthening EU citizenship rights, election of MEPs, conferring jurisdiction on CEU and altering number of Commissioners – s. 7 EUA)

s. 3 EUA
- Decisions adopted by the European Council under the simplified revision procedure under Art. 48(6),TEU
- Exceptions similar to s. 2 but narrower

s. 6 EUA
- Certain changes to voting rules (e.g. extension of QMV on CPSP). Exercise of general and specific '*passerelle*' clauses under Art. 48(7) TEU and specific *passerelle* clauses in social policy etc., UK entry into single currency, decision under Schengen to remove UK border controls, approval of European Council decision to adopt a common EU defence policy
- There are **no** exceptions under s. 6

Figure 6.4 Measures requiring both a national referendum and an Act of Parliament under the European Union Act

APPLICATION

Imagine the Member States agree to amend the TFEU to increase the number of MEPs in the European Parliament and to give the EU power to determine Member States' housing policies to ensure adequate provision of housing across the EU. Under the exceptions to section 2 EUA the increased number of MEPs would require an Act of Parliament but not a referendum. The housing powers amendment would require both an Act of Parliament and a referendum in the UK under section 2 EUA as it gives a new power to the EU and is not covered by an exception.

Section 9 EUA states that the UK may not support certain measures in the Area of freedom, security and justice without the approval of Parliament. Section 10 provides 'light touch' scrutiny involving parliamentary approval without an Act of Parliament of measures in certain areas including increasing the number of Advocate-Generals, amending the statute of the Court of Justice and the Union's accession to the ECHR.

> While it is too early to assess the impact of changes under the EUA, the UK Prime Minister, David Cameron, in December 2011 vetoed amendments to the Treaties following the Eurozone crisis. As a result, the other 26 Member States entered into a separate intergovernmental treaty, the Stability Pact. While this action did *not* follow from invoking a referendum lock under the EUA, Gordon and Dougan have suggested (2011) that the political impact of the EUA has generated a 'powerful political rhetoric' for a referendum on almost any change affecting the relationship of the UK and the EU. No referendum has yet been held, although David Cameron has promised a referendum on the UK's future membership of the EU after the next general election in 2015 (speech on role of the UK in the EU, 23 January 2013).

REFLECTION

EU LAW IN OTHER MEMBER STATES

Belgium

Belgium has both monist and dualist features. EU law is incorporated into Belgian law by statute, but the constitution does not provide for supremacy to international law. The constitutional status of EU law in Belgium was uncertain until the decision of the Cour de Cassation (Appeal Court) in *Minister for Economic Affairs* v. *Fromagerie Franco-Suisse 'Le Ski'* (1972). The Court of Justice had ruled previously that import duties on dairy products contravened the prohibition under Article 12 EEC (now Article 30 TFEU) on imposition of customs duties. The Belgian Parliament abolished the duties but passed a statute preventing return of money paid, leading to a challenge in the Belgian courts. The Cour de Cassation ruled that the rule that a later statute repeals an earlier one did not apply to an international treaty, being a higher legal norm. It followed that in the event of a conflict between the EEC Treaty and domestic law, the Treaty must prevail; a position which has been accepted in the Belgian courts.

France

There has long been tension in the French courts over recognition of the supremacy of EU law. The Cour de Cassation (highest appeal court) has been more willing than the Conseil d'Etat (supreme administrative court) to give precedence to EU law. Two cases illustrate their differing approaches: *Café Jacques Vabre* and *Cohn-Bendit*.

In *Directeur Général des Douanes* v. *Société Café Jacques Vabre* (1975, Cour de Cassation) Vabre had imported coffee extract into France from the Netherlands. Under a French statute passed *after* membership of the Community, Vabre had to pay customs duties, while coffee extract produced in France was taxed at a lower rate. Vabre claimed that payment of duties infringed Article 95 EEC (now 114 TFEU). The Cour de Cassation upheld his claim, holding that the Treaty had created a separate legal order binding Member States. Lack of reciprocity in enforcement by the Netherlands was not a ground for refusing to apply Community law. This approach was followed a year later in *Von Kempis* v. *Geldof* (1976) when the Cour de Cassation held that the Treaty also takes precedence over earlier French legislation.

The *Cohn-Bendit* decision (1975, Conseil d'Etat) arose from deportation of a German citizen resident in France where he was a student. Cohn-Bendit, a leader of the 1968 student uprising, was deported following an order from the Minister of the Interior as a threat to public policy. In 1975 he sought to return to France to take up a job. The Minister refused to rescind the deportation order without reason. Cohn-Bendit challenged the decision in the Tribunal Administratif which made a referral. The Minister appealed to the Conseil d'Etat against the order of reference to clarify the public policy exception in Directive 64/221. Before judgment was given the Minister revoked the deportation order. Despite the revocation the Conseil d'Etat delivered its judgment and allowed the appeal, holding that directives cannot be invoked by individuals to challenge administrative decisions under the Treaty. As Cohn-Bendit could not invoke the directive its interpretation was irrelevant.

Doubt remained after *Cohn-Bendit* over recognition of the direct effect of directives by French administrative courts until *Application of Georges Nicolo* (1989), a series of cases before the Conseil d'Etat on alleged irregularities in elections to the European Parliament. The Conseil d'Etat declared it was prepared to accept the supremacy of the EC Treaty over French law on the election of MEPs. The Conseil d'Etat confirmed its acceptance of the supremacy of Community law in *Boisdet* in 1990 where it gave precedence to an EC regulation on the common organisation of the dessert apples market over a later French law.

This was not to be the last word. Another French court, the Conseil Constitutional (empowered to examine constitutionality of legislation) declared provisions of the Maastricht Treaty incompatible with the Constitution which was amended to enable France to ratify it. Several further cases were heard by the Conseil Constitutional, with three treaties found to require constitutional amendments, the Treaty of Amsterdam (decision of 1997), the (failed) Constitutional Treaty (decision of 2004) later rejected by the French people in a referendum, and the Lisbon Treaty (2007). The Conseil Constitutional left no doubt in those decisions that it considers that the French Constitution takes precedence over EU law in France.

National reviews of constitutionality

The legitimacy of a French requirement to refer to the Conseil Constitutional when faced with a question of constitutionality was considered by the Court of Justice in Case C-188 & 189/10 *Melki and Abdeli* over two Algerian nationals unlawfully resident in France and subjected to a police control under the French Code of Criminal Procedure. Melki and Abdeli claimed the provision contravened the French Constitution and Article 67(2) TFEU requiring the removal of border controls within the EU. The Court of Justice found that a procedure requiring national review of constitutionality infringed EU law if it prevented the reviewing court (e.g. the Conseil Constitutional) from making a referral under Article 267 TFEU. Such a procedure was compatible with EU law if it did not prevent other national courts from making a referral at any point. It held that national courts remain free to adopt any necessary provisional measures to ensure the provisional judicial protection of rights under EU law and to disapply the national law at the end of an interim procedure if it conflicts with EU law.

·· **APPLICATION**

Imagine the UK adopts the Constitutional Review Act requiring constitutional treaties to be considered by the High Court for compliance with UK constitutional requirements. Such a provision does not necessarily infringe EU law following *Melki and Abdeli* as it does not prevent referral to the Court of Justice. However, if the provision stated that *only* a UK court could rule on constitutionality, it would itself infringe EU law as it would deny UK courts access to the preliminary reference procedure on validity.

Germany

Membership of the Community posed particular constitutional problems for Germany, due to the special protection of fundamental human rights in the German constitution, demonstrated in the *Internationale Handelsgesellschaft* (1974) decision. The applicant had sought annulment in an administrative court of a decision of a German agency under two Community regulations, claiming the regulations were invalid under the constitution as they infringed fundamental human rights. The Court of Justice held that the validity of Community provisions should be determined according to Community not national, law. The administrative court then referred the matter to the German Constitutional Court.

A potential challenge to the supremacy of Community law was posed by the German Constitutional Court's statement that until fundamental rights were adequately protected in Community law, Community measures would be subject to the provisions of the German constitution. No such measures were found to contravene the German constitution and in 1986 the Constitutional Court ruled in *Wünsche Handelsgesellschaft (Solange II)* that provided the general protection of human rights in Community law remained adequate, it would hear no further test cases comparing Community law with the German constitution. This ruling was not the end of the matter, as later Constitutional Court decisions continued to find EU law subject to the German constitution on fundamental rights.

Apart from the Federal Constitutional Court, Germany has five separate systems of courts: the ordinary courts and specialised courts dealing with administrative matters, social security, labour and tax, each headed by a Federal Supreme Court. The Federal Tax Court refused in 1981 and 1986 to recognise the direct effect of directives. Both cases arose out of claims by taxpayers for a tax exemption provided under a VAT directive which had not been implemented in Germany. In the second, Case 70/83 *Kloppenburg*, the Federal Tax Court contradicted a ruling of the Court of Justice in the same case that the directive was directly effective and refused the exemption. Kloppenburg appealed to the Constitutional Court which upheld the supremacy of Community law, annulling the decision of the Federal Tax Court as violating the German constitution which provides that no one shall be deprived of his 'lawful judge' (in this case, the Court of Justice). The Federal Tax Court should either have followed the Court of Justice ruling or made a second reference.

Kompetenz-Kompetenz

Further constitutional turmoil was experienced over ratification of the Maastricht Treaty. The Constitutional Court accepted in *Brunner* v. *European Union Treaty* (1993) that the Court of Justice holds primary responsibility for protecting fundamental rights, but found that the Community lacked what it called *Kompetenz-Kompetenz* (capability to determine the extent of its own powers). As the authority of the Community derived from the Member States, it could only act within the competence given. The Constitutional Court therefore reserved the right to review the legal measures of the Community institutions if they appeared to be outside the Treaties. It exercised this right in 2005 when it found that German legislation implementing the framework decision on the European Arrest Warrant was invalid as it infringed the German constitutional code prohibiting the extradition of German citizens.

Ratification of the Lisbon Treaty led to another challenge in 2009 in the Constitutional Court where it was argued that the Treaty infringed the German Constitution, relying on what came to be known as the 'identity lock' (including the political formation of economic, social and living conditions). The Constitutional Court found the Treaty was compatible with the German constitution, with sovereignty remaining with Member States who were 'masters of the Treaties', as the Lisbon Treaty did not create a federal state to which Germany could not belong.

In 2010 the Constitutional Court provided another ruling on the status of EU law in *Honeywell*. The challenge was based on the claim that the EU had exceeded its authority by recognising the principle of age discrimination without a basis in the Treaties in Case C-144/04 *Mangold* where the Court held that non-discrimination on grounds of age was a general principle of EU law. The Constitutional Court asserted that it should be able to disapply EU law outside the principle of conferral. However, it found that there was a presumption that the Union would normally act within its competences. Thus the '*ultra vires* lock' may only trigger a review of the legality of EU law where the EU institutions have 'transgressed the boundaries of their competences in a manner specifically violating the principle of conferral'. The act must be 'manifestly in violation of competences' and 'highly significant' in the division of competences between the EU and Member States. Such conditions are hard to satisfy, making the review of EU law by the Constitutional Court rather less likely in future.

Italy

The leading case is *Frontini* (1974) in which a cheese importer claimed that a levy imposed by an EC regulation contravened Article 23 of the Italian constitution stating that taxes may only be imposed by statute. Since Article 241 of the EEC Treaty (now 288 TFEU) provided for direct applicability of regulations, he argued that the Treaty was incompatible with the Italian constitution. The Italian Constitutional Court ruled that Community law is separate from both international and Italian law, and that the Italian constitution does not apply to legislation enacted by the Community institutions. It follows that Article 23 of the Italian constitution does not apply to measures under EU law today.

Nevertheless in *Fragd* v. *Amministrazione delle Finanze dello Stato* (1989) the Italian Constitutional Court considered whether a declaration of invalidity by the Court of Justice under the preliminary reference procedure was consistent with Italian constitutional principles of judicial protection when it had no effect in proceedings before the national court. The Court of Justice had declared invalid EC regulations containing the criteria under which the applicant had made payments to the Italian customs authorities over powdered glucose exported to Germany. Despite the ruling, payments made before the judgment could not be recovered. The court in Venice which referred to the Court of Justice refused to accept the ruling and referred the case to the Italian Constitutional Court. The Constitutional Court held there was no unconstitutionality but only after assessing the consistency of rules of Community law with protection of fundamental rights under the Italian constitution. Such an approach provides the Italian Constitutional Court with the basis for further reviews of EU law relative to Italian fundamental rights in future.

Poland

According to Sadurski (2008), the position of the Polish courts resembles the German courts in the early years of the Community when the German Constitutional Court considered protection of fundamental rights in EC law inferior to German law. Poland's membership of the EU under the Accession Treaty was challenged before the Polish Constitutional Tribunal (2005) in Case K 18/04. Although the Tribunal found the Accession Treaty conformed to the Polish constitution, it held that if there was 'irreconcilable inconsistency' between the constitution and the Treaties the decision to resolve the inconsistency 'belongs to the Polish constitutional legislator'. The Tribunal did not accept that the Communities and EU are 'supranational organisations'. Emphasising the 'relative autonomy' of EU and national law, the Tribunal identified areas in which an inconsistency might arise. Were this to happen, the Tribunal stated that the duty to interpret national law in compliance with EU law has limits and must not conflict with a 'minimum guaranteed function' under the constitution.

The Tribunal went further in 2005 in the *European Arrest Warrants (EAW I)* Case P 1/05, holding that the domestic law implementing a framework decision creating the European Arrest Warrant (EAW) was incompatible with the Polish constitution prohibiting extradition of a Polish citizen. Given that the time limit for implementation had passed, the Tribunal deferred cancellation of the implementing legislation to allow time to amend the constitution. While the decision shows lack of acceptance of EU law supremacy over the Polish constitution, the Constitutional Tribunal has shown some flexibility in deferring cancellation of domestic law implementing the EAW.

Case IKZP 30/08 *Criminal Proceedings against Jacob T* (EAW II) in 2009 also involved a constitutional complaint to the Polish Constitutional Tribunal. The case arose from a complaint by an individual sentenced to life imprisonment in the UK and sent back to Poland to serve his sentence. The applicant challenged the legality of the surrender procedure by asking the Tribunal whether provisions of the Polish Criminal Code complied with the Polish constitution. Although the Tribunal found the relevant provision of the Polish constitution did not accord with EU law, it followed EAW I, confirming surrender as a form of extradition within the Polish constitution, and held that the provisions complied with the constitution.

The Polish Constitutional Court again considered the status of EU law in its ruling on ratification of the Lisbon Treaty in Case K 32/09 in November 2010, holding that Article 90 of the Polish constitution determines the Union's competence limits. The Tribunal held it was permissible to confer competences on the Union relating to identity and state sovereignty only as far as they did not infringe the constitutional basis of the state. It found that the EU model under the Lisbon Treaty ensures respect for protection of state sovereignty in the process of integration. There was no conflict between the Polish constitution and the Treaty which was duly ratified.

REFLECTION

Academic commentators on supremacy tend to fall into two main schools of thought. Pluralists such as MacCormick acknowledge that not all legal problems have a legal solution. In his view (1995), both the Court of Justice and national courts should interpret EU law having regard for the political consequences of the judgment. National courts likewise should not reach decisions without reference to their position in the Union. MacCormick later modified his position (1999), advocating referral of conflict between national courts and the Court of Justice to international arbitration or adjudication.

Other commentators such as Kumm (2005) have adopted a different approach, emphasising the underlying commitment to constitutionalism of both EU and national law. This commitment, he argues, is based on four central elements: commitment to the rule of law, protection of fundamental rights, federalism and a commitment to the specific nature of the national community. While Kumm's perspective may provide a useful approach to the resolution of disputes between the national courts and the Court of Justice, it fails to take account of the broader questions surrounding such disputes, particularly where long-established traditional practices are overtaken by EU requirements.

Since the 2004 and 2007 enlargements much commentary has focused on the constitutional position of the new Member States. Sadurski (2008) argues there is a democracy paradox in resisting the supremacy of EU law when accession was supposed to guarantee human rights and democracy. Lazowski (2011), in a survey of Polish decisions on EU law, finds limitations of judicial expertise, with reluctance to make referrals to the Court of Justice. The relationship between the German Constitutional Court and the Court of Justice continues to provoke discussion. Pliakos and Anagnostaras (2011) see the battle over supremacy between the two courts as shifting from '*ultra vires*' to constitutional identity as a trigger for constitutional review. Payandeh (2011) asks whether the German Constitutional Court will exercise its identity review function responsibly or disrupt the process of European integration.

The supremacy of EU law over national law is a long-established doctrine in the Court of Justice. However, the same cannot be said of the constitutional courts of established and new Member States which continue to resist the primacy of EU law.

KEY POINTS

- EU law takes precedence over national law in the EU legal order.
- The Court of Justice has played a central role in developing the principle of supremacy.
- Where a national law conflicts with EU law, it should not be applied.
- The European Communities Act 1972 gave effect to EC [EU] law in the UK.
- The European Union Act requires a referendum and/or Act of Parliament in the UK under certain circumstances.
- The supremacy of EU law in a number of Member States including Germany, France and Poland is not fully acknowledged by the national constitutional court.

CORE CASES AND STATUTES

Case	About	Importance
Case 26/62 *Van Gend en Loos*	Imposition of customs duty contrary to EEC Treaty (now TFEU).	Declared that EC law is 'new legal order', taking precedence over national law and creating rights for individuals before national courts.
Case 6/64 *Costa* v. *ENEL*	Refusal to pay electricity bill, claiming that nationalisation statute infringed EC law and Italian constitution.	Clarified nature of 'new legal order', under which Member States had 'transferred their sovereign rights' to Community in areas covered by Treaty.
Minister for Economic Affairs v. *Fromagerie Franco-Suisse 'Le Ski'* (Belgian Cour de Cassation 1972)	Status of EC law in Belgium.	The Treaty must prevail in clash with domestic law.
Frontini v. *Ministero delle Finanze* (Italian Constitutional Court, 1973)	Claim that Italian statute incorporating EC Treaty was incompatible with Italian constitution, making levy imposed by EC regulation invalid.	Constitutional Court held that EU law was separate from Italian constitution, which does not apply to secondary legislation adopted by EU institutions.
Directeur Général des Douanes v. *Société Café Jacques Vabre* (French Cour de Cassation, 1975)	Status of EC law in France.	Individual may rely on Treaty to defeat French customs duty imposed after joining EC. Shows acceptance of supremacy of EC law by Cour de Cassation.
Case 106/77 *Simmenthal (No. 2)*	Clash between EC law on free movement of goods and Italian law adopted after joining EC.	Conflicting national law should not be applied, even if adopted after joining EU.

→

Case	About	Importance
Fragd v. *Amministrazione Delle Finanze dello Stato* (Italian Constitutional Court, 1989)	Claim that declaration of invalidity by CJEU infringed entitlement under Italian constitution to bring legal proceedings to protect rights and interests.	Italian Constitutional Court reserved right to review EC secondary legislation to ensure no infringement of human rights under Italian constitution.
Application of Georges Nicolo (Conseil d'Etat, 1989)	Relationship between French and EC law. Irregularities in EP elections.	Conseil d'Etat accepted supremacy of EC law over national law on election of MEPs.
Case C-213/89 *R* v. *Secretary of State for Transport, ex p. Factortame (No. 2)*	Spanish fishermen sought injunction to prevent UK from applying Merchant Shipping Act 1988 requiring vessels to be registered as British.	CJEU required courts to grant interim relief, even though this meant setting aside a national prohibition, overturning UK law which did not allow injunction against the Crown.
Case C-48/93 *Factortame (No. 3)*	Preliminary ruling from claim for losses suffered by Spanish fishermen excluded from fishing by UK law contrary to EU law.	State liability may arise in relation to *any* breach of EU law where rule is intended to confer rights on individuals, breach is sufficiently serious and caused the damage.
Brunner v. *European Union Treaty* (BVerf G, 1993)	Challenge to legality of Maastricht Treaty under German constitution.	German Federal Constitutional Court held that EC can only exercise competence given by Member States and cannot determine its own power. Reserved power to review legality of EU measures if they appear to be outside the Treaties.

Statute	About	Importance
Article 4 TEU	Principle of cooperation.	Requires Member States to fulfil their obligations under the Treaties.
Section 2(1) ECA 1972	Direct applicability and effect.	Provides for direct applicability and direct effect in UK law.
Section 2(2) ECA 1972	Implementation of EU law.	Provides for implementation in UK of EC (EU) law where it is not directly effective.
Section 2(4) ECA 1972	Indirect effect.	Provides for relationship between UK and EC (EU) law without making express provision for supremacy.

Statute	About	Importance
European Union Act (EUA) 2011 section 18	So-called sovereignty section.	Does not alter existing position that supremacy of EU law over UK law derives from Act of Parliament.
EUA section 2	'Referendum lock': Treaties to amend TEU or TFEU under ordinary revision procedure, or to replace the Treaties.	Require both national referendum and an Act of Parliament, with some exceptions (Act of Parliament alone required).
EUA section 3	'Referendum lock': decisions adopted by European Council under simplified revision procedure.	Require both referendum and Act of Parliament, with some exceptions (Act of Parliament alone required).
EUA section 6	'Referendum lock': changes to voting rules, exercise of 'passerelles'.	Require both referendum and Act of Parliament – no exceptions.
EUA section 7	Measures not amending the Treaties but of almost the same importance	Require Act of Parliament. Covers areas such as extending citizenship rights.
EUA section 9	Certain measures in Area of Freedom, Security and Justice (AFSJ)	Require Parliamentary approval.

FURTHER READING

Gordon, M. and Dougan, M. 'The United Kingdom's European Union Act 2011: "Who won the bloody war anyway?"' (2011) 37 *European Law Review* 3
Critical assessment of European Union Act 2011, including so-called sovereignty clause in section 18.

Kumm, M. 'The jurisprudence of constitutional conflict: constitutional supremacy in Europe before and after the Constitutional Treaty' (2005) *European Law Journal* 262
Worth reading for views on constitutional pluralism.

Lazowski, A. 'Half full and half empty glass: the application of EU law in Poland (2004–2009)' (2011) 48 *Common Market Law Review* 503
Thorough analysis of decisions on EU law in the Polish courts.

MacCormick, N. 'The Maastricht *Urteil*: sovereignty now' (1995) 1 *European Law Journal* 259

MacCormick, N. *Questioning Sovereignty* (Oxford University Press: Oxford, 1999).
Journal article and book provide a masterly exposition of the pluralist position.

Oppenheimer, A. *The Relationship between European Community Law and National Law: The Cases* (Grotius: Cambridge, Vol. I, 1994, Vol. II, 2003)
Annotated compilation of national law reports in English, not otherwise readily available.

Payandeh, M. 'Constitutional review of EU law after Honeywell: Contextualising the relationship between the German Constitutional Court and the EU Court of Justice', (2011) 48 *Common Market Law Review*
Assesses whether the Court of Justice or the German Constitutional Court is final authority on constitutionality of EU legal acts.

Pliakos, A. and Anagnostaras, G. 'Who is the ultimate arbiter? The battle over judicial supremacy in EU law' (2011) 36 *European Law Review* 109
Explores tensions between the Court of Justice and the German Constitutional Court since its *Lisbon* ruling.

Sadurski, W. '"Solange Chapter 3": constitutional courts in Central Europe – democracy – European Union' (2008) *European Law Journal* 1
Examines approach to EU law in post-Communist states in Eastern and Central Europe, focusing on role of Constitutional Courts in Czech Republic, Hungary and Poland.

CHAPTER 7
Direct and indirect effect

BLUEPRINT

Direct and indirect effect

LEGISLATION

- Article 4(3) TEU

CONTEXT

- New legal order
- Privatisation of utilities in 1980s UK

CONCEPTS

- Direct applicability and direct effect
- Vertical and horizontal effect
- Public body
- Indirect effect

- Should directives be horizontally effective?

- How should the Court of Justice develop the EU legal order in the absence of provision in the Treaties?

CASES

- *Van Gend en Loos*
- *Van Duyn*
- *Defrenne*
- *Marleasing*
- *Marshall*
- *Foster*
- *Pfeiffer*
- *Mangold*

SPECIAL CHARACTERISTICS

- Lack of horizontal effect for directives

REFORM

- No reform planned as development is through the case law of the Court of Justice

CRITICAL ISSUES

Setting the scene

Imagine the UK has adopted the Pork (Import Prohibition) Act 2013 forbidding importation of pork from outside the UK and imposing criminal penalties on importers infringing the prohibition. The government claims the measure is justified by the threat from Pig Disease in France and Italy. The Commission has investigated and found no need for restrictions on the pig movement as the outbreak has ended and control measures in affected Member States are sufficient. Tom has been charged with importing pork contrary to the 2013 Act. The UK action infringes Article 34 TFEU prohibiting measures restricting the free movement of goods. As this provision is *directly effective*, Tom can rely on it before the UK courts, giving him a *defence* to the criminal charge. This chapter considers the rules on direct effect as well as position when laws are not directly effective.

THE ROLE OF THE COURT OF JUSTICE

The Court of Justice has played a dynamic role in defining the EU legal order, using the preliminary reference procedure under Article 267 TFEU imaginatively to clarify the law. With no provision for supremacy in the Treaties, the Court filled the gap in 1963 in Case 26/62 *Van Gend en Loos* (referral by Dutch courts over importer's refusal to pay a new customs duty introduced contrary to Article 12 EEC). *Van Gend en Loos* is a landmark decision in which the Court developed the twin principles of supremacy and direct effect. Where a provision is directly effective, it may be relied upon by individuals before the national courts.

> Before *Van Gend en Loos*, Member States did *not* perceive Community law as creating rights for individuals. The Court sent out a strong signal to Member States and the international community that Community law represented a 'new legal order' in both national and international law.

CONTEXT

This chapter examines the rules on *direct effect*, as well as those on *indirect effect* where the requirements for direct effect are not satisfied. The Court of Justice has also developed a third type of remedy known as *State liability* where Member States are in breach of EU law in certain circumstances (covered in Chapter 8).

DIRECT APPLICABILITY AND DIRECT EFFECT

The terms 'direct applicability' and 'direct effect' are not defined in the Treaties. In the early years of the Community the Court of Justice treated them as interchangeable, according to Pescatore

(1983), a judge at the Court. The distinction between the two was first made by the legal academic, Winter (1973), as follows:

- *Directly applicable* provisions take effect in the legal systems of the Member States without the need for further enactment.

- *Directly effective* provisions give rise to rights or obligations on which individuals may rely before their national courts.

The only reference in the Treaties to direct applicability is in Article 288 TFEU (ex 249 TEC) referring to regulations as 'directly applicable'. The Court of Justice ruled in cases starting with *Van Gend en Loos* that Treaty Articles and other types of EU law may create direct effects, enabling individuals to rely on them in the national courts. *All* directly effective laws are directly applicable (i.e. not requiring further enactment), but *not all* directly applicable rights are directly effective as they may not be suitable for individuals to enforce.

APPLICATION

Assume the EU adopts a regulation providing for cooperation over the common external tariff. It is directly applicable without further enactment. However, as it is not intended to benefit individuals, it is not directly effective – unlike a directive on equal treatment in the workplace, which is intended to benefit individuals and is directly enforceable in the national courts if it satisfies the conditions for direct effect.

It is important to appreciate that directly effective Treaty provisions can be relied on by individuals *as of right* before the national courts, whereas enforcement by the Commission under Article 258 TFEU (ex 226 TEC) against a Member State in breach of EU law is at the Commission's discretion, providing *no remedy* for the individual.

The direct effect of Treaty Articles

As the Treaties do not provide for direct effect, it is only possible to be certain a particular EU law is directly effective when the Court of Justice has ruled. The first ruling on the direct effect of Treaty provisions was in Case 26/62 *Van Gend en Loos* in 1963 when the Court gave a landmark ruling on the nature of Community law, introducing the concepts of the 'new legal order' and of 'direct effect'.

CORNERSTONE

Conditions for direct effect

A Treaty provision which is intended to benefit individuals is directly effective when it is sufficiently clear, precise and unconditional (*Van Gend en Loos*, as amended by later decisions).

Van Gend en Loos arose from an importer's refusal to pay a customs duty imposed by the Dutch government contrary to (old) Article 12 EEC which prohibited new customs duties. The national court referred to the Court of Justice which held that the Treaty provision was directly effective, creating rights which the national courts must respect. It also declared that the EU was a 'new legal order' in national and international law in which Member States had limited their sovereign rights. It followed from *Van Gend* that the importer had a defence to the criminal charge in the national court as the Dutch law imposing the duty was invalid under Community law.

INTERSECTION

When considering single market law, you should remember that most TFEU provisions at the heart of the EU legal order are expressed in direct, straightforward and often brief terms and have been found by the Court to be directly effective (see Chapters 11–15). This has enabled individuals to enforce their rights before the national courts, including those on citizenship (Article 21), the free movement of persons (Article 45), right of establishment (Article 49), services (Article 56), goods (Articles 34–36) as well as equal pay (Article 157) and competition (Articles 101 and 102 TFEU).

'Clear and precise'

Lack of clarity or precision prevents a Treaty provision from being directly effective. Some Treaty provisions are worded in general or aspirational language, and are not intended to be directly effective. Articles 1–4 TEC (pre-Treaty of Lisbon) which set out the aims and purposes of the Community were held to be incapable of conferring individual rights in Case 155/73 *Sacchi* (a competition case on television broadcasting).

While Article 2 TEU provides that, 'the Union is founded on the values of respect for human dignity, freedom, democracy, equality, the rule of law and respect for human rights, including the rights of persons belonging to minorities', this Article is unlikely to be directly effective as the wording is too broad and general.

'Unconditional'

The requirement for the measure to be unconditional was relaxed by the Court of Justice. In Case 41/74 *Van Duyn* v. *Home Office* – in which the UK had denied a Dutch national entry to the UK to work for the Church of Scientology of which it disapproved – the Court held that Article 48 EEC (now 45 TFEU) on free movement of workers was directly effective despite being subject to derogations (exceptions) on grounds of public policy, public security and public health. Thus 'unconditional' now means little more than where there is no need for action by another body or further legislation at EU level or by the Member States to give it effect.

APPLICATION

A consignment of cheeses moving from Member State X to state Y is seized by state Y as it considers that the labelling of cheeses in X does not satisfy Y's consumer protection laws. The importer could rely on the prohibition against restrictions on imports in Article 34 TFEU even though that provision is subject to derogations in Article 36.

The Court in *Van Gend en Loos* stated that provisions would only be directly effective if they required no further action to give them effect.

The requirement has been overtaken by later decisions, particularly Case 43/75 *Defrenne* v. *Sabena*, an equal pay action based on Article 119 EEC referring to action on equal pay 'during the first stage' (1962). The Court found that the Article could be relied on after that date. It follows that a provision may be directly effective after any implementation date has been reached.

Vertical and horizontal direct effect

It is particularly important to identify whether any action is *vertical* or *horizontal* to determine its effects:

- *Vertical direct effect* arises where a provision may be enforced by an individual in the national courts against the state or a public body.

- *Horizontal direct effect* arises where a provision may be enforced by an individual in the national courts against other individuals including private bodies.

> **Take note**
>
> The original requirements for direct effect in *Van Gend en Loos* were that the measure was clear, unconditional and not dependent on further action by the Member States. These requirements have been reduced by the Court of Justice to whether it is essentially *practical* to enforce a particular measure, that is, whether it is *sufficiently clear and precise* for the national courts to apply.

Treaties like the TFEU are agreements between states. As *Van Gend en Loos* established, a Treaty obligation may give rise to enforceable rights for individuals where the conditions for direct effect are satisfied. Although the expression 'vertical direct effect' was not used by the Court of Justice in *Van Gend*, the decision provides an example of vertical effect, as the action was against the state. It followed that as the importer could rely on the Treaty Article against the state, he had a defence to the criminal charge in the national court arising from non-payment of import duty.

The Court addressed the enforceability of Treaty provisions between individuals (*horizontal direct effect*) in *Defrenne* (No. 2).

CORNERSTONE

Treaty provisions may be enforced horizontally as well as vertically (Case 43/75 *Defrenne* v. *SA Belge de Navigations Aérienne (SABENA) (No. 2)*).

Gabrielle Defrenne, an air stewardess, invoked Article 119 EEC (now Article 156 TFEU) in an equal pay claim in the Belgian Courts against her employers, Sabena, a private airline. She was paid less than a male steward and had to retire earlier. The Court of Justice held that (old) Article 119 EEC (equal pay for men and women) was directly effective. It was not limited to public authorities but also covered the relationship between individuals.

Article 18 TFEU (ex 12 TEC) prohibiting discrimination on grounds of nationality exemplifies a Treaty provision which is both horizontally and vertically effective. In Case 33/74 *Van Binsbergen* a legal adviser was prevented by a residence requirement from representing his client before the courts in the Netherlands when he moved from that country to Belgium. The Court found that such a restriction infringed the principle of non-discrimination but left it to the national court to see whether it was justified. The principle can be invoked either against a public or private body.

International treaties

International treaties are agreements between sovereign states. It is difficult to formulate a general rule in EU law about the direct effect of international treaties due to the different circumstances in which Treaties are adopted. In Case 104/81 *Kupferberg* the Court of Justice found Article 1 of the Free Trade Agreement between Portugal and the Community to be directly effective, creating enforceable rights for individuals. However, the Court ruled in Opinion 1/91 that the draft *EEA Agreement* was not directly effective as it was intended only to create rights and obligations between the contracting parties (states). The old General Agreement on Tariffs and Trade (GATT) was not directly effective as it was too vague (Cases 21–24/72 *International Fruit*). The World Trade Organization (WTO) Agreement replacing the GATT may arguably be directly effective as it has a stronger enforcement mechanism than the GATT, although Cases C-120/06P & 121/06P *FIAMM* v. *Council and Commission* casts doubt on this possibility.

> **Take note**
>
> The legal position of directives has generated an extensive body of case law. This is an area to which students should pay particular attention as it is very important.

DIRECT EFFECT OF ACTS OF THE INSTITUTIONS

The Treaties provide broad principles but not detailed rules which are found in the acts of the institutions – that is, secondary legislation in the form of regulations and directives (general laws addressed to the Member States), and decisions (addressed to individuals). Clarification may be found in the decisions of the Court of Justice.

Table 7.1 gives an overview of which provisions are vertically and/ or horizontally effective.

Regulations

Regulations are adopted by EU institutions to provide detailed uniform rules for the Member States in areas such as the Common Agricultural Policy. Article 288 TFE (ex 249 TEC) states that a regulation is of general application. In Case C-253/00 *Muñoz* the Court confirmed that a regulation on quality standards for grapes could be enforced in the national courts. The nature of regulations does not prevent them from containing provisions for implementation by Member States. Thus a regulation is not directly effective if worded too vaguely, leaving important features to be devised and implemented by Member States. In Cases C-42 & 45/10 *Vlaamse Dierenartsenvereniging VZW* the Court held that Regulation 998/2003 establishing a model passport for pet dogs, cats and ferrets to move around the EU was not directly effective as it provided for Member States to inscribe data unconnected to EU law.

Table 7.1 Vertical and horizontal effect

	Treaty articles	Regulations	Directives	Decisions	General principles	International agreements
Vertical effect	Yes	Yes	Yes	Yes	Yes	Uncertain
Horizontal effect	Yes	Yes	No	Yes	Yes (probably)	Uncertain

Directives

Directives are addressed to Member States. They are usually expressed in broad terms and may be less detailed than regulations. Directives are binding as to the result to be achieved (such as an obligation to achieve a safe standard of water safety), leaving Member States discretion as to how to implement them ('choice as to form and method') under Article 288 TFEU (ex 249 TEC). Unlike regulations, directives are not described in Article 288 as 'directly applicable'.

CORNERSTONE

Conditions for direct effect

Directives may be directly effective when they are:

- unconditional
- sufficiently precise (Case 41/74 *Van Duyn* v. *Home Office*).

Ms Van Duyn, a Dutch national, was prevented by the Home Office from taking up employment in the UK with the Church of Scientology, an organisation seen as socially harmful but not illegal. The UK government relied on the derogation in Article 48 EEC on free movement of workers on grounds of public policy and public security, set out more fully in Article 3 of Directive 64/221 (replaced by Directive 2004/38). The Court held it would be incompatible with the binding effect of directives if they could not be relied on directly by individuals as it would weaken their useful effect. The Court also held that where implementation is not required, a directive may take effect immediately if the criteria for direct effect are met, ruling that Article 3 of Directive 64/221 enabling a Member State to depart from the principle of free movement of workers was directly effective.

Implementation of directives

A directive may only be enforced directly before the national courts *after the expiry of any deadline for implementation*. In Case 148/78 *Pubblico Ministero* v. *Ratti* an Italian solvent manufacturer sought to defend himself against charges under Italian legislation on labelling of dangerous products, claiming that the products were labelled in accordance with two directives not implemented by the Italian government. The time limit for implementation had expired in relation to one of the two directives. The Court held that although the directives required implementation, they could be directly effective once the deadline had expired. Ratti thus had a defence to one charge but not the other.

After implementation a directive may be invoked to allow individuals access to the courts to whether the implementing authorities acted within their powers (Case 51/76 *Verbond van Nederlands Ondernemingen*) (in relation to a VAT directive where national authorities had some discretion).

Direct effect and national procedural requirements

The relationship between national procedural requirements and directly effective EU law arose relative to limitation periods in Case C-208/90 *Emmott* v. *Minister for Social Welfare*) and upper limits of financial claims in Case C-271/91 *Marshall* v. *South West Hampshire Area Health Authority (No. 2)*. In *Emmott* the applicant had applied for disability benefit in Ireland under Directive 79/7 before the implementation date but was informed by the Irish government that it could not make a decision until the Court of Justice ruled in Case C-377/89 *Cotter and McDermott*. The Court held in *Cotter* that a

Member State cannot take advantage of its unlawful conduct to deprive someone of a remedy under EU law. (The Irish government had relied on a national principle depriving married women of social security benefits contrary to an EU directive). By the time the applicant in *Emmott* applied to the Irish courts for judicial review the action was out of time. The Court held that a Member State cannot rely on a national time limit for proceedings for rights under a directive before the directive has been properly implemented.

In Case C-271/91 *Marshall* v. *South West Hampshire Area Health Authority (No. 2)*, an equal treatment claim over loss suffered from enforced early retirement for women, the Court held that the amount of damages available under a directly effective right in EU law may not be limited under a national statute, leading to removal of upper limits to claims based on EU law in employment tribunals in the UK.

Despite the emphasis in *Emmott* and *Marshall (No. 2)* on *effectiveness* of EU law over national procedural requirements, the Court of Justice distinguished *Emmott* on the facts in Case C-338/91 *Steenhorst-Neerings* (a claim for disability benefit before implementation of Directive 79/7 payable under Dutch law for a maximum period of a year). It ruled that the one-year limitation was not an absolute restriction but served a legitimate purpose of preserving financial balance. The Court reached a similar decision in Case C-410/92 *Johnson* v. *CAO* that a national rule limiting the period for claiming arrears of benefit under Directive 79/7 was compatible with EU law although the directive had not been properly implemented by the deadline.

How far is it possible for an individual to rely on a directive?

While it has been clear since *Defrenne* on equal pay that Treaty provisions may be horizontally effective, the Court of Justice avoided ruling for years on whether a directive may create horizontal direct effect. Instead it developed the principle of indirect effect whereby Member States must interpret national law in accordance with the relevant EU directive (Case 14/83 *Von Colson* v. *Land Nordhein Westfalen*) (see p. 158).

⊕ CORNERSTONE

Vertical effect of directives

Directives may be relied on *vertically* against the state or a public body *but not horizontally* against an individual (Case 152/84 *Marshall* v. *Southampton and South West Area Health Authority (Teaching) (No.1)*.

Take note

Ms Marshall succeeded in her claim under Directive 76/207 in the UK courts because she was employed by an area health authority, found to be a public body. Had she worked for a private body, her claim would have failed.

Marshall (No. 1) resolved uncertainty over the direct effect of directives. Ms Marshall brought an action against her employer when compelled to retire at sixty while male employees could work to sixty-five. She relied on Article 5 of the Equal Treatment Directive 76/207 as English law permitted different retirement ages for men and women under the Sex Discrimination Act 1975. The Court of Appeal sought guidance from the Court of Justice which held that a directive may be enforced against the state or a public body. The ruling means that a directive produces *vertical but not horizontal* direct effects, a significant limitation for the rights of individuals reflecting the unwillingness of Member States to diminish the status of national laws implementing directives.

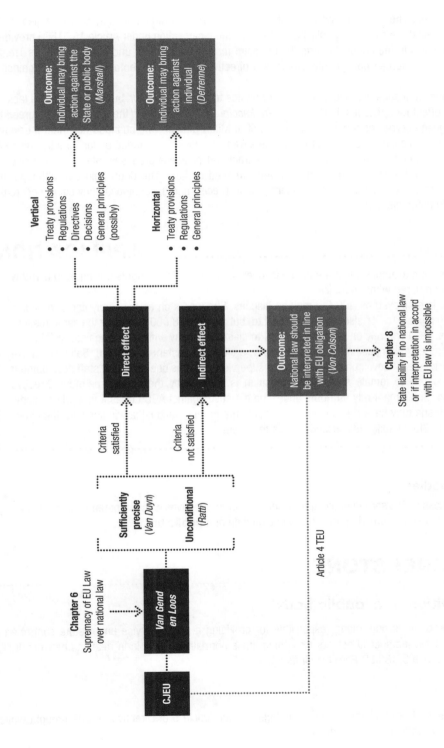

Figure 7.1 The principles of direct and indirect effect

Marshall was the first decision in which the Court ruled that directives may only be relied upon vertically against the state or a public body. Thus an equal pay action under Article 157 TFEU provides a stronger basis in the national courts than a claim for equal treatment under a directive, as Treaty rights may be enforced horizontally, whereas a directive may only be enforced vertically against a public body.

The Court of Justice has had several opportunities to review *Marshall*, but has upheld the lack of horizontal effect for directives. In Case C-91/92 *Faccini Dori* v. *Recreb Srl* the applicant had agreed to buy a language correspondence course on credit at Milan Station. She changed her mind four days later and tried to cancel the contract within the seven-day cooling off period under Directive 85/577, a consumer protection measure applying to contracts off business premises. She could not rely on national law as the directive had not been implemented by Italy. The Court held that although the relevant parts of the directive were sufficiently clear, precise and unconditional they could *not* create horizontally enforceable rights.

APPLICATION

The following examples illustrate the consequences of the different rights arising from a Treaty Article compared with a directive.

Jane is employed by ABC Ltd making biscuits. She works on an assembly line and is paid £22,000 a year. Trevor also works for ABC Ltd, but is paid £28,000 a year for the same responsibilities. Jane can rely on Article 157 TFEU to claim equal pay with Trevor against ABC Ltd.

Compare Jane's position with that of Sally, a clerical assistant at ABC Ltd. Sally would like to undertake staff development to train as a supervisor, but has been told that staff development is unavailable to female staff. Sally's position is covered by the Equal Treatment Directive 2006/54. She cannot rely on rights under the directive against ABC Ltd as it is a private body, although she may have rights in indirect effect (interpreting national law in line with the directive) or in State liability (discussed later in the chapter).

Public bodies

The harshness of *Marshall* in denying horizontal effect to directives was tempered to some degree by the Court of Justice's broad approach to the definition of a **public body**.

CORNERSTONE

Definition of a 'public body'

A 'public body' is one 'made responsible for providing a public service under state control and which possessed special powers exceeding those normally applicable in relations between individuals' (Case C-188/89 *Foster* v. *British Gas*).

Foster arose from a claim for equal treatment under Article 5 of Directive 76/207 brought while British Gas was still in public ownership.

CONTEXT

The UK Conservative government under Margaret Thatcher in the 1980s undertook a major programme to privatise state-run bodies supplying gas, electricity, water and telephone services, leading to the creation of bodies such as British Telecoms, formed as companies with shareholders. Aware that UK privatisation was imminent, the Court of Justice provided guidance on the meaning of 'public body' in *Foster*.

Ms Foster was employed in the UK by British Gas where female employees had to retire at sixty whereas men could continue to work until sixty-five under the Sex Discrimination Act 1975. She brought an action against her employer, seeking to rely on Directive 76/207 providing for equal treatment for men and women. The application was dismissed by the Employment Appeal Tribunal as British Gas was not a public body. The House of Lords referred to the Court of Justice to clarify the meaning of 'public body'. The Court established that a 'public body' must:

1. provide a public service under a measure adopted by the state;
2. be controlled by the state;
3. hold special powers greater than those normally held between individuals.

The House of Lords found that British Gas was a public body. The applicant could therefore rely on Directive 76/207 which took precedence over conflicting provisions of the Sex Discrimination Act 1975.

APPLICATION

Consider the status in EU law of a company responsible after privatisation for transporting prisoners between prison and court. The company provides a public service under state control. It has special powers to restrain prisoners. The company would satisfy the definition in *Foster* and would be treated as a public body under a directive.

Foster was criticised by academic commentators such as Curtin (1990) for providing only limited assistance with the definition of a public body. Later decisions of the Court of Justice have supplied examples of public bodies including:

- the Chief Constable of the Royal Ulster Constabulary when acting as an employer or as an organ of the state (Case 222/84 *Johnston* v. *RUC*, an equal treatment claim brought by a woman police officer employer by the RUC);

- a university (Cases C-250 & 268/09 *Georgiev* v. *Tehnicheski Universitet-Sofia*, an age discrimination claim in relation to compulsory retirement by a professor against a university in Bulgaria);

- a hospital receiving public funding and performing a public service but run autonomously with its own directors (Case C-180/04 *Vassallo* v. *Azienda Ospedaliera Ospedale San Martino di Genova*).

Most privatised utilities in the UK, such as British Telecoms and providers of water, gas and electricity, are public bodies within the ruling in *Foster*. In *Griffin* v. *South West Water* (1995) the UK High Court held that a privatised water company was covered. The Court of Appeal, however, found that Rolls-Royce was not a public body as it lacked the necessary special powers and responsibilities despite being wholly owned by the Crown at the time (*Doughty* v. *Rolls-Royce plc*) (1992). The Court

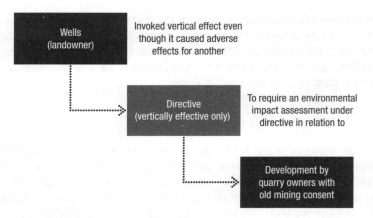

Figure 7.2 'Triangular' situations: *Wells*

of Appeal ruled in an unfair dismissal case in *NUT* v. *St Mary's Church of England Junior School* (1997) that governors of a voluntary-aided school were a public body 'charged by the state with running the school' which was part of the state system and regulated by Act of Parliament.

'Triangular' situations

The Court of Justice has acknowledged that vertical direct effect may be invoked against the state even where it gives rise to adverse consequences for another individual, as in Case C-201/02 *Wells* (see Figure 7.2) where a landowner sought to invoke a directive to deny the owner of a nearby quarry the right to extract minerals. An old mining permission had been granted in 1947 when competent authorities could give consents due to the need for building materials after the Second World War. In 1991 the Planning and Compensation Act provided that if no substantial development (i.e. mining) had taken place in the previous two years, mining could only be undertaken after registration. The quarry owners applied for registration which was granted subject to later conditions by the Secretary of State. These did *not* include an environmental impact assessment (EIA) required under Directive 85/337 for projects likely to have significant effects on the environment, although the quarry was near sites designated as environmentally sensitive. Mrs Wells whose house was on the other side of the road from the quarry applied for judicial review of the Secretary of State's failure to undertake an EIA. The UK High Court sought guidance from the Court of Justice which held that the directive could be relied on by the applicant to require an EIA, even though it would cause adverse repercussions on third parties (the quarry owners).

Decisions

Unlike regulations and directives, a generalised form of legislation, decisions are particular and limited in their scope under Article 288 TFEU (ex 249 TEC), being addressed to individuals rather than Member States. Nevertheless, it has been accepted in principle that decisions may be directly effective where the criteria for direct effects are satisfied, as the Court held in Case 9/70 *Grad* v. *Finanzamt Traunstein*. A company challenged a tax imposed by the German government which it claimed contravened a VAT directive and a decision setting a time limit for implementation. The Court held that decisions are capable of creating direct effects.

Article 288 TFEU provides that a decision is binding 'in its entirety upon those to whom it's addressed'. It is thus necessary to examine decisions individually to determine whether they are directly effective – usually only where the decision had some sort of legislative character. While it is hard to find examples of decisions found to create horizontal direct effects, there are several decisions found by the Court *not* to do so such as Case C-80/06 *Carp Snc* v. *Ecorad Srl*. This case arose from a dispute before the Italian courts between a builder and a supplier of building materials. The builder, Carp, claimed that doors supplied by Ecorad did not meet European harmonised CE standards in an EC decision adopted under a directive as no certificate of compliance had been issued. The decision was an act of general application addressed to Member States and could not be relied upon in an action between individuals. However, it appears to follow that if the decision had been addressed to individuals, it could have been horizontally effective.

General principles of law

General principles such as equality derive from the general principles of the Member States and from international law. (General principles as a source of law are covered in Chapter 5.) The scope of general principles for creating direct effects was regarded as limited until the decision of a Grand Chamber of the Court in Case C-144/04 *Mangold* v. *Helms*. This case arose from a referral by a German court seeking clarification of the law on age discrimination under Directive 2000/78 providing a general framework for equality legislation. Mangold, a fifty-six-year-old German lawyer, entered into a contract of employment with Helms for a fixed term from 2003 to 2004, under German law which allowed fixed-term contracts for workers over fifty-two years to encourage employment of older workers, although such contracts were subject to the EU Framework Agreement 1999/70. He claimed in the German courts that the agreement discriminated on grounds of age contrary to Directive 2000/78. The German court referred to the Court of Justice which held it was the national courts' responsibility to guarantee effectiveness of the principle of non-discrimination on grounds of age by setting aside any conflicting provision of national law, even before the expiry of the period for transposition. The Court ruled that *non-discrimination on grounds of age was a general principle of Union law* deriving from international treaties and the Member States, an approach which neatly sidestepped the problem of declaring the directive to be horizontally effective. It then found that the directive had to be applied by the German courts.

Although *Mangold* was not cited in several later decisions on age discrimination, the Court of Justice upheld it in Case C-555/07 *Kücükdeveci* v. *Swedex*, ruling that non-discrimination on grounds of age is a general principle of EU law, to which Directive 2000/78 gives expression. It followed in *Kücükdeveci* that national legislation failing to recognise work done below the age of twenty-five when calculating the notice period for dismissal was incompatible with the principle and should not be applied. The Court repeated the duty to interpret national law in line with EU law under *Marleasing* (discussed below), a duty implied in the Treaties, enabling national courts to give full effect to EU law when deciding cases.

Despite *Mangold* and *Kücükdeveci*, uncertainty remains on how far general principles are horizontally effective.

The Court of Justice's acknowledgment of the horizontal effect of general principles has been criticised for providing 'an excuse for "competence creep" via judicial activism' (i.e. acquisition of more powers for the EU through decisions of the Court without Treaty reform). Laenaerts and Gutiérez-Fons (2010) defend the Court, observing that '[F]or general principles to carry out their constitutional task properly the role of the judiciary cannot simply be that supported by Montesquieu [under the traditional doctrine of the separation of powers] according to which judges are limited to acting as mouthpieces for the law. The application of general principles entails a more proactive type of adjudication whereby courts are often called upon to address politically charged questions left unsolved by the political process.' It is clear that the Court has adopted a more creative role in developing the law than is open to the national courts. More decisions on the relationship between general principles and discrimination will surely follow.

INDIRECT EFFECT

Take note

Article 5 EEC was an important provision, requiring Member States to take 'all appropriate measures, whether general or particular, to ensure fulfilment of the obligations arising out of this Treaty'. Article 4(3) TEU repealed and replaced Article 10 TEC following the Treaty of Lisbon.

You have already seen in this chapter that only provisions of EU law which satisfy the requirements laid down by the Court of Justice are regarded as directly effective. This does not mean that Member States may disregard provisions lacking direct effect as they are bound by the obligation to observe EU law, now contained in Article 4 TEU, known as the *principle of effectiveness or sincere cooperation*. It requires Member States:

- to assist each other in carrying out their tasks under the Treaties;
- to ensure fulfilment of their obligations under the Treaties or acts of the institutions;
- to facilitate the achievement of the Union's tasks;
- to refrain from measures which could jeopardise the Union's tasks.

The Court relied on Article 5 EEC (later Article 10 TEC, now Article 4 TEU) to develop the principle of indirect effect in Case 14/83 *Von Colson* v. *Land Nordhein-Westfalen*.

Von Colson arose from a claim under the Equal Treatment Directive 2006/207 by an unsuccessful female applicant for a job in a male prison in Germany. When not appointed she claimed damages in the German courts which found that the rejection was based on gender but was justifiable and awarded damages limited to travelling expenses. The applicant argued that the award contravened Article 6 of the Equal Treatment Directive 76/207 (requiring Member States to introduce the necessary remedies to enable equal treatment claims to be pursued through the judicial process). The Court of Justice held that Article 6 was not clear enough to be directly effective. It ruled that the national courts were bound by Article 10 TEC to achieve the result in the directive. It follows that Member States must interpret national law so as to give effect to the obligations under the directive.

The duty of consistent interpretation

Indirect effect arises when a national court is faced with the need to interpret national law implementing a directive or predating it. The principle requires national courts to interpret national law in light of the wording and purpose of the directive, sometimes called the *duty of consistent interpretation*. *Von Colson* was decided before the ruling in *Marshall* that directives may only be enforced vertically, and represents an alternative way of ensuring that EU law may be enforced in the national courts. The duty has been upheld in decisions such as Case C-106/89 *Marleasing* v. *La Comercial* and Case C-91/92 *Faccini Dori*.

In Case C-106/89 *Marleasing* a Spanish company (Marleasing) brought an action before the Spanish courts to annul the memorandum and articles of association of the defendant company, La Comercial. The applicant claimed that the defendant had been established to put its assets beyond the reach of creditors including Marleasing, and that the company was null and void for infringement of the Spanish Civil Code due to 'lack of cause'. La Comercial argued that lack of cause was not specified in Directive 68/151 which exhaustively lists the grounds for the invalidity.

The Court of Justice held that a national court must interpret national law *as far as it is possible to do so in the light of the wording and purpose of the directive, regardless as to whether the law was adopted before or after the directive.* This obligation derives from the need to achieve the result required by the directive under Article 249 TFEU. It followed that the Spanish court was obliged to interpret the Civil Code so as to rule out a declaration of nullity on grounds other than those listed in the directive.

The clarification of the duty of consistent interpretation in *Marleasing* is important as it is clear that it applies to national laws adopted both *before* and *after* the relevant EU law. However, the wording in the ruling 'as far as possible' provides an escape route for a national court unable to interpret national law consistently with EU law, in which the state may incur liability if the conditions in *Brasserie* are satisfied (see Chapter 8).

CORNERSTONE

Pfeiffer

The duty of consistent interpretation covers the whole system of national law, not merely implementing legislation (Case C-397/01 *Pfeiffer* v. *Rotes Kreuz*).

Pfeiffer arose from a requirement for emergency workers to work more than forty-eight hours a week contrary to Article 6 of the Working Time Directive 93/104. The applicants were employed by the German Red Cross, a private body, as ambulance drivers. The directive had been transposed into German law which provided an exception for emergency workers who had to spend significant periods of time on stand-by awaiting call-out. The German court sought guidance from the Court of Justice on the meaning of Article 6 of the directive. The Court (sitting as a Grand Chamber) held that Article 6 of Directive 93/104 had vertical but not horizontal effect.

The Court clarified the scope of indirect effect in such circumstances, repeating the duty to interpret national law in accordance with the directive under *Von Colson*. It noted that this duty 'is inherent in the system of the Treaty, since it permits the national court . . . to ensure the full effectiveness' of EU law when deciding disputes. This time the Court went further, adding a requirement for courts to give full effectiveness to EU law by taking national law *as a whole* into consideration, not merely the implementing provision. It held that:

It is the responsibility of the national court, hearing a dispute involving the principle of non-discrimination in respect of age, to provide . . . the legal protection which individuals derive from the rules of Community [EU] law and to ensure that those rules are fully effective, setting aside any provision of national law which may conflict with that law.

It follows that national courts must make full use of *all* available existing approaches to statutory interpretation, following a purposive rather than a literal approach; a requirement described by Klamart (2006) as giving the interpretation obligation 'a new level of urgency'.

APPLICATION

Imagine that a directive requires Member States to introduce a new procedure to resolve employment disputes. Italy does not introduce legislation as a similar procedure is already in use under legally binding collective bargaining agreements (covering terms of employment between employers and the unions) provided union members of the biggest unions agree that the dispute is 'serious'. A dispute occurs, but union members do not agree it is 'serious'. A disaffected union member claims he has been denied access to dispute resolution procedure and brings an action in the national courts, claiming that the collective bargaining agreement should be interpreted in accordance with the directive. Applying *Pfeiffer*, the national court should not adopt a restrictive approach to statutory interpretation but should interpret the collective bargaining agreements in accordance with the directive. If this is impossible, the agreements should be set aside.

Limits on the duty of consistent interpretation

The Court of Justice has imposed limits on the duty of consistent interpretation. Case 80/86 *Kolpinghuis Nijmegen* arose from a referral from criminal proceedings against a café proprietor in the Netherlands where tap water and carbon dioxide was sold as 'mineral water' under a local regulation interpreted in light of an unimplemented EC directive. This required Member States to adopt measures to ensure that only water extracted from the ground as natural mineral water may be sold as such. The Court held that a directive cannot have indirect effect in criminal proceedings when it would cause the accused to be convicted when he would otherwise have been acquitted.

In Case C-168/95 *Arcaro* the Court held that the obligation to interpret national law in line with a directive *reaches a limit where the obligation has not been transposed*. Here Italian law had failed to implement directives requiring prior notification of *all* rather than merely *new* discharges of cadmium, a highly poisonous substance. Criminal liability could not be imposed on the basis of an obligation under the directive.

Another limitation arises in relation to the deadline for implementation. The Court held in Case C-212/04 *Adeneler* that the *full duty of consistent interpretation only applies after the deadline has been reached*. Before the implementation date, national courts should interpret in accordance with the ruling in Case C-129/96 *Environnement Wallonie* v. *Région Wallone* which requires Member States not to adopt legislation which could seriously compromise achieving the result required by the directive.

APPLICATION

Imagine that the EU has adopted a directive imposing new standards for discharge of sewage into rivers within specified limits for implementation by 1 January 2013. The UK adopts a statute regulating discharge into rivers from 1 June 2012, but allowing discharge above the limits permitted in the directive. Such action would infringe EU law under *Environnement Wallonie* as it compromises the objectives of the directive. If the UK had adopted a law permitting discharge of sewage into rivers 'within reasonable limits', it should be possible to interpret the national law in accordance with the directive, but only after 1 January 2013.

Incidental horizontal effect

While the Court's position that directives do not create horizontal direct effects has been maintained in *Marleasing* and *Webb* v. *EMO*, some academic commentators have seen later decisions of the Court of Justice as supporting the possibility that directives may incidentally create horizontal effects for third parties. (Tridimas (2000) examines the differing explanations.) The case law is inconclusive.

Case C-194/94 *CIA Security* v. *Signalson and Securitel* arose from Belgium's failure to notify a national regulation implementing a technical standards directive to the Commission. CIA Security had brought an action in the Belgian courts against Signalson and Securitel to stop their unfair trading practices. CIA argued it had been libelled by the two companies when they claimed the alarm system marketed by CIA had not been approved under Belgian law. While acknowledging that it had not sought approval, CIA claimed that the Belgian requirement contravened the free movement of goods under EU law and had not been notified to the Commission under Directive 83/189. The Court ruled that a breach of the duty to notify implementing legislation rendered the national law *inapplicable*, holding that the directive was intended to protect the free movement of goods from preventive control. As the national law had not been notified, it would enhance effectiveness of the control if it were *not* applied to individuals. The decision provided the applicant with an *incidental benefit*, enabling CIA to rely on the directive in the national courts even though it did not impose direct obligations on Signalson and Securitel.

A similar ruling followed in Case C-443/98 *Unilever Italia SpA* v. *Central Food SpA*. The Court of Justice was asked to consider the status of technical regulations notified to the Commission but which infringed Directive 83/189. The parties had a contract to deliver olive oil. The applicant delivered oil in compliance with the directive's labelling requirements but not with Italian regulations. While acknowledging that directives cannot create horizontal effects, the Court found that case law such as *Faccini Dori* was not relevant where a technical regulation is inapplicable because a Member State has failed to comply with EU requirements. A national court must refuse to apply a technical regulation adopted contrary to a directive.

Another possible, though not necessarily accepted, explanation for the impact of directives on national law derives from the distinction identified by Advocate-General Saggio in Cases C-240–244/98 *Océano Grupo Editorial* v. *Roció Murciana Quintero* between the so-called *exclusionary* and *substitution* effects of directives. The exclusionary effect arises when a directive rules out conflicting national legislation, whereas the substitution effect introduces new rules under the directive, which cannot be relied upon by individuals. *CIA Security* and *Unilever* may be seen as examples of the exclusionary approach.

UK decisions on indirect effect

In *Duke* v. *Reliance Systems Ltd* (HL, 1987) the plaintiff sought damages under the Sex Discrimination Act 1975 which had been amended to comply with the Equal Treatment Directive 76/207. As the amendment was retrospective the House of Lords refused to allow a claim arising out of the period before amendment on the basis that the language of the statute was clear. The *Von Colson* approach was rejected as the basis for interpretation of a UK statute.

INTERSECTION

The inability of the House of Lords to interpret the Act in accordance with Directive 76/207 would potentially have given rise to liability but the decision preceded recognition of State liability in relation to directives in Case C-6/90 *Francovich*. The conditions for State liability were clarified in Case C-46 & 48/93 *Brasserie/Factortame* (considered in Chapter 8).

Unlike *Duke*, the House of Lords in *Litster* v. *Forth Dry Dock Engineering* (HL, 1989) was able to interpret a UK regulation implementing Directive 77/187 safeguarding employee rights on transfer of the undertaking in compliance with the directive. *Litster* is an example of a national court adopting a *purposive* approach to statutory interpretation; that is, construing the English law so as to comply with EU law, even where this involves departing from a strict, literal approach.

REFLECTION

The status of directives continues to generate academic commentary. Do they give rise to incidental horizontal effects? Most commentators think not. According to Dougan (2000) who criticises the exclusionary and substitution theories, *CIA Security* and *Unilever* should be treated as ad hoc exceptions to the rule in *Faccini Dori*, as they belong to a time when the judges were divided on the resolution of direct effect and supremacy in relation to directives and were willing to experiment. Arguably these two awkward decisions are best seen as limited to technical directives rather than as a general basis for the incidental horizontal effect of directives.

Craig (2009) critically examines the arguments underpinning denial of horizontal direct effect to directives. He rejects the Court of Justice's justification of legal certainty in *Wells*, preferring the view of Advocate-General Jacobs that denial of direct effect and ensuing complex exceptions lead to *legal uncertainty*.

The Court of Justice continues to make bold decisions such as its recognition in *Mangold* that general principles may be horizontally effective. However, it seems unlikely that Member States will accept the loss of sovereignty necessary to give directives horizontal effect. The Court has punctured the limitations on the direct effect of directives by allowing for occasional incidental horizontal effect and by acknowledging that they may cause consequences for third parties. There remains little immediate prospect it will declare directives to be horizontally effective.

KEY POINTS

- The Court of Justice has played a central role in developing direct effect, an essential element of the EU legal order under *Van Gend en Loos*, enabling individuals to enforce EU law in the national courts.

- Individuals may rely on Treaty provisions to bring actions in the national courts both vertically against the state or public body and horizontally against another individual (*Defrenne*).

- Regulations may be enforced both vertically and horizontally (*Grad*).

- Decisions (*Grad*) as well as general principles (*Mangold*) can probably be enforced horizontally as well as vertically.

- Directives are vertically effective only (*Marshall*), so cannot be enforced against private individuals, although the Court has mitigated this rule by defining 'public body' widely in *Foster* v. *British Gas*.

- The Court of Justice has developed the concept of indirect effect in *Von Colson*, requiring courts to interpret national law in accordance with the relevant EU obligation. The duty applies as far as it is possible to do so whether the national law was adopted before or after the relevant EU law (*Marleasing*), and must take account of national law as a whole (*Pfeiffer*).

- Failure to implement EU law or adopt a national law which is capable of being interpreted in accordance with the EU obligations may give rise to State liability under *Brasserie/Factortame*.

CORE CASES AND STATUTES

Case	About	Importance
Case 26/62 *Van Gend en Loos* v. *Nederlands Administratie de Belastigen*	Imposition of customs duties in the Netherlands contrary to Article 12 EEC.	EC was 'new legal order' in national and international law based on direct effect and supremacy. It set out criteria for direct effect, modified by its own later decisions.
Case 41/74 *Van Duyn* v. *Home Office*	Dutch national prevented from entering UK to work for Church of Scientology. UK relied on derogation in Article 48(3) EEC and Directive 64/221	Directives can be directly effective where criteria for direct effect are met.
Case 43/75 *Defrenne* v. *Sabena (No. 2)*	Female air stewardess sought to rely on principle of equal pay in Article 119 EEC (now 157 TFEU) when required to retire earlier than male air steward.	Treaty provisions satisfying requirements for direct effect are horizontally effective, so may be enforced by individuals against other individuals.
Case 14/83 *Von Colson* v. *Land Nordrhein-Westfalen*	Female applicant denied job in male prison sought to rely on Article 6 of Equal Treatment Directive 76/207 (requirement for remedies in equal treatment claims).	CJEU relied on Article 5 EEC (now Art. 4 TEU) requiring national courts to provide a remedy by interpreting national law in accord with EC [EU] law.

→

Case	About	Importance
Case C-106/89 *Marleasing SA* v. *La Comercial Internacional de Alimentacion*	Marleasing sought annulment of memorandum and articles of another company under Spanish Civil Code for 'lack of cause', although this was not listed in Directive 68/151 which provides exhaustive list of grounds of annulment.	Develops duty of interpretation – CJEU held that national courts must interpret national law as far as possible in light of wording and purpose of directive, regardless as to whether it was adopted before or after the directive.
Case C-188/89 *Foster* v. *British Gas*	Action brought under Equal Treatment Directive by women employed by British Gas before privatisation.	'Public body' defined as 'made responsible for providing a public service under state control' with special powers greater than those normally applicable between individuals.
Case C-271/91 *Marshall* v. *South West Hampshire Area Health Authority (No.1)*	Woman employed by an area health authority challenged the different retirement ages for men and women under Equal Treatment Directive.	Directives may only be enforced vertically against state or public body.
Cases C-397–403/01 *Pfeiffer and others* v. *Deutsches Rotes Kreuz* (Grand Chamber)	Requirement in Germany for emergency workers to work more than forty-eight hours – the maximum under Working Time Directive 93/104.	National courts must take national law *as a whole* into consideration. They must therefore make use of all available existing approaches to statutory interpretation.
Case C-144/04 *Mangold* v. *Helms*	Claim arising in Germany under Directive 2000/78 providing general framework for equality legislation including age.	Non-discrimination on grounds of age is general principle of EU law deriving from international law and law of Member States.

Statute	About	Importance
Article 4(3) TEU (repealed and replaced Article 10 TEC)	Principle of 'sincere cooperation' requiring Member States to support each other in achieving the Union's tasks or resulting from acts of the institutions, to take general or particular measures to ensure fulfilment of these obligations.	Important underlying obligation. Old Article 10 TEC was invoked to justify development of indirect effect and State liability.
Article 288 TFEU (ex 249 TEC)	Defines 'legal acts of the Union' (regulations, directives and decisions). Provides that regulations are directly applicable.	Directives and decisions may also be directly applicable and directly effective.

FURTHER READING

Craig, P. 'The legal effect of directives: policy, rules and exceptions' (2009) 34 *European Law Review* 349
Reconsiders the legal effect of directives in EU law, critically examining the policy underlying denial of horizontal effect.

Curtin, D. 'The province of government: Delimiting the direct effect of directives in the common law context' (1990) 15 *European Law Review* 195
Includes consideration of meaning of 'public body' after *Foster*.

Dashwood, A. 'From *Van Duyn* to *Mangold* via *Marshall*: Reducing direct effect to absurdity' (2006–7) 9 *Cambridge Yearbook of European Legal Studies* 81
Critical analysis of reasoning in these important decisions.

Dougan, M. 'The disguised vertical direct effect of directives?' (2000) 59 *Cambridge Law Journal* 586
Considers whether 'disguised' vertical direct effect of directives offers a way to reconcile judgments such as *CIA Security* with *Marshall* and *Dori*.

Drake, S. 'Twenty years after *Von Colson*: the impact of indirect effect on the protection of individuals' community rights' (2005) 30 *European Law Review* 329
Analyses the case law of the Court of Justice on indirect effect.

Laenaerts, K. and Gutiérez-Fons, J. A. 'The constitutional allocation of powers and general principles of EU law' (2010) 47 *Common Market Law Review* 1629
Examines the role of general principles in filling the gaps left by the Treaties and secondary legislation.

Pescatore, P. 'The doctrine of direct effect: an infant disease of community law' (1983) 8 *European Law Review* 155
Influential analysis of direct effect by a judge in the Court of Justice.

Tridimas, T. 'Black, white and shades of grey: horizontality of directives revisited' (2002) 21 *Yearbook of European Law* 327
Examines the circumstances in which an unimplemented directive may give rise to horizontal effect.

Winter, T. A. 'Direct applicability and direct effects: two distinct and different concepts in community law' (1973) 8 *European Law Review* 425
This article published forty years ago remains important as it identified the distinction between direct applicability and direct effect, concepts often (confusingly) used interchangeably.

CHAPTER 8

The principle of State liability

BLUEPRINT

The principle of state liability

LEGISLATION

- Article 4(3) TEU
- Article 19(1) TFEU

CONTEXT

- Animal welfare

CONCEPTS

- State liability
- Transposition
- 'Sufficiently serious' breach
- Wide and narrow discretion

- Are national courts reluctant to make rulings against their own government awarding damages for state liability?

- Why should a Member State be free to ignore its obligations under EU law when they are not directly effective?

CASES

- *Francovich*
- *Brasserie/Factortame (No. 3)*
- *Hedley Lomas*
- *Köbler*

SPECIAL CHARACTERISTICS

- Need for effective judicial protection and a complete set of remedies

REFORM

- None proposed

CRITICAL ISSUES

Setting the scene

The Spanish fishermen prevented from fishing by the Merchant Shipping Act 1988 contrary to Community law (see Chapter 6) benefited from a momentous decision (*Factortame (No.5)*) in 1996 when the Court of Justice confirmed that Member States were liable for loss arising from action by a national legislature. The consequences were immense. Member States could be liable for *any* breach of EU law where the conditions were satisfied. This chapter examines the establishment and development of State liability by the Court.

THE ROLE OF THE COURT OF JUSTICE IN DEVELOPING STATE LIABILITY

The Court of Justice has played a central role in developing remedies in EU law as the Treaties do not provide for individuals to have rights in the national courts. The introduction of State liability is the latest remedy developed by the Court to complement the principles of direct and indirect effect.

INTERSECTION

To understand State liability it is essential that you appreciate the role of the Court of Justice in developing direct and indirect effect (see Chapter 7).

Francovich – State liability in relation to directives

Before the introduction of State liability a Member State could evade liability in the national courts under a directive which was not directly effective by failing to implement it. Indirect effect did not help where no national law had been adopted. Even where a directive was directly effective, lack of horizontal effect deprived individuals of a remedy against a private body (Case 152/84 *Marshall*). The Court of Justice developed State liability to fill these gaps, relying on the principle of sincere cooperation in (what is now) Article 4TEU.

CORNERSTONE

Article 4 TEU

Member States shall take any appropriate measure, general or particular, to ensure fulfilment of the obligations under the Treaties or from acts of the EU institutions (Article 4 TEU (ex 10 TEC)).

The principle of State liability was recognised by the Court in Joined Cases C-6, 9/90 *Francovich* and *Bonifaci* v. *Italy*, arising from Italy's failure to implement a directive protecting workers on their employer's insolvency. Francovich and Bonifaci had brought claims in the Italian courts against their employers, a company later declared insolvent. The Court found the directive insufficiently precise

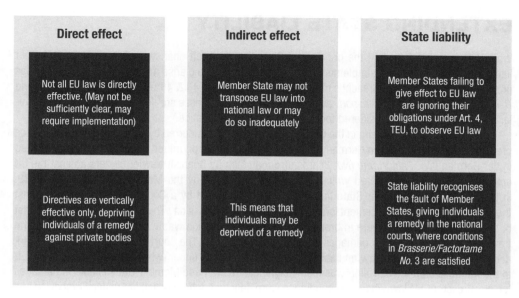

Figure 8.1 Why is State liability necessary?

to be directly effective. As there was no national law, indirect effect provided no remedy. The Court considered it wrong for a Member State to benefit from failing to observe EU law. It turned to the principle of sincere cooperation in Article 5 TEC (now 4 TEU) requiring Member States to observe Community law, finding that the real fault lay with the Member State's failure to implement the directive.

CORNERSTONE

Francovich

Member States are liable for loss under a directive when three conditions are satisfied (Cases C-6, 9/90 *Francovich* and *Bonifaci* v. *Italy*).

The conditions for liability identified by the Court in *Francovich* are:

(a) The directive confers rights for the benefit of individuals.

(b) The content of the rights is identifiable from the directive.

(c) There is a causal relationship between the damage suffered and the breach.

Francovich represents a landmark in EU law, enabling individuals to claim damages in the national courts against a Member State for loss arising under a directive without establishing direct effect. *Francovich* removed any incentive for a Member State to profit from its own default by failing to implement a directive fully or on time. The decision has frequently been upheld including Case C-91/92 *Faccini Dori* (discussed in Chapter 7).

EXTENDING STATE LIABILITY

While *Francovich* established the principle of State liability it left unanswered the question whether liability was restricted to non-implementation of a directive or could arise more widely. Clarification was provided in a ruling on two breaches of EU law, Joined Cases C-46 & 48/93 *Brasserie du Pêcheur* and *R* v. *Secretary of State for Transport, ex p. Factortame (No. 3)*. (Cases are 'joined' when they raise similar issues which can be considered together by the Court of Justice.)

Brasserie arose from a claim in the German courts for losses incurred by a French exporter in Alsace prevented from selling beer in Germany as it contained additives permitted under EU law but prohibited under German law. *Factortame (No. 3)* arose from a claim by Spanish trawler owners against the UK government for losses suffered while prevented from fishing by the Merchant Shipping Act 1988. In both cases the actions for State liability had been preceded by a Court of Justice ruling against the Member State in enforcement proceedings by the Commission. Thus there was no doubt that both Germany and the UK were in breach of EU law. The question was whether the importer and the trawler owners could recover damages from the Member States. The Court of Justice made a landmark decision, applying its case law on liability of the EU institutions under (what is now) Article 340 TFEU to the Member States. The ruling was highly significant as it made Member States liable in damages for *any* breach of EU law where the conditions were satisfied, whereas liability under *Francovich* had only been identified for loss under a directive.

INTERSECTION

The liability of the EU institutions under Article 340 TFEU (ex 288 TEC) is examined in Chapter 10. Where an institution has wide discretion (i.e. freedom of action) the institution is liable if there is a *sufficiently serious* breach.

The Court emphasised in *Brasserie/Factortame (No. 3)* that the same approach to the exercise of discretion should apply to both Member States and the institutions, holding that the 'decisive test' to establish that a breach is sufficiently serious is whether the Member State or institution had 'manifestly and gravely disregarded the limits on its discretion'. Four years later the Court applied this approach to the EU institutions in Case C-352/98P *Laboratoires Pharmaceutiques Bergaderm* v. *Commission* (an unsuccessful damages claim against the Commission by a company making sun protection products for losses under a directive banning an ingredient they alone used). It ruled that what was important was *whether the act involved the use of discretion* and adopted the wording of *Brasserie/Factortame (No. 3)* to define a sufficiently serious breach.

The conditions for State liability

The Court of Justice decided in *Brasserie and Factortame* and *Factortame* that Member States are liable for infringement of EU law where three conditions are satisfied. The main change from *Francovich* is the requirement for the breach to be 'sufficiently serious'.

CORNERSTONE

Brasserie/Factortame (No. 3)

A Member State is liable for a breach of EU law where:

(a) the rule of law breached is intended to confer rights on individuals;

(b) the breach is sufficiently serious;

(c) there is a direct causal link between the breach and the damage suffered by the injured party.

When is a breach 'sufficiently serious'?

The Court in *Brasserie/Factortame* identified six criteria by which national courts should decide whether the breach is sufficiently serious. Whether:

1. the EU rule breached is clear and concise;

2. Member States have any discretion;

3. the breach or damage was intentional;

4. the mistake was excusable;

5. the institutions contributed to the breach;

6. any national measures contrary to EU law have been retained.

The criteria were upheld in later decisions including Case C-5/94 *R* v. *Minister of Fisheries and Food, ex p. Hedley Lomas* (discussed below).

Other aspects of the ruling in Brasserie/Factortame

Brasserie/Factortame (No. 3) also established that Member States may not demand a higher standard than a 'sufficiently serious breach' for liability. Compensation must be proportionate to the loss or damage suffered and should be determined by national law in the absence of EU law. Specific damages such as exemplary damages may be awarded if available in similar national claims.

> **Take note**
>
> Actions for State liability should be brought in the national courts, not in the Court of Justice, a mistake students often make. Most State liability actions are contested and referred to the Court of Justice. Member States cannot limit their liability to damages sustained after delivery of a judgment by the Court of Justice in enforcement proceedings as individuals have a right to bring proceedings in the national courts.

Although the Court of Justice in *Brasserie/Factortame (No. 3)* found that *national courts* should determine what constitutes a breach, it indicated that both cases arose in the context of 'wide discretion'. The Court stated that the UK's breach in *Factortame* should be regarded as 'sufficiently serious' to incur liability, whereas the position in relation to Germany in *Brasserie* was less clear. This guidance proved influential as the Spanish trawler owners succeeded in their action against the UK whereas the importer in *Brasserie* did not.

Clarifying 'sufficiently serious breach'

After *Brasserie/Factortame (No. 3)* the Court of Justice clarified what constitutes a sufficiently serious breach in later rulings, in view of the *discretion* which the Member State possesses. 'Discretion' means

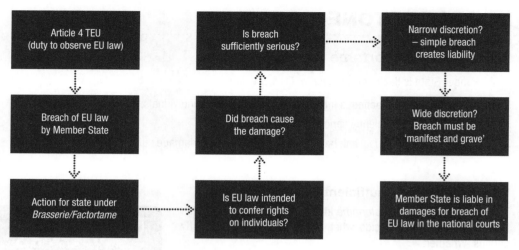

Figure 8.2 Actions for State liability in the national courts

the degree of freedom, determined by the EU, for the Member State to choose how it achieves an EU obligation. Discretion may be *narrow, non-existent* or *wide*. Thus a directive requiring Member States to label foods which include specified additives would involve narrow discretion, whereas another directive requiring a 'reasonable standard of safety' in selling foods would allow wide discretion.

The rules for narrow or non-existent discretion make it easier to establish State liability than where the discretion is wide.

CORNERSTONE

Breach with narrow or no discretion

Mere infringement of EU law may be a sufficiently serious breach where the Member State is in no position to make legislative choices and has little or no discretion (Case C-5/94 *R* v. *Minister of Fisheries and Food, ex p. Hedley Lomas*).

The referral in *Hedley Lomas* followed refusal by the Ministry of Agriculture, Fisheries and Food (MAFF) to grant licences to export live animals to Spain for slaughter due to concern over slaughterhouse conditions there.

Concern in Europe about possible cruelty to animals due for slaughter led the EU to adopt a directive in 1974 to ensure that animals were stunned before they were slaughtered. The UK did not accept that the directive was being observed in Spain.

While the export ban imposed by the Ministry of Agriculture restricted the freedom to export goods contrary to Article 35 TFEU, the UK sought to rely on a derogation (exception) in Article 36 on grounds of the life or health of animals. However, the UK had *no* discretion to impose such a ban as the EU had adopted a directive on slaughterhouse conditions. Although the UK had complained to the Commission about Spanish slaughterhouses, the Commission dropped its investigation after Spain provided assurances it would comply. The Court of Justice upheld the conditions for liability in *Brasserie/Factortame*, repeating that the test for a sufficiently serious breach is whether the Member State has 'manifestly and gravely' disregarded the limits of its discretion. It follows that when a Member State with little or no freedom of action infringes EU law, *any* breach of EU law will be sufficiently serious to result in State liability.

....APPLICATION

Imagine the EU adopts a directive in 2011 requiring Member States to compensate farmers with crops affected by Wheat Mould. The UK adopts regulations in 2012 to implement the directive but repeals them in 2013, claiming that the scheme is unaffordable in a recession. Harry, a farmer, has gone out of business due to losses from Wheat Mould, but has been told by the UK government that compensation is no longer available. He may bring an action for State liability against the UK for its breach in repealing the regulations. As the UK had no discretion, its action was a sufficiently serious breach of EU law to incur liability.

The Court of Justice followed *Hedley Lomas* in Case C-470/03 *AGM-COS.MET Srl* v. *Suomenvaltio and Tarmio Lehtinen* over an EU directive requiring Member States to grant market access to enable certain types of equipment to be sold. A state official in Finland wrote a report, later appearing on television declaring that vehicle lifts from Italy were unsafe. The Italian producers sued the Finnish state and the official. The Court held that as the directive left Member States with no discretion, failure to comply made the breach sufficiently serious. It also found that the State could incur liability from statements made by public officials where they could be attributed to the State.

Cases 178 etc./94 *Dillenkofer* v. *Federal Republic of Germany* arose from Germany's failure to implement the package holidays directive (adopted to protect tourists on the tour operator's insolvency). The Court held that *failure to implement a directive on time* amounts to a sufficiently serious breach. In Case C-140/97 *Rechberger* v. *Austria*, on the same directive, the Court found that *incorrect transposition* of a directive into national law may be sufficiently serious where the Member State has no discretion.

In Case C-452/06 *R* v. *Licensing Authority of the Department of Health, ex p. Synthon* the UK refused to allow a drug produced in the Netherlands to be marketed although it had been approved by the Dutch authorities. The refusal was sufficiently serious as the UK had no discretion, having failed to invoke a special procedure on marketing drugs for human consumption.

Breach with wide discretion

It is more difficult to establish liability where there is considerable national discretion, as Case C-392/93 *R* v. *HM Treasury, ex p. British Telecommunications plc* illustrates. The UK had transposed an ambiguously worded directive on procurement (tendering for contracts) in telecommunications. BT claimed it lost an order due to the UK's approach to implementation. The Court held that the UK's misunderstanding of the directive was excusable as it had unsuccessfully sought help on interpretation from the Commission and had acted in good faith. Such a breach was insufficiently serious to produce State liability.

Lack of clarity also prevented a directive from giving rise to State liability in Case C-278/05 *Robins* v. *Secretary of State for Work and Pensions*. This case concerned a claim against the UK government for losses from failure to transpose fully Directive 80/987 on inter-company pension schemes on insolvency. The Court found that Article 8 of the directive lacked clarity and precision. State liability would only arise if the Member State had manifestly and gravely exceeded the limits of its discretion, which was not the case. The Court adopted similar reasoning in Case C-283etc/94 *Denkavit International* v. *Bundesamt für Finanzen* concerning incorrect transposition of a directive on taxation by the German government. It was influenced by the fact that most other Member States had adopted the same approach as Germany and that there was no case law on the subject. The breach was not sufficiently serious for State liability.

> **REFLECTION**
>
> Tridimas (2001) has noted that most references to the Court on State liability come from a limited number of states with a reasonably good record for observing EU law such as Austria, Germany, Sweden and the UK, suggesting that some Member States are not making references when they should. As State liability cases are normally contested by Member States, this may mean that national courts are not giving full effect to EU law. While it is difficult to assess *inaction* by national courts unless it is reported, failure by national courts to give full effect to EU law may itself give rise to an action for State liability, as Case C-224/01 *Köbler* v. *Austria* confirmed.

CORNERSTONE

State liability and the national courts

The principle of State liability applies to all organs of state including the judiciary, but 'only in the exceptional case where the court has manifestly infringed the law' (Case C-224/01 *Köbler* v. *Austria*).

Köbler arose from an entitlement for professors to a long-service increment if they had worked fifteen years in Austria. Professor Köbler claimed for time spent at universities in Austria and other Member States. The Austrian court referred the case to the Court of Justice but withdrew it on the advice of the Court Registrar who had assumed the question had been resolved by another ruling that such an increment conflicted with the free movement of workers. The Austrian court then reclassified the increment as a 'loyalty bonus', resulting in loss of payment to the applicant who sued the Austrian government. The Court of Justice was asked to rule whether the Austrian court had 'manifestly infringed' EU law by failing to make a second referral which would effectively have determined compatibility of the national provision with the Treaties. The Court held that a national court of last resort may incur State liability if it fails to make a reference only where it has 'manifestly infringed the applicable law'. Liability should be assessed in view of all the factors before the court including the degree of clarity and precision of the rule infringed, whether the infringement was excusable, the position taken by any EU institution and non-compliance with an obligation to refer under Article 267(3) TFEU.

Köbler was followed in Case C-173/03 *Traghetti del Mediterraneo*, arising from the Italian government's attempt to restrict State liability of courts of last resort. The Court of Justice held that under no circumstances may a national law impose criteria for State liability stricter than a 'manifest infringement of the applicable law', as stated in *Köbler*. Under *Traghetti* the standard of a 'manifest infringement' must not be too high for applicants to achieve.

It is clear that an individual suffering loss from infringement of EU law may claim against the Member State where the conditions in *Brasserie/Factortame* are satisfied in a range of circumstances including breaches by the national courts of last resort.

APPLICATION

State liability is often raised in the context of an unimplemented directive. Imagine an individual becomes ill after bathing in polluted water following failure of the UK government to transpose an EU directive establishing a clearly worded water quality standard. The failure to transpose the directive is a sufficiently serious breach in an area of narrow discretion (*Dillenkofer*). A directive relating to water standards would be seen as creating rights for individuals. Provided the illness was caused by the pollution, the individual should have a remedy against the UK government. Liability would be unlikely to arise if the directive were ambiguously worded and the Member State had tried, but failed to implement its obligations fully, as in *R* v. *HM Treasury, ex p. British Telecommunications plc*. If the national proceedings raised doubt about the meaning of EU law and the dispute progressed through the national courts to the Supreme Court which refused to refer to the Court of Justice, that refusal too could give rise to State liability.

NATIONAL REMEDIES AND EFFECTIVE JUDICIAL PROTECTION

No requirement to exhaust national remedies

Case C-445/06 *Danske Slagterier* v. *Bundesrepublik Deutschland* arose from Germany's failure to transpose a directive on health conditions for producing and marketing fresh meat, excluding pork from Danish slaughterhouses which did not comply with (illegal) German requirements. The Court found it is not a breach of EU law for a Member State to prevent an individual from claiming compensation where he has wilfully or negligently failed to avoid loss by using a legal remedy provided the national court considers it reasonable to use such a remedy. The ruling meant that a similar provision in the German constitution does not infringe EU law where its use was reasonable.

Case C-118/08 *Transportes Urbanos y Servicios Generales SAL* v. *Administración del Estado* involved an action for damages from Spain's administration of a VAT Directive, which had been found to infringe EU law in Case C-204/03 *Commission* v. *Spain*. The Court applied the principle of equivalence by which the same rules are applied to actions based on EU law as apply to national law. It held that there was no requirement to exhaust national remedies for judicial review before bringing an action for State liability after the fault of the Member State has been established when such a rule is not applied to a comparable action for damages from an alleged breach of the national constitution in the competent national court.

The principle of effective legal protection in EU law

The introduction of State liability is an important development of the principle of effective legal protection in Article 19(1) TEU, requiring Member States to provide sufficient legal remedies in areas covered by EU law. The principle initially emerged through the case law of the Court on direct and indirect effect and was developed and applied in relation to State liability. Together these principles should provide the individual with a complete set of remedies before the national courts in relation to substantive rights such as the exercise of free movement of goods and procedural rights such as the right to be heard.

State liability was introduced by the Court of Justice to fill the gaps left by direct and indirect effect where the loss resulted from the fault of the Member State. However, it has proved difficult in practice for individuals to succeed in actions before the national courts for State liability, begging the question as to whether the set of remedies really is 'complete'.

Academic commentators are divided as to whether State liability in conjunction with direct effect and indirect effect completes the package of national remedies to the detriment or advantage of the national courts and the individual. Tridimas (2001) argues that, having established State liability as a remedy, the Court of Justice is unwilling to leave discretion to the national courts despite its preparedness to use State liability as a model for EU liability. Dougan (2000) considers there is a danger of the Court of Justice losing confidence in its own capacity to exercise effective judicial supervision over enforcement of Union rights by being too deferential to the national courts. These views reflect a perception that the Court is failing to demonstrate sufficient leadership to the national courts, particularly in recent decisions on State liability. While there is some justification for these criticisms it could be argued that the EU is at a more advanced stage in its development today than in the early years of State liability, and Member States should be trusted to reach their own decisions effectively.

REFLECTION

Approach of the national courts to State liability

Few applications have succeeded in establishing State liability before the national courts despite the growing body of case law in the Court from preliminary referrals. Most State liability cases have turned on whether the breach was sufficiently serious. The German Bundesgerichtshof (Federal Supreme Court) in *Brasserie du Pêcheur* v. *Germany* (1997) found the breach insufficiently serious to award damages. It considered that the act causing loss to the applicants was the denial of the right to sell beer containing additives, and that there was no causal connection between this act and their loss. In the UK, however, the Spanish trawler owners succeeded in obtaining damages against the UK government in *R* v. *Secretary of State for Transport, ex p. Factortame (No. 5)*. The House of Lords confirmed liability, holding that adoption of legislation which discriminated on grounds of nationality over registration of British fishing vessels was sufficiently serious to give rise to liability where individuals suffered loss as a result.

The action in *Three Rivers District Council* v. *Governor and Company of the Bank of England* (1997) failed when the UK High Court held that the First Banking Directive did not intend to confer rights on individuals. This would otherwise have imposed a duty on the Bank of England to protect depositors in BCCI (a failed bank). The Italian courts in *Francovich* found the applicant to be outside the group on whom the Insolvency Directive conferred rights and so unable to claim.

While the introduction of State liability plugged a gap in principle, few claims have led to awards of damages. Actions based on direct and indirect effect stand a much higher chance of success in the national courts as there is no need to prove that the breach is sufficiently serious.

KEY POINTS

- The Court of Justice established the liability of Member States in *Francovich* for loss under a directive based on Article 10 TEC (now Article 4 TEU).
- The Court extended State liability in *Brasserie/Factortame (No. 3)* for all breaches of EU law satisfying certain conditions, particularly the requirement for the breach to be 'sufficiently serious', applying the Court's case law on liability of the EU institutions under Article 340 TFEU to the Member States.
- Liability under *Brasserie/Factortame (No. 3)* depends on the extent of Member States' discretion. A mere breach of EU law may be sufficiently serious where discretion is narrow, whereas, the breach must involve a 'manifest and grave' disregard of limits where discretion is wide.
- Later decisions of the Court have upheld *Brasserie/Factortame (No. 3)* in decisions such as *Hedley Lomas* (wide discretion) and *BT* (narrow discretion).
- State liability was extended to national courts of last resort (*Köbler*) where they fail to refer to the Court of Justice in breach of EU law.

CORE CASES AND STATUTES

Case	About	Importance
Cases C-6 & 9/90 *Francovich* and *Bonifaci* v. *Italy*	Failure to implement directive protecting employees on employer's insolvency.	Established principle of State liability where individual suffers loss from failure to implement directive.
Joined Cases C-46& 48/93 *Brasserie du Pêcheur* v. *Federal Republic of Germany* and *R* v. *Secretary of State for Transport, ex p. Factortame (No. 3)*	*Brasserie* concerned refusal of Germany to allow importation of beer containing additives permitted by EU law. *Factortame* arose from loss suffered by Spanish trawler owners excluded from sharing UK 'catch quota' by UK statute contrary to EU law.	Extended State liability to loss from any provision of EU law where: • rule of law breached is intended to confer rights on individuals; • breach is sufficiently serious; • there is direct causal link between breach and damage. Provided guidance on 'sufficiently serious breach'.
Case C-392/93 *R* v. *HM Treasury, ex p. British Telecommunications plc*	Damages action by BT which claimed it had failed to win contract due to UK's transposition of directive.	UK had wide discretion and had acted in good faith to transpose ambiguously worded directive without assistance from the Commission. Breach was not sufficiently serious.

→

Case	About	Importance
Case C-5/94 *R* v. *Minister of Fisheries and Food, ex p. Hedley Lomas*	Damages claim by exporter refused licence to export live animals to Spain due to UK concern over conditions in Spanish slaughterhouses. UK sought to rely on exception to free movement of goods.	UK had no discretion as EU had adopted directive and Commission had investigated. Simple breach was enough to establish liability.
Cases 178 etc./94 *Dillenkofer* v. *Federal Republic of Germany*	Damages claim from failure by Germany to implement Package Holidays Directive.	Member State had no discretion. Simple breach (failure to implement directive) was sufficiently serious.
Case C-224/01 *Köbler* v. *Austria*	Austrian court of last resort failed to request preliminary ruling under Article 267 TFEU to clarify law on salary increments earned in other Member States.	State liability may result from decisions of national courts in exceptional cases where they have manifestly infringed EU law.

Statute	About	Importance
Article 4(3) TEU (ex 10 TEC)	Requires Member States to: • ensure fulfilment of their obligations under Treaties or acts of institutions; • facilitate achievement of Union's tasks; • refrain from measures which could jeopardise Union's tasks.	Underlying obligation invoked by CJEU to justify State liability.
Article 19(1) TEU	Member States shall provide remedies sufficient to ensure effective legal protection in fields covered by Union law.	Developed by CJEU in relation to direct and indirect effect and State liability. Added to TEU by Treaty of Lisbon.

FURTHER READING

Beutler, R. 'State liability for breaches of community law by national courts: is the requirement of manifest infringement of the applicable law an insurmountable obstacle?' (2009) 46 *Common Market Law Review* 773
Examines State liability by national courts in view of *Köbler* and *Traghetti*.

Dougan, M. 'The *Francovich* right to reparation: reshaping the contours of community remedial competence' (2000) 6 *European Public Law* 103
Analyses the case law on State liability, particularly *Francovich* and *Brasserie*.

Nassimpian, D. '. . . and we keep on meeting: de-fragmenting state liability' (2007) 32 *European Law Review* 819
Critically assesses case law on State liability, drawing parallels between decisions on State liability, Community torts and personal liability.

Scott, H. and Barber, N. 'State liability under *Francovich* for decisions of national courts' (2004) 120 *Law Quarterly Review* 403
Analyses implications of *Köbler* for domestic legal systems.

Tridimas, T. 'Liability for breach of community law: growing up and mellowing down?' (2001) 38 *Common Market Law Review* 301
Critically examines case law since *Francovich* in the context of the Court of Justice's policy on remedies.

CHAPTER 9

Enforcement actions against Member States

Enforcement actions against Member States

LEGISLATION

- TFEU, Articles 258–260

CONTEXT

- Infringements of EU law by Member States such as the long-standing dispute between the UK and Spain over Gibraltar

CONCEPTS

- Pre-litigation procedure
- Reasoned opinion
- Defences
- Reciprosity
- Interim measures
- Direct actions
- Arbitration
- Lump sum and penalty payments
- Mitigation

- How is the balance to be maintained between observance of the EU legal order and good relations between Member States and the EU institutions?

- How is the duty of Member States to observe EU law to be enforced?

CASES

- *Lütticke*
- *Star Fruit*
- *Commission Italy* (Statistical Returns)
- *Commission* v. *France*
- *Commission* v. *Greece*
- *France* v. *UK*
- *Spain* v. *UK*

SPECIAL CHARACTERISTICS

- Discretion of Commission as to whether to proceed with enforcement
- Two-stage procedure (pre-litigation and judicial)

REFORM

- Treaty of Lisbon removed need for reasoned opinion under Art. 260

CRITICAL ISSUES

Setting the scene

In August 2013 a long-standing dispute between the UK and Spain over the status of Gibraltar came to a head. Spain increased its border controls on individuals entering Gibraltar, claiming justification from border abuses such as smuggling. The move followed creation of an artificial reef of concrete blocks near the shore which Spain argued disturbed access to fishing. The UK Prime Minister, David Cameron, complained to the EU Commission that lengthy delays from Spanish border controls infringed EU law. This chapter looks at the central role of the Commission in enforcing EU law where such disputes arise, both informally (as with the Gibraltar dispute) and through the Court of Justice, under Article 258–260 TFEU (ex 226–228 TEC).

A dispute such as that between the UK and Spain over Gibraltar would be discussed informally in a 'pre-litigation' procedure with the Commission. (It is always better to resolve disputes informally, where possible.) If negotiation does not resolve matters, the Commission may issue a reasoned opinion setting out the breach and the necessary steps to remedy it. Failure to comply enables the Commission to bring proceedings in the Court of Justice under Article 258 TFEU (ex 226 TEC). If a breach is found, the Court will declare that Spain (or the UK) has infringed EU law, with scope for a fine or penalty under Article 260 TFEU (ex 228 TEC) for ignoring the ruling. If the Commission decides not to proceed, the UK may bring proceedings under Article 259 TFEU (ex 227 TEC). Such actions are rare as they damage relations between Member States.

> Gibraltar is a small but strategically important territory, guarding access to the Mediterranean for commercial shipping and military purposes. It was captured from Spain by Anglo-Dutch forces in 1704, ceded to the UK indefinitely under the Treaty of Utrecht in 1713 and given the status of Crown colony in 1830. Spain has never accepted UK sovereignty. The Gibraltar constitution provides that its sovereign status can only be changed with the consent of its people. In a referendum in 2002, voters in Gibraltar rejected a plan for the UK and Spain to share sovereignty. Tension over border controls in Gibraltar has dominated relations between the UK and Spain for many years.

CONTEXT

Take note

Enforcement procedures under Articles 258 to 260 do not provide a remedy for individuals. While those who complain to the Commission that a Member State has allegedly infringed EU law may hope that enforcement will end an apparent breach, there is no guarantee that the Commission will act. Individuals may pursue remedies in the national courts through direct effect, indirect effect and State liability (see Chapters 7 and 8).

ENFORCEMENT AND THE LEGAL ORDER OF THE EU

Article 4 TEU (ex 10 TEC) requires Member States to observe EU law. The Commission has a duty under Article 17 TEU to ensure that the Treaties and measures adopted under them are applied. This chapter is mainly concerned with direct actions by the Commission against Member States to enforce EU law under Article 258 and 260 TFEU.

This chapter also covers the procedure under Article 259 TFEU (ex 227) by which Member States may bring enforcement proceedings, and Article 260 TFEU (ex 228 TEC) which enables the Commission to seek imposition of financial penalties where an infringement has been established by the Court of Justice.

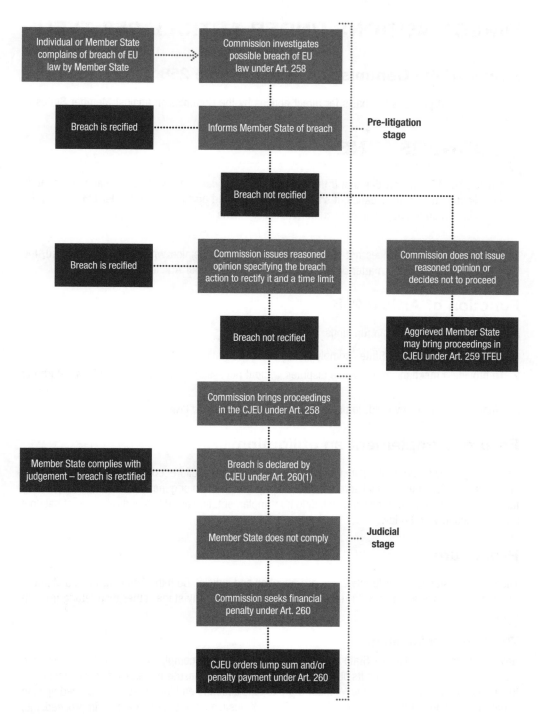

Figure 9.1 Enforcement under Articles 258–260 TFEU

DIRECT ACTIONS UNDER ARTICLE 258 TFEU

Power of the Commission under Article 258

Article 258 TFEU provides the basis for direct actions by the Commission against Member States in breach of EU law.

CORNERSTONE

Article 258(1) TFEU provides that if the Commission considers a Member State has failed to fulfil an obligation under the Treaties, it shall deliver a reasoned opinion on the matter after giving the state concerned the opportunity to submit its observations.

If the state concerned does not comply with the reasoned opinion within the period stated, the Commission may bring the matter before the Court of Justice under Article 258(2).

Function of Article 258

Article 258 serves three main functions:

1. To ensure that Member States comply with their EU obligations.
2. To provide a mechanism to resolve disputes without necessarily involving proceedings before the Court.
3. Where the Court is involved, to provide general guidance on EU law.

Failure to implement an obligation

Proceedings may be brought against any state or state agency. 'Failure' covers any breach of EU law, under the Treaties, international agreements, secondary legislation or general principles of law. It may take the form of an act or omission, including non-implementation of EU law and retention of national laws conflicting with EU law.

Procedure

There are two stages under Article 258 – pre-litigation and judicial. Both the Commission and Member State involved have an interest in resolving the dispute at an early stage rather than letting it reach the Court.

The pre-litigation stage

Having informed the Member State concerned of the grounds of complaint under Article 258(1), the Commission invites it to submit its observations. The Commission issues a *reasoned opinion* recording the infringement and requiring the Member State to take action to end the breach. A reasoned opinion cannot be challenged in the General Court or Court of Justice as it is merely a step in proceedings, not a binding act (Case 48/65 *Alfons Lütticke GmbH* v. *Commission* where the applicant challenged a reasoned opinion over a tax which the company claimed infringed EU law).

If a Member State does not accept the opinion it may move to the second stage before the Court of Justice. In deciding whether or not to issue a reasoned opinion, and bring proceedings in the Court, the Commission acts as a college. Such decisions cannot be taken by a Commissioner alone but 'must be the subject of collective deliberation by the college of Commissioners' (Case C-191/95 *Commission* v. *Germany*). Germany challenged the reasoned opinion issued by the Commission over alleged infringement of a directive on disclosure of information in company accounts. The Court found that the Commission had indeed acted as a college when they decided to issue a reasoned opinion as they had acted collectively with knowledge of all the necessary information on facts and law.

The Commission usually imposes a *time limit for compliance* in the reasoned opinion. If no time is stated, a Member State should comply within a reasonable time. While the Court may dismiss an action where the Commission has allowed insufficient time (as it did in Case 293/85 *Commission* v. *Belgium (Re University Fees)*), the period may be shorter in urgent cases. A period of seven days to respond to the formal letter and fourteen to the reasoned opinion was accepted in Case C-328/96 *Commission* v. *Austria*. The Court cannot change the limit imposed by the Commission (Case 28/81 *Commission* v. *Italy*, where Italy had failed to implement a directive on requirements for road haulage operators. Its request to extend the time for compliance in the reasoned opinion was rejected.)

The Commission is not obliged to disclose a draft reasoned opinion where it does not proceed as it is merely a preparatory document. In Case T-309/97 *Bavarian Lager Company Ltd* v. *Commission* the CFI found that refusal of access to a draft reasoned opinion was justified to safeguard Member States' confidentiality. The applicant, a beer importer, prevented from selling beer in public houses by the UK system of 'tied' houses, had complained to the Commission that UK law infringed EU law on the free movement of goods. The Court accepted that disclosure of the draft reasoned opinion could undermine possible enforcement proceedings against the UK.

No party may *require* the Commission to act under Article 258. Failure to act under Article 258 is not an omission under Article 265 (ex 232 TEC) (Case 247/87 *Star Fruit* v. *Commission*). Star Fruit, a banana trader in Belgium, tried unsuccessfully to challenge the Commission's failure to act under (what is now) Article 265 after complaining about organisation of the banana market in France. As the Commission has complete discretion under Article 258, it is not surprising that the Court dismissed the request in Case C-87/89 *Sonito* v. *Commission* for the Commission to bring enforcement proceedings against Greece and Italy over alleged fraud over aid to tomato producers.

The judicial stage

If a Member State fails to comply with the reasoned opinion within the stated time limit, the Commission may bring proceedings before the Court which conducts a full examination and may review the legality of the Commission's action, as in Case 293/85 *Commission* v. *Belgium*. Enforcement proceedings had been brought over Belgium's failure to remove higher fees charged to students from other EU Member States. Belgium objected to the short periods of time for a response – eight days to reply to the formal notice and fifteen to the reasoned opinion. The Court of Justice considered the periods too short and dismissed the action.

While interested states are entitled to be heard, individuals are not (Case 154/85R *Commission* v. *Italy (Re Import of Foreign Motor Vehicle)*, where vehicle importers were not allowed to intervene in proceedings against Italy).

Defences

Defences to actions under Article 258 rarely succeed, mainly because the pre-judicial stages act as a filter so that only the more difficult to defend cases reach the Court. The Court's Annual Report for

2012 shows that it declared an infringement in 83 cases (87.4%) in 2010, 72 (88.9%) in 2011 and 47 (90.4%) in 2012 in actions for failure to fulfil its obligations, mostly under Article 258. Member States are required by Article 4 TEU to implement EU law fully. Occasionally a state establishes it is not bound by the obligation, for example, where the deadline for implementation of a directive has not yet expired or where the Commission has introduced grounds not in the reasoned opinion, as in Case C-545/10 *Commission* v. *Czech Republic*. The Czech Republic was found to be in breach of a directive on allocating railway infrastructure capacity, but criticism that the Czech Office for the Protection of Competition had not been given sufficient powers was dismissed as it had not been raised in the pre-litigation procedure.

It is unusual for the Court to disagree with the Commission's interpretation of the law. However, Italy succeeded in its defence in Case C-531/06 *Commission* v. *Italy* over alleged infringement of EU law requiring all private pharmacies to be owned and operated by qualified pharmacists. The Court found that Member States were entitled to exercise discretion to protect the public over reliability and quality of medicinal products.

Unsuccessful defences

Member States have submitted a wide range of defences but few have succeeded. Failed defences include:

- *Necessity* (Case 101/84 *Commission* v. *Italy (Re statistical returns)*). The Commission brought proceedings for failure to submit statistical returns since 1979 on carriage of goods by road. The Italian government claimed their records had been destroyed in a bomb attack by a terrorist organisation and put forward a defence of necessity based on *force majeure* ('act of God'). The Court held that the bomb attack did not justify failure to submit returns for four and a half years. While necessity might have been a defence immediately after the attack, it was not available after a lapse of time.

- *Constitutional or political difficulties* (Case 28/81 *Commission* v. *Italy*). Italy unsuccessfully argued that frequent changes of government making it difficult to complete its legislative programme should be a defence in proceedings over failure to implement a directive.

- *Trade union opposition* (Case 128/78 *Commission* v. *United Kingdom (Re Tachographs)*). The UK unsuccessfully claimed that its failure to implement an EU regulation requiring lorry drivers to record hours on the road and rest breaks was due to pressure from trade unions.

- *Claiming that national provisions achieved a higher standard* than their obligations under EU law (Case C-194/01 *Commission* v. *Austria* (failure to transpose a hazardous waste directive)).

- *Introducing the obligation in practice but not in law* (Case 167/73 *Commission* v. *France (Re French Merchant Seamen)*). The French Maritime Code provided for French merchant ships crews to comprise three French nationals for every one non-French, contrary to the principle of non-discrimination in EU law. The French government claimed it did not apply the provision in practice.

- *Reciprosity by another Member State* (i.e. another state also in breach) (Case 232/78 *Commission* v. *France ('Lamb Wars')*). France applied levies and import restrictions to UK lamb. Its defence that the UK operated similar restrictions to protect its own market was rejected.

- *Reciprosity by the EU institutions* (i.e. EU institutions in breach) (Cases 90 & 91/63 *Commission* v. *Luxembourg* and *Belgium*). France and Luxembourg claimed that their charges on imported skimmed milk powder were necessary as the Council had failed to adopt a regulation on the common organisation of the milk products market within the prescribed time. The Court found that a breach by the Council did not justify Member States taking such action.

- *Taking measures claimed to reduce the impact of a breach of EU law without addressing it* (Case C-265/95 *Commission* v. *France*). The Commission brought proceedings following failure of the French authorities to respond adequately to violent action by its farmers who had systematically disrupted movement of agricultural produce from other Member States including strawberries from Spain and tomatoes from Belgium. The French government claimed it had condemned the violence and taken measures to reduce the number of incidents. The Commission considered these steps were not enough. The failure of the French government to act infringed Article 34 TFEU (then 30 TEC) as well as Article 4 TEU (then 10 TEC). While inaction might have been justified by a threat to public order, the Court found no such threat on the facts.

APPLICATION

Imagine that Greece adopts a law requiring employers to give Greek nationals priority in employment after overwhelming parliamentary support to change the law. When the pre-litigation procedure fails, the Commission brings proceedings in the Court. Greece submits a defence that it cannot comply with the principle of non-discrimination under Article 18 TFEU during a recession as the Greek parliament would refuse to repeal the law. Such a defence would fail. It raises questions of necessity (dismissed in Case 101/84 *Commission* v. *Italy*) and constitutional difficulties (dismissed in Case 28/81 *Commission* v. *Italy*). Such political and economic problems should be resolved in compliance with EU law.

Poland put forward an unusual defence in Case C-165/08 *Commission* v. *Poland* based on *religious or ethical grounds*. It claimed to have prohibited circulation of genetically modified seed varieties and banned their inclusion in the national catalogue of seed varieties on Christian and humanist principles on conception of life which was opposed to manipulation of living organisms. The Court held these claims did not establish that the national legislation had been inspired by ethical and religious considerations, especially as Poland had based its objections in the pre-litigation procedure on risks to health and the environment. It found Poland to be in breach of the directive without specifically considering this defence (for further discussion see Prete and Smulders, 2010).

General and persistent infringements

The Court accepted in Case C-494/01 *Commission* v. *Ireland ('Irish waste')* that the Commission may bring proceedings against a Member State not only over a specific breach of EU law but also against general and structural infringements of EU law. The Commission obtained a declaration under Article 260 against Ireland for general and persistent breaches in applying the directive. While the Court did not provide much guidance in the Irish waste case, it held in Case C-88/07 *Commission* v. *Spain ('Medicinal Herbs')* that a general administrative practice (systematic classification of medicinal herbs as medical products or food supplements without detailed analysis, leading to withdrawal of the products from Spanish market) was a general and persistent breach.

PARALLEL PROCEEDINGS AND INTERIM MEASURES

Enforcement proceedings under Article 258 often run in parallel with proceedings in the national courts which may lead to a preliminary reference before the Court of Justice under Article 267. The Court is empowered under Article 279 TFEU (ex 243) in any cases to order any necessary interim order such as an order to suspend a national law infringing EU law where the matter is urgent and there appears to be a strong case.

APPLICATION

Imagine the EU adopted Directive 2011/00 on 1 June 2011 on vehicle exhaust emissions, specifying the level of carbon monoxide which may be discharged from new vehicles. Spain adopts the Vehicle Emissions Regulations on 1 July 2011 permitting a higher level of carbon monoxide in exhaust gases. Airwatch, a national pressure group, challenges the Regulations in the Spanish courts on the basis that they contravene EU law. The Commission has begun proceedings under Article 258 against Spain for its failure to comply with the directive. It would be open to the Court of Justice to make an interim order under Article 279 in conjunction with either the Article 267 or 258 proceedings temporarily suspending the Regulations. If it can establish standing (see Chapter 10), Airwatch could seek suspension of the Regulations in the Spanish national courts, as the measure clearly conflicts with EU law.

The exclusion of the Spanish fishermen from sharing the UK fishing catch quota gave rise to a series of cases before the Court including enforcement proceedings under Article 258 in Case 246/89R *Commission* v. *UK (Re Merchant Shipping Rules)* where the Commission obtained suspension of the Merchant Shipping Act 1988. These proceedings took place in parallel with Case C-213/89 *R* v. *Secretary of State for Transport, ex p. Factortame*, arising from the House of Lords' request for a preliminary ruling on availability of an interim remedy. After ruling against the UK in Case 246/89R the Court of Justice held in Case C-213/89R that national courts should temporarily suspend any national provisions which may be in breach of EU law.

INTERSECTION

The series of cases on the Spanish fishermen are considered in relation to the supremacy of EU law (see Chapter 6).

ACTIONS BY MEMBER STATES AGAINST OTHER MEMBER STATES UNDER ARTICLE 259 TFEU

Article 259 TFEU (ex 227 TEC) enables one Member State to bring an action against another in the Court of Justice.

CORNERSTONE

> Where a Member State considers that another Member State has failed to fulfil an obligation under the Treaties it may bring the matter before the Court of Justice under Article 259(1).

The procedure resembles Article 258, namely notification to the Commission (Article 259(2)), followed by delivery of a reasoned opinion (Article 259(3)) and the right to bring the matter before the Court. If the Commission fails to deliver an opinion within three months, the Member States may bring the matter being brought before the Court.

Article 259 provides a procedure which the UK may use if the Commission does not take enforcement proceedings against Spain over border controls with Gibraltar.

Actions before the Court of Justice

Few cases have proceeded to judgment under Article 259 as Member States prefer to settle their differences through diplomacy or leave enforcement to the Commission. There is only one ruling under Article 259 although several unsuccessful applications have been made. In Case 141/78 *France* v. *United Kingdom* France brought an action against the UK government over use of fishing nets with mesh which was too small (catching more fish than permissible) after the Commission did not proceed with enforcement. The Court of Justice found the UK to be in breach.

Rejected claims under Article 259

The Court rejected claims under Article 259 in two cases:

1. Case C-388/95 *Belgium* v. *Spain*, an action based on a claim by Belgium that a Spanish law requiring Rioja wine to be bottled where it is grown and forbidding bulk exportation contravened EU law.

2. Case C-145/04 *Spain* v. *UK* arose from UK action to implement the judgment by the European Court of Human Rights (ECtHR) in *Matthews* v. *UK* that the UK was in breach of the ECHR by not giving voting rights in the European Parliament to Gibraltar residents (see Chapter 5). Spain objected to the UK giving voting rights to Commonwealth citizens who were not EU citizens and complained to the Commission which decided not to issue a reasoned opinion, given the sensitivity of the dispute between the two countries over Gibraltar. The Court of Justice found that the UK could not be criticised for compliance with the ECtHR judgment and dismissed the action.

Arbitration under Article 273 TFEU

Article 273 TFEU (ex 239) provides an alternative mechanism by which Member States may agree to submit any dispute within the Treaties to the Court of Justice.

PENALTIES AGAINST MEMBER STATES UNDER ARTICLE 260 TFEU

Before the Maastricht Treaty the Court could only declare that a Member State was in breach under
Article 260 TFEU (ex 228), providing no incentive to comply as Member States ignoring a ruling were
not subject to any penalty. The limitations of the pre-Maastricht position may be illustrated by France's
willingness to defy the Court in Case 232/78 *Commission* v. *France ('Lamb Wars')*. France continued
to exclude British beef despite a ruling against it by the Court of Justice until the Commission agreed
a new system of subsidies to benefit French farmers. As Kilbey (2010) points out, by the time the
Maastricht Treaty was being negotiated, 'it was clear that the Community could no longer rely on
Member States being shamed into compliance'.

The imposition of financial penalties under Article 260

The revised, post-Maastricht procedure under Article 260 TFEU enables the Commission to seek
imposition of a financial penalty (a lump sum or penalty payment).

CORNERSTONE

Article 260

Article 260(1) TFEU provides that if the Court decides that a Member State has failed to fulfil
an obligation under the Treaties, the State shall be 'required to take the necessary measures to
comply with the judgment of the Court'. Article 260(2) empowers the Commission to bring the
case before the Court if the Member State does not comply after being given the opportunity to
submit its observations.

The Treaty of Lisbon removed the need for a reasoned opinion, introducing a new procedure for
failure to transpose a directive. Article 260(3) TFEU empowers the Commission to specify in the
original Article 258 proceedings the lump sum or penalty payment if a breach is found. If the Court
finds that the Member State has not complied, it may impose a lump sum or penalty payment which
must not exceed the amount specified by the Commission.

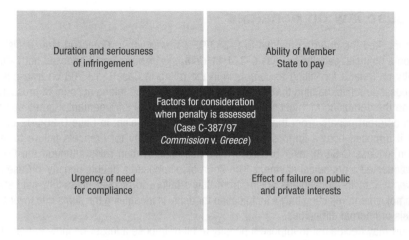

Figure 9.2 Factors affecting financial penalties

Factors to be taken into account

The Commission has used the procedure extensively in recent years. It provided a Memorandum in 1996 and guidelines in 1997, 2005 and 2010 on factors to be taken into account in assessing the penalty, including seriousness of the infringement, duration and the need to ensure deterrence.

The Court applied the guidance in Case C-387/97 *Commission* v. *Greece*, imposing a penalty payment on Greece for failure to comply with the judgment in Case C-45/91 over non-implementation of directives on disposal of waste. The Commission brought proceedings under Article 260 following non-compliance with the ruling in Case C-45/91.

The earlier ruling had found Greece in breach of its obligations under a waste disposal directive, particularly over a rubbish tip in Crete. The Commission proposed that the Court should impose a periodic penalty until the breach was remedied. The Court held that the basic criteria to be taken into account are duration of infringement, degree of seriousness and ability of the Member State to pay. In applying the criteria, regard should be had to the effects of failure to comply on public and private interests, as well as urgency of need for compliance. The Court ruled that Greece should pay a daily penalty until it had complied with the judgment in Case C-45/91. It stated that the guidance, while not binding, should ensure that action by the Commission is transparent, foreseeable and consistent with the principle of legal certainty.

APPLICATION

Assume that Spain has failed to transpose a directive on coordination of bus timetables. The Commission brings proceedings in the Court of Justice under Article 258, specifying the imposition of a fine of 500,000 euros. Spain ignores the ruling for three years due to the economic crisis. The Commission may bring further proceedings seeking imposition of a financial penalty in the Court. As the breach by Spain has continued for three years since the judgment, the Court is likely to view it as serious and deliberate. It is unlikely to award a lesser penalty but cannot increase it under Article 260(3).

Later case law on penalties

The Court invoked the criteria provided in C-387/97 *Commission* v. *Greece* in later decisions when deciding on a financial penalty. In Case C-374/11 *Commission* v. *Ireland* it imposed both a lump sum and penalty on Ireland for failing to comply with the ruling in Case C-188/08 on transposition of a waste disposal directive, holding that the penalty must be decided taking account of pressure needed to persuade the defaulting Member State to comply and end the infringement. Sometimes the Court imposes a different penalty from that requested by the Commission. In Case C-304/02 *Commission* v. *France* it imposed both a lump sum and a periodical penalty for France's failure to implement its decision in Case C-64/88 over breach of fisheries conservation rules although the Commission had only requested a periodical payment. The Court also imposed a double penalty in Case C-496/99 *Commission* v. *Italy* in proceedings arising from Italy's failure to recover unlawfully paid state aid to promote employment, rejecting Italy's justification for delay in identifying the sums due (over two years) on the basis of internal difficulties.

The Court may decide not to impose a penalty at all or impose a lesser penalty. In Case C-503/04 *Commission* v. *Germany* the Commission asked the Court to impose a periodical penalty. This time the Court decided that as the breach had been rectified by the time of the Article 258 hearing, it was inappropriate to impose a financial penalty, making a declaration only of failure to comply in time with the reasoned opinion under Article 258. The Court of Justice also refused to impose a periodic penalty in Case C-119/04 *Commission* v. *Italy* (from a finding against Italy of discrimination on grounds of nationality in foreign-language posts in universities) as Italy appeared to have complied by the time the case was considered by the Court.

Mitigating factors in assessing a penalty

Despite the good record of the Nordic states for compliance with EU law, Sweden was subject to enforcement proceedings when it was unable to transpose Directive 2006/24 on electronic communications owing to controversy over privacy. It was found to be in breach in Case C-185/09 *Commission* v. *Sweden*, with a lump sum penalty imposed in Case C-270/11. The Court applied the guidance in its earlier case law but also took account of Sweden's conduct in having never previously failed to comply with a judgment under Article 258. It considered the duration of the infringement (twenty-seven months) and imposed a fine of three million euros.

Academic writing on enforcement was scarce before the Maastricht Treaty introduced financial penalties. The gap has been filled by a growing body of commentary. Harlow and Rawlings' (2006) analysis of the accountability of Member States through Articles 226–228 TEC questions how far the current model of centralised enforcement can meet the demands of citizens for accountability. Prete and Smulders (2010) have a more optimistic view of Articles 258–260 as 'one of the most important means available to ensure the timely and correct application of EU law', seeing the alternative to centralised infringement proceedings as 'reducing Europe to a power game' which is unsustainable.

Other analysis (Kilbey, Escudero, Theodossiou) has focused largely on the impact of introducing financial penalties, shown to be effective in compelling Member States to address their obligations under EU law. The latest changes under the Treaty of Lisbon under Article 260 should continue to facilitate enforcement.

REFLECTION

KEY POINTS

- The Commission may bring enforcement proceedings under Article 258 TFEU against Member States where they infringe EU law.
- Many disputes are resolved during pre-legislative proceedings. Only stronger cases against Member States are brought before the Court of Justice.
- Where a Member State fails to comply with a judgment, the Commission may bring further proceedings in the Court, seeking imposition of a periodic payment or lump sum under Article 260 TFEU.
- Member States are entitled under Article 259 TFEU to bring enforcement proceedings against other states where the Commission decides not to act or takes no action, but such cases are rare as they disturb good relations between states.

CORE CASES AND STATUTES

Case	About	Importance
Case 141/78 *France v. United Kingdom*	France brought action under Article 259 against UK over fishing net mesh size after Commission did not proceed with enforcement.	UK found to be in breach – a rare example of a ruling under Article 259.
Case 28/81 *Commission* v. *Italy*	Italy argued it could not transpose directive due to frequent changes of government.	Difficulties of constitutional or administrative nature are no defence.
Case 101/84 *Commission* v. *Italy*	Enforcement proceedings against Italy for failure to submit statistical returns after terrorist bomb destroyed building housing them.	Defence of *force majeure* rejected as several years had elapsed, leaving time for Italian government to comply.
Case 247/87 *Star Fruit* v. *Commission*	Commission took no action under Article 258 after trader complained about common organisation of banana market. It then challenged inaction under Article 265.	Applicant could not rely on Article 265. Commission has complete discretion whether to bring enforcement proceedings. Failure to act cannot be reviewed by CJEU.
Case C-265/95 *Commission* v. *France*	Enforcement action against France for failing to respond to violent action by French farmers disrupting movement of agricultural products.	France was found in breach of Articles 10 and 30 TEC (now 4 TEU and 34 TFEU) having failed to take sufficient action. Preventive measures were not enough.

➔

Case	About	Importance
Case C-387/97 *Commission* v. *Greece*	Action to impose a financial penalty after Greece failed to comply with earlier ruling to implement waste disposal directive.	CJEU laid down criteria when awarding penalty (duration of infringement, seriousness, ability of Member State to pay). Should also consider urgency and effect of non-compliance on public and private interests.
Case C-145/04 *Spain* v. *UK*	Spain brought proceedings over UK's implementation of ECtHR decision after Commission declined to give reasoned opinion in dispute over voting rights of Gibraltar residents.	CJEU dismissed action, holding that UK could not be criticised for compliance with ECtHR decision.

Statute	About	Importance
Article 258 TFEU (ex 226 TEC)	Procedure for Commission to enforce EU law against Member States which appear to be in breach.	Enables Commission to bring proceedings in CJEU after preparatory negotiations.
Article 259 TFEU (ex 227 TEC)	Procedure for Member State to bring action in CJEU for breach of EU where Commission decides not to proceed or takes no action.	Rarely invoked as it damages relations between Member States.
Article 260(1) TFEU (ex 228)	Enables CJEU to declare that Member State is in breach of EU law following proceedings under Article 258 TFEU.	Declaratory order requiring Member State to rectify the breach.
Article 260(2) TFEU	Enables Commission to bring proceedings in CJEU requesting imposition of financial penalty where Member States has failed to comply with ruling that it has infringed EU law. Empowers CJEU to rule and impose penalty.	Commission should specify amount of lump sum or penalty payment sought. The Court is not bound by Commission's suggested penalty but may increase it, decrease it or decide not to award penalty.
Article 260(3) TFEU	Empowers Commission to specify amount of lump sum or penalty payment where Member States has failed to transpose directive.	CJEU cannot award heavier penalty than specified by Commission.

FURTHER READING

Escudero, M. L. 'Case C-154/08 *Commission* v. *Spain*, judgment of the Court (Third Chamber) of 12 November 2009' (2011) 48 *Common Market Law Review* 227
Examines the first infringement proceedings in the Court of Justice from a national Supreme Court decision.

Harlow, C. and Rawlings, R. 'Accountability and law enforcement: the centralized EU infringement procedure' (2006) 31 *European Law Review* 447
Analyses accountability in relation to Commission enforcement under (old) Article 226 to 228 TEC.

Kilbey, I. 'The interpretation of Article 260 TFEU (ex 228 EC)' (2010) 35 *European Law Review* 370
A comprehensive assessment of the Article 160 procedure. Critically examines the first twelve decisions of the Court on financial penalties and considers the changes introduced under the Treaty of Lisbon.

Prete, L. and Smulders, M. 'The coming of age of infringement proceedings' (2010) 47 *Common Market Law Review* 9
A thorough assessment of procedures under (what is now) Articles 258–260 by a member and director of the Legal Service of the Commission, writing in their personal capacity, with examination of defences submitted by Member States.

Theodossiou, M. 'An analysis of the recent response of the community to non-compliance with Court of Justice judgments: Art. 228' (2002) 27 *European Law Review* 25
Assesses the impact of financial penalties on the EU legal order, with particular reference to a ruling against Greece.

Wenneras, P. 'A new dawn for commission enforcement under Arts. 226 and 228: general and persistent (GAP) infringements, lump sums, and penalty payment' (2006) 43 *Common Market Law Review* 31
Examines the use of penalties with particular reference to two rulings against Ireland and France involving general and persistent infringements.

CHAPTER 10

Judicial review and damages claims

BLUEPRINT

Judicial review and damages claims

KEY QUESTIONS

LEGISLATION

- Article 263 TFEU
- Article 265 TFEU
- Article 340 TFEU

CONTEXT

- 'War against Terror'
- Treaty reform

CONCEPTS

- Standing
- Privileged and non-privileged applicants
- Direct and individual concern
- Non-contractual liability

- Does the limited standing of individuals under Article 263 infringe their fundamental human rights?

- To what extent should individuals be able to challenge EU acts and receive damages if EU institution causes loss?

CASES

- *Plaumann*
- *Bergaderm*

REFORM

- Introduction of regulatory acts not requiring implementation after Lisbon Treaty – may be challenged without individual concern

SPECIAL CHARACTERISTICS

- *Plaumann* formula for individual concern under Article 263
- Importance of discretion in determining liability under Article 340

CRITICAL ISSUES

Setting the scene

Imagine that Peter makes and sells ice cream made from hazelnuts in the UK. Last week the EU adopted a regulation prohibiting the use of nuts in ice cream due to the risk of allergic reaction. Peter wishes to challenge the regulation. This scenario raises various issues, particularly whether Peter has standing (right to challenge) in the General Court under Article 263 TFEU. It is hard for individuals to challenge a measure not addressed to them as the rules on standing are very demanding. If Peter can persuade the UK government to bring a challenge, the position would be different, as Member States and EU institutions can challenge any EU act in the Court of Justice where there are grounds. A total ban appears disproportionate when labelling would warn consumers of the presence of nuts. There may also be scope for a damages action against the EU institutions under Article 340 TFEU (ex 288 TEC).

CHALLENGING AN ACT OF THE EU INSTITUTIONS

Only the Court of Justice can determine whether legislative acts of the EU institutions are valid. National courts cannot rule on validity as EU law takes precedence over national law (Case 26/62 *Van Gend en Loos*) and should refer to the Court of Justice for a ruling on validity under Article 267. There are three main provisions under which the Court may review acts:

1. *Article 263 TFEU (ex 230 TEC)* is the main basis for *annulment* of a legislative act and the most important procedure to understand.

2. *Article 265 (ex 232 TEC)* enables the Court to consider *inactivity* of the institutions, i.e. failure to act where the institution has a legal duty to act.

3. *Article 277 (ex 241 TEC)* enables an act to be *indirectly reviewed*. An applicant may challenge the legality of a general act on which a later act or omission is based.

ACTION FOR ANNULMENT UNDER ARTICLE 263 TFEU

Overview

Article 263(1) TFEU provides for annulment of an act of the EU institutions. Article 263(2) empowers the Court of Justice to hear actions by Member States and the EU institutions on specified grounds. These 'privileged' applicants are not subject to restrictive rules on standing and may challenge any reviewable act. Article 263(4) provides a restricted right of challenge for individuals, usually known as 'non-privileged applicants'. Both types of applicant must bring their challenge within two months of adoption of the act under Article 263(6).

Only actions by privileged applicants under Article 263(2) are heard in the Court of Justice. Non-privileged applicants must bring their actions in the General Court (formerly CFI), with appeal to the Court of Justice which may review decisions of the General Court affecting the unity and consistency of EU law (Article 13(1) of Annex to Statute of the Court of Justice).

Five questions will be considered here in relation to Article 263:

1. Which acts may be reviewed?
2. Who has the right to challenge?
3. What are the relevant time limits?
4. On which grounds may an act be challenged?
5. What are the effects of annulment?

Which acts may be reviewed?

CORNERSTONE

Article 263(1) TFEU

The Court of Justice shall review the legality of legislative acts, of acts of the Council, of the Commission and of the European Central Bank, other than recommendations and opinions, and of acts of the European Parliament and European Council intended to produce legal effects vis-à-vis third parties.

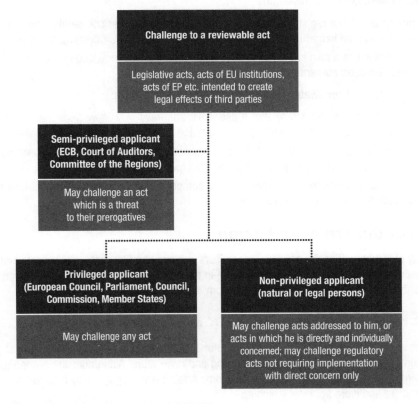

Figure 10.1 Actions for annulment under Article 263

Article 263(1) TFEU identifies three types of reviewable acts:

1. Legislative acts
2. Acts of the Council, Commission and European Central Bank (ECB) other than recommendations and opinions
3. Acts of the European Parliament, European Council and of bodies, offices and agencies of the Union intended to create legal effects vis-à-vis third parties.

Legislative acts

The category of 'legislative acts' was introduced by the Treaty of Lisbon. It is defined under Article 289(3) TFEU as a 'legal act which has been adopted by a legislative procedure', i.e. under either the ordinary legislative procedure in Article 289(1) or a special legislative procedure where the Treaties provide. It follows from Article 289(3) that it is the *process by which the act is adopted* which determines its status, not its description as a regulation, directive or decision. (Classification of non-legislative acts is considered in Chapter 4.)

Reviewable acts are not limited to regulations, directives and decisions. Before the Treaty of Lisbon the Court of Justice was concerned with *substance rather than form* and considered as reviewable all acts of the institutions designed to have legal effect, however designated. In Case 22/70 *Commission v. Council (Re European Road Transport Agreement)* concerning 'discussions' of guidelines before signing the Road Transport considered reviewable as intended to establish a binding course of action. The following were held to be reviewable:

- A 'communication' in a registered letter from the Commission under competition rules stating that the company was no longer immune from fines (Cases 8–11/66 *Re Noordwijk's Cement Accord*).
- Notice of vacancy for a post in the Parliament, requiring a 'perfect knowledge of Italian' (Case 15/63 *Lassalle* v. *European Parliament*).

The following were not reviewable as they did not create legal effects:

- A reasoned opinion under Article 258 (Case 7/61 *Commission* v. *Italy (Pigmeat)*), enforcement proceedings against Italy over restriction on importing pork).
- A Commission letter containing a statement of objections in a competition case (Case 60/81 *IBM v. Commission*), considered as an informal step in proceedings.
- Preliminary observations by the Commission in a competition investigation (Case T-64/89 *Automec v. Commission*), also a step in proceedings.

Effect of the Treaty of Lisbon

The Treaty of Lisbon unified the previous three pillars into one (the EU), making more acts reviewable. Some shadows of the pre-Lisbon position remain in the scope for review under the Common Foreign and Security Policy (CFSP) and the Area of freedom, security and justice (AFSJ).

INTERSECTION...

The three-pillar structure is considered in Chapter 1. Before Lisbon only acts under the first pillar (the European Community) were legally binding and reviewable. Acts under the second (CFSP) and third pillars (Cooperation in Justice and Home Affairs) were regulated by intergovernmental cooperation, and were not legally binding.

Acts under the Common Foreign and Security Policy

Article 24 TEU excludes from review acts under the CFSP, a sensitive policy area, with two exceptions where acts are reviewable:

1. Monitoring compliance with the common security and defence policy under Article 40.
2. Legality of Council decisions against natural or legal persons under Article 275 TFEU.

> The UN has adopted resolutions since the 1990s in response to the 'War against Terror' including freezing the assets of organisations and individuals associated with Osama bin Laden and Al-Qaeda identified on a list produced by the UN Sanctions Committee. The EU implemented the UN resolutions in Regulation 881/2002.

CONTEXT

The Court of Justice held in Cases C-402 & 415/05P *Kadi* v. *Council and Commission* (*Kadi I*) that such actions are reviewable even when pursuant to a UN resolution. The Court overturned a CFI decision in 2008, allowing individuals whose assets had been frozen as suspected Al-Qaeda supporters to challenge Regulation 881/2002. It annulled the regulation as the applicants had been denied a fair hearing and access to a judicial remedy even though the regulation had been adopted to implement a UN resolution. In July 2013 a Grand Chamber of the Court of Justice dismissed three further appeals against the General Court's annulment of an EU regulation in Cases C-584 etc./10 *Commission and UK* v. *Kadi (Kadi II)*.

The CFI followed *Kadi I* in 2009 in Case T-318/01 *Othman* v. *Council and Commission*. It annulled an EU regulation as far as it imposed sanctions on the applicant, a Jordanian national (better known as 'Abu Quatada') detained in the UK under anti-terrorist legislation – deportation to Jordan having been suspended pending his application to the European Court of Human Rights. He was deported in July 2013.

Action under the Area of freedom, security and justice

The Treaty of Lisbon brought the old third pillar (Cooperation and Justice in Home Affairs) into the main body of the Treaties. Articles 67–89 TFEU now cover the Area of freedom, security and justice (AFSJ) which is subject to review by the Court. The AFSJ requires the Union to remove border controls between Member States and frame a common policy on asylum, immigration and external border controls. Validity and proportionality of actions by police or law enforcement agencies and Member States to maintain law and order or internal security are excluded from review under Article 276 TFEU.

Acts of the EU institutions

Under the EC Treaty only acts of the Council and Commission were explicitly reviewable. Amendment under the Maastricht Treaty enabled the European Parliament's acts to be challenged where intended to produce legal effects in relation to third parties, reflecting Case 230/81 *Luxembourg* v. *European Parliament* (challenge by Luxembourg to Parliament's resolution to move from Luxembourg to Brussels and Strasbourg) and Case 294/83 *Partie Ecologiste ('Les Verts')* v. *European Parliament* (challenge to allocation of campaign funds to the Green Party for the 1984 elections). An act of the Parliament with only internal effect on authorisation of expenditure was found inadmissible in Case 190/84 *'Les Verts'* v. *European Parliament*. Later Treaties added acts of the European Central Bank (ECB) and Parliament, with the European Council added by the Treaty of Lisbon, as well as 'bodies, offices and agencies of the Union intended to create legal effects vis-à-vis third parties', reflecting changes to the EU institutional structure.

Who has the right to challenge?

The right to challenge depends on whether the applicant is privileged or non-privileged. EU institutions and Member States are privileged and may challenge any reviewable act under Article 263(2). Non-privileged applicants (individuals) have restricted rights to challenge under Article 263(4).

Privileged applicants

CORNERSTONE

Article 263(2)

The Court of Justice has jurisdiction under Article 263(2) in actions [for annulment] brought by Member States, the European Parliament, the Council or the Commission.

Take note

The term 'prerogatives' should not be confused with its usage in English law. In EU law it refers to participation in the legislative process. Acts adopted on the wrong legal base were usually by the Council alone, denying Parliament opportunity to influence the legislation.

Article 263(2) enables Member States, Parliament, Council and Commission to challenge. Originally Parliament could not challenge, but its status changed under the Maastricht Treaty reflecting Case C-70/88 *Parliament* v. *Council ('Chernobyl')* when the Court recognised Parliament's right to 'safeguard its own prerogatives' (usually where acts were adopted on the wrong legal base). The Treaty of Nice put Parliament on a par with the other privileged applicants.

Semi-privileged applicants

The ECB, Court of Auditors and Committee of the Regions have gradually gained recognition as semi-privileged applicants entitled under Article 263(3) to bring an action where there is a threat to their prerogatives.

APPLICATION

Imagine the EU adopts a directive under Article 114 TFEU (ex 95 TEC) harmonising telephone networks. The Committee of the Regions (COR) considers the directive should have been adopted under Article 170 TFEU (ex 154 TEC) providing for establishment of 'Trans-European Networks' in areas including telecommunications, and requiring consultation with the COR, whereas Article 114 does not. The COR could challenge the measure under Article 263(4) as a threat to its prerogatives.

Non-privileged applicants

CORNERSTONE

Article 263(4) TFEU

A natural or legal person can only challenge 'an act addressed to that person or which is of direct and individual concern to them, and against a regulatory act which is of direct concern to them and does not entail implementing measures'.

Under Article 263(4) individuals ('natural or legal person') have restricted rights as non-privileged applicants to challenge an act such as a decision addressed to them.

APPLICATION

Imagine that 'A' plc, a major UK pharmaceutical producer, wants to merge with 'B' GmbH, a similar German company. If the firms' turnover is above a certain level they must notify the merger to the Commission under Regulation 139/2004. When the Commission has considered the application it will issue a decision addressed to both firms approving or rejecting the merger. Both A and B may challenge the decision in the General Court.

Acts not addressed to the applicant

Where an act is *not* addressed to the applicant, the individual has to establish standing to challenge by showing 'direct and individual concern'. Failure to do so leads to the application being declared 'inadmissible' which means that the General Court will not consider it.

The act must be of direct concern

A measure is of *direct concern* to the applicant when his position is decided by the act itself without exercise of further discretion such as a national implementation measure (Case 69/69 *SA Alcan* v. *Commission*). *Alcan* arose before the customs union was achieved so that duties were paid when goods moved between states. An exception was provided for unprocessed aluminium, for which a 'tariff quota' (reduced rate of duty) had applied. The applicant sought to annul a Commission decision refusing a tariff quota to Belgium and Luxembourg. The Court found that the decision did not concern the applicant as it only affected Member States.

Any discretion exercised by a third party is fatal to establishing standing, as the applicant's position is not determined by the act alone. In Case T-341/02 *Regione Siciliana* v. *Commission* the Region of Sicily sought to annul a Commission decision ending financial assistance for a motorway project on the island addressed to the Italian government. The CFI in a decision upheld by the Court of Justice (Case C-417/04P) refused to admit the application, finding that the national government had significant discretion in implementing the measure.

The act must be of individual concern to the applicant

It is hard, if not impossible, for most applicants to establish standing before the General Court in relation to an act not addressed to them due to difficulty in showing individual concern.

APPLICATION

Continuing with the scenario in the Application above, imagine the Commission has approved the merger between A and B in a decision addressed to them. Their main competitor, C, seeks to challenge the decision as it is adversely affected by the merger. It would only be able to do so if it satisfies the criteria for individual concern as the decision is not addressed to it.

The problem of establishing standing has led to criticism that denial of access to the Court infringes the fundamental rights of individuals including the right of effective judicial protection. Nevertheless the Treaty of Lisbon made only modest adjustment to the requirement for individual concern where the applicant is not the addressee, for which the test remains the formula adopted in Case 25/62 *Plaumann & Co.* v. *Commission*.

CORNERSTONE

The *Plaumann* formula

'In order for a measure to be of individual concern to the person to whom it applies, it must affect their legal position because of a factual situation which differentiates them from all other persons and distinguishes them individually in the same way as the person to whom it is addressed' (the *Plaumann* formula, as restated in Case 26/86 *Deutz und Geldermann* v. *Council*, where an application to annul a regulation by a producer of sparkling wines was dismissed for lack of individual concern).

The applicant in *Plaumann* was a major importer of clementines claiming to be individually concerned in a Commission decision addressed to the German government refusing permission to reduce customs duties on clementines from outside the Community. The Court refused to accept the applicant had standing. It held that the test for individual concern requires the applicant to prove that *the decision affects him because of factors which are peculiarly relevant to him*, not merely because he belongs to a class affected by the act. In this case the class was that of importer of clementines and anyone, in principle, could import clementines.

APPLICATION

Imagine the EU has adopted a regulation during an outbreak of 'foot and mouth' disease prohibiting movement of cattle and sheep within a thirty-mile radius of an outbreak. John's farm is twenty-eight miles from an outbreak but his livestock are unaffected by the disease. He seeks to annul the measure as it has prevented him taking his animals to market. John should be able to show *direct concern* as there is no discretion over animal movements within the thirty-mile zone, so the consequences for John are entirely determined under the regulation. For *individual concern* he must show the regulation affects him in a way which distinguishes him from all other persons as if addressed to him personally. This depends on whether the Court regards the scope of the regulation (farmers within thirty miles of outbreak) as sufficient to identify *all* members of the class. This should be possible, so John should be seen as both directly and individually concerned. If the measure had prohibited *all* movement of cattle and sheep in a Member State without a geographical restriction, the class would be farmers in a Member State with an outbreak of 'foot and mouth', i.e. an *open* class. John would be unable to challenge.

Decisions in which the applicant established standing

The following cases provide examples of actions where both direct and individual concern were recognised because the applicant belonged to a *closed, identifiable group*:

(a) Cases 106 and 107/63 *Toepfer KG* v. *Commission*. The applicant, an importer of cereals, had applied unsuccessfully to the German government for a licence to import cereals. The refusal was confirmed in a Commission decision. As the decision affected only *existing* applicants it was of individual concern.

(b) Case 11/82 *Piraiki-Patraiki* v. *Commission*. The applicants who manufactured and exported cotton yarn sought to challenge a decision addressed to the French government authorising an import quota on Greek cotton yarn. The Court held that the decision was of individual concern to those who had entered into contracts *before* the decision but performed after it.

(c) Case C-152/88 *Sofrimport SARL* v. *Commission*. The Court held that importers with goods *in transit* when a Commission regulation banning importation of fruits was adopted were individually concerned. The regulation had been adopted under a Council regulation requiring the Community to have regard for the interests of importers with goods in transit.

(d) Joined Cases T-218 to 240/03 *Boyle and others* v. *Commission* arose from a request to the Commission by fishing vessel owners in the Irish fleet to increase its capacity. The Commission refused in a decision addressed to Ireland. As the number and identity of vessel owners could be established before the decision was made, the CFI found it affected a *closed group of identified persons* within the meaning of *Plaumann*.

Decisions in which the applicant failed to establish standing

Most applicants fail to establish standing, with the Court declaring the application inadmissible where the applicant appears to belong to an *open class*. In Case 231/82 *Spijker Kwasten NV* v. *Commission* the Commission had issued a decision to the Dutch government requiring it to ban importation of Chinese brushes. Despite the fact that the applicant had previously applied for a licence to import Chinese brushes, the Court held that the decision was *not* of individual concern.

The following cases provide examples of where applicants such as *environmental groups, trade associations* and *regional authorities* have found it particularly hard to satisfy the *Plaumann* formula:

(a) In Case C-321/95P *Stichting Greenpeace Council (Greenpeace International)* v. *Commission* the applicants (an alliance between an environmental group, local residents, fishermen and farmers) sought to annul a Commission decision providing aid to build two power stations on the Canary Islands. The Court of Justice applied *Plaumann* and upheld the CFI decision not to recognise individual concern, finding the applicants could not be differentiated from residents generally or others working in the area.

(b) In Case T-37/04 *Região autónoma dos Açores* v. *Council* the regional authority responsible for the Azores sought to annul a fisheries management regulation, claiming it adversely affected the marine environment. The CFI held it was not individually concerned as Member States not regional authorities are entitled to defend the general interest in their territories. Natural or legal persons cannot rely on collective interests to bring a challenge.

(c) In Case C-355/08P *WWF-UK Ltd* v. *Council and Commission* the applicant sought to annul Regulation 41/2007 fixing total allowable catches of cod. The CFI declared the action inadmissible, a decision upheld by the Court of Justice where the applicant was found not to be individually concerned. The regulation provided for Regional Advisory Councils (RACs) to advise the Commission on fisheries. WWF-UK Ltd, a member of the Executive Council of the North Sea RAC, had contributed to a minority report refusing to support the Commission's proposal to permit fishing in view of an international recommendation for a zero catch for North Sea cod. The Court found that reliance on a procedural right such as the right to be heard does not normally provide standing to challenge the substance of an EU act.

Establishing standing before the Treaty of Lisbon

It is useful to be aware of the standing of non-privileged applicants *before* the Treaty of Lisbon as some traces of the old law remain. Before the Lisbon amendment, non-privileged applicants could only challenge under Article 230(4) TEC (now Article 263(4) TFEU) where the measure was *a decision* or *equivalent to a decision*, as well as being of direct and individual concern. The Lisbon Treaty amended the wording to 'acts', apparently removing the distinction between regulations and decisions. However, it is likely to remain harder to establish individual concern under *Plaumann* where the act is a general measure (i.e. regulation or directive) than where it is a decision.

According to Cases 789 & 790/79 *Calpack*, a 'true' regulation applies generally and objectively to categories of persons, whereas a decision binds those to whom it is addressed (i.e. named or identifiable individuals). Where the Court found that an act described as a regulation had the characteristics of a decision it could be challenged where individual concern could be shown, as in Cases 41–44/70 *International Fruit NV* v. *Commission (No. 1)*, a decision in the form of a regulation prescribing the number of import licences for a particular period on the basis of previous applications and so applying to a finite number of people.

Even where a regulation was deemed a 'true' regulation, it might be of individual concern where the applicant's *right* had been infringed. In Case C-309/89 *Codorniu* v. *Council* the applicant sought to challenge a regulation reserving the word '*crémant*' for high-quality sparkling wines from parts of France and Luxembourg. The applicant was a major producer of sparkling wines in Spain and the largest producer of quality sparkling wines in the EU, holding a Spanish trademark for one of its products. The Court found the measure was a true regulation of general application. Although not part of a fixed group, the applicant was individually concerned because the regulation affected the firm in a different way from other producers by removing its trademark rights. While *Codorniu* was welcomed as a relaxation on individual concern, it should be seen as exceptional.

Back to the future – *Jégo Quéré* and *UPA*

The CFI set off a short-lived flurry of excitement in 2002 in Case T-177/01 *Jégo Quéré* by adopting a more liberal approach to individual concern. The applicants sought to challenge an EU regulation imposing a fishing net mesh size which would have prevented them using their nets to fish off Ireland where they had previously fished. As the regulation was a measure of general application, it would not normally have been open to challenge by a non-privileged applicant. However, the CFI found the action admissible, holding that failure to recognise the applicants' standing would deprive them of a remedy contrary to the ECHR (Article 6, right to a fair trial, and Article 13, right to an effective remedy before the national courts). In a decision given *after* Advocate-General Jacobs' submissions in *UPA* and *before* the Court of Justice ruling, the CFI put forward a new test for individual concern (not upheld by the Court of Justice), that an applicant should be regarded as individually concerned in a measure of general application where it 'affects his legal position in a manner which is both definite and immediate, by restricting his rights or by imposing obligations on him'.

A few months later the Court of Justice reached a very different conclusion in Case C-50/00P *Unión de Pequeños Agricultores (UPA)* v. *Council.* The applicant was a trade association seeking to challenge a regulation on common organisation of the market in olive oil. It claimed that as it could not readily use the preliminary reference procedure to seek a ruling on validity, it should be able to challenge the regulation under Article 230 TEC or it would be deprived of a remedy. Advocate-General Jacobs argued that the Court should depart from its narrow interpretation of standing in the interests of effective judicial protection. He submitted that the only satisfactory solution was to recognise the applicant as individually concerned 'where the measure has, or is liable to have a substantial effect on his interests'. This wide interpretation was *not* accepted by the Court, which ruled that it remained necessary for a natural or legal person to establish direct and individual concern under the *Plaumann* formula. To adopt a more liberal interpretation would set aside the condition in Article 230(4), exceeding the Court's jurisdiction and requiring amendment to the Treaties by the Member States. The Court also held that Member States were responsible for establishing a 'system of legal remedies which ensure the right to effective judicial protection' (now recognised in Article 19(1) TEU).

INTERSECTION

Part of the rationale for the *UPA* decision was that annulment actions operate within a wider system of remedies including preliminary rulings on validity under Article 267 (considered in Chapter 3). However, this mechanism can only be invoked where there are proceedings before the national courts.

The Court of Justice followed *UPA* when hearing the appeal in *Jégo Quéré*. It rejected the test for standing put forward by the CFI, finding that the rules could not be relaxed even where national law provided no remedy. It is therefore clear that the standing of non-privileged applicants remains governed by the strict requirements of the *Plaumann* test.

Concern that opening up access to individuals would overwhelm the Court and disturb the legal order underlies the reaffirmation of the *Plaumann* test. The Court of Justice expressed confidence in *UPA* that individuals have access to a 'complete set of remedies', thereby not infringing Articles 6 and 13 of the ECHR, as national courts may request a ruling on the validity of a measure under Article 267 (then 234 TEC), although it did not consider that the absence of national proceedings would prevent this possibility. *UPA* led to extensive academic criticism. Albors-Llorens (2003) saw it as showing the Court's reluctance to intrude on Member States as the main actors in Community law by opening up the categories of challengers, a change being best left to Treaty reform. Usher (2003) considered the Court had adopted a 'conventional solution', with some advantages for the litigant (use of the preliminary reference procedure to challenge validity) but also disadvantages (where a litigant wishes to challenge general legislation not the subject of national implementation, leading to a gap in the system of judicial protection).

REFLECTION

Pressure for reform continued after *UPA* as the Treaties were under review.

The Convention process leading to the Constitutional Treaty (CT) was underway between 2001 and 2003, focusing Treaty-drafters, academics and judiciary on the possibility of increasing access for individuals to challenge EU acts. While the CT was abandoned in 2005, the Treaty of Lisbon followed a similar approach on the standing of non-privileged applicants in Article 263(4) TFEU.

CONTEXT

Establishing standing after the Treaty of Lisbon

The Treaty-drafters resisted the call to liberalise standing, introducing a modest change by adding a new category of *regulatory acts* which may be challenged without showing individual concern.

CORNERSTONE

Article 263(4) TFEU

Any natural or legal person may . . . institute proceedings against an act addressed to that person or which is of direct and individual concern to them, and against a regulatory act which is of direct concern to them and does not entail implementing measures.

The new wording of Article 263(4) falls far short of Advocate-General Jacobs' call for standing to be extended to *those whose interests are adversely affected* by an act. While it may indicate the start of a gradual relaxation of the standing rules, individuals still have to satisfy the *Plaumann* test where they seek to challenge a legislative act addressed to someone else or a regulatory act requiring implementation. Non-privileged applicants may now challenge three categories of act under Article 263(4) TFEU:

1. acts addressed to them

2. acts not addressed to them but of direct and individual concern

3. regulatory acts of direct concern to them not entailing implementing measures.

The first category ('acts addressed to them') represents little change from the pre-Lisbon position, as it is unlikely that acts other than decisions would be addressed to individuals. The second category maintains the pre-Lisbon requirement for direct and individual concern, but extends the type of review-able act as it is no longer necessary to show that the measure was equivalent to a decision. The third category is new, with no requirement for individual concern. The standing of non-privileged applicants remains controversial as individuals still struggle to fulfil the criteria under Article 263(4) if they are not the addressee. While the Treaty of Lisbon widened the scope for a challenge in relation to regulatory acts not requiring implementation, criticism remains that individuals are denied a remedy in breach of their fundamental rights.

Meaning of 'regulatory act'

The term 'regulatory act' is not defined in the Treaties but was interpreted in Case T-18/10 *Inuit Tapiriit Kanatami* v. *Parliament and Council (Inuit I)* (upheld by the Court of Justice in Case C-583/11P) where the General Court held that regulatory acts are 'acts of general application apart from legislative acts' (arising from an application by Inuit traders in Canada to annul an EU ban on the marketing of seal products). This means that legislative acts cannot be reviewed in proceedings by individuals without individual concern. *Legislative acts* are defined in Article 289(3) TFEU as 'acts adopted by legislative procedure', such as regulations or directives. The General Court had a second opportunity to con-sider the regulation forbidding marketing of seal products in Case T-526/10 *Inuit Tapiriit Kanatami* v. *Commission (Inuit II)*. It found no grounds and dismissed the application without ruling on admissibility 'in the circumstances of the case and for the sake of economy of procedure', presumably mindful of the Court of Justice's pending judgment in *Inuit I*.

INTERSECTION

Chapter 4 on EU sources and competences provides more detailed consideration of the categories of acts introduced by the Treaty of Lisbon, including regulatory acts in the light of *Inuit* and *Microban* (below).

Acts outside the definition in Article 289(3) or (4) are *non-legislative acts*, which nevertheless may lay down legally binding general rules. Non-legislative acts of general application may be adopted by the Commission under delegated powers provided by Article 290(1) TFEU. Article 291 provides for implementation by the Member States, Commission or Council. Case T-262/10 *Microban International Ltd* v. *Commission* found that the act (a decision prohibiting a substance used to make plastics) was a regulatory act. With no Member State discretion, it did not require implementing measures. The applicant was therefore directly concerned and could challenge the decision under Article 263(4) without showing individual concern.

APPLICATION

Imagine the Commission adopts a decision prohibiting the sale of fifty poisonous plants under powers delegated by the Council and Parliament in a regulation under the ordinary legislative procedure. Susan owns a garden centre specialising in the sale of exotic plants, many of which feature on the Commission list of prohibitions. She is worried she will go out of business as so many of her specialist plants cannot be sold and she cannot find substitutes. She wishes to challenge the decision in the General Court. Under *Inuit* the Commission decision is a regulatory act. Susan should be able to demonstrate direct concern as her position is determined by the decision itself with no scope for exercise of discretion. Lack of discretion is also central to establishing that the measure does not require implementing measures (*Microban*). Susan should be able to challenge the regulation in the General Court under Article 263(4) without individual concern.

Criticism of the Treaty of Lisbon changes

Academic commentators on the Lisbon amendments on standing have tended to view the changes as pragmatic, given the Court's concern not to open the acts of the EU institutions to the 'floodgates' of review in actions by private individuals, and its conviction in *UPA* that that EU law offers a complete set of remedies when the preliminary reference on invalidity under Article 267 is considered.

Usher (2003) suggests that the wording of Article 230(4) TEC might not have been revised under the draft CT (with the same wording as Lisbon) without the impetus of *UPA* and *Jégo Quéré*, but sees the distinction between legislative and regulatory acts as artificial, given that there are no such restrictions on individuals raising questions on validity before the national courts. Koch (2005), also commenting on the draft CT, describes the amendment as limited progress in the right direction, but with a long way to go before the gaps in individual protection are closed. Arnull (2011) considers that effectiveness of judicial protection for individuals under the new wording depends on how far the Court of Justice adopts an activist position in interpretation. The hopes expressed by Balthasar (2010) and Albors-Llorens (2012) of a liberal interpretation of 'regulatory act' were not realised by the Court of Justice's decision in *Inuit I*, upholding the narrow approach of the General Court.

REFLECTION

What are the relevant time limits?

The period of time in which to bring a challenge under Article 263 is very short. Article 263(6) provides that an applicant, whether privileged applicant or not, must bring a claim for annulment within *two months* of:

(a) publication; or

(b) notification to the applicant; or

(c) the day in which it came to the applicant's knowledge (in the absence of notification).

As Article 297 TFEU (ex 254 TEC) requires regulations to be published, time runs from the date of publication in the *Official Journal* (or date of notification for directives and decisions). The date of knowledge is the date when the applicant became aware of the measure. A limited extension takes account of the distance of the applicant's place of residence from the Court of Justice (ten days for the UK).

After the two-month period has expired, the measure cannot be challenged by other means such as Article 277 (ex 241 TEC) (Case C-188/92 *TWD Textilwerke Deggendorf GmbH* v. *Germany*). In *TWD* a polyester yarn producer was in dispute with the German Minister for Foreign Affairs over action to recover an EC subsidy. The German government had failed to notify the aid to the Commission which required Germany to recover it in a decision not challenged by TWD. The Court held that an applicant could not bring an indirect challenge under Article 277 when it had been notified of a decision which it failed to challenge under Article 263.

On which grounds may an act be challenged?

Article 263(2) provides four grounds for annulment:

1. lack of competence;

2. infringement of an essential procedural requirement;

3. infringement of the Treaties or of any rule relating to their application;

4. misuse of power.

Lack of competence

The EU institutions may adopt measures only where empowered by the Treaties or secondary legislation. Thus a measure may be challenged where the adopting institution lacked the necessary competence. In Case 22/70 *Commission* v. *Council (Re European Road Transport Agreement (ERTA))* the Commission unsuccessfully challenged the Council over participation in drafting the Road Transport Agreement, as Article 228 EEC (now 218 TFEU) authorised the Commission to negotiate international agreements and the Council to conclude them.

Infringement of an essential procedural requirement

Infringement of an essential procedural requirement follows from the obligation to use correct procedures under the Treaties or secondary legislation when adopting acts, such as the obligation to *state the reasons* for a decision in Article 296 TFEU (ex 253 TEC). In Case 24/62 *Germany* v. *Commission (Re Tariff Quotas on Wine)*

Take note

These grounds derive from French administrative law where they are known respectively as *incompetence, vice de forme, violation de la loi* and *détournement de pouvoir*. They are not mutually exclusive but overlap, making it possible to plead more than one ground.

an application by Germany to import wine for blending was partially unsuccessful, with the Commission stating that there was enough of such wine already within the Community. The Court of Justice annulled the decision, holding that reasons provided must not be too vague or inconsistent, but must set out clearly the main issues on which they are based.

Failure to state the legal basis was found to infringe an essential procedural requirement under Article 293 TFEU (then 253 TEC) in Case 45/86 *Commission* v. *Council* (Commission challenge to two regulations adopted by the Council under the General System of Preferences (tariffs to developing countries)).

Failure to consult the Parliament where required by the Treaties also infringes an essential procedural requirement (Case 138/79 *Roquette Frères SA* v. *Council* and Case 139/79 *Maizena GmbH* v. *Council*). These cases involved challenges to a regulation under Article 43 EEC (now 43 TFEU) adopted by the Council *before* receiving Parliament's opinion, when consultation was obligatory. The regulation was annulled.

It is similarly a breach to choose the *wrong legal basis* where it denies Parliament the right to participate in the legislative process. In Case C-300/89 *Commission* v. *Council* (*'Titanium Dioxide'*) the Council based a measure harmonising the titanium dioxide waste regime on former Article 130s EEC (now Article 192 TFEU) rather than on Article 100a EEC (now 114 TFEU). Action under Article 130s required unanimity, whereas Article 100a required QMV and consultation with Parliament. The Court held that Article 100a should have been used, enabling Parliament to participate in decision-making. Choice of legal base has become less controversial following extension of the ordinary (previously co-decision) procedure to most areas.

No action lies where the result of applying the measure is unaffected by the defect, nor where the defect is trivial. In Case 30/78 *Distillers Co. Ltd* v. *Commission* the applicant had failed to notify an agreement to the Commission under competition rules at the time to seek exemption (approval). The Court held that it would still have refused exemption even if there had been no procedural irregularity.

Infringement of the Treaties or rule relating to their application

Infringement of the Treaties or of any rule relating to their application covers the provisions of all relevant Treaties, acts of the EU institutions and general principles common to the laws of the Member States. Since the Charter of Fundamental Rights was given the same legal status as the Treaties following the Treaty of Lisbon, infringement of the Charter as well as *any of the general principles* recognised by the Court of Justice provide grounds for annulment. Proportionality is frequently invoked. In Case C-353/99P *Council* v. *Hautala*, for example, a journalist sought access to a Council document on arms exports but was refused as it might damage relations with third countries. The Court found the decision was subject to the principle of proportionality requiring the Council to consider partial access.

INTERSECTION

General principles include fundamental rights, proportionality, legal certainty, equality, as well as principles under the Treaties such as transparency and subsidiarity. As infringement of *any* general principle of law or fundamental right is a ground for annulment, you should refer to Chapter 5 for more examples, particularly infringements of the ECHR and Charter of Fundamental Rights.

Misuse of powers

The term 'misuse of powers' has been interpreted by the Court to include improper, though not illegal use of powers. In Case 105/75 *Giuffrida* v. *Council* a competition for a senior administrative post in the Council was set up with a job description worded to fit the profile of an internal candidate who was then appointed. An unsuccessful applicant challenged the appointment decision. The Court found the appointment was a misuse of powers and annulled it.

APPLICATION

Assume the Commission has adopted a decision with immediate effect changing the rules on compensation to farmers after an outbreak of 'pig flu' (a respiratory disease in pigs). No reason is given, although the Commission has issued a press release stating that new scientific evidence shows that humans and animals are at risk. Under previous rules farmers had to vaccinate their herds when their pigs suffered from pig flu and could obtain compensation from the Commission. The new rules restrict compensation to pig farmers who slaughter their entire herd where an outbreak occurs anywhere in the Member State. The UK objects to the measure which it claims is an over-reaction, unsupported by scientific evidence.

As a privileged applicant the UK government can challenge the decision under Article 263(2) without individual concern. Possible grounds include infringement of an essential procedural requirement (failure to give reasons) and infringement of the Treaties or rule relating to their application. The second type of infringement may arise where there is a breach of a general principle of EU law, including proportionality or legitimate expectations. The UK government may claim the decision is disproportionate if the disease could be controlled by vaccination rather than slaughter. However, this ground may fail as the precautionary principle applies where there is scientific uncertainty enabling the Commission to act to protect humans and animals (see Chapter 12 on the free movement of goods). Bringing the decision into effect immediately may infringe the principle of legitimate expectations (*Mackprang*), as the 'reasonably prudent' farmer would not expect such a significant change without notice.

What are the effects of annulment?

Article 266 TFEU (ex 233 TEC) requires institutions whose act has been declared void to take the necessary measures to comply with the judgment. Where the act is a regulation or directive, Article 264 TFEU (ex 231 TEC) empowers the Court to declare whether parts of the act should remain in force, as in Case 81/72 *Commission* v. *Council* where the Court ordered that staff salaries should still be paid under an annulled regulation until a new regulation was issued.

ACTION FOR INACTIVITY UNDER ARTICLE 265 TFEU

Article 265 TFEU (ex 232 TEC) complements Article 263 by providing a remedy where an EU institution has failed to act when it is under a duty to do so. In Case 13/83 *Parliament* v. *Council (Re ERTA)* Parliament brought an action under Article 175 EEC (now 265 TFEU) complaining of the Council's failure to implement a common transport policy. The Court upheld the action in part but rejected the complaint where the obligation was too vague to be enforceable.

CORNERSTONE

Article 265(1) TFEU

Article 265(1) provides that if the Parliament, European Council, Council, Commission or ECB fail to act in infringement of the Treaties, Member States and the other EU institutions may bring an action before the Court of Justice to have the infringement established.

Inconsistency between Articles 263 and 265 may be resolved by applying the 'unity principle', adopting the same approach to both Articles by applying decisions under Article 263 to Article 265 and vice versa (Case 15/70 *Chevalley* v. *Commission*). This case involved an application by a landowner for a declaration under Article 175 EEC (now 265 TFEU) that the Commission had failed to address a decision to him providing detailed rules on agricultural leases. He brought an alternative action under Article 173 EEC (now 263 TFEU) as the Commission had informed him no action would be taken. The Court dismissed the action as inadmissible but stated that, 'The concept of a measure capable of giving rise to an action is identical in Articles 173 and 175, as both provisions merely prescribe one and the same method of recourse.' The Court has not been entirely consistent in following the 'unity' principle as in Case 302/87 *Parliament* v. *Council ('Comitology')* it allowed Parliament to bring an action under Article 175 over the Council's failure to adopt a measure which was not itself a reviewable act.

Who may bring an action under Article 265?

Privileged applicants

Member States and EU institutions may challenge any omission on the part of the Parliament, European Council, Council or ECB to adopt a binding act where there is a legal duty to act under Article 256(1). Parliament was first recognised as one of the 'other institutions' in Case 13/83 *Parliament* v. *Council*.

Non-privileged applicants

Article 265(3) gives natural and legal persons the right to complain to the Court that an institution had failed to address any act other than a recommendation or an opinion to that person. Where the decision is addressed to a third party the legal position is less clear. It would be consistent with Article 263 if an applicant could challenge an omission relating to a third party where he or she is directly and individually concerned. Such a right was implied by the Court in Case 246/81 *Bethell* v. *Commission* although the claim failed. The applicant, an MEP and chairman of an air transport pressure group, had complained to the Commission about airline price fixing. He was not satisfied by the response and commenced proceedings under Articles 173 and 175 TEC. The Court declared the claim inadmissible as he was not the addressee of a decision under Article 173 or a potential addressee under Article 175.

Similar reasoning was employed in Case 15/71 *Mackprang* v. *Commission* where action was also declared inadmissible. The applicant complained that the Commission had failed to address a measure to the Member States on import levies on goods from Algeria, so he had to pay the higher rate of levy payable on goods from third countries. The Court found the application amounted to a request for the Commission to adopt an act which could not be addressed to the applicant under Article 175 due to its form.

Procedure

No action may be brought under Article 265 unless the institution has first been called upon to act, after which it has two months to act in accordance with the request or define its position. If it fails to comply, the applicant may bring an action within two months. In Case 48/65 *Alfons Lütticke GmbH* v. *Commission* the applicants had asked the Commission to take a decision against Germany over imposition of a tax. The Commission refused in a letter to the applicant, stating it did not consider the tax infringed the Treaty. The applicant sought to annul the definition of position in the letter under Article 173 EEC, while alternatively claiming that the Commission had failed to act under Article 175. The Court found the action was inadmissible as the Commission had defined its position and notified it to the applicant within two months of being called on to act.

.... APPLICATION

Imagine that a recent international study shows the number of insect species in the EU has dropped dramatically in the last ten years. If nothing is done insects like the honey bee may die out. The UK is concerned that the EU has failed to adopt a policy protecting insect diversity under Article 191 TFEU (ex 174 TEC) and calls on the Commission to produce a draft policy. The Commission has two months to respond. If it fails to do so, the UK may bring proceedings in the Court under Article 265 to establish the infringement.

Effects of successful action

Article 266 TFEU (ex 233 TEC) lays down the effects of a successful action under both Articles 263 and 265. The institution concerned must take the necessary measures to remedy its failure in accordance with the judgment. No sanctions are available, although a further action may be brought under Article 265.

INDIRECT REVIEW UNDER ARTICLE 277 TFEU

Under Article 277 TFEU (ex 241 TEC) an applicant may challenge the legality of a general act on which a subsequent act or omission is based without restrictive time limits. Article 277 provides that:

> Notwithstanding the expiry of the time limit laid down in Article 263(3), any party may, in proceedings in which a regulation of the Council or the Commission is in issue, plead the grounds specified in Article 263(2) . . . to invoke before the Court of Justice the inapplicability of that act.

The plea of illegality does not give rise to an independent cause of action but may only be invoked where there are already proceedings before the Court of Justice (Cases 31 & 33/62 *Wöhrmann* v. *Commission*). This usually means bringing an action under Article 277 where there are other proceedings under Article 263 for annulment or Article 267 for a ruling on validity in the same case. In *Wöhrmann* the applicant unsuccessfully sought to challenge a regulation imposing a charge outside the two-month limit which applied under (what is now) Article 263. The Court declared that the sole purpose of the procedure under (what is now) Article 277 TFEU was to protect interested parties against the application of illegal regulations, not to circumvent the time limit in Article 263. It found that proceedings before a national court should be suspended for a preliminary referral on validity.

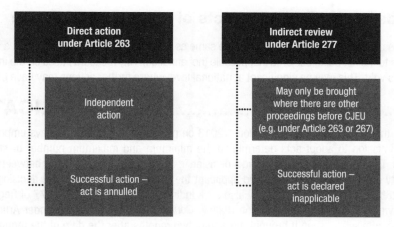

Figure 10.2 Results of successful actions under Articles 263 and 277

The Court of Justice refused to consider a plea under (what is now) Article 277 in the context of preliminary reference proceedings in Case 44/65 *Hessische Knappschaft* v. *Maison Singer et Fils* over interpretation of a social security regulation. The Court held that it was for national courts to determine whether a preliminary reference should be made. Thus the Court of Justice could not be compelled by the parties to hear a request for a preliminary reference or a claim under Article 277 TFEU.

A plea under Article 277 may be brought by the applicant or defendant provided there is a direct judicial link between the act or omission affecting the applicant and the act in question. In Case 32/65 *Italy* v. *Council and Commission* Italy sought to have parts of two competition regulations declared inapplicable in an action to annul a third. The Court of Justice held that the regulation called into question must apply to the issue with which the application is concerned. Finding no such connection between the third regulation and the other two, it dismissed the application.

Who may bring an action under Article 277?

The reference to 'any party' in Article 277 clearly covers individuals. The Court held in Case C-442/04 *Spain* v. *Council* that a Member State may bring an action under Article 277 even where it had failed to act within the two-month limit under Article 263. Spain sought to raise the validity of several Articles of a regulation under the Common Fisheries Policy after expiry of the time limit for annulment. The Court of Justice found it followed from the wording of (what is now) Article 277 that 'any party' including a Member State can invoke the inapplicability of a regulation. The Court held there was no misuse of powers and the plea failed.

Reviewable acts

Before amendment by the Treaty of Lisbon, old Article 241 (now 277) was stated to apply only to regulations. To be consistent with Article 263, where substance rather than the form determined the remedy, the Court of Justice held in Case 92/78 *Simmenthal SpA* that a general notice of invitation to tender (forming the basis of a decision to the Italian government in which the applicant was directly interested) could be challenged. The decision was annulled.

Article 277 TFEU broadened the scope of reviewable acts to cover 'acts of general application', extending the scope of review to directives under the ordinary or special legislative procedures and possibly delegated acts under 290 TFEU.

Grounds of review and effects of a successful action

The grounds of review under Article 277 are the same as those under Article 263, although a successful action leads to the act being declared inapplicable (not annulled). Any measure based on the inapplicable regulation is void. This may be significant at national level where further actions may have been taken.

·· APPLICATION

Imagine the EU has adopted Regulation 1/2013 on provision of statutory holidays empowering the Commission to adopt acts determining the minimum and maximum number of statutory holidays. The Commission has adopted a decision in January 2014 providing for between fifteen and thirty days a year. As a privileged applicant the UK may seek to annul the decision under Article 263 within two months. It may also seek indirect review under Article 277 of Regulation 1/2013 which is linked to the decision (*Italy* v. *Council*), so the application under Article 277 would be admissible, even if brought more than two months after the date of the regulation. If the action succeeds the regulation would be declared inapplicable.

LIABILITY OF THE EU INSTITUTIONS UNDER ARTICLE 340 TFEU

Article 340 TFEU (ex 288 TEC) provides the basis for a damages claim against the EU institutions. Circumstances may give rise to both an action for annulment under Article 263 and damages under Article 340. While it is easier to establish standing under Article 340 than Article 263, damages claims usually fail as the criteria for liability are not satisfied.

CORNERSTONE

Article 340(2) TFEU

Article 340(2) provides that the Union shall make good any damage caused by its institutions or its servants in the performance of their duties, in accordance with the general principles common to the laws of the Member States.

Article 340(2) imposes *non-contractual liability* (i.e. liability in tort) on the EU institutions for losses arising from their acts and omissions where they are under a duty to act. The EU institutions comprise the Parliament, European Council, Council, Commission, Court of Justice, ECB and Court of Auditors (Article 13 TEU). There are no restrictions on standing of persons who may bring an action under Article 340(2), unlike judicial review under Article 263 (Case 48/65 *Alfons Lütticke GmbH* v. *Commission*). Applicants have five years from the alleged wrongful act or omission to bring an action (Article 46 of the Statute of the Court of Justice).

Requirements for claiming damages under Article 340

The Court of Justice decided in Cases C-46 & 48/93 *Brasserie/Factortame (No. 3)* that the liability of the EU institutions and Member States is based on the same principles.

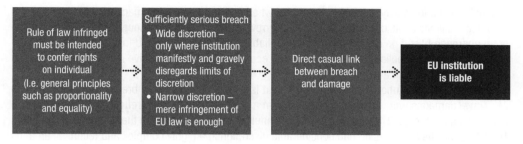

Figure 10.3 Liability of the EU institutions under *Bergaderm*

INTERSECTION

The conditions for liability in *Brasserie/Factortame* are examined in Chapter 8, including the requirement for the breach to be sufficiently serious, which was applied from the case law on Article 340.

In Case C-352/98P *Laboratoires Pharmaceutiques Bergaderm* v. *Commission*, the Court of Justice confirmed its approach in *Brasserie/Factortame* on the EU institutions (see Figure 10.3).

CORNERSTONE

Liability of the EU institutions depends on their use of discretion, not whether the act is legislative or administrative (*Bergaderm*).

Before *Bergaderm* the Court of Justice distinguished between liability from administrative (i.e. non-legislative) acts requiring only a wrongful act, damage and a causal connection, and from legislative acts requiring breach of a superior rule of law for the protection of the individual and for the breach to be sufficiently serious. *Bergaderm* abolished that distinction. The case arose from the Commission's adoption of a directive prohibiting a substance in suntan lotions considered to cause cancer. Bergaderm, the only company using the substance, claimed it was driven into liquidation as a result. It sued the Commission unsuccessfully for damages in the CFI. On appeal to the Court of Justice Bergaderm argued the measure was an administrative rather than a legislative act, so it should only be necessary to establish illegality, without showing that the breach was sufficiently serious. The Court of Justice upheld the CFI decision, ruling that it was immaterial whether the act was legislative or administrative. What mattered was whether the act involved the use of discretion.

The Court held that three conditions must be satisfied for an EU institution to be liable in damages:

1. The rule of law infringed must be intended to confer rights on the individual.

2. The breach must be sufficiently serious.

3. There must be a direct causal link between the breach of the obligation and the damage sustained.

The importance of discretion in establishing liability

Bergaderm removed the artificial distinction between legislative and administrative acts, placing the focus instead on the exercise of discretion. Where discretion is wide, the breach must be sufficiently serious to result in liability, for which the test is whether the EU institution manifestly and gravely disregarded the limits on its discretion. Where it is narrow, a simple breach is enough. The Court's adoption of an approach based on discretion to establish liability is logical, as the EU institutions exercise discretion when making policy choices about social, economic and administrative matters, just as they do when deciding to adopt a legislative act.

Where the EU institution has *wide discretion*, it is difficult to establish a breach. In Case T-212/03 *My Travel* damages were claimed for losses from a Commission decision refusing clearance for two undertakings to merge. The decision was later annulled by the CFI although the damages claim failed. The CFI found the Commission had considerable discretion in a highly complex and technical area. Its errors of economic analysis were not considered manifest and grave and so not a sufficiently serious breach, as any other decision would have unreasonably restricted the Commission's regulatory role.

Where the EU institution has *little or no discretion*, a mere infringement of EU law is enough for liability, as the CFI confirmed in Case T-178/98 *Fresh Marine* v. *Commission*. (The Commission had misread a report and imposed anti-dumping penalties on a company for selling salmon in the EU below the price on the Norwegian market.)

APPLICATION

Imagine that a long-established subsidy paid to a farmer growing barley in the UK is suddenly withdrawn by the Commission. The farmer goes bankrupt, suing the Commission in the General Court for damages, claiming infringement of legitimate expectations and of the principle of proportionality. The Commission argues it has considerable discretion under the scheme, as it must use its resources to support farming across the EU. It can demonstrate it has conducted a careful analysis of barley growing, although its findings are disputed by some experts. It is unlikely the General Court would award damages in favour of the farmer as the Commission does not appear to have committed a grave and manifest infringement of its discretion.

Liability from a lawful act

Several unsuccessful claims for losses from a lawful act ('no fault' liability) have been made. It is clear from Case C-233/99P *Dorsch Consult* v. *Council* that unusual and special damage would have to be established. The applicant failed to show such damage in a 1995 claim after the first Gulf War for loss under an EU trade ban with Iraq following a UN resolution, having chosen to contract with the government of a country known to be 'high risk' in commercial terms. The Court of Justice remains reluctant to acknowledge 'no fault' liability. In Cases C-120/06P & 121/06P *FIAMM* v. *Council and Commission* (damages claim by banana exporters against the Council and Commission) the exporters were caught up in a protracted dispute between the EU and WTO leading to imposition of penal duties on EU products entering the USA. The Court found that 'no fault' liability was not an established principle of EU law, but if it were, it would require unusual and special damage.

Causation and damages

Damage must not be too remote (*Lütticke*) and must be a direct consequence of the unlawful conduct of the institution (Cases 64 etc./76 *Dumortier Fils SA* v. *Council*, where damages were awarded for refunds withheld under a discriminatory regulation on maize). Applicants must act as reasonably prudent business people. In Case 169/73 *Compagnie Continentale* v. *Council* a French cereal exporter failed to recover damages after claiming to be 'misled' under a Council resolution on compensation as the company should have known of conditions at the time as a reasonably prudent business person.

Contributory negligence

The Court does not usually reduce an award due to contributory negligence, although in Case 145/83 *Adams* v. *Commission* damages for loss and emotional distress from breach of confidence by the Commission were reduced by 50 per cent due to the applicant's failure to protect himself by warning of his return. (He had 'blown the whistle' on competition breaches by his employers in Switzerland before returning and being charged with industrial espionage. During his imprisonment his wife committed suicide.)

The applicant must mitigate his loss. In Cases C-104/89 and C-37/90 *Mulder* v. *Commission and Council* damages were reduced by the amount the applicants, dairy farmers, would have earned if they had undertaken alternative commercial activities while unable to produce and sell dairy products under an EC scheme. Losses which could have been passed on to customers cannot be recovered (Cases 261 and 262/78 *Interquell Stark-Chemie GmbH* v. *Commission*, on damages for abolition of production refunds for *quellmehl*, a form of German black bread).

Damage

Compensation can only be recovered for damage which is actual or imminent and foreseeable with sufficient certainty rather than speculative (Cases 5 etc./66 *Kampffmeyer* v. *Commission*, where a claim for loss from refusal of import licence by the Commission was not specific). A damages claim in Case 253/84 *GAEC* v. *Council and Commission* for alleged losses of a French farmer from German farm subsidies after a Council decision also failed as prices had already dropped.

ROLE OF THE NATIONAL COURTS

Concurrent liability

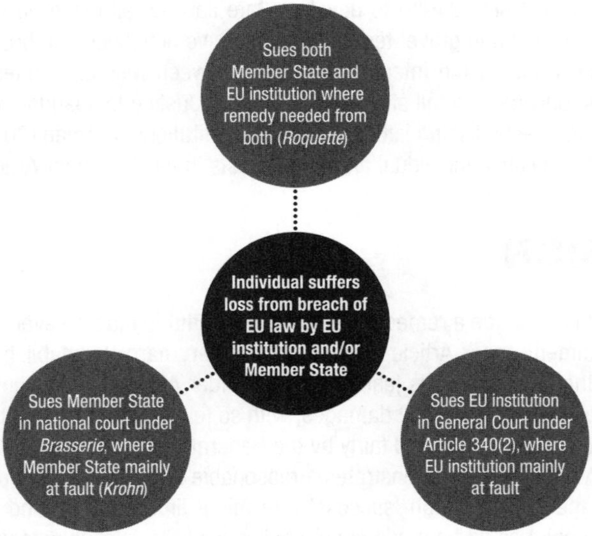

Figure 10.4 Concurrent liability of the EU institutions and the Member States

It may be unclear whether an action should be brought against the Member State in the national courts or an EU institution in the General Court, as many claims, particularly over agriculture, concern schemes administered by national intervention agencies. In Case 96/71 *Haegemann Sprl* v. *Commission* an action was brought in the Belgian courts to recover a charge on wine imported from Greece into Belgium. The Court held that where the national authority is primarily at fault, the action should be brought in the national courts. Losses directly caused by an EU institution should be the subject of a damages claim under Article 340(2) (Case 175/84 *Krohn* v. *Commission*).

··**APPLICATION**

Imagine the EU Commission provides assistance to hill farmers in a scheme which it changes without notice, withdrawing all financial support. Aggrieved hill farmers could sue the Commission for infringement of legitimate expectations. If the scheme had been set up by the Commission but administered by the Member States which decided to withdraw support, the hill farmers could sue the Member State. The principles of State liability would be the same as those applying to the institutions.

Where a remedy is needed from *both* national courts and the General Court, applicants should bring actions before both sets of courts. In Case 26/74 *Roquette* v. *Commission* the applicant successfully sued the French government for damages over compensation payments under the CAP but was not awarded interest, failing in later proceedings to recover the interest as damages. If there is no effective remedy at national level, failure to bring an action before the national courts does not prevent an action under Article 340(2) (Cases 197 etc./80 *Ludwigshafener Walzmühle Erling KG* v. *Council and Commission*) (national remedy only available to importers of wheat, not makers of pasta like the applicant).

Most recent writing on liability of the EU institutions has focused on the approach of the Court of Justice after *Brasserie/Factortame* and *Bergaderm*. The use of discretion is the paramount consideration. Tridimas (2001) finds inconsistencies between the Court's approach to State liability relative to liability of the institutions, arguing that the Court has not made enough use of case law under Article 340(2) to develop State liability, although he welcomes the extension of the 'manifest and grave' test to administrative acts based on broad discretion. Hilson (2005) argues that in the interests of parity between Member States and the EU institutions it would only be a 'small step' for the Court of Justice to abandon the concept of discretion in relation to establishing liability of the EU institutions. Gutman (2011), however, points to the need to balance individual and EU interests in liability under Article 340.

REFLECTION

CONCLUSION

The individual seeking to enforce a remedy against an EU institution faces severe barriers, particularly in an action for annulment under Article 263 where it is very hard to establish standing unless the act is addressed to the individual. It is just as difficult under Article 340 to show that the breach is sufficiently serious to justify an award of damages, with so few actions succeeding that questions are raised as whether individuals are treated fairly by the General Court. Gutman (2011) may be right that the case law under Article 340(2) demonstrates a reasonable balance between protecting individuals and the interests of the EU, as a high 'success' rate might limit capacity and confidence of Union legislators. The same point could be made about challenges to legislative acts under Article 263.

KEY POINTS

- Any act intended to be legally binding is reviewable under Article 263 TFEU.
- Privileged applicants (EU institutions and Member States) may challenge *any* act under Article 263.
- Non-privileged individuals may only challenge acts addressed to them or acts in which they are directly and individually concerned unless the measure is a regulatory act not requiring implementation which only requires direct concern to challenge.
- Article 263(2) provides the grounds for annulment such as infringement of the Treaties including breach of general principles and fundamental rights.
- Where an EU institution fails to act when under a duty to do so, its inaction may be challenged under Article 265 TFEU.
- A declaration that an act is inapplicable under Article 277 may be sought in conjunction with other proceedings before the Court of Justice.
- Article 340 TFEU provides the basis for an action in damages against the EU institutions, with liability determined in relation to use of discretion.

CORE CASES AND STATUTES

Case	About	Importance
Case 25/62 *Plaumann & Co* v. *Commission*	Applicant (clementine importer) sought to challenge decision addressed to German government on customs duties. CJEU found applicant not individually concerned as member of open class.	Established test for individual concern under Article 230(4) TEC – measure must affect applicant's legal position by differentiating him from other persons and distinguishing him individually as if addressed to him.
Case C-309/89 *Codorniu* v. *Council*	Application for annulment under Article 230(4) TEC (now 263) of 'true' regulation by applicant not within closed group.	Applicant was (exceptionally) held individually concerned as regulation affected firm in different way from other producers.
Case C-50/00P *Unión de Pequeños Agricultores (UPA)* v. *Council*	Attempt by trade association to challenge general regulation.	Although A-G Jacobs submitted there should be a more liberal test on standing, CJEU reaffirmed restrictive test in *Plaumann*.
Case T-177/01 *Jégo Quéré* v. *Commission*	Challenge to regulation of general application found admissible by CFI but overturned by CJEU.	CFI formulated more liberal test for standing than *Plaumann*, but was overruled by CJEU in Case C-263/02P after *UPA* ruling.
Case T-18/10 Inuit *Tapiriit Kanatami* v. *Parliament and Council*	Definition of 'regulatory acts' under Article 263(4) TFEU as 'acts of general application apart from legislative acts', upheld by CJEU in Case C-583/11P.	Regulatory act not requiring implementation may be challenged by directly concerned non-privileged applicant without individual concern.

→

Case	About	Importance
Case C-352/98P *Laboratoires Pharmaceutiques Bergaderm and Goupil* v. *Commission*	Prohibition in directive of substance considered carcinogenic, used only by applicant.	Applied same approach to liability of EU institutions as Member States. Placed liability for non-legislative acts on par with legislative acts.

Statute	About	Importance
Article 263(1) TFEU (ex 230(1) TEC)	Annulment of acts of EU institutions.	Defines which acts are reviewable.
Article 263(2) TFEU	Empowers Member States, EP, Council and Commission to challenge on specified grounds.	'Privileged' applicants under Article 263(2) can challenge any EU act.
Article 263(4) TFEU	Natural or legal persons can challenge acts addressed to them or in which they are directly and individually concerned, and regulatory acts not requiring implementing measures in which they are directly concerned.	Individuals seeking to challenge acts not addressed to them must show *both* direct and individual concern under *Plaumann*. Regulatory acts not requiring implementation only require direct concern.
Article 263(6) TFEU	Provides two-month period for annulment.	Measure may not be challenged outside time limit by other means such as Article 277 where applicant could have challenged under Article 263 (*TWD*).
Article 277 TFEU (ex 241 TEC)	'Any party' may plead grounds in Article 263(1) TFEU before CJEU to invoke inapplicability of act of EU institution, despite expiry of time limit in Article 263(6).	May be invoked in relation to acts of general application where there are other linked proceedings before CJEU, with no restrictive rules on standing or time limits. Successful action leads to declaration of inapplicability.
Article 340(2) TFEU (ex 288(2) TEC)	Requires EU to make good damage caused by its institutions or servants performing their duties, in accordance with general principles common to laws of Member States.	Enables individuals to sue EU institutions in tort. CJEU applied case law under Article 340 to Member States' liability on same terms as EU institutions in *Brasserie/Factortame*.

FURTHER READING

Albors-Llorens, A. 'The standing of private parties to challenge community measures: Has the European Court missed the boat?' (2003) 62 *Cambridge Law Journal* 72
Examines position of private parties wishing to challenge an act of the institutions after *UPA* and *Jégo Quéré*.

Albors-Llorens, A. 'Sealing the fate of private parties in annulment proceedings? The General Court and the new Standing Test in Article 264(4) TFEU' (2012) 71 *Cambridge Law Journal* 52
Case note analysing *Inuit* and *Microban*.

Arnull, A. (2001) 'Private applicants and the action for annulment since *Codorniu'* (2001) 38 *Common Market Law Review* 7
Assesses standing of non-privileged applicants after *Codorniu* but before Lisbon.

Arnull, A. 'The principal of effective judicial protection in EU law: an unruly horse?' (2011) 36 *European Law Review* 51
Worth reading for discussion of judicial effectiveness in *UPA* and *Kadi*.

Balthasar, S. '*Locus standi* rules for challenges to regulatory acts by private applicants: the new Article 263(4) TFEU' (2010) 35 *European Law Review* 542
Written after Lisbon but before *Inuit* and *Microban*. Argues for a liberal interpretation of 'regulatory acts'.

Gutman, K. 'The evolution of the action for damages against the European Union and its place in the system of judicial protection' (2011) 48 *Common Market Law Review* 695
Comprehensive evaluation of case law on damages.

Hilson, C. 'The role of discretion in EC Law on non-contractual liability' (2005) 42 *Common Market Law Review* 677
Compares use of discretion in liability of EU institutions and Member States.

Koch, C. '*Locus standi* of private applicants under the EU Constitution: preserving gaps in the protection of individuals' right to an effective remedy' (2005) 30 *European Law Review* 511
Written about the CT, but relevant as Lisbon wording follows CT.

Tridimas, T. 'Liability for breach of community law: growing up and mellowing down?' (2001) 38 *Common Market Law Review* 301
Mainly focuses on Member States' liability, but also relevant to EU institutions.

Usher, J. 'Direct and individual concern – an effective remedy or a conventional solution' (2003) 28 *European Law Review* 575
Incisive analysis of A-G Jacobs' submissions in *UPA* and the CFI decision in *Jégo Quéré*.

PART 2

Free movement and the single market

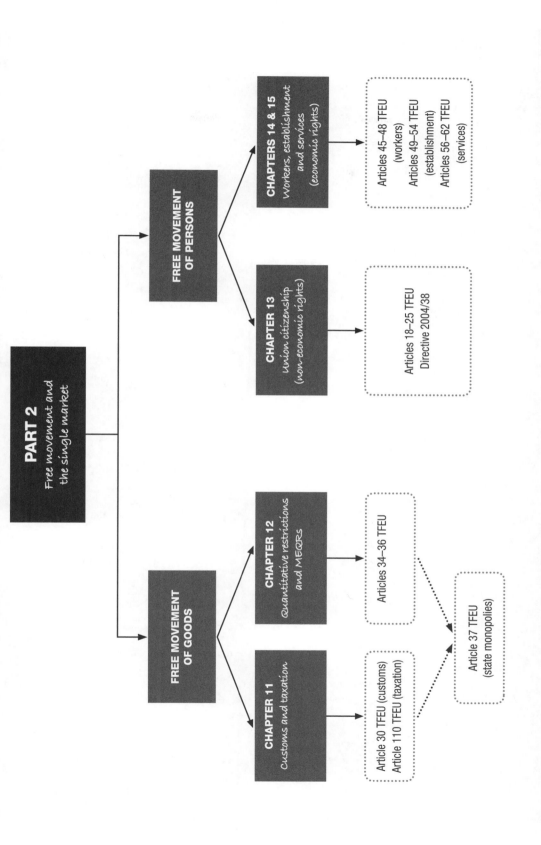

CHAPTER 11

Customs duties, discriminatory taxation and state monopolies

BLUEPRINT

Customs duties, discriminatory taxation and state monopolies

KEY QUESTIONS

LEGISLATION

- Article 28 TFEU
- Article 30 TFEU
- Article 37 TFEU
- Article 110 TFEU

CONTEXT

- EU is the biggest world trading space
- Threats from organised crime and terrorism
- Impact of e-commerce

CONCEPTS

- Customs duty
- Charge having equivalent effect
- Discriminatory taxation
- State monopolies

- Should Member States be able to impose charges which are not protectionist but benefit domestic products?

- How does the customs union contribute to the single market?

CASES

- *Sociaal Fonds voor de Diamantarbeiders*
- *Fratelli Cucchi*

REFORM

- Regulation 450/2008 and the Modernised Customs Code

SPECIAL CHARACTERISTICS

- Need to distinguish charges disguised as a tax from a genuine tax
- 'Similar' products for tax purposes should be taxed alike.
- State monopolies are normally considered under Art.110 or 34–36

CRITICAL ISSUES

Setting the scene

In May 2013 the Court of Justice celebrated the fiftieth anniversary of a remarkable ruling – Case 26/62 *Van Gend en Loos* v. *Nederlandse Administratie der Belastingen*. On 9 September 1960 a transport company in the Netherlands known as Van Gend en Loos imported from Germany a quantity of urea formaldehyde, used to make glue. The Dutch authorities imposed a duty of 8%. Eleven days later the company lodged an objection as the duty was 5% higher than expected, the Netherlands government having increased the duty three years after the EEC Treaty came into force.

The case was sent to the Court of Justice to clarify the position on customs duties, leading to a ruling in February 1963 which became the best known decision in the Court of Justice's history. The Court did not confine itself to the narrow point – the legality of an increase in customs duty – but held that the EEC Treaty created a 'new legal order', creating rights and duties on which individuals could rely. It ruled that the Treaty provision prohibiting increases in customs duty was directly effective, giving the importer a defence before the Netherlands court. Since the decision the Community has developed dramatically, removing customs duties in 1968, completing the single market in 1992, introducing the European Union in 1993 and enlarging from six Member States to twenty-eight. Nevertheless the ruling in *Van Gend en Loos* continues to provide the basis for the EU legal order (see Chapter 7).

This chapter examines the customs union, discriminatory taxation in relation to goods and state monopolies. Free movement of goods is covered in Chapter 12.

FREE MOVEMENT, THE CUSTOMS UNION AND THE TREATIES

> ### Take note
>
> It would be useful at this stage to reread Chapter 1 to ensure you understand the rationale for the development of the single market and its role in 'deepening' the EU.

The free movement of goods, persons, services and capital provides the original economic rationale for the European Economic Community (EEC) under the Treaty of Rome and remains at the heart of the EU. Article 26 TFEU (ex 14 TEC) provides for an *internal market* comprising an area within which the free movement of goods, persons, services and capital is ensured in accordance with the Treaties. Articles 34–36 TFEU (ex 28–30 TEC) require removal of all restrictions on free movement of goods.

The EU is a *customs union* and a single market. Article 28 TFEU (ex 23 TEC) provides for the Union to comprise a customs union prohibiting customs duties and measures of equivalent effect (CEEs) between Member States and providing for a common external tariff (rate of duty) on goods entering the Union from outside. While the customs union is within the EU's exclusive competence under Article 3 TFEU, internal taxation is a matter for the Member States unless it infringes EU law. Thus Article 110 TFEU (ex 90 TEC) enables Member States to administer their own system of taxation provided it is not discriminatory or protectionist in relation to goods.

The meaning of 'goods'

The Court of Justice uses the term 'goods' interchangeably with 'products'. In Case 7/68 *Commission* v. *Italy (Re Export Tax on Art Treasures)* the Court defined 'goods' as covering anything capable of

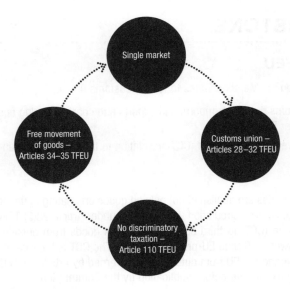

Figure 11.1 Free movement of goods under the TFEU

money valuation and of being the object of commercial transactions. Thus gold and silver collectors' coins no longer in circulation were 'goods' in Case 7/78 *R* v. *Thompson* (arising from a prosecution for exporting gold and silver coins from the UK). An export ban to prevent a threat to the coinage from melting down the metal was legitimate.

'Goods' may have a negative value such as shipments of non-recyclable waste in Case C-2/90 *Commission* v. *Belgium* (*Walloon Waste*) (proceedings against Belgium for banning storage and dumping of hazardous waste from other Member States contrary to a directive). The term was held to cover goods in a contract for work and materials as well as in a contract of sale in Case 45/87R *Commission* v. *Ireland* (*Re Dundalk Water Supply*) (proceedings against Ireland for stipulating a national product standard in a public works contract).

The customs union

A customs union is a limited form of integration requiring removal of tariff barriers between participating States with little loss of sovereignty. It was achieved by the European Community in 1968. Under the original Treaty of Rome, Article 12 EEC prohibited new customs duties and equivalent charges, while Article 13 EEC required Member States to abolish existing duties. Reclassification of goods with a higher rate of duty was found by the Court to contravene Article 12 in Case 26/62 *Van Gend en Loos*. As the Court found the Article directly effective, individuals could rely on it to resist paying higher rates of duty. Articles 12 to 17 EEC were repealed by the Treaty of Amsterdam since the distinction between new and existing duties had become out-dated. Article 30 TFEU retains the essence of the prohibition in Article 12. The customs union today is covered by Articles 28 to 32 TFEU (ex 23 to 27 TEC).

CORNERSTONE

Article 28 TFEU

Article 28 TFEU requires Member States to form a customs union:

- prohibiting customs duties on imports and exports and charges having equivalent effect (CEEs) between Member States
- adopting a common customs tariff (CCT) in relation to third countries (non-Member States).

In a customs union duties are abolished not only on goods originating in the contracting States but also from third countries in free circulation within the EU under Article 28(2) TFEU. The application of a common customs tariff (CCT) to third countries prevents goods from outside the EU entering the internal market at a lower tariff than EU-produced goods. The CCT is the rate at which customs duty is applied to goods entering the EU from outside. It is governed by Article 31 TFEU (ex 26 TEC) which requires the Council to fix the rate before publication by the Commission.

> The EU is the biggest trading space in the world, with 245 million customs declarations completed in 2011 according to the Commission. Enlargement, the threat of terrorist attacks, internationalisation of organised crime and the development of e-commerce pose new challenges for customs authorities supervising the EU's international trade.

CONTEXT

Coordination on customs between the EU and Member States is essential as the EU does not operate its own customs service but works through the national authorities. The EU issued the Modernised Customs Code in 2008 under Regulation 450/2008 to simplify legislation and procedures, while the Commission issued a Communication setting out its strategic objectives including increasing business competitiveness by modernising working methods.

PROHIBITION OF CUSTOMS DUTIES AND CHARGES OF EQUIVALENT EFFECT

CORNERSTONE

Article 30 TFEU

Article 30 TFEU (ex 25 TEC) prohibits customs duties on imports and exports and charges having equivalent effect (CEEs) between Member States.

What are customs duties and charges having equivalent effect?

Customs duties are financial charges applied when goods cross a border. In some cases duties are identified as such while other instances may be less obvious. Article 30 TFEU provides for the abolition of *charges having an effect equivalent to customs duties*. The Court defined a charge having equivalent effect (CEE) in Case 24/68 *Commission* v. *Italy ('Statistical Levy')*, declaring that:

> [A]ny pecuniary charge . . . which is imposed unilaterally on domestic or foreign goods by reason of the fact that they cross a frontier and which is not a customs duty in the strict sense constitutes a charge having equivalent effect within the meaning of Articles 9, 12, 13 and 16 of the Treaty.

The case concerned proceedings over a charge levied by the Italian government to compile statistical data in trade patterns. The Court of Justice found the advantage of the data to traders too uncertain to be an identifiable benefit, so the charge was held to be a CEE contrary to Articles 9–16 EEC.

CORNERSTONE

Disguised charges

The imposition of any charge on goods crossing a frontier is an obstacle to free movement of goods (Cases 2 & 3/69 *Sociaal Fonds voor de Diamantarbeiders*).

CEEs come in many forms and may be disguised as a tax or levy. *Diamantarbeiders* concerned a levy on imported diamonds imposed by the Belgian government. The levy was not protectionist as Belgium did not produce diamonds, but was intended to provide social security benefits for diamond workers. The Court held that customs duties on goods between Member States are prohibited independently of their purpose and destination.

In Case C-293/02 *Jersey Produce Marketing Organisation Ltd* v. *States of Jersey and others* the Court found that the Jersey Potato Export Marketing Board's imposition of a 'contribution' by reference to the amount of potatoes for export to the UK contravened Articles 23 and 25 TEC (now 28 and 30 TFEU). The contribution was regarded as a CEE even though the potatoes were intended for export to the UK (i.e. not crossing a border) as they might be re-exported to other Member States. Likewise in Case C-72/03 *Carbonati Apuani Srl* v. *Comune di Carrara* a tax proportionate to weight was levied on marble excavated within a municipality in Italy on transportation across municipal boundaries as a contribution to road maintenance costs. This tax was also a CEE because it was levied regardless of destination (i.e. whether staying in Italy or for export).

There are no exceptions to the prohibition in Article 30 TFEU. In Case 7/68 *Commission* v. *Italy (Re Export Tax on Art Treasures)* the Court held that Article 36 EEC (now 36 TFEU) could not be invoked to justify an illegal tax levied by the Italian government to protect the national artistic heritage.

Payments for services

A charge levied by a Member State to pay for services is permissible under Article 30 TFEU but may be difficult to justify. In Case 46/76 *Bauhuis* v. *Netherlands Inspection* the Court held that inspection charges payable on crossing a border may only be recovered by the Member States if levied under a *mandatory* EU scheme. Thus charges for veterinary and other inspections required by EU law and imposed by the Netherlands when live animals were exported were not CEES and could be recovered if they did not exceed the cost of inspection. Where a Member State seeks to recover an inspection charge which is merely *permissible* under EU law, it will be regarded as a CEE, as in Case 314/82 *Commission* v. *Belgium (Re Health Inspection Service)* (imported but not domestically produced poultry meat subject to inspection charge).

Charges which are reimbursed to domestic producers

CORNERSTONE

A charge levied both on imported and domestic goods may infringe Article 30 TFEU if:

- its sole purpose is to provide financial support for the specific advantage of the domestic product;
- the taxed product and the domestic product benefiting are the same;
- charges imposed on the domestic product are refunded in full (Case 77/76 *Fratelli Cucchi* v. *Avez SpA* and Case 105/76 *Interzuccheri*).

A levy had been imposed on imported and domestically produced sugar, but the proceeds were intended for the exclusive benefit of national sugar refineries and sugar beet producers. The Court ruled that such a charge was a CEE contrary to Article 30.

Where a charge does not infringe Article 30, it may breach Article 110 if it amounts to discriminatory taxation or Article 107 (ex 87 TEC) if it is an unlawful state aid (Case 73/79 *Commission* v. *Italy (Re Reimbursement of Sugar Storage Costs)*). Sums paid under an illegal charge must be repaid in full by the Member State (Case 199/82 *Amministrazione della Finanze dello Stato* v. *San Giorgio*), where the Court ruled that a remedy had to be put in place to allow recovery of health inspection charges levied contrary to EU law.

Non-discriminatory charges

A non-discriminatory charge taxed at the same rate regardless of source should be assessed under Article 110 to establish whether it is a genuine tax. If the proceeds of the charge are applied to the exclusive benefit of the domestic product, it will be a CEE contrary to Article 30 if the conditions in *Fratelli Cucchi* are satisfied.

APPLICATION

Imagine the UK imposes a charge on growing sisal to make rope following pressure from domestic growers concerned about competition. A full rebate is payable to sisal growers based in the UK. While the charge might appear to be a non-discriminatory tax, the real purpose is to protect UK growers from competition from imports. The charge is, in effect, payable when the sisal enters the UK and should be considered as a CEE as it satisfies the conditions in *Fratelli Cucchi*. It is therefore prohibited under Article 30.

PROHIBITION OF DISCRIMINATORY TAXATION UNDER ARTICLE 110 TFEU

CORNERSTONE

Article 110 TFEU

Article 110 TFEU (1) (ex 90 TEC) prohibits Member States from imposing, directly or indirectly, on the products of the other Member States any internal taxation greater than that imposed directly or indirectly on similar domestic products. It also prohibits in Article 110(2) the imposition of any internal taxation on the products of other Member States which affords indirect protection to other products.

Member States may impose taxes which are *genuine and non-discriminatory* under Article 110 TFEU. A 'genuine tax' was defined in Case 90/79 *Commission* v. *France (Re Levy on Reprographic Machines)* as a measure relating to a system of internal dues applied systematically to categories of products in accordance with objective criteria irrespective of the origin of the products.

Article 110 allows Member States to establish the taxation system for each product provided there is no discrimination against imported products or indirect protection of domestic products. The purpose of the Article is to abolish discrimination against imported products, not to accord them tax privileges as the Court held in Case 253/83 *Kupferberg* (German tax on wine was found not to be applicable to Portugal under the Free Trade Agreement with the EU before Portuguese accession).

Internal taxation may be imposed on imported products where the charge relates to the whole class of products irrespective of origin, even where there is no domestically produced counterpart (Case 90/79 *Commission* v. *France* in which a 3% levy on reprographic equipment to buy books for a National Book Fund and address copyright problems was covered by Article 110). Taxes discouraging importation relative to sale of domestic products are illegal. In Case C-402/09 *Tatu* v. *Statul român prin Ministerul Finanțelor și Economiei and Others* a pollution tax payable on first registration of motor vehicles infringed Article 110 as it discouraged placing imported second-hand motor vehicles into circulation without doing so for their domestic equivalent.

'Similar' products

To be covered by Article 110 products need not be *identical* if they are *similar*, in which case they should be taxed in the same way. Conversely products which are not similar may be taxed at different rates without infringing Article 110. The case law of the Court, mostly on alleged discrimination over the taxation of alcoholic drinks, illustrates 'similarity'.

In Case 243/84 *John Walker* the Court compared *fruit liqueur wines and whisky*, holding that it was not enough that both contained alcohol. To be 'similar', alcohol would have to be present in more or less equal quantities. As whisky contained twice as much alcohol as fruit liqueur wines it was *not* similar within Article 110 (2) TFEU. In Case 170/78 *Commission* v. *UK (Re Excise Duties on Wine)* beer produced in the UK and wine mostly produced outside the UK were compared. Wine is more highly taxed and less widely drunk than beer in the UK. Allowing for changing habits and the growing popularity of wine, the Court held it was possible to compare beer with lighter, cheaper wines, and found the tax system discriminatory. It confirmed the similarity of beer and light wines for taxation purposes in Case C-167/05 *Commission* v. *Sweden* but found the higher price charged for certain categories of wine was justified.

'Similar' products may be taxed differently where the difference is based on objective criteria to achieve acceptable economic objectives. In Case 196/85 *Commission* v. *France* 'traditional' natural sweet wines were taxed at a lower rate than ordinary wine. The Court accepted the justification (economic assistance to rural areas dependent on wine production). There was no contravention of EU law in the absence of protectionist or discriminatory motives.

·· APPLICATION

Assume the UK is a major producer of gin taxed at a lower rate than brandy from other EU states. Alcotrader Ltd, a UK-based importer, objects to the high rate of tax on brandy and brings an action in the UK courts. To assess whether the higher tax on brandy infringes Article 110(1), the UK court should compare brandy and gin for similarity by examining patterns of consumption, alcohol levels and price. If the products are regarded as similar, the differential tax rates would be illegal under Article 110(1) unless objectively justified. On the facts there is no indication of justification.

Indirect discrimination against imports

Internal taxation contravenes Article 110(2) if it discriminates against imports by providing indirect protection to domestic products. Unlike Article 110(1), Article 110(2) does not provide for a direct comparison between domestic and imported products. Indirect protection will occur where imported products are taxed more heavily than their domestic competitors (Case 27/67 *Fink-Frucht GmbH*). In Case 170/78 *Commission* v. *UK* (beer/wine comparison) the Court of Justice held that whichever criteria for comparison were adopted, the tax system benefited domestic production.

Indirect discrimination

Particular risk of indirect discrimination under Article 110 arises using a sliding scale of taxation distinguishing between imports and exports, as the following cases show:

(a) The German government taxed small brewers, mostly German, on a scale which benefited them to the detriment of larger brewers, normally importers, charged at a fixed rate. The Court of Justice held that the possibility of discrimination infringed the prohibition (Case 127/75 *Bobie* v. *HZA Aachen-Nord*).

(b) The French government applied road tax on a sliding scale with a significantly higher rate on cars over 16 c-v (horsepower). No cars over 16 c-v were made in France. A French taxpayer who imported a 36 c-v Mercedes from Germany sought repayment in the French courts of the tax differential. The Court held that such a tax system amounted to indirect discrimination based on nationality, contrary to Article 110 TFEU (Case 112/84 *Humblot* v. *Directeur des Services Fiscaux*).

(c) In an attempt to remedy the discrimination in *Humblot* the French government amended the system to introduce nine new categories under the sliding scale for tax purposes, although the rate increased sharply at 16 c-v. The Court of Justice found that the discrimination had been modified but not removed (Case 433/85 *Feldain* v. *Directeur des Services Fiscaux*).

Taxation has long been an area over which Member States have prized their national sovereignty, reflected in the requirement for unanimity on EU harmonisation measures. While EU law does not control direct taxation such as income tax unless it restricts free movement and/or is discriminatory, it plays a more significant role in relation to indirect taxation, such as VAT. The EU is trying to achieve greater coherence in its taxation policy, but has the difficult task of reconciling the freedom of Member States to determine their own internal taxation policies with the need to harmonise indirect taxation to remove obstacles to free movement.

The Court of Justice has adopted a wider approach in decisions on free movement to include national restrictions which are not discriminatory but which pose obstacles to free movement, raising the question as to whether a similar approach should be adopted when taxation is being examined in the context of the free movement of services or capital. Academic commentators differ as to how far it is appropriate to apply this perspective to taxation. Snell (2007) considers that the Court has been more cautious over fiscal obstacles than those arising through regulation, possibly reflecting ambiguity about the nature of the 'internal market' after the SEA which he argues allows greater national discretion on taxation than the 'common market' under the Treaty of Rome, requiring elimination of distortion of competition as well as removal of barriers to free movement. This is not universally accepted. Advocate-General Leger in Case C-293/02 *Jersey Produce Marketing* took the view that the two expressions were the same. Snell advocates greater legislative intervention on taxation and the introduction of QMV.

Banks (2008), unlike Snell, argues strongly in favour of the Court of Justice acknowledging discrimination as the central notion underlying fundamental rights, making discrimination a criterion of any restriction on a fundamental freedom. Such a move would, she claims, overcome the criticism of inconsistency in the Court's treatment of national tax measures under Article 90 TEC (now 110 TFEU) relative to taxation in the context of infringement of fundamental freedoms.

REFLECTION

STATE MONOPOLIES

CORNERSTONE

Article 37 TFEU

Under Article 37(1) TFEU (ex 31(1) TEC) Member States must adjust state monopolies of a commercial character to ensure that no discrimination exists between nationals of Member States affecting conditions under which goods are procured and marketed. Article 37(2) prohibits the introduction of any new measures contrary to Article 37(1).

An organisation need not enjoy *exclusive* control over the market in particular goods to be a state monopoly. Case 6/64 *Costa* v. *ENEL* provides guidance on the application of Article 37 EEC (now 37 TFEU) in a referral by the Italian courts following nationalisation of electricity (discussed in Chapter 6). The Court held that an undertaking is covered by Article 37 if its object is to enter into transactions involving a commercial product which can be traded between Member States, and to play an effective part in such trade. Article 37(1) was held to be directly effective in Case 59/75 *Pubblico Ministero* v. *Flavia Manghera* (Italian monopoly on making, selling and importing tobacco) and Article 37(2) in Case 6/64 *Costa* v. *ENEL*.

State monopolies in services

State monopolies in *services* were held to be outside Article 37 in Case 155/73 *Italy* v. *Sacchi* (state monopoly in television advertising). However, the Court recognised in Case 271/81 *Société d'Insémination Artificielle* that a monopoly in services may indirectly influence trade in goods, holding that legislation on artificial insemination of cattle did not indirectly establish a monopoly infringing free movement of goods. State monopolies in services may infringe other Treaty provisions, including Article 18 TFEU (non-discrimination) and Articles 56–62 TFEU (services).

State monopolies, differential taxation and the free movement of goods

There is little need today to invoke Article 37 in relation to *differential taxation*, which is normally assessed under Article 110. In Case 148/77 *Hansen* (differential rates of tax applied by the German Federal Monopoly Administration) the Court decided it was preferable to examine the issue from the perspective of Article 110 TFEU rather than Article 37.

> ### Take note
>
> Several Member States including Sweden and Finland operate state monopolies regulating the sale of alcohol, generally justified on public health grounds under Article 36 TFEU.

Article 37 is sometimes raised where there are restrictions on free movement of goods under Articles 34–36 TFEU. In Case 120/78 *Rewe* v. *Bundesmonopolverwaltung für Branntwein* ('*Cassis de Dijon*') arising from a minimum alcohol requirement for spirits imposed by Germany the Court of Justice found that Article 37 only applied to monopolies exercising a commercial function such as marketing, which the German authority was not. The restriction was instead assessed under the free movement of goods provisions. Article 37 may still be applied with the other provisions on the elimination of quantitative restrictions, customs duties and CEEs. In Case C-189/95 *Harry Franzén* the Court of Justice found that restricting the sale of alcohol to a state monopoly of retail outlets such as those in Sweden did not contravene Article 37.

The Court considered the alcohol monopoly provisions again in Case C-170/04 *Rosengren and others*, finding the ban on direct imports of alcoholic drinks into Sweden by private individuals outside Article 37 TFEU as it did not relate to the existence or operation of the monopoly on sale of alcohol. It was assessed under Article 34 and held to be disproportionate and unjustifiable under Article 36.

KEY POINTS

- The EU has operated as a customs union since 1968.
- Customs duties are financial charges payable when goods cross a border. They are illegal when goods move between Member States, as are charges equivalent to customs duties.
- Member States may administer their own system of taxation provided it does not discriminate against goods from other Member States.
- To appreciate whether a different rate of taxation is justified, goods should be assessed for 'similarity' under Article 110 TFEU.
- Article 37 TFEU may still be invoked in the free movement of goods but internal taxation should be assessed under Article 110 TFEU.

CORE CASES AND STATUTES

Case	About	Importance
Case 7/68 *Commission v. Italy (Re Export Tax on Art Treasures)*	Italian tax (found to be CEE) on exportation of goods with artistic, historical, archaeological or ethnographic value.	Defines 'goods' as anything capable of money valuation and being the object of commercial transactions.
Case 26/62 *Van Gend en Loos*	Imposition of customs duty contrary to Article 12 EEC.	Article 12 EEC was held to be directly effective, and criteria for direct effect established in first case defining 'new legal order'.
Cases 2 & 3/69 *Sociaal Fonds voor de Diamantarbeiders*	Levy on imported diamonds to provide social security benefits for diamond workers.	Levy was CEE – charge on goods crossing border, so illegal.
Case 77/76 *Fratelli Cucchi* v. *Avez SpA*	Levy on imported and domestically produced sugar refunded to domestic producers.	Such charge is CEE if sole purpose is to provide financial support for domestic product when taxed and domestic product benefiting are the same and charges imposed on the domestic product are fully refunded.
Case 90/79 *Commission v. France (Re Levy on Reprographic Machines)*	Definition of 'genuine tax'.	'Genuine tax' relates to system of dues applied systematically to categories of products according to objective criteria regardless of origin.
Case 170/78 *Commission* v. *UK (Re Excise Duties on Wine)*	Whether wine is 'similar' to beer for taxation under Article 110 TFEU.	As beer may be compared with lighter, cheaper wines, UK's higher rate of tax on wine infringed Article 110 TFEU.

Statute	About	Importance
Article 26 TFEU (ex 14 TEC)	Defines internal market.	Internal market is 'area without internal frontiers in which free movement of goods, persons, services and capital is ensured in accordance with the Treaties'.
Article 28 TFEU (ex 23 TEC)	Defines customs union.	Article 28(1) provides that Union comprises customs union covering all trade in goods, prohibiting customs duties and CEEs between Member States.
Article 30 TFEU (ex 25 TEC)	Prohibition on customs duties and CEEs.	Prohibits customs duties on imports and exports and CEEs between Member States, as well as customs duties of fiscal nature.
Article 37 TFEU	Requires Member States to adjust state monopolies of commercial character to ensure no discrimination affecting conditions under which goods are procured and marketed.	May be invoked in free movement under Articles 34–36 TFEU, but state monopolies involving differential taxation are considered under Article 110.
Article 110 TFEU (ex 95 TEC)	Prohibition on discriminatory taxation.	Prohibits Member States from imposing taxation (1) discriminating against products of other Member States or (2) affording indirect protection to domestic products.

FURTHER READING

Banks, K. 'The application of the fundamental freedoms to Member State tax measures: guarding against protectionism or second-guessing national policy choices?' (2008) 33 *European Law Review* 482
Examines case law of the Court on taxation, with particular reference to discrimination in national measures.

Kingston, S. 'A light in the darkness: recent developments in the ECJ's direct tax jurisprudence' (2007) 44 *Common Market Law Review* 1321
Examines decisions under Article 93 TEC (now Article 113 TFEU) on tax harmonisation.

Snell, J. (2007) 'Non-discriminatory tax obstacles in Community law' (2007) 56 *International and Comparative Law Quarterly* 339
Compares the Court of Justice's approach on taxation with its general case law on free movement restrictions.

CHAPTER 12

The free movement of goods

BLUEPRINT

The free movement of goods

LEGISLATION

- Article 34 TFEU
- Article 35 TFEU
- Article 36 TFEU

CONTEXT

- Declining share of world trade in 1980s prompted the single market programme

CONCEPTS

- Quantitative restrictions and MEQRs
- Distinctly and indistinctly applicable measures
- 'Rule of reason'
- Selling arrangements
- Product requirements
- Dual burden and equal burden
- Derogations

- Should Member States be able to apply stricter standards to imports than domestic goods (e.g. when indecent or obscene)?

- In what circumstances may Member States restrict the free movement of goods?

CASES

- *Dassonville*
- *'Cassis de Dijon'*
- *Keck and Mithouard*

REFORM

- Further harmonisation of intellectual property rights

SPECIAL CHARACTERISTICS

- Distinctly applicable measures only justifiable under Article 36, whereas indistinctly applicable measures are justifiable under *Cassis*

CRITICAL ISSUES

Setting the scene

Imagine that Swash Ltd, a UK company making shampoo, is prevented from selling its products in France as they contain ingredients forbidden under French law. The scenario raises questions over the validity of restrictions on free movement of goods under Articles 34 to 36 TFEU, a central element of the single market. Under the principle of mutual recognition developed by the Court of Justice in *Cassis de Dijon* (considered in the chapter), goods made in one Member State (the UK) should be recognised as meeting the standard in another Member State (France). The restriction is illegal unless one of the grounds for exception, such as a serious health risk, applies and the measure is not discriminatory.

PRINCIPAL PROVISIONS ON THE FREE MOVEMENT OF GOODS

The principal provisions on the free movement of goods are in Articles 34 to 36 TFEU (ex 28–30 TEC):

- Article 34 TFEU (ex 28) prohibits **quantitative restrictions** on imports, and all measures having equivalent effect;
- Article 35 TFEU (ex 29) prohibits quantitative restrictions on exports and all measures having equivalent effect;
- Article 36 TFEU (ex 30) provides that the prohibitions in Articles 34 and 35 will not apply to import and export restrictions justified on specific grounds.

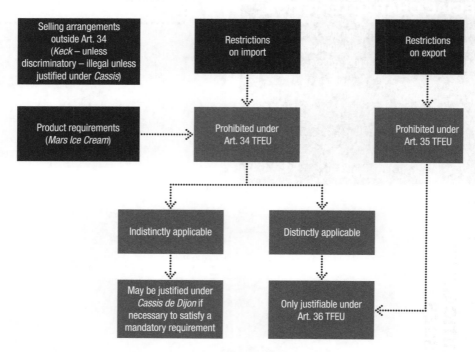

Figure 12.1 Restrictions on free movement of goods under Articles 34–36 TFEU

Quantitative restrictions and measures having equivalent effect

A *quantitative restriction* is a measure restricting the import of a product by amount, number, volume or value, such as a restriction permitting importation of 1,000 tonnes of wheat in a particular year. **Measures having equivalent effect (MEQRs)** are usually legal or administrative measures restricting free movement, such as a requirement to package a product in a particular way. While quantitative restrictions are easier to identify than MEQRs, both types restrict the free movement of goods. (These terms are discussed in more detail below.)

'Measures taken by Member States'

While Articles 34–36 TFEU refers to 'measures taken by Member States', it would be wrong to think that only the action of Member States may lead to a breach. The expression has been interpreted widely to cover the activities of *any public or semi-public body*, such as measures adopted by professional bodies with regulatory powers (Cases 266 and 267/87 *R* v. *Royal Pharmaceutical Society of Great Britain*, concerning a body regulating sale of pharmaceutical products over-the-counter). In Case 222/82 Apple and Pear Development Council the Court held that a body established and funded by the government to develop fruit growing was also covered. Ireland was unable to avoid liability under Article 34 by claiming that the 'Buy Irish' campaign was conducted by the Irish Goods Council, a private undertaking, as the Court of Justice held that the Council could influence traders through its promotional activities (Case 249/81 *Commission* v. *Ireland*).

Failure to act

A Member State may infringe Article 34 by omissions as well as actions. In Case C-265/95 *Commission* v. *France* the Commission brought proceedings against France for failing to act against individuals disrupting the free movement of agricultural products from other Member States, such as Spanish strawberries. Lorries transporting the goods were intercepted, loads destroyed and drivers threatened. The Court held that by failing to adopt all necessary and proportionate measures to prevent obstruction, France was in breach of Article 34, Article 10 TEC (now 4 TEU) and provisions on the common organisation of markets in agricultural products.

When considering omissions it is important to examine *how much discretion* the Member State may exercise. In Case C-112/00 *Schmidberger* v. *Austria* the Austrian government decided not to ban a demonstration by an environmental group, leading to closure of the Brenner motorway for thirty hours. Schmidberger, a German-based undertaking transporting steel and timber between Germany and Italy, brought an action against the Austrian authorities for losses from the motorway closure.

INTERSECTION

The conditions for State liability established in Cases C-46 & 48/93 *Brasserie/Factortame* include the requirement for the breach to be *sufficiently serious* (see Chapter 8), including analysis of discretion enjoyed by the Member State in the area of the breach. Where there is little or no discretion, a simple breach may be enough. Where a Member State has wide discretion, the breach must be 'manifest and grave', considering factors such as whether the action was excusable.

The Court of Justice in *Schmidberger* was faced with conflicting fundamental principles – free movement of goods, and expression and assembly under the ECHR and the Austrian constitution. It held that the decision not to ban the road closure was a MEQR. However, the Austrian authorities had a *wide margin of discretion* which they had exercised proportionately according to legitimate objectives to protect fundamental rights. The decision did not infringe Article 34.

PROHIBITION OF QUANTITATIVE RESTRICTIONS ON IMPORTS AND OF MEQRS

CORNERSTONE

Article 34 TFEU

Quantitative restrictions on imports and measures having equivalent effect are prohibited between Member States under Article 34 TFEU (ex 28 TEC).

The prohibition on quantitative restrictions MEQRs is directly effective (Case 74/76 *Iannelli & Volpi*, involving restrictions on importing paper from France into Italy), enabling restrictions imposed by Member States to be challenged in the national courts.

Quantitative restrictions

The Court of Justice interpreted 'quantitative restrictions' in Case 2/73 *Geddo* v. *Ente Nazionale Risi* (levy by Italian authorities on movement of rice) as measures amounting to a total or partial restraint on imports, exports or goods in transit. Examples include a quota system (Case 13/68 *Salgoil SpA* v. *Italian Minister of Trade*, refusal by the Italian authorities to licence importation of a quantity of Fuller's earth, used for filtering and cleansing), a ban (Case 7/61 *Commission* v. *Italy (Re Ban on Pork Imports)*, a complete prohibition by Italy on importing various pork products) and Case 34/79 *R* v. *Henn and Darby* (a ban on importing pornographic materials). However, a national prohibition on selling sex articles from unlicensed premises, applied without distinction to domestic and imported products, was not to be a quantitative restriction (Case C-23/89 *Quietlynn* v. *Southend Borough Council*).

Measures having equivalent effect to quantitative restrictions on imports

The term 'measures having equivalent effect to quantitative restrictions on imports' (MEQRs) has been more widely interpreted than quantitative restrictions. It may be applied to domestic goods as well as imports and exports and covers regulatory measures such as standards on size, quality and weight as well as inspection or certification requirements (Case 249/81 *Commission* v. *Ireland*, involving a campaign to promote goods made in Ireland).

Distinctly and indistinctly applicable measures

Directive 70/50 was issued by the Commission to guide Member States by providing a non-exhaustive list of MEQRs. Measures are divided into:

1. *Distinctly applicable measures* – measures not applying equally to domestic or imported products that hinder imports which could otherwise take place, including those 'which make importation more difficult than the disposal of domestic production' (Article 2(1)).

2. *Indistinctly applicable measures* – measures applying equally to domestic and imported products (Article 3). These measures only contravene Article 34 'where the restrictive effect of such measures on the free movement of goods exceeds the effect intrinsic to trade rules' (Article 3). Such measures are valid unless they are disproportionate.

Put simply, distinctly applicable measures target imports whereas indistinctly applicable measures apply to both goods produced at home and imported goods. Distinctly applicable measures are thus more damaging to the single market. Not surprisingly, they are harder to justify than indistinctly applicable measures.

APPLICATION

Imagine the UK is concerned about health risks from soft cheeses and bans all imported soft cheeses – a distinctly applicable measure, as it does not apply to domestically produced cheeses. If the UK had passed a law requiring all soft cheeses to conform to a particular production standard to avoid health problems, the measure would be indistinctly applicable, applying to both imported goods and domestically produced goods. The first measure would be harder to justify than the second.

The *Dassonville* formula

The Court defined measures having equivalent effect (MEQRs) in broad terms in Case 8/74 *Procureur du Roi* v. *Dassonville*.

CORNERSTONE

'All trading rules enacted by Member States which are capable of hindering directly or indirectly, actually or potentially, intra-Community trade' are measures equivalent to quantitative restrictions (*Dassonville*).

The defendants in *Dassonville* had imported Scotch whisky into Belgium purchased from French distributors without the certificate of origin required by Belgian law. They argued in criminal proceedings that the requirement contravened Article 34 TFEU. The Court of Justice held that such a requirement constituted a MEQR as it favoured direct imports from the country of origin over imports from another Member State where the goods were in free circulation.

Decisions after *Dassonville*

The definition in *Dassonville* was confirmed in later decisions including Case 82/77 *Van Tiggele* where the defendant was charged with selling gin below the national minimum price in the Netherlands. The Court of Justice held that a minimum price was an MEQR preventing imports from being sold at a lower price. In Case 130/80 *Kelderman* a national measure on dry materials in bread was found to be an MEQR even though the Netherlands claimed to administer the restriction flexibly. The Court has consistently upheld that free movement of goods should not depend on a national authority's discretion.

It is unnecessary to show that a measure has an *appreciable* effect on trade between Member States if it is *capable of producing such effect*, as in Case 16/83 *Prantl* (German restriction on use of traditional form of wine bottle to German producers of high-quality wine). The same approach applies where the hindrance is slight, as in Case 177 & 178/82 *Van der Haar* where the Court left the national courts to decide whether a Dutch law fixing the price of tobacco was a MEQR.

A measure which is *incapable* of hindering trade between Member States will not contravene Articles 34 and 35 even where the sale of domestic goods is affected. Thus a Belgian law to improve working conditions, banning production and delivery of bread during the night while competing bakers in adjoining Member States were not similarly controlled (Case 155/80 *Oebel*) was not a MEQR, nor was a Dutch law regulating the permitted ingredients in cheese produced in the Netherlands but not outside (Case 237/82 *Jongeneel Kaas BV* v. *Netherlands*).

Cassis de Dijon

The next significant development came in Case 120/78 *Rewe-Zentral AG* v. *Bundesmonopolverwaltung für Branntwein*, known as '*Cassis de Dijon*', a ruling of great importance to the free movement of goods. The Court in *Cassis* identified the *grounds* ('mandatory requirements') on which Member States may adopt *indistinctly applicable* measures to restrict free movement as well as the *principle of recognition* which underpins the completion of the single market.

The *Cassis* ruling arose in the context of a German law providing for a minimum alcohol content of 25 per cent for spirits including cassis (blackcurrant-flavoured liqueur), a requirement satisfied by liqueurs made in Germany but not in France where the alcohol level was only 15 to 20 per cent. The measure thus excluded French cassis from the German market. It was challenged by importers in the German courts which referred to the Court of Justice. The Court held that the requirement was a MEQR. It rejected German claims relating to public health (a higher alcohol level would prevent increased consumption), the fairness of commercial transactions (weak imported cassis would have an unfair commercial advantage over the more expensive German product) and protection of the consumer. Nevertheless, it acknowledged possible justification to depart from Article 34 where it is *necessary* to satisfy one of the *mandatory requirements* relating particularly to effectiveness of fiscal supervision, protection of public health, fairness of commercial transactions and defence of the consumer (considered below).

Cassis and the 'rule of reason'

This principle whereby a restriction may be upheld where mandatory requirements are satisfied is sometimes known as 'the rule of reason'.

CORNERSTONE

The 'rule of reason' in *Cassis*

Obstacles to movement within the Community arising from disparities between national laws relating to the marketing of the product in question must be accepted in so far as those provisions may be recognised as being necessary in order to satisfy the mandatory requirements relating in particular to the effectiveness of fiscal supervision, the protection of public health, the fairness of commercial transactions and the defence of the consumer.

The alcohol requirement in *Cassis*, though mandatory, failed because the Court of Justice found it was not *necessary*. The objectives could have been achieved by less restrictive means such as labelling. It follows that 'necessary' means *no more than necessary* under the principle of proportionality.

Cassis is an important decision for a number of reasons. It displaced the previous assumption that Article 34 does not apply to a national measure unless it can be shown that it discriminates between imports and domestic products or between different forms of trade between Member States. It also provides a basis to justify national measures provided they applied to both domestic and imported goods. After *Cassis* the Court applied the rule of reason to indistinctly applicable rules, but not to distinctly applicable measures, seen as more damaging to the single market. The current position is as follows:

> **Take note**
>
> The principle of proportionality involves weighing the objective of a law against the means adopted to achieve it. If legislation is more restrictive than it needs to be to achieve its objective, it infringes the principle of proportionality.

- *Indistinctly applicable measures* may be justified under *Cassis* where necessary to protect a mandatory requirement.

- *Distinctly applicable measures* normally contravene Article 34 but may be justified under the derogation (exception) in Article 36, a more demanding standard than that under *Cassis* (considered on p. 254.)

Justification in the interests of consumers

Justification in the interests of consumers is one of the most frequently invoked mandatory requirements. In Case 238/82 *Duphar BV* v. *Netherlands* a drug company challenged exclusion of its product from a list of approved drugs available from public funds under a government measure. The Court of Justice ruled out economic justification but accepted that such a measure may be necessary in the interests of consumers provided the list of drugs did not discriminate against imports. It ruled that the list must be drawn up under objective criteria, without reference to the origin of products and verifiable by the importer.

The Court upheld national consumer protection measures restricting free gifts as a sales promotion, despite the risk that such legislation could impede inter-Member trade in Case 286/81 *Oosthoek's Uitgeversmaatschappij BV*. However, in Case C-362/88 *GB INNO-BM* v. *Confédération du Commerce Luxembourgeois* the justification failed. A Belgian company had distributed leaflets in supermarkets in Luxembourg advertising cut-price products. Such advertising was lawful in Belgium but not in Luxembourg where they were seized and the supermarket prosecuted. The Court of Justice found that the measure restricted the free movement of goods but was not justified on grounds of consumer protection as the ban was prejudicial to small importers who were denied a particularly effective means of advertising.

Dual-burden and equal burden rules

A further distinction may be made between 'dual-burden' and 'equal burden' rules.

(a) *Dual-burden rules* are applied to imported goods by the host state, even though they have already been subject to regulation in the home state. Rules relating to the product itself such as its packaging (e.g. a requirement to sell margarine in cube-shaped boxes in Case 261/81 *Walter Rau*) involve a dual burden as the producer or seller must satisfy the rules of both the home and host State. A similar dual burden results from rules on product composition such as Italy's permissible ingredients in pasta in Case 407/85 *Drei Glocken* v. *USL*.

(b) *Equal burden rules* apply to all goods, regardless of origin, and are not protectionist. The Court of Justice has not been entirely consistent, tending to treat as outside Article 34 equal burden rules on conditions under which goods are sold, as it did in a ban on employment of labour on Sundays in France in Case C-312/89 *Union Départementale des Syndicats CGT* v. *Sidef Conforama* and Case C-332/89 *Marchandise*. In other cases the Court has found an equal burden rule within Article 34 but justifiable under *Cassis*. In Cases 60 and 61/84 *Cinéthèque SA* a French rule to protect the cinema industry by prohibiting distribution of video cassettes within a year of the film's release was not expressly found to be a mandatory requirement, but the Court held that the rule was justifiable and not contrary to Article 34. Uncertainty over equal burden cases was not addressed by the Court until its decision in Cases C-267 and 268/91 *Keck and Mithouard* on selling arrangements (discussed below).

Mandatory requirements identified since *Cassis*

The list of mandatory requirements in *Cassis* is not exhaustive. It has been supplemented by the Court to include:

* Improvement of working conditions by limiting night working (Case 155/80 *Oebel*) in relation to a national restriction on hours worked in bakeries.

* Protection of the environment (Case 302/86 *Commission* v. *Denmark (Re Disposable Beer Cans)*) in a national requirement for beer and soft drinks to be sold in reusable containers. The Court found that protection of the environment was a mandatory requirement. However, the prohibition (allowing only a limited amount of drinks to be sold in non-reusable containers) discriminated against imports and was disproportionate.

* Protection of fundamental rights (Case C-112/00 *Schmidberger* v. *Austria*) in which the right to demonstrate conflicted with the free movement of goods.

* Pluralism of the press (Case C-368/95 *Vereinigte Familiapress Zeitungsverlags- und vertriebs GmbH* v. *Heinrich Bauer Verlag*). Prizes offered in magazines were seen as potentially eliminating competition from smaller papers which could not afford such inducements.

* Public safety (Case C-110/05 *Commission* v. *Italy*). This case concerned proceedings against Italy over a prohibition on using a motor tricycle to tow trailers. Although the prohibition was a MEQR it was necessary to protect road safety. Public safety was invoked again in Case C-142/05 *Mickelsson and Roos* over a prohibition on using personal watercraft on waterways not designated for general navigation. The Court left it to the national courts to determine whether access to the domestic market was restricted, but accepted that the measure could be justified to protect the environment if certain conditions were satisfied.

A restriction on purely economic grounds *cannot* be justified (Case 238/82 *Duphar BV* v. *Netherlands*, where the Netherlands had denied access to pharmaceutical products considered 'too expensive'). Other restrictions not justifiable under *Cassis* were nevertheless held to be covered under Article 36, including:

* imposition of a labelling requirement (Case 27/80 *Fietje*, arising from a Netherlands requirement to label the alcoholic content of liqueurs);

* a requirement that silver goods be hallmarked (Case 220/81 *Robertson*, arising from a prosecution for failing to hallmark silver-plated goods);

* prohibition on retail sale of products unless marked with their country of origin (Case 207/83 *Commission* v. *United Kingdom*, proceedings against the UK over a requirement for all new goods to be marked with a certificate of origin).

The approach of the Court in *Cassis* was modified in Case 788/79 *Gilli* v. *Andres*. Italian law prohibited the sale of vinegar containing acetic acid unless produced by wine fermentation, excluding cider vinegar. The Court suggested a modification to the *Cassis* principle, namely that it applied only where national rules do not discriminate in application between domestic and imported goods. It found that legislation such as the Italian prohibition contravened Article 34 by discriminating against goods not satisfying the national vinegar requirement.

....**APPLICATION**

Imagine that Croatia, a new EU Member State, has adopted laws needing to be assessed for compatibility with EU law. Law A requires producers to maintain a 'satisfactory standard of product safety' in products sold through the internet. Law B requires producers of foodstuffs for sale in supermarkets to be packaged in materials which can be recycled. Law C prohibits the sale of cars without inbuilt satellite navigation systems as a study showed that confusion over road navigation contributed to road accidents. All three laws have been adopted in areas identified as mandatory requirements. Law A would be covered by the consumer protection requirement under *Cassis* itself provided it is proportionate (it should be, as it is not unreasonably restrictive). However, it may discriminate against imports (*GB INNO* – restriction on distribution of leaflets in supermarkets), in which case it would not be justified. Law B would be compatible with EU law as protection of the environment was recognised in *Commission* v. *Denmark* provided it is proportionate. (Could the environment be protected in this context without a requirement for all supermarket goods to be sold in recyclable packaging?) Law C may be compatible as protection of road safety was recognised in *Commission* v. *Italy*. However, it seems unlikely that a requirement for a built-in navigation system is proportionate, as improving safety through navigation could be achieved through better sign-posting and road maps.

Failure to establish 'necessity'

The following measures were not found to be necessary:

- In Case 16/83 *Prantl* an importer was charged with infringing a German law intended to prevent unfair competition after importing Italian wine in a bulbous bottle of similar shape and design to a traditional German quality wine. The Court of Justice held that as long as the imported wine conformed to fair and traditional practice in its state of origin its exclusion could not be justified.

- In Case 182/84 *Miro BV* the name 'jenever' in the Netherlands was restricted to gin with a minimum 35 per cent alcohol volume, whereas Belgian 'jenever' had a 30 per cent level. The Court of Justice held the name could not be reserved for one national variety provided the import had been lawfully produced and marketed in the exporting state.

- Case C-531/07 *Fachverband der Buch-unde Medienwirtschaft* v. *LIBRO Handelsgesellschaft* concerned an Austrian measure providing for the sale of German-language books at a price fixed by the publisher. The measure was found to be a MEQR as it prevented importers from fixing minimum retail prices according to the market, whereas Austrian publishers could do so. While the Court accepted that protection of books as cultural objects may be a mandatory requirement justifying restriction, it was disproportionate as the objective could be achieved by less restrictive means.

- Other prohibited restrictions include national rules on permitted ingredients in various food such as the Netherlands' requirements for bread (Case 130/80 *Kelderman*), and Italian requirements for pasta (Case 407/85 *Drei Glocken* v. *USL*).

In the 1980s the European Community was losing its share of world trade to other trading blocs such as North America and the Far East. It could not afford to allow barriers to trade between Member States to worsen its position further. The Commission led by its President, Jacques Delors, responded by producing the White Paper 'Completing the Internal Market' (COM (85) 310) calling for a new strategy to remove remaining barriers by the end of 1992. The *Cassis de Dijon* principle of mutual recognition played a significant part in the new approach, requiring Member States to recognise that goods produced to the standards of one Member State could circulate freely throughout the Community.

CONTEXT

Mutual recognition

To clarify the implications of *Cassis* the Commission issued a statement recognising the need for mutual recognition

CORNERSTONE

'There is no valid reason why goods which have been lawfully produced and marketed in one of the Member States should not be introduced into any other Member State' (Commission statement, 1980).

The statement means that goods lawfully marketed in one Member State will be regarded as complying with the mandatory requirements of the state into which they are being imported unless the measure is necessary. The Court of Justice adopts a rigorous approach to determining what is 'necessary' and will not allow any measure which is disproportionate.

INTERSECTION

The principle of mutual recognition is the lynchpin of the Commission's internal market programme. It has been applied outside the free movement of goods, particularly to the recognition of professional qualifications (considered in Chapter 15).

Article 34 as a defence

Article 34 has frequently been invoked before the national courts as a defence to charges involving regulatory offences, including prosecutions for breaches of the Sunday trading law in England and Wales before its limited relaxation under the Sunday Trading Act 1994. The first ruling from the Court of Justice was in Case 145/88 *Torfaen BC* v. *B&Q plc*. A DIY retail company in the UK charged with trading on a Sunday contrary to the Shops Act 1950 argued that the measure infringed Article 34 TFEU. The Court of Justice held that such measures are a legitimate part of social and economic policy to accord with national or regional socio-cultural characteristics and do not contravene Article 34 provided their restrictive effect is not disproportionate. Sunday trading is thus a legitimate area for legislation by Member States provided the measure is proportionate.

The emphasis on proportionality was maintained in other Sunday trading cases such as Case C-169/91 *Stoke-on-Trent City Council* v. *B&Q plc*, where the Court of Justice held that national rules on shop opening hours were not disproportionate to the aim of regulating working hours in accordance with national or regional socio-cultural characteristics even though the prohibition reduced turnover. It similarly held that bans on employment on Sundays in France and Belgium did not infringe Article 34 in Case C-312/89 *Union Départementale des Syndicats CGT* v. *Sidef Conforama* and Case C-332/89 *Criminal Proceedings* v. *Marchandise*.

Selling arrangements: calling 'time' on Article 34 as a defence

After the Sunday trading cases there was a danger that the free movement provisions were being used to undermine national legislation with little or no relevance to imports. The Court of Justice signalled its determination to identify the limits of Article 34 in Cases C-267 & 268/91 *Keck and Mithouard* in relation to selling arrangements. Keck and Mithouard resold goods at a loss contrary to French law. They argued that the law infringed Article 34 by restricting the volume of imported goods. After expressing the need to reappraise its previous jurisprudence under Article 34, the Court ruled that:

> The application to products from other Member States of national provisions restricting or prohibiting certain selling arrangements is not such as to hinder directly or indirectly, actually or potentially, trade between Member States, provided that the provisions apply to all affected traders operating within the national territory and provided that they affect in the same manner, in law and in fact, the marketing of domestic products and those from other Member States.

CORNERSTONE

Keck

Once a measure is identified as a selling arrangement, it is outside Article 34 (*Keck and Mithouard*).

When is a selling arrangement outside Article 34?

After *Keck* it was clear that Member States can determine their own selling arrangements provided they do not affect imports and are not discriminatory. The following provide examples of selling arrangements held to be outside Article 34 and so enforceable under national law:

(a) Dutch restrictions on petrol station opening hours (Cases 401 & 402/92 *Tankstation 't Heukske Vof and Boermans*).

(b) German restrictions on promotion of 'quasi-pharmaceutical products' such as medicated shampoo outside pharmacies (Case C-292/92 *Hünermund* v. *Landesapotheker Baden-Württemburg*).

(c) Italian rules reserving the retail sale of tobacco products to approved suppliers (Case C-387/93 *Giorgio Domingo Banchero*).

(d) Belgian rules prohibiting sales at very low profit margins (Case C-63/94 *Belgapom*).

(e) A French ban on televised advertising of the distribution sector: Case C-412/93 *Société d'Importation Edouard Leclerc-Siplec* v. *TF1 Publicité SA and M6 Publicité SA*.

Decisions on advertising

Decisions on advertising as a selling arrangement are less clear. In Cases C-34–36/95 *Konsumentombudsmannen* v. *De Agostini* the Court considered a Swedish ban on types of television advertising. Actions had been brought against traders in the Swedish courts for infringing the restrictions, in one case by advertising a magazine entitled *Everything You Need to Know About Dinosaurs* contrary to a ban on advertising to children under twelve, and in the other for marketing a soap called 'Body de Lite' considered to be misleading advertising. The Court found that an outright ban on advertising would have infringed Article 34, but left the national court to decide whether the restriction operated unequally on imported goods relative to domestic products, when television advertising was virtually the only way for a new entrant to break into the market.

In Case C-405/98 *Konsumentombudsmannen* v. *Gourmet International Products* the Court again had to consider a Swedish advertising ban, this time of drinks above 2.25 per cent alcohol. Gourmet International Products had published three pages of advertisements of whisky and red wine in a magazine largely intended for the restaurant trade. The Court decided that such a ban infringed Article 34 as it affected the marketing of products from other Member States more severely than home products and was an obstacle to trade between Member States. Nevertheless, it held that the ban may be justified on public health grounds if it was proportionate – a matter left to the national courts to decide.

Distinguishing selling arrangements from restrictions infringing Article 34

It is important to be able to distinguish selling arrangements and restrictions that are illegal under Article 34. A national restriction will *not* be regarded as a selling arrangement when it imposes a 'dual burden' of regulation where the goods are produced and where they are sold. In such a case the purpose and context of the national legislation should be assessed for possible infringement of Article 34.

Case C-254/98 *Schutzverband gegen unlauteren Wettbewerb* arose in relation to an Austrian law which only allowed bakers, butchers and grocers to sell their goods in a given area if they traded from a permanent establishment in the same district. The Court found that the requirement imposed an additional burden on traders from outside Austria. It did not accept that the measure was justified on grounds of public health as it was seen as disproportionate (refrigeration in the delivery vans would have avoided deterioration).

Product requirements

A 'dual burden' often arises as a specific **product requirement**, as where a national law on unfair competition made it necessary for importers to repackage the goods. Case C-315/92 *Verband Sozialer Wettbewerbe V* v. *Clinique Laboratoires SNC*) concerned a German prohibition of the name 'Clinique' for cosmetics, preventing lawfully made imported goods from being sold there unless they were repackaged. The Court of Justice was not convinced that customers were misled into thinking the goods possessed pharmaceutical properties. The Court took a similar line on repackaging in Case C-470/93 *Verein gegen Unwesen in Handel und Gewerbe Köln* v. *Mars GmbH* where Mars GmbH had increased the quantity of ice cream in an individual packet as a publicity promotion. The company was prevented under German law from distributing its products with the expression '+10%' on the basis that it gave the consumer a misleading impression that more of the product was offered without a price increase. Again the effect was to require the company to repackage in order to sell the product in Germany. The Court of Justice held that such a requirement infringed Article 34 TFEU by making the importer incur additional costs.

However, in Case C-244/06 *Dynamic Medien Vertriebs GmbH* v. *Avides Media AG* the Court found that German requirements that image storage media such as photographs must be subject to examination and classification to protect young persons was *not* a selling arrangement. Such rules did not infringe Article 34 where the procedure was transparent and the decision open to challenge.

As the case law on selling arrangements continues to build it may be seen that the Court has tended to leave significant decisions to the discretion of the national authorities where there is no obvious discrimination or effect on trade between Member States, as it did in Case C-441/04 *A-Punkt*. The Court of Justice decided that it should be the national courts' responsibility to determine whether a national prohibition on the doorstep selling impeded market access of products from other Member States.

APPLICATION

Imagine the UK has adopted the Foodstuffs and Herbal Medicines Statute requiring all foodstuffs for consumption by children to contain vitamin X, helping to prevent a range of childhood diseases. The Act prohibits the sale of herbal medicines to children under the age of fourteen as some products cause side effects dangerous to young children. The requirement to add vitamin X is a product requirement, posing a dual burden on producers in other Member States. It is a MEQR which would be illegal under Article 34 unless justified under *Cassis* (on grounds of health or consumer protection). The prohibition on the sale of herbal medicine to children, however, is a selling arrangement outside Article 34 unless it discriminates against imports, which it does not appear to do.

The Court's case law on selling arrangements has been the subject of extensive scrutiny and comment by Advocates-General in the Court of Justice and academic commentators.

REFLECTION

The *Keck* ruling was criticised by Advocate-General Jacobs in Case 412/93 *Leclerc-Siplec* (involving a prohibition on television advertising for distribution). He submitted that the Court should not make a rigid distinction between different types of measure, and that a discrimination test was inappropriate. In his view advertising was of central importance, enabling producers in other Member States to penetrate the market. The Court nevertheless found the ban to be a selling arrangement outside Article 34. Advocate-General Geelhoed in Case C-239/02 *Doewe Egberts* (a Belgian prohibition on advertising the slimming qualities of a product) submitted that a general prohibition on advertising tended to discriminate against imports and so should be assessed under Article 34 rather than being seen as a selling arrangement. This time the Court agreed.

Academic commentators have also criticised *Keck* as failing to protect market integration. Some have proposed a new test focusing on *market access*; that is, whether the measure imposes a direct or substantial restriction on trade within States. Such an approach would enable selling arrangements like those on advertising which restrict market access to be covered and assessed under Article 34. Both Shuibne (2002) and Wilsher (2008) argue that selling and marketing restrictions should be presumed to restrict trade unless they are minimal. Snell (2010), however, questions the place of market access. In his view the central question remains whether the focus of the law is on *discrimination*, in which case a comparative test based on impact is appropriate, or on *economic freedom*, in which case there is no need for a comparison. A focus on market access implies a third approach but has not been supported by the Court. Davies (2010) sees discrimination and market access as not necessarily opposed, since non-discriminatory measures usually affect market access equally. Meanwhile the Court's case law continues to evolve, with every indication that it is responding flexibly, both to academic commentary and new types of selling arrangements.

PROHIBITION OF QUANTITATIVE RESTRICTIONS ON EXPORTS AND OF MEQRS

Article 35 TFEU prohibits restrictions on exports.

CORNERSTONE

Article 35

Quantitative restrictions on exports and all measures having equivalent effect shall be prohibited between Member States (Article 35 TFEU (ex 29TEC)).

Case 53/76 *Bouhelier* provides an example of a national measure contrary to Article 35. A French requirement that watches for export should undergo a quality inspection to obtain an export licence was found to infringe Article 35 as it was not imposed on watches for the home market.

The principles relating to imports under Article 34 also apply to exports under Article 35. Until the decision in *Gysbrechts* in 2008 it was thought that indistinctly applicable measures only infringed Article 35 when they discriminated against exports by providing an advantage to the home product or market to the disadvantage of the EU import. In Case 15/79 *P.B. Groenveld BV* manufacturers of meat products banned possession of horsemeat to prevent its export to countries where such trade was prohibited. The Court of Justice held that the measure which was indistinctly applicable did not contravene (what is now) Article 35.

However, in Case C-205/07 *Gysbrechts* v. *Santurel Inter BVBA*, the Court considered the legality of a rule prohibiting sellers of goods at a distance (through the internet or by post) from requiring purchasers to pay in advance or provide details of their payment card, making it difficult for sellers to pursue defaulting customers based abroad. The Court found that such a rule operated as a MEQR on exports. It held that the prohibition on advance payment was justified to protect consumers, but it was disproportionate to demand details of payment cards. Although the measure in *Gysbrechts* was indistinctly applicable, the Court found it was covered by Article 35, *contrary* to its earlier approach in *Groenveld*.

The following restrictions were found *not* to infringe Article 35:

- Indistinctly applicable Dutch rules on the content and quality of Dutch cheeses. While not overtly protectionist, the rules benefited importers not bound by the same standards. The Court held that there was no breach of Article 35 as the rules were not intended to benefit domestic production (Case 237/82 *Jongeneel Kaas BV*).
- Restrictions on night working in bakeries (Case 155/80 *Oebel*).
- A prohibition on free gifts as a sales promotion (Case 286/81 *Oosthoek's*, arising from a publisher's use of incentives such as encyclopaedias to encourage purchasers to buy books, contrary to a Dutch prohibition on such free gifts).

Approach of the UK courts

The House of Lords in *R* v. *Chief Constable of Sussex, ex p. International Traders' Ferry Ltd* (1999) considered the legality under Article 35 TFEU of policing arrangements for the port of Shoreham in Sussex without referring to the Court of Justice. International Trader's Ferry (ITF) had operated from

Mandatory requirements under *Cassis*	Derogation under Article 36, TFEU
• Applies to indistinctly applicable measures • Easier to satisfy than Article 36 • Court of Justice may add more exceptions	• Applies to distinctly and indistinctly applicable measures • Strictly interpreted • List of exceptions is exhaustive

Figure 12.2 Exceptions to the free movement of goods

Shoreham since 1995, transporting live animals across the Channel. A long protest campaign by animal rights groups made it difficult for lorries to reach the port facilities without police protection. The Chief Constable reduced the level of policing, stating that deployment of police at the port was significantly affecting his resources to police other areas. He informed ITF that lorries seeking access to the port at times when policing was unavailable would be turned away. ITF sought judicial review of the decision to reduce policing on grounds of unreasonableness (in English law) and as a measure having equivalent effect under Article 35.

The House of Lords held that the Chief Constable had not acted unreasonably in English law as the rights to trade and protest lawfully were not absolute. Assuming the Chief Constable's acts to be MEQRs under Article 35, the House of Lords held they were justified under Article 36 on grounds of public policy. His actions were found to be proportionate and reasonable, having regard to available resources.

DEROGATION FROM ARTICLES 34 AND 35 TFEU UNDER ARTICLE 36 TFEU

Article 36 TFEU (ex 30 TEC) provides the basis for derogation (departure) from the prohibitions on restrictions on imports and exports under Articles 34 and 35.

CORNERSTONE

Article 36 TFEU

The provisions of Articles 34 and 35 shall not preclude prohibitions or restrictions on imports, exports or goods in transit justified on grounds of public morality, public policy or public security; the protection of health and life of humans, animals or plants; the protection of national treasures possessing artistic, historic or archaeological value; or the protection of industrial and commercial property.

As an exception to one of the basic freedoms of the single market Article 36 TFEU must be *interpreted strictly*. The Article provides the only justification for distinctly applicable measures, which are seen as particularly divisive to the market since they are not applied to goods produced in the home State. Thus it is not surprising that the Court of Justice held the list of exceptions to be exhaustive in Case 95/81 *Commission* v. *Italy*. This contrasts with exceptions arising under *Cassis*, where the Court of Justice has added over the years to the mandatory requirements identified in *Cassis* itself in relation to the less-damaging indistinctly applicable measures.

The following were held *not* to justify derogation as they are not listed in Article 36:

(a) consumer protection (Case 113/80 *Commission* v. *Ireland* – in which the Irish government unsuccessfully sought to justify its origin-marking rules as consumer protection measures);

(b) protection of cultural diversity (Case 229/83 *Association des Centres Distributeurs Edouard Leclerc* v. *'Au Blé Vert' Sarl* – concerning a French law allowing booksellers and importers to fix the price of books);

(c) economic policy (Case 238/82 *Duphar* – concerning a prohibition on buying pharmaceutical products on grounds of cost).

Justification and arbitrary discrimination

Member States may derogate from the free movement of goods as far as a measure is *justified to achieve the objectives* in Article 36. 'Justified' means 'necessary' (Case 227/82 *Leendert van Bennekom*, restriction on holding concentrated pharmaceutical products), with the onus on the national authorities to prove necessity. Thus Article 36 may only be invoked subject to the principle of proportionality. It cannot be relied upon to facilitate administrative tasks or reduce public expenditure unless alternative arrangements would place an excessive burden on the authorities (Case 104/75 *Officier van Just* v. *De Peijper*, criminal proceedings against a trader for supplying UK medicinal preparations to pharmacies in Rotterdam without authorisation).

Measures must not only be necessary. They must not amount to a means of *arbitrary discrimination* or a *disguised restriction on inter-Member trade*, for example by providing an advantage to the marketing of one state, including the domestic state, over the other state.

Public morality

There have been three preliminary references to the Court of Justice from UK courts in which the public morality ground was raised:

1. Case 34/79 *R* v. *Henn and Darby*
2. Case 121/85 *Conegate Ltd* v. *Customs and Excise Commissioners*
3. Case C-23/89 *Quietlynn* v. *Southend Borough Council*.

Henn and Darby arose from a prosecution under customs legislation of importers who had attempted to bring pornographic materials from the Netherlands into the UK. The legislation banned material which was 'indecent or obscene' whereas domestic legislation prohibited material only where it was likely to 'deprave or corrupt', a distinction which discriminated against imported goods as indecency is a less rigorous concept than obscenity. A reference to the Court of Justice was made on appeal to the House of Lords. The Court held:

- There was a breach of Article 34 but it was justified under Article 36. A Member State under Article 36 can prohibit imports from another Member State of articles of an obscene or indecent nature in accordance with its domestic laws.
- If a prohibition on imported goods is justifiable on grounds of public morality and imposed for that purpose, enforcement cannot be a means of arbitrary discrimination or disguised restriction on trade contrary to Article 36 unless there is a lawful trade in the same goods within the Member States concerned.

Henn and Darby should be contrasted with *Conegate*, in which the UK Customs and Excise seized inflatable rubber 'love dolls' on the ground that they were indecent and obscene. The importers claimed the seizure contravened Article 34, the sale of such dolls being restricted but not banned in the UK. The Court of Justice held that the seizure was not justified in the absence of a general prohibition on making and selling such goods in the UK and of effective measures to restrict domestic distribution.

In *R* v. *Bow Street Magistrates, ex p. Noncyp Ltd* (1990) the Court of Appeal decided *not* to refer to the Court of Justice the question of whether seizure of a book deemed obscene but published in the public interest was permitted by Article 36. The Court of Appeal held that such books remained 'obscene' and liable to forfeiture under Article 34 in the absence of lawful UK trade. The Crown Court did refer to the Court of Justice in Case C-23/89 *Quietlynn* v. *Southend Borough Council* following a prosecution under UK licensing legislation. The Court of Justice interpreted Article 34, holding that national provisions prohibiting the sale of lawful sex articles from unlicensed sex establishments did not constitute a MEQR.

APPLICATION

Assume that Ireland is opposed to the availability of pornography on religious grounds. It adopts a law banning importation of pornographic books and other materials, which it claims is necessary to protect the morality of its citizens. Such a measure is illegal under Article 34 as a quantitative restriction discriminating against imports unless it can be justified on grounds of morality under Article 36. While *R* v. *Henn and Darby* appears to recognise that Member States have some discretion over the public morality justification, the *Conegate* decision where there was no national prohibition points to the likelihood that the Irish measure would not be justified.

Public policy

Public policy has rarely been successfully invoked as a derogation under Article 36. However, in Case 7/78 *R* v. *Thompson and others* the Court of Justice held that silver alloy coins minted before 1947 were not legal tender and so not a 'means of payment' but 'goods'. Restrictions on exportation of such coins to prevent their being melted down were found to be justified on grounds of public policy (the need to avoid debasing the coinage).

The public policy exception in relation to goods has been strictly construed by the Court which has ruled it may *not* be invoked to:

(a) serve economic ends (Case 231/83 *Cullet* v. *Centre Leclerc* – fixing a minimum price for petrol to ensure sufficient commercial margins for all retail outlets);

(b) restrict criminal behaviour (Case 16/83 *Prantl* – sale or importation of wine from outside a specified region in a traditional bottle);

(c) protect consumers (Case 177/83 *Kohl* – use of a trade symbol by a pharmaceutical company resembling another older pharmaceutical company's symbol might have misled consumers).

Public security

Public security was successfully invoked before the Court of Justice only in Case 72/83 *Campus Oil* v. *Minister of State for Industry and Energy*. The Irish government sought to justify an order instructing petrol importers to buy up to 35 per cent of their needs from INPC (the Irish National Petroleum Co.) at government-fixed prices. The Court found that although petroleum products were of fundamental national importance the measure contravened Article 34. While rejecting claims based on public policy or economic objectives the Court held that the measure was justified on grounds of public security to maintain continuity of essential oil supplies in times of crisis.

Protection of the health and life of humans, animals and plants

The protection of public health outweighs all other considerations, particularly economic concerns, as the CFI (now General Court) declared in Cases T-125&126/96 *Boehringer* v. *Council* (upholding a directive prohibiting administration of growth-promoting drugs to food-producing animals). Discriminatory measures on public health grounds include import bans, import licences, health inspections and prior authorisation requirements.

Import bans are hard to justify as they are usually unnecessary to protect health, such as that in Case 153/78 *Commission* v. *Germany (Meat Preparations)* a national ban on imported meat products not made from meat produced in the country of manufacture of the finished product, as meat from animals slaughtered in third countries may have been used.

When may a restriction be justified on health grounds?

⊕ CORNERSTONE

For a restriction to be justified under Article 36, the following conditions must be satisfied:

- there must be a real, not a slight, health risk;
- the measure must form part of a seriously considered health policy;
- the measure must not operate as a disguised restriction on trade (Case 40/82 *Commission* v. *UK (French Turkeys)*).

In *French Turkeys* a licensing system had been established by the UK government to exclude poultry imported from countries following a policy of vaccination rather than slaughter in response to Newcastle disease, a contagious poultry disease. The measure had been adopted by the government in the run-up to Christmas after lobbying by UK poultry producers. The Court held that such a ban could not be justified on grounds of animal health as it was not part of a seriously considered health policy but a disguised restriction on inter-Member trade.

A requirement to obtain an import or export licence constitutes a MEQR. In Case 124/81 *Commission* v. *UK (UHT Milk)* the Court accepted the UK argument that an import licensing system was necessary to regulate the heat treatment of imported milk and trace the origins of infected milk, but held that a system which involved retreating and repackaging imported milk was not justified as milk in all Member States was subject to equivalent controls. In Case 74/82 *Commission* v. *Ireland (Re Protection of Animal Health)*, a case involving similar licensing requirements was accepted as justified by the Court, because British poultry did not match the high standards of Irish poultry – demonstrating the need to examine each case on its merits to assess whether a restriction is justifiable.

Examples of justified restrictions

The following cases provide examples of restrictions justified under Article 36:

(a) A plant health inspection to control a plant pest applied to imported but not domestically produced apples was justified as only imported apples posed a threat (Case 4/75 *Rewe-Zentralfinanz GmbH*).

(b) The rules of a national pharmaceutical society prohibiting substitution by pharmacists of equivalent drugs instead of proprietary prescribed brands discriminated against imports, but was necessary to avoid anxiety from product substitution and to maintain confidence (Cases 266 & 267/87 *R* v. *Royal Pharmaceutical Society of Great Britain*).

(c) Case C-141/07 *Commission* v. *Germany* concerned the legitimacy of a German requirement for a local pharmacist to be given responsibility for all tasks involved in supplying medicinal products to German hospitals, making it more difficult for medicinal products to be supplied from another Member State. The Court held that the requirement was a MEQR, but proportionate and justified under Article 36 to achieve a high level of health protection.

(d) A national measure restricting bee-keeping on a Danish island to a particular species was a MEQR, justified under Article 36 to preserve an endangered sub-species (Case C-67/97 *Ditlev Bluhme*).

Health inspections

Member States may carry out random but not systematic health checks at frontiers. In Case 42/82 *Commission* v. *France* three out of four wine consignments from Italy into France were sampled for analysis, causing excessive delays in customs clearance. The Court held that the checks were systematic not random, as well as disproportionate and discriminatory. Health inspections may only be justified if reasonably proportionate to the aim pursued and health protection may not be achieved by less restrictive means (Case 73/84 *Denkavit Futtermittel* v. *Land Nordrhein-Westfalen*, where a requirement for importers of animal foodstuffs to produce a certificate from the veterinary authorities of the exporting state or a licence from the importing state was covered by Article 36 provided the licence was issued on proportionate terms).

In the absence of harmonisation Member States have considerable discretion in protecting the health and life of humans, animals and plants. National authorisation schemes have been upheld on pesticides, fungicides, bacteria and additives. Factors taken into account may include the harmful effect of the substance, eating habits in the importing country and national storage habits (Case 53/80 *Officier van Justitie* v. *Koninklijke Kaasfabriek Eyssen*, arising from prosecution of a processed cheese producer for supplying cheese containing an additive not permitted under Dutch law).

Disproportionate national requirements cannot be justified under Article 36. In Case C-120/95 *Decker* v. *Caisse de Maladie des Employées Privés* the Court considered a requirement for prior authorisation by a national sickness fund before claiming the cost of spectacles made outside the Member State. The Court found the requirement restricted the free movement of goods by curbing importation of spectacles. It was not justified on grounds of public health as spectacles may only be purchased on prescription from a qualified ophthalmologist. In Case 178/84 *Commission* v. *Germany (Re Beer Purity Laws)* the Court held that a ban traditionally imposed in Germany on additives in beer was disproportionate and unjustified on health grounds.

The precautionary principle in relation to health

Where scientific opinion is divided as to the health risk, a Member State can determine the degree of protection for its citizens in the absence of harmonisation (Case 174/82 *Officier van Justitie* v.

Sandoz BV). The Dutch authorities had refused to allow muesli bars to be sold with added vitamins, on the ground that they were dangerous to health although the bars were freely sold in Germany and Belgium. It was unclear from scientific evidence at what point adding vitamins could cause harm. The Court held that a requirement for prior authorisation to sell foodstuffs where vitamins had been added did not infringe Article 34 provided it was not disproportionate, but allowed the Member State to authorise its marketing where addition of vitamins meets a need, especially a technical or nutritional one.

A French requirement for prior authorisation for processing aids and foodstuffs from other Member States was found to be a MEQR in Case C-333/08 *Commission* v. *France*. The French government sought to justify the requirement on the precautionary principle. However, the Court found the scheme disproportionate as it systematically prohibited marketing any processing aids or foodstuffs involving aids lawfully made in other Member States without distinguishing the aids or level of risk to health.

....**APPLICATION**

Imagine that the German government is alarmed about risk to the general public from genetically modified organisms (GMOs) entering the food chain. A recent scientific report by a leading scientific authority, Agrivice, has shown that crops grown from GMOs are contaminating non-GMO crops in the EU. The German government prohibits the sale of any products derived from GMOs. Food producers in Bulgaria, which favours crops from GMOs, objects to the prohibition as it prevents them exporting their products to Germany. Bulgaria's own scientific experts have reported that GMOs are the most efficient way to maximise crop production, with no significant risks to the population. In such circumstances Germany could rely on the precautionary principle to exclude products derived from GMOs as there is genuine scientific doubt as to their safety. If there had been no scientific support for the German position, the prohibition would infringe Article 34 and would be unjustified under Article 36. A ban would be disproportionate, as informing consumers on the packaging would alert them that the goods derived from GMOs.

Protection of national treasures possessing artistic, historic or archaeological value

The protection of national treasures with artistic, historic or archaeological value has not been successfully invoked to justify derogation under Article 36. Italy tried but failed to rely on it to justify a tax on exporting works of art in Case 7/68 *Commission* v. *Italy (Re Export Tax on Art Treasures)*. While the Court's case law remains undeveloped, Regulation 116/2009 imposes uniform controls at borders on exporting protected goods and Directive 93/7 provides that Member States retain the right to define their national treasures unlawfully removed from States and for cooperation between national authorities.

Protection of industrial and commercial property

The protection of industrial and commercial property, or 'intellectual property', is listed in Article 36 as a derogation from Articles 34 and 35. The exception covers property rights usually protected under national law such as trademarks, patents and copyright. The granting of intellectual property rights was largely left to the Member States until the single market programme, supported by

Article 345 TFEU (ex 295 TEC) which provides that: 'The Treaties shall in no way prejudice the rules in Member States governing the system of property ownership.' Some harmonisation of trademarks, patents, copyright and other forms of intellectual property has taken place, but many holders of rights prefer to use national law to ensure their rights are protected fully.

Harmonisation of intellectual property rights

Articles 114TFEU (ex 95 TEC) provides a general basis for approximation of single market law, with new Article 118 TFEU (post-Lisbon) introducing an obligation on the EU to harmonise intellectual property rights, providing a uniform procedure throughout the EU and centralised arrangements for authorisation and supervision. This led the Commission to propose a recast (revised) Trademark Directive 2008/95 and the Regulation on the Community Trademark 207/2009. Directive 2001/29 harmonised some aspects of *copyright* and related rights in the information society, with Directive 2006/116 (amended by Directive 2011/77) protecting copyright for seventy years.

Directive 91/250 requires Member States to harmonise *computer programmes and databases*. The Court of Justice confirmed in Case C-406/10 *SAS* (arising from UK High Court proceedings for infringement of copyright in computer programmes and manuals) that only the *expression* of a computer programme is protected under the directive, not underlying thinking and programming languages.

Decision 2011/167 confirmed EU willingness to establish enhanced cooperation for *unitary patent protection*, implemented in Regulations 1257 and 1260/2012 (in force on 1 January 2014 when the Unified Patent Court Agreement takes effect).

Counterfeit goods and piracy (e.g. of DVDs) is a significant problem worldwide. The EU adopted Directive 2004/48 on enforcement of intellectual property rights requiring harmonisation at a high level to protect the internal market. This directive only provides for procedures under civil law after a later proposal to harmonise criminal law was dropped.

The Court of Justice and 'exhaustion of rights'

The Court of Justice continues to hear preliminary references from disputes before the national courts over the extent to which national protection infringes EU law on free movement. The Court has developed the concept of 'exhaustion of rights' by which the holder of an intellectual property right under national law cannot invoke that law to prevent importation of products in circulation in another Member State. The theory of exhaustion does not apply to marketing counterfeit goods or products marketed outside the EEA under Article 6 TRIPS Agreement (an international agreement on Trade-related Aspects of Intellectual Property Rights). This was confirmed by the Court of Justice in Case C-355/96 *Silhouette International* v. *Hartlauer* over importation into Austria of high-quality spectacles by a cut-price distributor with the Silhouette trademark in Bulgaria before it joined the EU. The Court held that national rules on exhaustion of trademarks did not apply, enabling Silhouette to obtain an injunction in the UK courts to prevent importation.

.... APPLICATION

Imagine that Luxe Cases Ltd. owns a UK trademark for high quality suitcases sold through a smart range of shops. Pilem High Ltd purchases a quantity of Luxe suitcases legitimately in Italy and seeks to reimport them into the UK for sale in their cut-price shops. Luxe could not prevent their reimportation and sale as the rights in the goods were exhausted when they were put into circulation. However it could do so if Pilem High had obtained the suitcases in the USA rather than the EU or if they were counterfeit copies.

Free movement of capital

The free movement of capital is one of the four freedoms of the single market although it developed more slowly than the other three freedoms, with barriers removed only in the context of the single market programme in 1992. Article 63(1) TFEU (ex 56(1) TEC) prohibits restrictions on free movement of capital between Member States, as well as between Member States and third countries (non-Member States). This enables companies to invest in businesses in other Member States and individuals to open bank accounts or move their savings around the EU.

KEY POINTS

- Quantitative restrictions and measures equivalent to quantitative restrictions are prohibited under Articles 34 and 35 TFEU.
- Distinctly applicable measures are more damaging than indistinctly applicable ones as they target imports directly.
- Indistinctly applicable measures may be justified as mandatory requirements under *Cassis de Dijon* provided they are necessary.
- The principle of mutual recognition under *Cassis de Dijon* lies at the heart of the single market programme.
- Selling arrangements do not infringe Article 34 TFEU.
- Article 36 provides an exhaustive list of the grounds to depart from the principles of free movement in Articles 34 and 35.

CORE CASES AND STATUTES

Case	About	Importance
Case C-265/95 *Commission* v. *France*	Proceedings against France for failing to prevent obstruction to free movement of goods.	Omission to act infringed Articles 34 TFEU and 4 TEU.
Case 8/74 *Procureur du Roi* v. *Dassonville*	Importation of Scotch whisky from France into Belgium without certificate or origin.	Defines MEQRs as all trading rules enacted by Member States which may hinder trade between Member States directly or indirectly, actually or potentially.
Case 120/78 *Rewe-Zentral ('Cassis de Dijon')*	Exclusion of liqueur produced in France from German market as below minimum permitted level in Germany.	Very important decision providing basis by which indistinctly applicable measures may be upheld where necessary to satisfy mandatory requirements. Also provides for principle of mutual recognition whereby goods produced to standard of one Member State may circulate freely throughout EU.

Case	About	Importance
Cases C-267 & 267/91 *Keck and Mithouard*	Prohibition under French law on reselling goods at loss.	Restriction was selling arrangement outside Article 34 provided it did not affect imports and was not discriminatory.
Case C-405/98 *Konsumentombudsman* v. *Gourmet International Products*	Swedish prohibition on television advertising of alcoholic drinks above certain strength.	Prohibition infringed Article 34 as it affected marketing of products from other Member States more severely than domestic products, although justifiable on public health grounds if proportionate – left to national courts.
Case C-470/93 *Verein gegen Unwesen in Handel und Gewerbe Köln*	German requirement for repackaging.	Product requirement contrary to Article 34.
Case C-205/07 *Gysbrechts* v. *Santurel Inter BVBA*	Prohibition on requiring advance payment from consumer in distance selling transactions and on requesting customer's credit card number.	Both prohibitions were restrictions on exports under Art. 35 TFEU, although indistinctly applicable (major change from *Groenveld*). The first prohibition was justified as consumer protection measure, but second infringed Article 35 as disproportionate.
Case 34/79 *R* v. *Henn and Darby*	Difference in standard of prohibition between imported goods ('indecent or obscene') and domestic goods ('likely to deprave or corrupt').	Prohibition on imported goods was MEQR justified on grounds of public morality under Article 36. Enforcement is discriminatory only where there is lawful domestic trade in same goods.
Case 40/82 *Commission* v. *UK (French Turkeys)*	Proceedings against UK which had banned imported French turkeys before Christmas after lobbying by UK producers.	Ban was not justified under Article 36 on health grounds. Established three conditions: 1. must be real not slight health risk; 2. must be part of seriously considered health policy; 3. must not operate as disguised restriction on trade.
Case 174/82 *Officier van Justitie* v. *Sandoz*	Netherlands' ban on sale of muesli bars with added vitamins, although such bars could be sold in Germany and Belgium.	As scientific opinion was divided, Member State could act to protect its citizens, in absence of harmonisation, provided action was proportionate (precautionary principle).

Statute	About	Importance
Article 34 TFEU (ex 28 TEC)	Prohibits restrictions on imports and MEQRs.	Central provision of single market law.
Article 35 TFEU (ex 29 TEC)	Prohibits restrictions on exports and MEQRs.	Prohibits restrictions on exports.
Article 36 TFEU (ex 30 TEC)	Derogation (departure) from prohibition in Articles 34 and 35 on specified grounds.	Strictly interpreted. May not be invoked where there is arbitrary discrimination or disguised restriction on inter-Member trade.
Directive 70/50 Article 2(1)	Defines distinctly applicable measures.	Invalid unless justified under Article 36.
Directive 70/50 Article 3	Defines indistinctly applicable measures.	Invalid unless necessary to satisfy mandatory requirement under *Cassis* or justified under Article 36.

FURTHER READING

Davies, G. 'Understanding market access: exploring the economic rationality of different conceptions of free movement law' (2010) 11 *German Law Journal* 67, available at http://www.germanlawjournal.com/pdfs/FullIssues/PDF_Vol_11_No_08_Complete%20Issue.pdf
Considers whether free movement law should be based on discrimination or market access in analysis of post-*Keck* case law.

Oliver, P. and Enchelmaier, S. 'Free movement of goods: recent developments in the case law' (2007) 44 *Common Market Law Review* 649
Critical review of case law after *Keck*.

Shuibhne, N.N. 'The free movement of goods and Article 28EC: an evolving framework' (2002) 27 *European Law Review* 408
Examines the case law of the Court, reassessing *Keck* in relation to discrimination and market access.

Snell, J. 'The notion of market access: a concept or a slogan?' (2010) 47 *Common Market Law Review* 437
Critically reviews the significance of market access in decisions including *Keck*.

Tryfonidou, A. 'Further steps on the road to convergence among the market freedoms' (2010) 35 *European Law Review* 36
Examines the Court's progress towards convergence among the market freedoms, with reference to recent decisions on free movement of goods.

Wilsher, D. 'Does *Keck* discrimination make any sense? An assessment of the non-discrimination principle within the European single market' (2008) 33 *European Law Review* 3
Analyses post-*Keck* case law with a view to providing a general framework to understand discrimination in internal market law.

CHAPTER 13
Union citizenship

BLUEPRINT
Union citizenship

KEY QUESTIONS

LEGISLATION

- Articles 18, 20(1) TFEU
- Articles 27(1) and 27(2) Directive 2004/38

CONTEXT

- '9/11' and the 'war on terror'

CONCEPTS

- Union citizenship
- Family members
- Political rights
- Residence rights
- Equality of treatment
- Restrictions on free movement

- Do Union citizens identify with the EU?
- Should economically inactive citizens be free to reside throughout the EU?

- Should Union citizens be free to live anywhere in the EU?
- How far should Member States be able to restrict these rights?

CASES

- *Grzelczyk*
- *Metock*

SPECIAL CHARACTERISTICS

- Requirement for lawful residence to rely on principle of non-discrimination
- Importance of proportionality

REFORM

- Directive 2004/38 only in force since 2006, but based on case law of CJEU, which continues to build.

CRITICAL ISSUES

Setting the scene

Nina, a twenty-year-old Bulgarian national and student, wants to live in London. As a Union citizen Nina can live in the UK for up to three months with a valid passport or identification card, after which the position becomes more complex. As a student she could participate in the EU's ERASMUS exchange programme. If she studies at a UK university, she would be entitled to live in the UK for the duration of her studies, after which she can look for work. If Nina becomes ill while studying, she would be entitled to receive medical services in the same way as a UK national. This chapter explores the rights of Union citizens like Nina, including their freedom to move and reside throughout the EU.

INTRODUCTION TO UNION CITIZENSHIP

Citizenship is a badge of political and legal identity demonstrating where an individual 'belongs'. While individuals readily identify with being British or French nationals, for example, there is little identification so far with Union citizenship, the concept introduced under the Maastricht Treaty to recognise the new political entity, the European Union. It represents an important move *away* from the previous market focus which enables economically active individuals such as workers, the self-employed and their families to move around the EU.

The importance of Union citizenship was recognised by the Court of Justice in Case C-184/99 *Grzelczyk*, as the 'fundamental status of nationals of the Member States' (see p. 278). Union citizenship operates in parallel with national citizenship, providing individuals who are nationals of EU Member States with rights of movement and residence throughout the EU, as well as political rights.

The rights of Union citizens are covered by Articles 18–25 TFEU (ex 12–22 TEC) under the heading 'Non-Discrimination and Citizenship of the Union', with detailed rights in Directive 2004/38.

DEFINING UNION CITIZENSHIP

Article 20(1) TFEU (ex 17(1) TEC) provides for the establishment of citizenship of the Union, but leaves it to national law to determine who is a Union citizen.

CORNERSTONE

Article 20(1) TFEU

Every person holding the nationality of a Member State shall be a citizen of the Union. Citizenship shall be additional to and not replace national citizenship.

Article 20(2) TFEU states that 'Citizens of the Union shall enjoy the rights and be subject to the duties provided for in the Treaties', including the right to move and reside freely within the territory of the Member States, and various political rights relating to participation in local and European Parliamentary elections. The rights are exercised 'in accordance with the conditions and limits defined by the Treaties and by measures adopted thereunder'.

Acquiring and losing the nationality of a Member State

Member States can lay down the conditions for acquiring and losing nationality provided they exercise their powers with due regard for EU law. So far there has only been one referral to the Court of Justice involving loss of nationality. In Case C-135/08 *Janko Rottmann* v. *Freistaat Bayern* an Austrian national had moved to Germany after investigation into alleged fraudulent activities for which an arrest warrant was issued. Once in Germany, Rottmann applied successfully for naturalisation without mentioning the proceedings for which he lost his Austrian nationality. The German authorities withdrew his national-isation retroactively, leaving him stateless and no longer a Union citizen. The Court of Justice held that a Member State can withdraw nationality from a Union citizen acquired by naturalisation where it was obtained by deception subject to the principle of proportionality. However, Article 17 TEC (now 20 TEU) requires the Member State of origin to interpret its national law to avoid loss of Union citizenship by allowing the individual to recover his original nationality. The ruling effectively required the Austrian authorities to restore Rottman's original Austrian nationality.

Initial hesitation over citizenship

Member States were afraid of being overwhelmed by economically inactive citizens claiming social assistance after the introduction of Union citizenship. No secondary legislation was adopted for nine years until Directive 2004/38 fleshed out the Treaty provision. While the Court initially adopted a cautious approach, it recognised Union citizenship in 1998 as a significant right in Case C-85/96 *Martinez Sala* v. *Freistaat Bayern*, applying the principle of non-discrimination.

⊕ CORNERSTONE

The principle of non-discrimination (Article 18 TFEU (ex 12 TEC))

Within the scope of the Treaties, and without prejudice to any special provisions contained therein, any discrimination on grounds of nationality shall be prohibited.

The principle of non-discrimination has always been central to EU law, its symbolic importance recognised by the transfer under the Treaty of Lisbon to the new Part Two TFEU headed 'Non-Discrimination and Citizenship of the Union'. Directive 2004/38 makes further provision for equal treatment in Article 24(1), extending the right to family members.

Martinez Sala: a blueprint for citizenship

Martinez Sala established that Union citizens may rely on the principle of non-discrimination to claim equal treatment with the nationals of the host State. The applicant, a Spanish national long resident in Germany, had worked intermittently before giving birth. The German authorities rejected her claim for child-rearing allowance as she did not have a current residence permit although she had applied for one. The Court held that a Union citizen lawfully resident in the territory of the host State may rely on the principle of non-discrimination in all areas within the material scope of the Treaties (i.e. areas

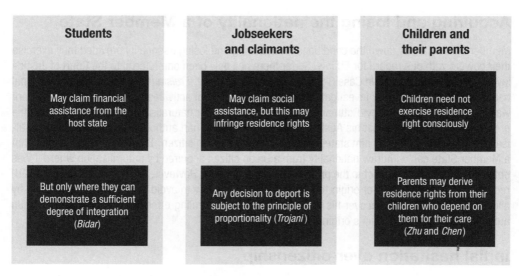

Students	Jobseekers and claimants	Children and their parents
May claim financial assistance from the host state	May claim social assistance, but this may infringe residence rights	Children need not exercise residence right consciously
But only where they can demonstrate a sufficient degree of integration (*Bidar*)	Any decision to deport is subject to the principle of proportionality (*Trojani*)	Parents may derive residence rights from their children who depend on them for their care (*Zhu* and *Chen*)

Figure 13.1 Rights of the economically inactive

covered by EU law). The ruling enabled any lawfully resident Union citizen to claim equal treatment on a par with nationals of the host State in relation to rights under EU law such as the child-rearing allowance in *Sala*.

Citizenship as a 'fundamental status'

The Court of Justice applied its reasoning in *Sala* in Case C-184/99 *Grzelczyk* v. *Centre public d'aide Sociale d'Ottignies-Louvain-la-Neuve-Louvain-la-Neuve*, a referral following a claim for financial relief by a French national studying in Belgium. The applicant claimed it was discriminatory to refuse relief for being outside the applicable secondary legislation, Regulation 1612/68, after the claim. The Court held that the requirement for 'sufficient resources' would be satisfied for students by a declaration at the start of the period of study. Although it held that a Member State may withdraw a residence permit where a student claims social assistance as he no longer fulfils the residence conditions, withdrawal should not follow automatically from applying for social assistance. The Court then made an important declaration about the 'fundamental status' of Union citizenship, repeated in many later decisions.

CORNERSTONE

Case C-184/99 *Grzelczyk*

Union citizenship is destined to be the fundamental status of nationals of the Member States, enabling those who find themselves in the same situation to enjoy the same treatment, irrespective of nationality, subject to such exceptions as are expressly provided for.

This statement makes it clear that Union citizenship is the key which unlocks the right to equal treatment across the EU, representing a significant move away from an economic to a *political* definition of status. Its verbatim repetition in later judgments shows that it continues to represent the Court's view of Union citizenship. The Court has developed a substantial body of case law on citizenship since *Sala*, extending existing rights by applying the principle of non-discrimination. Examples include:

(a) The right to give a minor child a surname under the law of another State where the child is resident in one State, holding dual nationality in the other (Case C-148/02 *Garcia Avello*. In Case C-353/06 *Grunkin and Paul* it held that Member States must recognise a child's surname in the form registered in another State where the child was born and the family live.

(b) The right to use the language of the Union citizen in proceedings in a border area (Case C-274/96 *Bickel and Franz*), over criminal proceedings against two applicants in a German-speaking part of Italy. The applicants complained that only German-speaking residents and not Union citizens from outside Italy had such a right. The Court found such action discriminatory and contrary to the rights of Union citizens.

(c) The right to privacy in relation to personal data (Case C-524/06 *Heinz Huber* v. *Germany*), where an Austrian national resident in Germany requested removal of personal data from a register of non-nationals introduced to fight crime. The Court held that a requirement to process personal data of non-national Union citizens infringed the principle of non-discrimination unless the system contained only data necessary to apply the law, enabling non-national EU citizens' residence rights to be more effectively applied – a matter left to the national court.

APPLICATION

Imagine that Mary, an eighteen-year-old UK national, is working in France as an au pair. Under French law (fictitious), all French nationals under twenty-one are entitled to a training grant to improve their employability skills. Mary's grant application is rejected as she is not a French national. The payment would be regarded as social assistance within the scope of EU law, non-payment of which infringes the principle of non-discrimination. As an EU citizen lawfully resident in France, Mary would be entitled to payment on the same basis as a French national.

A directly effective right

In the absence of national law individuals can only rely on Treaty provisions which are directly effective before the national courts. The Court established in Case C-413/99 *Baumbast and R* v. *Secretary of State for the Home Department* that the right of movement and residence in Article 21(1) TFEU is directly effective. Baumbast, a German national, lived in the UK with his wife (a Colombian national) and their two children, as an employed and then self-employed person. When his business failed Baumbast worked outside the EU while the rest of the family stayed on in the UK, travelling to Germany for medical treatment. He appealed against the UK government's refusal to renew residence permits for himself and his family. The Court held that a Union citizen who no longer enjoys residence rights as a migrant worker may enjoy such a right by direct application of Article 21(1) TFEU (then 18(1) TEC). The right of residence under Article 21(1) TFEU is thus horizontally effective (enforceable against individuals). While exercise of the right is subject to limitations and conditions, they must be applied in accordance with the general principles of Union law, particularly the principle of proportionality.

DIRECTIVE 2004/38 – THE CITIZENS' DIRECTIVE

Directive 2004/38 came into effect in 2006 to implement Article 18 TEC (now 21 TFEU), providing detailed rights for Union citizens and their family members, particularly the right to move freely and reside throughout the territories of the Member States. Directive 2004/38 enables Member States to restrict free movement and residence of EU citizens and their families on grounds of public policy, public health or public security under Article 27. The Directive consolidates legislation, repealing and replacing Directive 64/221, amending Regulation 1612/68, and repealing other directives on residence rights. It incorporates principles developed by the Court of Justice through preliminary references including the proportionality principle. New rights are introduced, notably the residence rights of registered partners as family members.

Three categories of residence rights

Directive 2004/38 introduces three new categories of residence rights:

1. residence rights up to three months;
2. residence rights for more than three months;
3. permanent residence rights.

Residence rights up to three months

Union citizens and their families are entitled to reside in another Member State for up to three months on production of a valid identity card or passport under Article 6(1) of Directive 2004/38, provided they do not become a burden on the social assistance of the host State. This means that Union citizens have no entitlement to social assistance during the three-month period.

Residence rights for more than three months

To establish residence rights after three months, the individual must demonstrate under Article 7(1) of Directive 2004/38 that he or she falls within one of the following categories:

Resident up to 3 months (Art. 6(1))	Resident more than 3 months (Art. 7(1))	Permanent resident rights (Art. 16)
• Valid ID card/passport • If not a burden on social assistance of host state • Not entitled to social assistance	• Worker/self employed • Not a burden on social assistance and has sickness cover • Student with sickness cover and declaration of means • Family member of one of the above	• Lawfully resident for 5 years or more • Not subject to conditions under Arts. 6–15 • Family members also benefit • May only be expelled on 'serious grounds' of public policy or security

Figure 13.2 Residence rights of Union citizens and their families under Directive 2004/38

(a) Union citizens who are workers or self-employed in the host State.

(b) All other Union citizens with sufficient resources to avoid becoming a burden on the social assistance system of the host State and comprehensive sickness cover in that State while they are resident.

(c) Union citizens following a course of study in the host State, provided they have comprehensive sickness cover in that State and give an assurance to the relevant authority, by a declaration or equivalent means, that they have sufficient resources for themselves and their family members not to become a burden on the social assistance system of the host Member State during their period of residence.

(d) The family members accompanying or joining an EU citizen who satisfies the conditions in (a), (b) or (c).

The right of residence for more than three months is subject under Article 14(2) to the requirement that the Union citizen and family members must continue to meet the conditions in Article 7. Applying the principle of proportionality, the directive provides in Article 14(3) that failure to do so should not lead automatically to deportation. The host State should consider whether the case is one of temporary difficulties, taking into account duration of stay, personal circumstances and the amount of aid granted. Persons with a genuine chance of finding employment or self-employment should not be expelled unless considerations of public policy or public security apply. Registration may be required for stays over three months.

Permanent residence rights

Permanent residence rights are granted to citizens who have resided lawfully for five years or more (Article 16) and are not subject to conditions otherwise imposed under Articles 6 to 15 (covering residence rights up to and beyond three months). Family members who are not nationals of a Member State but who have legally resided with the Union citizen in the host State for a continuous period of five years also benefit from permanent residence rights under Article 16(2).

Once permanent residence rights have been established, they may only be lost through absence from the host Member State over two years under Article 16(4). Article 28(2) provides that a Member State may only expel a Union citizen or family member where there are *serious grounds* of public policy or public security. Where the Union citizen has ten years' residence in the host State, it is even harder for the Member State to deport him or her as *imperative grounds* of public security are required – for example, where the individual poses a terrorist threat. (Expulsion on grounds of public policy/ public security is considered on p. 290.)

A shorter continuous period of three years' lawful residence may be enough for workers or the self-employed who reach the age of entitlement to a state pension in the host State provided they have worked for at least twelve months there (Article 17(1)(a)). An exception is made for individuals suffering industrial accidents, who only need two years' lawful residence (Article 17(1)(b)), as well as for frontier workers living in the host State but working in another after three years' continuous residence, provided they return to the host State at least once a week (Article 17(1)(c)).

Definition of 'family members'

Directive 2004/38 broadened the definition of 'family member' to include registered partners. Family members are defined by Article 2(2) of the directive (which replaced Article 10 of Regulation 1612/68) as:

(a) the spouse;

(b) the partner with whom the EU citizen has contracted a registered partnership on the basis of the legislation of a Member State if the legislation of the host State treats registered partnerships as equivalent to marriage and in accordance with the relevant legislation of the Member State;

(c) direct descendants who are under the age of twenty-one or are dependents and those of the spouse or partner, as defined in (b);

(d) dependent direct relatives in the ascending line and those of the partner or spouse.

.... APPLICATION

John, a UK national, married to Sue, a US national, has recently been offered a job in France where he wishes to move with his extended family. Sue's elderly invalid mother lives with John and Sue, as do the couple's twenty-two-year-old twins, Paul and Molly. Paul is disabled after a car crash. Molly works as a hairdresser. John is a Union citizen and a worker and is entitled to live in France under Article 7(2) of Directive 2004/38. He can bring with him those who qualify as family members under Article 2(2), even though they are not Union citizens. Thus Sue may live with him in France, as well as her mother (direct, dependent relative of the spouse in the ascending line). Although Paul is over twenty-one, he is entitled to live with John as he is dependent. Molly does not derive rights from her father, as she is not dependent on him. However, if she is a Union citizen, she would be entitled to move to France under the directive in her own right.

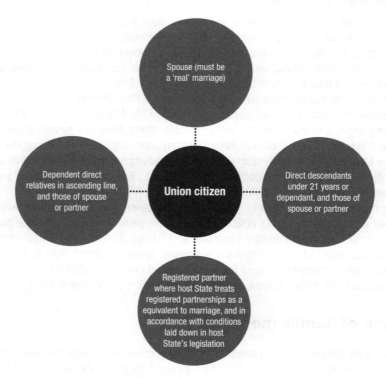

Figure 13.3 Definition of 'family members'

Who is a 'spouse'?

An individual married to a Union citizen and not separated is certainly covered by the term 'spouse'. It may be necessary to consider whether the marriage is recognised as providing residence rights by one of the Member States. (A marriage ceremony which did not comply with local rules would be invalid.) Where a residence right is recognised in one Member State, it must also be recognised in the other Member States under the principle of mutual recognition.

The position of non-EU nationals known as third-country nationals (TCNs) married to Union citizens is quite complex. The Court of Justice made an important ruling in Case C-127/08 *Metock and others* v. *Minister of Justice, Equality and Law Reform* that TCNs married to Union citizens who are not nationals of the host State may rely on Article 3(1) of Directive 2004/38 to join or accompany the Union citizen, regardless of when or where the marriage took place. Metock and nine other applicants were TCNs who arrived in Ireland claiming asylum. They later entered into genuine marriages with Union citizens who were not Irish nationals. As Irish law required TCNs to have lived in another Member State before moving to Ireland and claiming residence rights, the Irish authorities refused to issue residence cards. The Court held that the requirement for residence in another Member State before arrival in the host State infringed the directive. It found that Article 3(1) could be relied on to enable TCNs married to non-national Union citizens to join or accompany the Union citizen, regardless of when or where the marriage took place.

APPLICATION

Abdul is a national of Pakistan where he is introduced to Rina, a Belgian national visiting family in Lahore. They fall in love and marry in Pakistan. Rina returns to Belgium where Abdul later joins her. Under a (fictitious) Belgian law, non-Union citizens marrying Belgian nationals are only entitled to reside in Belgium if they have previously lived in another Member State. Abdul is refused a residence permit. As this is a genuine marriage, applying *Metock*, Abdul would be entitled under EU law to reside in Belgium, even though there has been no cross-border movement.

Metock followed Case C-1/05 *Jia* v. *Migrationsverket*, where the Court of Justice held that a TCN may acquire rights under EU law without having been previously resident in another Member State, enabling a TCN to move directly to the host State from a third country. *Metock* effectively overruled Case C-109/01 *Secretary of State for the Home Department* v. *Akrich* where the Court had found that a non-EU spouse could only benefit from EU residence rights when moving to another Member State to which the Union spouse was migrating where he or she could rely on the prior lawful residence of the Union spouse.

REFLECTION

Metock removed the artificial requirement for a TCN to move to Member State A (where he did not wish to go) to reside in Member State B (where he wanted to be in the first place). However, the decision was controversial as it made it harder for national authorities to exclude TCNs. Currie (2009) sees *Metock* as legally justified, but is concerned about the 'political reality' behind national immigration law, given the limited scope to exclude third country family members. Costello (2009) praises the judgment's boldness, while criticising it for basing family residence rights on cross-border movement rather than acknowledging the fundamental rights dimension which was decisive to the Court of Justice in *Carpenter* (see Chapter 15).

Marriages of convenience

Member States are entitled to question whether a marriage is 'real' under Article 35 of the directive. Rights conferred by the directive may be refused, withdrawn or terminated by Member States where there is abuse of rights or fraud such as a marriage of convenience, usually where a TCN marries a Union citizen to acquire residence and other rights. There is no case law on Article 35 yet but it is likely that an arranged marriage would be regarded as genuine if there is no compulsion.

Effect of divorce and separation

Before Directive 2004/38 the position on divorce and separation was unclear. Limited guidance was provided by Case 267/83 *Diatta* v. *Land Berlin* (involving a TCN separated from her EU national husband) where the Court ruled that separation does not dissolve the marital relationship as it has not been terminated by the competent authorities. Directive 2004/38 improved the position for divorced and separated spouses. Article 13(2) provides that 'Divorce, annulment of marriage or termination of the registered partnership . . . shall not entail loss of the right of residence of a Union citizen's family members who are not nationals of a Member State' in three circumstances:

1. before initiation of divorce proceedings or termination of the registered partnership . . . the marriage or registered partnership has lasted at least three years, including one year in the host Member State; or

2. by agreement . . . the spouse or partner who is not a national of a Member State has custody of the Union citizen's children; or

3. it is warranted by particularly difficult circumstances, such as having been the victim of domestic violence while the marriage or registered partnership was subsisting.

Cohabitees, registered partners and other family members

Before Directive 2004/38 cohabitees enjoyed no general right of residence in EU law, although entitlement might arise in specific instances under the principle of non-discrimination, as in Case 59/85 *Netherlands* v. *Reed* (UK national cohabiting with another UK national in circumstances from which residence rights would have arisen if one party had been a Dutch national).

Registered partners under Article 2(2) of Directive 2004/38 acquire the same residence and other rights as spouses provided the partnership is recognised as equivalent to marriage in the host State. A partnership validly registered in one Member State but not recognised by the host State will be outside Article 2(2). Cohabiting but non-qualifying partners may gain some rights under Article 3(2)(b) of the directive, which requires the host Member State, in accordance with national law, to *facilitate entry and residence* of the partner with whom the Union citizen has a durable relationship, duly attested.

Article 3(2)(a) provides for 'facilitated entry and residence' of other family members outside Article 2(2) where, in the country from which they have come, they are dependents of members of the household of the Union citizen having the primary right of residence, or where serious health grounds require the personal care of the family member by the Union citizen. The expression 'facilitated entry and residence' has not yet been interpreted by the Court, but suggests a lesser right than entry, with host State discretion on admission. Future referrals are likely to clarify the host State's obligation to 'undertake an extensive examination of the personal circumstances' and 'justify any denial of entry or residence to these people'. While the scope of Article 3(2) remains uncertain, it should be read subject to the fundamental right of family reunification.

APPLICATION

Imagine that Sally, a Canadian national, has been in a long-term relationship with Bruno, an Italian, for ten years. The couple live in Canada but have never married. Bruno accepts the offer of work in Italy where Sally wishes to join him. She is not covered by the definition of family member in Article 2(2), being neither a spouse nor in a same-sex registered partnership. As she is in a durable relationship, Sally is entitled to have her entry into Italy and residence 'facilitated' under Article 3(2)(b), an undefined right, falling short of entitlement to reside.

Union citizens and family members who are not EU nationals, lacking necessary travel documents or visas, should not be excluded by Member States but given a reasonable opportunity to obtain the necessary documentation or have them brought within a reasonable time under Article 5(4) of the directive, incorporating Case C-459/99 *MRAX* v. *Belgium*.

Equality of treatment

Under Article 24(1) of Directive 2004/38, Union citizens and their families, including TCNs, are entitled to equal treatment. Under Article 24(2) there is no duty on the host State to confer entitlement to social assistance during the first three months of residence, or provide a student loan or maintenance grant to Union citizens unless they are workers, self-employed or their families. Despite this lack of provision, the Court has recognised the possibility of financial support for students where the applicant has demonstrated a sufficient level of integration with the society of the host State (see p. 286).

RIGHTS OF EXIT AND ENTRY

Union citizens with a valid identity card or passport and their family members who are not EU nationals can leave the territory of a Member State to travel to another Member State under Article 4 of Directive 2004/38 and enter under Article 5. Administrative formalities for Union citizens are provided in Article 8 and for family members who are not EU nationals in Article 9.

The right to residence derives from the Treaties, not from possession of a residence permit. In Case 157/79 *R* v. *Pieck* (criminal proceedings against a Dutch national who had overstayed his residence permit in the UK) the Court of Justice held that a Member State is not entitled to require a general residence permit from a person enjoying the protection of Community law (i.e. a national of a Member State). This means that Union citizens holding a valid ID card or passport under Article 4 of Directive 2004/38 cannot be required to produce a visa to enter another Member State or be deported or subjected to criminal penalties because a residence permit expires.

In Case 48/75 *Procureur du Roi* v. *Royer* (criminal proceedings for illegal entry and residence in Belgium against a French national previously convicted of robbery) the Court of Justice found that the right to enter includes the right to search for work, although the host State may deport the Union citizen after a reasonable period of time. In Case C-292/89R *R* v. *Immigration Appeal Tribunal ex p. Antonissen* a period of six months before deportation was found to be sufficient where there was no evidence of a genuine attempt to find work. The right of entry and residence should now be read subject to Article 7 of Directive 2004/38 providing for a right of residence over three months where the Union citizen falls into a recognised category such as worker or family member. He or she should not be deported automatically if conditions are not met.

RIGHTS OF THE ECONOMICALLY INACTIVE

Individuals who are economically inactive fall into various categories and are not necessarily dependent on the state for support (see Figure 13.1).

Citizens who can support themselves

Article 7(1)(b) of Directive 2004/38 provides residence rights for Union citizens who have sufficient resources for themselves and their family members not to become a burden on the social assistance system of the host State while they are resident, provided they have comprehensive health insurance in the host State. This provision benefits people of any age who can support themselves such as retired citizens with a pension as well as citizens living off private means.

Students

Students who are Union citizens have residence rights for the duration of their studies under Article 7(1)(c) of Directive 2004/38, although Member States are reluctant to provide financial assistance to students from other Member States. In Case C-209/03 *Dany Bidar*, a French national had been refused a student loan despite having attended school in the UK for three years before taking up a university place at the London School of Economics. The Court held that introduction of Union citizenship had changed the position of students whose requests for assistance had previously been outside the Treaties. (In Case 197/86 *Brown* and Case 39/86 *Lair*, before the introduction of citizenship, the Court found education to be a social advantage under Regulation 16121/68. Entitlement to a maintenance grant only arose if the individual could establish he was a worker who had become involuntarily unemployed.)

The Court ruled In *Bidar* that lawfully resident students were covered by the principle of non-discrimination after the introduction of Union citizenship and could claim financial assistance provided they could demonstrate a *sufficient degree of integration* into the society of that State, for example through residence for a reasonable time. The Court was willing in *Bidar* to go further than Directive 2004/38 (not yet in force) which makes no specific provision for student financial support. Students from across the EU will continue to find it hard to gain financial assistance outside the home State due to the difficulty of establishing the necessary degree of integration. A national requirement for five years' lawful residence for a maintenance grant was found to be reasonable in Case C-158/07 *Förster*.

APPLICATION

Assume that the Republic of Ireland provides maintenance grants for students attending university there if they are 'sufficiently established' in Ireland. Colin, a UK national aged eighteen, moved to Ireland with his parents eight years ago, attending school locally. His grandparents live nearby, enabling him to visit them weekly. The words 'sufficiently established' should be interpreted in accordance with *Bidar*. Given the time Colin has lived in Ireland as well as his school attendance and family links, he should be able to show the necessary level of integration to qualify for a maintenance grant.

His position may be contrasted with that of Mary, also a UK national, who moved to Ireland for a gap year after completing her secondary education in London, hoping to qualify for a maintenance grant. During the year she worked part-time and travelled around Ireland. Mary would be unlikely to demonstrate the necessary degree of integration to qualify for a maintenance grant in Ireland.

Jobseekers and other claimants

The need for a suitably developed link was also a factor in claims by Union citizens for jobseeker's allowances. In Case C-224/98 *D'Hoop* v. *Office National de l'Emploi* a Belgian applicant was refused a 'tideover' allowance (payable when seeking a first job) because she had completed her secondary education in France. The link required was seen to be disproportionate (i.e. excessive in the circumstances).

The link with the host State was weaker in Case C-138/02 *Collins* v. *Secretary of State for Work and Pensions* where an Irish national who had moved to the UK to look for work unsuccessfully claimed a jobseeker's allowance. However, the Court found that a jobseeker was entitled to a financial benefit intended to facilitate access to the labour market of another Member State. The residence requirement imposed by the UK had to be interpreted in accordance with the principle of proportionality.

A short period of work may entitle a Union citizen to benefits. Cases C-22 & 23/08 *Vatsouras and Koupatantze* concerned Greek nationals living in Germany who had worked for only a short time (three months and one month) before claiming benefit. The ruling was given after introduction of Directive 2004/38 which provides in Article 24(1) for Union citizens to enjoy equal treatment subject to a derogation under Article 24(2), which the Court interpreted as requiring Member States to provide social assistance to jobseekers only for as long as they are entitled to reside. The Court also found that the principle of non-discrimination does not preclude national rules excluding nationals of other Member States from receiving social assistance benefits granted to nationals of non-member countries.

In Case C-456/02 *Trojani* v. *CPAS* the Court found that a Union citizen lawfully resident but not economically active may rely on the principle of non-discrimination in (what is now) Article 18 TFEU to claim social assistance on the same basis as a national of the host State. While it was open to the host State to find that reliance on social assistance infringed the right of residence, any decision to deport was subject to the principle of proportionality. Thus a short spell of claiming assistance should not automatically lead to deportation.

Citizens who have lost their job

Article 7(3) protects citizens who have lost their job or are no longer self-employed who may retain their status and residence rights in circumstances including temporary inability to work after an accident and involuntary unemployment after having been employed for more than a year and registered as a jobseeker.

Children and their parents

The beneficiary of residence rights under Article 21 TFEU need not exercise the right consciously – for example, where a child in its parents' care moves from Italy to Spain. Parents may derive rights from a child, as in Case C-200/02 *Zhu and Chen*. Mrs Chen had come to the UK from China to escape the 'one child' policy. She moved to Northern Ireland from Wales to give birth so the child would acquire Irish nationality. After the birth Mrs Chen and the child, Catherine, moved back to Wales where the family supported themselves. Mrs Chen challenged the UK government's refusal of residence rights. The Court found that although Catherine had never left the UK this was not a 'wholly internal situation' as she had the nationality of another Member State, Ireland. Mrs Chen's temporary move to Northern Ireland was not seen as an abuse of EU law, holding that the child could exercise the free movement rights as a Union citizen, and that her mother's rights derived from the child's need for her care.

In Case C-34/09 *Ruiz Zambrano* v. *Office national de l'emploi* the Court of Justice held that Member States were not permitted to refuse a TCN the right of residence or a work permit in the State where his minor children, who were Union citizens, were residing.

Internal situations

Union citizens cannot rely on residence rights under Article 21 TFEU in a 'purely internal' situation where the individual has never crossed a border. Case C-434/09 *Shirley McCarthy* v. *Secretary of State for the Home Department* concerned an application by an individual with dual Irish-UK nationality receiving state benefits who had never worked or travelled outside the UK. The referral arose from the UK government's refusal of a residence permit for the applicant and her husband, a Jamaican national. The Court of Justice ruled that Article 21 TFEU does not apply to a Union citizen who has never exercised free movement rights but has always resided in a Member State where she is a national while also holding nationality of another Member State. However, national measures must not deprive her of Union citizenship rights or make it harder to exercise movement and residence rights.

> The Scottish government can charge students from England and Wales to attend university in Scotland as this is an internal situation in EU law, provided Scotland remains part of the UK, but not students from other Member States which would discriminate against them relative to students from Scotland paying no fees. This anomaly raises the question as to whether students from Northern Ireland entitled to apply for an Irish passport would have to pay fees as they would hold the nationality of another Member State.

REFLECTION

POLITICAL RIGHTS OF UNION CITIZENS

Articles 22–24 TFEU

Union citizens enjoy political rights under Articles 22–24 TFEU (ex 19–21 TEC):

1. Article 22 – The right to vote and stand as a candidate in municipal elections and elections to the European Parliament (but not general elections to a national parliament) in a Member State where the Union citizen is resident but not a national (implemented for municipal elections by Directive 94/80 and for European Parliamentary elections by Directive 93/109). The Court found that Belgium had infringed Directive 93/109 in Case C-323/97 *Commission* v. *Belgium* by only permitting Belgian nationals to vote or stand in municipal elections. Voting rights in the European Parliament were considered in relation to Gibraltar residents in Case C-145/04 *Spain* v. *UK*. The UK was found not to be in breach of EU law when it amended the law to comply with a decision of the European Court of Human Rights on voting rights of Gibraltarians.

2. Article 23 – The right to receive diplomatic and consular protection in the State where the Union citizen is resident on the same terms as a national of that State (implemented by Directive 95/533).

3. Article 24 – The right to petition the Parliament and Union Ombudsman and write to the EU institutions in any of the official languages.

INTERSECTION

The Treaty of Lisbon encourages citizens to participate in the decision-making process, particularly through introduction of the citizens' initiative under Article 11(4) TEU, considered in Chapter 2 in relation to institutional reform. It enables a million Union citizens to submit a proposal for legislation to the Commission, but has not yet been implemented.

The Commission must report every three years on the application of citizenship provisions to the Parliament, Council and Economic and Social Committee (Article 25 TFEU (ex 21 TEC)), while the Council must adopt provisions which it recommends to Member States.

Participation in European Parliamentary elections is low. This may be due to EU citizens' lack of identification with the Union which has been criticised for lacking a 'demos' (i.e. people who are the subjects of a democracy), despite the automatic status of Union citizenship following from Member State nationality.

Various theories have been suggested to explain the basis of Union citizenship. According to the German sociologist and philosopher Habermas (1992), Union citizenship is not a new idea but can be traced back to the Swiss philosopher Rousseau. In his 'Social Contract' (1762) Rousseau argued that man should remove himself from a 'state of nature' by entering into a social contract with others by which everyone is free, having surrendered the same amount of rights and taken on the same duties as other citizens. According to Habermas, democratic societies like the EU operate through consensus, with political loyalty to constitutional principles in the Treaties as the basis for Union citizenship rather than a shared cultural identity. The American political scientist Weiler (1999) also sees rights under the Treaties as a 'social contract' between Union citizens, a view supporting the principle of direct effect whereby rights and duties may be created between individuals.

REFLECTION

LIMITATIONS ON GROUNDS OF PUBLIC POLICY, PUBLIC SECURITY OR PUBLIC HEALTH

Scope of the limitation

The rights of Union citizens to move and reside within the EU must be balanced against the threats posed by certain individuals. The extent to which such rights may be curtailed is covered in Directive 2004/38 which recognises that any restriction of movement and residence rights is subject to the principle of proportionality. As the directive consolidated earlier secondary legislation particularly Directive 64/221 and earlier case law, the principles established before the current directive remain relevant.

Overview of scope for restrictions under Directive 2004/38

Directive 2004/38 provides in Articles 27 to 33 for restrictions on the right of entry and residence of Union citizens and their family members on grounds of public policy, security or public health.

The restrictions apply regardless of category in which the individual exercises movement rights. (If a Member State needs to detain a suspected terrorist from another State, it is irrelevant whether he or she is there as a tourist, worker or family member.)

CORNERSTONE

Article 27(1) Directive 2004/38

Article 27(1) empowers Member States to restrict the free movement of Union citizens and their families on grounds of public policy, public security and public health.

Take note

'Public policy' is a translation of the French expression 'l'ordre public' in the original Treaty of Rome, possibly better translated as 'public order'. 'Public security' has often been invoked as an almost interchangeable alternative to public policy.

The area of discretion left to national authorities over the public policy/public security proviso may be examined by reference to decisions of the Court such as Case 36/75 *Rutili* v. *Ministre de l'Intérieur* and Case 30/77 *R* v. *Bouchereau* which are reflected in the wording of Article 27.

Article 27(1) also provides that such measures 'shall not be invoked to serve economic ends'. Thus Member States cannot restrict numbers of Union citizens entering from elsewhere in the EU, on account of a recession.

CORNERSTONE

Article 27(2) Directive 2004/38

Measures taken on grounds of public policy or public security must comply with the principle of proportionality and be based exclusively on the personal conduct of the individual concerned. Previous criminal convictions are not in themselves grounds for taking such measures.

'Measures' were defined in Case 30/77 *Bouchereau* as 'any action affecting the rights of persons coming within the field of application of Article 45 TFEU to enter and reside freely in a Member State on the same conditions as the nationals of the host State'. This is a broad definition from which it follows that any action making it difficult or impossible for a Union citizen to move freely within the EU such as detention, deportation or service of a notice of deportation is covered.

Bouchereau was a French national who came to work in the UK in 1975. He was convicted of unlawful possession of drugs in 1976, having pleaded guilty to a similar offence earlier in the year. The UK sought to deport him back to France but proceedings were suspended for a preliminary reference to the Court of Justice. The Court held that restrictions on the movement of an EU national may not be imposed unless the individual constitutes 'a genuine and sufficiently serious threat to one of the fundamental interests of society'. A *previous* criminal conviction may only be taken into account as evidence of personal conduct where it constitutes a *present threat* to the requirements of public policy by indicating a likelihood of recurrence. Past conduct alone may constitute a present threat where the conduct is sufficiently serious.

The need to assess the threat on an individual basis may be seen in Case 67/74 *Bonsignore* v. *Oberstadtdirecktor of the City of Cologne.* Bonsignore, an Italian working in Germany, had accidentally shot his brother. He was convicted and fined for unlawful possession of a firearm but challenged the deportation order in the German courts. The Court held that the public policy requirement can only be invoked to justify deportation or breaches of the peace and public security committed by the individual concerned and not for reasons of a general preventive nature. Someone like Bonsignore did not pose a sufficiently serious threat *himself* and was most unlikely to reoffend. What happened was a tragic accident, and thus did not provide the basis for deportation to discourage *other people* from possessing unlawful firearms.

Proportionality

The reference to proportionality in Article 27(2) reflects Case 48/75 *Procureur du Roi* v. *Royer* where the Court held that failure to comply with administrative requirements (e.g. to renew a passport or ID card) does not justify deportation although it may lead to a penalty, provided it is proportionate. Thus an administrative penalty such as a small fine might be appropriate but not a criminal penalty or deportation.

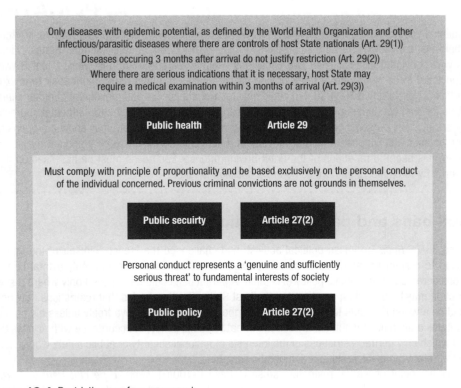

Figure 13.4 Restrictions on free movement

Personal conduct

Article 27(2) paragraph 3 provides that:

> The personal conduct of the individual concerned must represent a genuine, present and suffi-ciently serious threat affecting one of the fundamental interests of society. Justifications that are isolated from the particulars of the case or that rely on considerations of general prevention shall not be accepted.

This wording consolidates a body of case law in the Court of Justice, particularly in relation to the extent to which convictions may justify restrictions.

Criminal convictions

As criminal convictions do not in themselves constitute grounds for restrictions, national authorities must assess whether the personal conduct of the individual concerned poses a 'genuine and suffi-ciently serious threat to one of the fundamental interests of society', as the Court of Justice held in *Rutili* and *Bouchereau*. Thus expulsion *without* considering the merits of the case infringes EU law. In Case C-348/96 *Donatella Calfa* an Italian on holiday on Crete convicted of possession and use of prohibited drugs was sentenced to three months' imprisonment and expelled for life from Greece under a national policy of automatic expulsion for drugs offences. The Court held that automatic expulsion after conviction failed to take account of the individual's personal conduct and the extent to which it posed a threat.

.... APPLICATION

Imagine you are a UK solicitor asked to advise two clients, both Union citizens, worried whether their past convictions may cause problems if they wish to work in other Member States. Client A was convicted of assault on two occasions – eight years ago and last year. Client B was convicted three years ago of drink driving. In both cases the host State might seek to invoke Article 27 of Directive 2004/38, but could only restrict the access and movement of either client if he (or she) continues to pose a sufficiently serious threat to one of the fundamental interests of society. The personal conduct of Client A (twice convicted of assault) may show a propensity for violence justifying restriction of movement. Client B is less likely to be a present threat, as there has been no repetition of the drink-driving offence. Each case must be assessed on the merits by the national authorities before a decision is taken.

Total bans and partial restrictions

In Case 36/75 *Rutili*, an Italian political activist, had challenged the French Minister of the Interior's decision to restrict his activities to certain *départements*. The Court held that only a total ban may be considered under the public policy exception. A partial ban could be imposed only where a similar restriction may be placed on a national of the host State. The Court ruled that restrictions may not be placed on a worker's rights to enter another Member State, live and move freely unless his presence constitutes a genuine and sufficiently serious threat to public policy, in accordance with Articles 8–11 ECHR which only permit restrictions in the interests of national security or public safety where *neces-sary* to protect those interests in a democratic society.

A similar point on partial restriction arose in Case C-100/01 *Ministre de l'Interieur* v. *Olazabal* where the Court of Justice followed *Rutili*. Olazabal, a Spanish national and supporter of the Basque separatist organisation ETA, had been convicted in France of conspiracy to disturb public order by intimidation or terror. He was sentenced to imprisonment (partly suspended) and banned from residing in France for four years. The French Conseil d'Etat referred to the Court of Justice to clarify the scope for restrictions. The Court held that partial restrictions on residence rights may be imposed on nationals of other Member States where the host State imposes punitive measures 'or other genuine and effective measures' against its own nationals to combat such a threat.

In Case C-33/07 *Ministerul Administraţiei şi Internelor-Direcţia Generală de Paşapoarte Bucureşti v. Jipa*, the Romanian authorities had restricted the applicant's freedom to travel to Belgium for three years. Jipa left Romania in 2006 to travel to Belgium, where his residence was regarded as illegal. He was repatriated (sent back) to Romania under an agreement between the two countries providing for readmission of persons in an illegal situation. The Court held that a *restriction on freedom to travel* is not incompatible with EU law where the individual is illegally resident provided the individual's personal conduct constitutes a genuine and sufficiently serious threat to one of the fundamental interests of society, and the restrictions are appropriate and proportionate. However, it found that the Romanian authorities appeared to have relied solely on the repatriation measure without assessing personal conduct and the nature of any threat. The decision shows how important it is for each case to be considered fully on the merits before a restriction is imposed.

The scope of the public policy restriction must be determined by reference to EU law

While public policy varies from State to State, its *scope* may not be unilaterally determined by a Member State without reference to EU law (Case 41/74 *Van Duyn* v. *Home Office*). *Van Duyn* arose in relation to a Netherlands national prevented by the Home Office from taking up employment in the UK with the Church of Scientology, an organisation which was not illegal but regarded as socially harmful by the UK government. The Court of Justice held that *present* but not *past* association may be considered as personal conduct. While finding that Member States may not unilaterally determine the scope of public policy, the Court nevertheless permitted a *stricter* standard to be applied to an EU national in these circumstances than would have been applied to a UK national where the government deemed it to be necessary. This is perhaps surprising as it does not accord with the principle of non-discrimination.

Van Duyn was decided in 1974. Six and a half years later the Court adopted a stricter approach in Cases 115 & 116/81 *Adoui and Cornuaille*, arising from referrals in Belgium where two prostitutes, both EU nationals, had been denied residence permits although prostitution was not illegal there. Although the Court did not distinguish or overrule *Van Duyn* it held that Member States cannot refuse residence to EU nationals on account of conduct which is neither illegal nor controlled in the nationals of the host State.

It is difficult to reconcile *Adoui and Cornuaille* with *Van Duyn*, as *Van Duyn* allows Member States to adopt a stricter standard towards nationals of other Member States when *Adoui* does not. The Court of Justice chose not to overrule *Van Duyn* when it decided more or less the same point in *Adoui* – arguably the better decision in terms of the right of the individual. One possible explanation is that the Court was more in tune with the ethos of the single market in *Adoui* than *Van Duyn*.

REFLECTION

Supply of information

Article 27(3) requires the Member State of origin to supply information to the host Member State to assess whether an individual poses a threat. Where a person is expelled, he or she is entitled to re-enter the Member State issuing the passport or ID card without formality (Article 27(4)). Thus if the passport of the expelled person has expired, he or she should be readmitted to the home State.

Protection against expulsion

Article 28 provides for protection against expulsion. Host States must take account of considerations including length of residence, family and economic considerations, social and cultural integration into the host State and limits with the country of origin (Article 28(1)). Union citizens with a permanent right of residence or their family members, irrespective of nationality, may not be expelled unless there are serious grounds of public policy or public security (Article 28(2)).

Expulsion decisions may not be taken against Union citizens unless the decision is based on imperative grounds of public security if they:

(a) have resided in the Member State for the previous ten years; or

(b) are a minor, unless the expulsion is necessary for the best interests of the child under the UN Convention on the Rights of the Child 1989: Article 28(3).

Procedural safeguards

Article 30 requires notification in writing of decisions under Article 27(1) in clear language, informing the persons concerned of the grounds on which the action is taken and the relevant appeal mechanisms. Article 31 provides for procedural safeguards including access to judicial and administrative redress. Article 32 states that persons excluded on grounds of public policy, security or health may apply to have the order lifted after a reasonable period or three years from enforcement of the final exclusion order. Expulsion orders may not be issued by the host State under Article 32 as a penalty or consequence of a custodial sentence unless they conform to the requirements of Articles 27 to 29.

The public health exception

Article 29 covers the public health exception but has not yet been interpreted by the Court of Justice. Under Article 29(1) measures restricting freedom of movement may only be imposed where justified for diseases with epidemic potential as defined by the World Health Organization (WHO) and other infectious or contagious parasitic diseases where there are controls on host State nationals. Article 29(2) provides that diseases occurring *after* three months from arrival do not justify expulsion. Article 29(3) introduces a new provision where there are serious indications of a public health risk for a Member State to require persons entitled to residence to undergo, free of charge within three months from arrival, a medical examination certifying that they are not suffering from any of the conditions in paragraph 1. Such examinations cannot be required routinely.

··· **APPLICATION**

Albert, a Belgian national in Brussels, is HIV positive. Colette, a French national living in Paris, has recently been diagnosed with tuberculosis. Both would like to travel to the UK for treatment. Albert cannot be excluded under Article 29 as there are no restrictions on UK nationals who are HIV positive. As UK nationals with tuberculosis may be restricted, Colette may not be permitted to enter. If she is not excluded at the border, she may be subject to a medical examination within three months of arrival. If she is clear of the disease on arrival but contracts it four months later, she cannot be excluded on grounds of health. Union citizens suffering from a disease of epidemic proportions (as defined by the WHO) such as cholera may be subject to restrictions.

NATIONALS OF THIRD COUNTRIES

Although the host State may require TCNs to obtain a visa, it should give them 'every assistance' under Article 5(4) of Directive 2004/38.TCNs enjoy rights of entry and residence under various legal arrangements, including:

(a) *As a family member of a Union citizen under Article 2(2) of Directive 2004/38.* Often such rights arise in the context of marriage. A TCN married to a Union citizen is entitled to reside in their spouse's Member State under Article 2(2), although the host State may investigate to see whether the marriage is 'real' under Article 35 and refuse residence if it is not. However, in Case C-256/11 *Dereci and others* v. *Bundesministerium für Inneres* (where several TCNs were married to Austrians but had never left the country) the Court found that it is permissible for a Member State to refuse entry and residence to a TCN married to a Union citizen who has never exercised free movement rights provided the refusal does not deprive the citizen of 'genuine enjoyment' of his or her rights of citizenship.

(b) *As a beneficiary under an association agreement (international agreements between the EU and a non-Member State for trade links and limited access to the single market).* In Case C-340/97 *Nazli* v. *Nurnberg* a Turkish national was detained in custody for a year pending criminal proceedings after being lawfully employed in Germany for four years. The Court held that a TCN does not in such circumstances lose his status as a lawful member of the EU workforce under an association agreement and may apply for extension to his residence permit to seek access to employment.

(c) *As an employee of an undertaking established in the EU.* Such employees must be allowed to move with the undertaking with no more restriction than applied to nationals in the state of origin (Case C-113/89 Rush Portugesa).

(d) *Under a partnership agreement with a non-Member State.* In Case C-265/03 *Simutenkov* v. *Ministerio de Educacíon y Cultura*, professional sportsmen (Russian footballers) lawfully employed in the EU were entitled under the EC-Russia Partnership Agreement to equal treatment with nationals of the host State in terms of working conditions.

(e) *Under the EEA Agreement.* Nationals from Iceland, Norway and Liechtenstein enjoy full rights of free movement within the EU under EEA.

(f) *Under the Schengen Agreement.* Schengen established an area within which border facilities are relaxed between participating states.

(g) *Under the Area of freedom, security and justice.* Article 67(2) TFEU provides for the relaxation of border facilities, as well as common policies on matters including immigration and asylum.

The Schengen Agreement

The original idea in the Treaties was to allow individuals to travel and settle throughout the Union, but border controls made it difficult. Five EU Member States (Belgium, France, Germany, Luxembourg and the Netherlands) entered the Schengen Agreement in 1985 to create an area within which border formalities would be removed, followed in 1990 by the Schengen Convention implementing the Agreement (CISA). Gradually the area was extended to include all Member States except the UK, Ireland, Bulgaria, Croatia, Romania and Cyprus, which have remained outside due to concern about terrorism, drug trafficking and illegal immigration – although Bulgaria and Romania were due to join in 2014. Some non-EU states also belong to the Schengen Area (Iceland, Liechtenstein, Norway and Switzerland). Controls on the EU's external borders have been strengthened under a common set of rules.

Anyone, regardless of nationality, may cross internal borders within the Schengen Area without showing their passport or ID card. National police may carry out limited checks at borders, for example where a suspected criminal is crossing a border, and spot-checks to establish identity. Under the Schengen Information System (SIS) an information network was established at border posts, police stations and consular agents to enable Member States to access information about individuals, vehicles or objects.

The UK has participated since 1999 in some aspects of the Schengen Agreement (police and judicial cooperation in criminal matters, the fight against drugs and the SIS), with Ireland following in 2000. Case C-503/03 *Commission* v. *Spain* illustrates the relationship between CISA and EU law. The proceedings arose from refusal of the Spanish authorities to allow two TCNs (Algerians) married to Spanish nationals to enter the country because their names were included on the SIS list of persons excluded under an alert (notice warning other Member States). The Court made it clear that the Schengen *acquis* (i.e. body of law on the Schengen Agreement) must comply with Community law, including Directive 64/221 (then in force). It held that a country participating in the Schengen arrangements may issue an alert only after establishing that the individual represents a genuine and sufficiently serious threat to one of the fundamental rights of society. If that country consults the SIS, it must be able to prove that the individual's presence poses such a threat. The Court found against Spain as it had failed to verify that the individuals posed a threat before refusing entry.

Area of freedom, security and justice

The Area of freedom, security and justice originated in cooperation between Member States over terrorism, drug trafficking and immigration which became a formal area for cooperation in the third pillar under the Maastricht Treaty. The Amsterdam Treaty added a title headed 'Visas, asylum, immigration and other policies', moving it to the first pillar for regulation by law. The Lisbon Treaty introduced new Title V (ex Title IV) covering the Area of freedom, security and justice. Article 67(1) TFEU (ex 61 TEC and 29 TEU) provides, 'The Union shall constitute an area of freedom, security and justice with respect for fundamental rights and the different legal systems and traditions of the Member States.' Article 67(2) requires the Union to remove internal border controls and frame a common policy on asylum, immigration and external border control. Article 72 TFEU (ex 64(1) TEC and 33 TEU) provides that Title V does not affect the duty of Member States to maintain law and order and safeguard national security. The European Arrest Warrant (EAW) illustrates action taken under the Area of freedom, security and justice. It was created under a framework decision in 2002 and introduced in January 2004. EAWs have been used extensively as they enable a suspect to be surrendered and extradited from another Member State.

The attack on the Twin Towers in New York ('9/11') in September 2001 prompted an international drive against terrorism. Part of the EU response was to introduce the EAW, replacing separate extradition arrangements between Member States.

Poland has been particularly active in issuing EAWs and has been criticised for over-use in non-serious crimes. We consider two cases involving EAWs by Poland in relation to supremacy of EU law over national law (see Chapter 6).

CONCLUSION

The introduction of Union citizenship under the Treaty of Maastricht has been one of the most significant developments in providing individual rights in EU law. The Court of Justice has produced bold judgments clarifying those rights, even before adoption of Directive 2004/38. While Union citizens and their family members now benefit from extensive rights, TCNs enjoy only limited rights of residence and movement. The Area of freedom, security and justice offers scope for common policies including asylum and the status of refugees.

KEY POINTS

- An individual is a Union citizen if he or she holds the nationality of a Member State.
- The Court of Justice has played a central role in developing Union citizenship, by applying the principle of non-discrimination to rights under EU law.
- Directive 2004/38 provides for the rights of Union citizens and their family members, including entry and residence throughout the EU.
- Member States may restrict free movement rights on grounds of public policy, public security or public health.
- TCNs may acquire limited rights of entry and residence in the EU.
- The Schengen Agreement has removed the need for border controls between the participating states (not including the UK and Ireland).
- The Area of freedom, security and justice provides for removal of internal border controls, with common policies on asylum, immigration and external border controls.

CORE CASES AND STATUTES

Case	About	Importance
Case C-85/96 *Martinez Sala* v. *Freistaat Bayern*	Referral from claim for child-rearing allowance by Spanish woman living in Germany.	Where Union citizen is lawfully resident in another Member State, he or she is entitled equal treatment with nationals of host State in areas within EU law.
Case C-184/99 *Grzelczyk* v. *Centre public d'aide Sociale d'Ottignies-Louvain-la-Neuve*	Referral from claim for financial relief by French national studying in Belgium.	Member State may withdraw residence permit where student claims social assistance, subject to principle of proportionality. Demonstrates move from economic to political definition of status as Union citizenship is 'fundamental status' of nationals of Member States.
Case C-413/99 *Baumbast and R* v. *Secretary of State for the Home Department*	Referral following UK refusal to renew residence permit of German national, his wife (TCN) and their children after applicant's business failed.	Article 20(1) TFEU (then 18(1) TEC) held to be directly effective, entitling Union citizen to residence rights even where he has lost status as migrant worker.
Case C-209/03 *Dany Bidar*	Referral after UK refusal of student loan to French national studying at UK university after living and attending school there for three years.	Lawfully resident EU students are covered by principle of non-discrimination and may claim financial assistance if sufficiently integrated into society of host State.
Case C-456/02 *Trojani* v. *CPAS*	Destitute French national given accommodation in salvation army hostel in Brussels where he undertook tasks in return for keep and pocket money.	Where Union citizen is lawfully resident but not economically active in another Member State, he may rely on principle of non-discrimination to claim social assistance. While claim may infringe right of residence, any decision to expel is subject to proportionality.
Case C-200/02 *Zhu and Chen*	Mrs Chen came to UK from China to avoid its one-child policy. She moved to Ireland and gave birth to daughter who acquired Irish nationality. Both moved back to UK where mother was refused residence permit.	Parents may derive residence rights through their minor children. Mrs Chen derived right to reside in UK though baby daughter who needed to be cared for by her.
Case C-127/08 *Metock and others* v. *Minister of Justice, Equality and Law Reform*	Metock and others moved to Ireland where they claimed asylum, later marrying Union (non-Irish) citizens. As Irish law required them first to have lived in another Member State, they were refused residence rights.	TCNs married to non-national Union citizens may rely on Article 3(1) of directive to join or accompany Union citizen wherever marriage took place. Requirement for prior residence in another Member State infringed directive.

Case	About	Importance
Case 30/77 *R* v. *Bouchereau*	UK government sought to expel French national convicted of drugs offences while in UK.	Restrictions may only be imposed on an individual posing genuine and sufficiently serious threat to one of fundamental interests of society. Past conviction is only relevant where it represents present threat (i.e. likely to recur).
Case 41/74 *Van Duyn* v. *Home Office*	Dutch woman prevented from entering UK to work for Church of Scientology, organisation of which UK government disapproved but not illegal.	Only present (not past) association may be considered as personal conduct. CJEU ruled that Member State may apply stricter standard to nationals from other Member States than to own nationals in some circumstances.
Cases 115 & 116/81 *Adoui and Cornuaille*	Belgium refused residence permits to two nationals from other Member States working as prostitutes in Belgium where prostitution was not illegal.	CJEU did not overrule *Van Duyn*, but applied stricter standard, holding that Member States cannot refuse residence to nationals from other Member States on account of conduct not illegal in own nationals.

Statute	About	Importance
Article 18 TFEU (ex 12 TEC)	Prohibits discrimination on grounds of nationality within scope of Treaties.	May be relied on by Union citizen lawfully resident in another Member State for rights under EU law.
Article 20(1) TFEU (ex 17(1) TEC)	Establishes Union citizenship.	Anyone with nationality of Member States also holds Union citizenship.
Article 20(2) TFEU (ex 17(2) TEC)	Union citizens enjoy rights and are subject to duties under Treaties.	Exercise of rights and duties is subject to conditions under Treaties and secondary legislation (mainly Directive 2004/38).
Article 21(1) TFEU (ex 18 TEC)	Union citizens can move and reside freely within territory of Member States.	The most important right of Union citizens. Detailed provision is made in Directive 2004/38.
Article 2(2) Directive 2004/38	Defines 'family member' for purpose of residence rights.	Definition includes registered partners under Article 2(2)(b), provided partnerships are treated as equivalent to marriage in host State under that state's laws.
Article 6(1) of Directive	Provides residence right up to three months for Union citizens in other Member States.	No formalities other than production of valid passport or ID card. Extends to TCN family members with passport or ID under Article 6(2).

→

Statute	About	Importance
Article 7(1) of Directive	Provides residence rights beyond three months for Union citizens if they are workers, have sufficient resources not to be burden on state and sickness insurance, or are enrolled in accredited course of study.	Economic categories of residence rights, extended to family members under Article 7(2).
Article 16(1) of Directive	Provides for permanent residence right for Union citizens with five years' continuous residence in host State.	Not subject to administrative formalities in Chapter III. Also covers family members with five years' continuous residence with Union citizen (Art.16(2)).
Article 24(1) of Directive	Union citizens and family members enjoy equal treatment with nationals of host State within scope of Treaties.	Incorporates CJEU case law on equal treatment with no entitlement to financial assistance during first three months (Article 24(2)).
Article 27(1) of Directive	Enables Member States to restrict freedom of movement on grounds of public policy, public security and public health.	The only grounds for restriction of movement. Cannot be invoked for economic ends.
Article 27(2) of Directive	Measures under Article 27(1) must be proportionate and based exclusively on personal conduct of individual concerned. Previous criminal convictions do not in themselves constitute grounds. Personal conduct must represent genuine, present and sufficiently serious threat to one of fundamental interests of society.	Consolidates CJEU case law including *Bouchereau*. Past association is not enough unless it shows present threat (*Van Duyn*). Individuals cannot be restricted to deter others (*Bonsignore*). Conviction must be assessed in order to determine nature of threat.
Article 28(1) of Directive	Protection against expulsion.	Host State must take into account factors including length of residence, family and economic considerations, social and cultural integration into host State and links with country of origin.
Article 29(1) of Directive	Diseases justifying measures restricting free movement	Only covers diseases with epidemic potential defined by WHO and other infectious/contagious diseases controlled in host State nationals.

FURTHER READING

Costello, C. '*Metock*: Free movement and "normal family life" in the Union' (2009) 46 *Common Market Law Review* 587
Critically analyses *Metock*, including relationship to family reunification, position of TCNs and extent to which EU law requires a cross-border element.

Currie, S. 'Accelerated justice or a step too far? Residence rights of non-EU family members and the court's ruling in *Metock*' (2009) 34 *European Law Review* 310
Criticises *Metock*, particularly the Court's reasoning on protection of family life.

Dougan, M. (2006) 'The constitutional dimension to the case law on Union citizenship' (2006) 31 *European Law Review* 613
Examines the constitutional implications of *Baumbast*, especially the requirement for proportionality when applying restrictions.

Habermas, J. 'Citizenship and national identity: some reflections on the future of Europe' (1992) 12(1) *Praxis International* 1
Influential study of EU citizenship by renowned political theorist.

O'Leary, S. 'Equal treatment and EU citizens: A new chapter on cross-border educational mobility and access to student financial assistance' (2009) 34 *European Law Review* 612
Commentary on *Förster* providing insight into post-*Bidar* case law.

Weiler, J. *The Constitution of Europe* (Cambridge University Press: Cambridge 1999)
Examines constitutional nature of EU after Maastricht.

Wiesbrock, A. 'Free movement of third country nationals in the European Union: the illusion of inclusion' (2010) 35 *European Law Review* 455
Critically examines mobility rights of TCNs in the EU.

CHAPTER 14
The free movement of workers

BLUEPRINT

The free movement of workers

LEGISLATION

- Article 45(1) and (2) TFEU
- Article 45(4) TFEU
- Article 7(1) Regulation 492/2011

CONTEXT

- Collapse of communism and accession of new Member States, subject to transitional restrictions.

CONCEPTS

- 'Workers'
- Accession States

- Should workers and their families from new Member States be given immediate access to the EU labour market?
- Is the EU approach to 'social advantage' too restrictive?

- How to remove barriers to the free movement of worker?

CASES

- *Lawrie-Blum*

SPECIAL CHARACTERISTICS

- Particularly important to this topic area, may include rules, tests, principles, defences, institutions, processes, other.

REFORM

- Modernisation of rules governing social security systems in Member States in regulation 883/2004 (in force 2010)

CRITICAL ISSUES

Setting the scene

Imagine that three EU nationals wish to work in the UK. Carlos, a Spanish national, arrived in London two months ago on holiday hoping to get a job. He is staying in a hostel rent free in return for unpaid two hours' washing-up a day. Agneza, a Croatian national, has just arrived and would like to work as a waitress. Liisa, a Finnish national and qualified teacher, has been told that jobs in state schools are reserved for UK nationals. The right to work anywhere in the EU lies at the heart of the single market, but the position of these three individuals differs.

It is important to establish exactly who is a worker, as the self-employed and individuals who are not working are covered by different Treaty provisions. The Court of Justice has ruled that there has to be an economic element to be considered a worker. If the washing-up undertaken by Carlos has an economic value he should be able to stay in the UK as a worker. Agneza's situation is different as Croatia joined the EU in July 2013. Transitional restrictions may be applied until 2020, enabling Member States to limit access of Croatian nationals to the labour market. Liisa has a right to work across the EU. Any attempt by the UK to restrict access to employment in schools is invalid under EU law.

OVERVIEW

The free movement of workers is an important element of the single market, enabling Union citizens to move from a Member State where work is scarce to another where there may be a labour shortage. While this freedom was originally seen as an economic right, enabling the worker to live and work throughout the EU on the same terms as host State workers, the social importance of the worker has been increasingly recognised, particularly by the Court. As Advocate-General Trabucchi stated, 'The migrant worker is not to be viewed as a mere source of labour, but as a human being' (Case 7/75 *Mr and Mrs F.* v. *Belgian State*, on right to social assistance of an Italian worker living in Belgium with his wife and disabled son). Articles 45–48 TFEU (ex 39–42 TEC) provide for free movement of workers, complemented by the right of establishment in Articles 49–56 TFEU (ex 43–55 TEC) and **freedom to provide services** in Articles 56–62 (ex 49–55 TEC) (considered in Chapter 15). The free movement rights are underpinned by the principle of non-discrimination on grounds of nationality in Article 18 TFEU (ex 12 TEC).

> **Take note**
>
> The Treaty provisions on free movement of workers have been renumbered twice, under the Treaties of Amsterdam and Lisbon. As the changes were minor, the current numbering under the Treaty of Lisbon is used throughout the chapter.

Market and non-market actors

It is important to appreciate that workers, like the self-employed, are *market actors* with rights under the Treaties relating to their economic status. These rights have been recognised since the creation of the European Community and have been subject to secondary legislation and interpretation by the Court of Justice. The EU increasingly also recognises the rights of *non-market actors*; that is, individuals who are economically inactive. The Maastricht Treaty acknowledged the significance of this move by introducing Union citizenship, a category determined by nationality rather than economic status. In Case C-184/99 *Grzelczyk* the Court declared that citizenship is destined to be 'the fundamental status of nationals of the Member States'.

INTERSECTION

Chapter 13 examines the development of Union citizenship including the introduction of Directive 2004/38 consolidating secondary legislation and decisions of the Court of Justice.

Workers are subject to derogations (exceptions) to free movement rights under Article 45(3) TFEU and, as Union citizens, under Article 27 of Directive 2004/38 on grounds of public policy, public security and public health. Workers and their families also benefit from rights under Directive 2004/38, including permanent residence after five years of residence under Article 16 and entitlement to a state pension after three years of lawful residence under Article 17(1)(a). Article 45(4) TFEU (ex 39(4)) provides for a further exception for employment in the public service.

Although Union citizenship rights are intended to provide a 'safety net', they have been criticised as inferior to workers' rights. O'Brien (2009) argues there should be greater alignment between the two concepts. She claims that the discrepancy in protection is particularly apparent when workers lose their status, for example by becoming temporary carers, which may lead to unequal treatment under national law. In her view this difference in treatment is symptomatic of failure to integrate social objectives (occupational mobility) with EU law (equal treatment) and that a more liberal definition of 'worker' is needed. Tryfonidou (2009) claims that the Court of Justice has developed an approach to workers by extending the scope of market freedoms to cover all economically active citizens even if their activity is within the home State provided there is some cross-border element. She too recognises that those outside the scope of market freedoms depend on citizenship rights under a less favourable regime.

REFLECTION

Social security and social assistance rights of workers are covered by Regulations 883/2004 and 987/2009 (considered later in the chapter).

CORNERSTONE

Article 45 TFEU

Article 45(1) TFEU provides that freedom of movement of workers shall be secured within the Union. This freedom under Article 45(2) requires the abolition of discrimination based on nationality between workers of the Member States in relation to employment, remuneration and other conditions of work and employment.

Under Article 45(3) freedom of movement entails the right, subject to limitations justified on grounds of public policy, public health or public security to:

- accept offers of employment actually made;
- move freely within the territory of Member States for this purpose;
- stay in a Member State for the purpose of employment under the same provisions governing employment of nationals of that State;
- remain in the territory of a Member State after employment, subject to conditions in secondary legislation.

Scope of Article 45

'Workers'

The Treaties do not define the term 'worker'. The Court has interpreted the term liberally, holding that the concept of 'worker' is a Community (Union) one, which may not be determined by the laws of Member States (Case 53/81 *Levin* v. *Staatssecretaris van Justitie*, a referral following denial of a residence permit to a UK national working part-time as a waitress).

CORNERSTONE

Case 66/85 *Lawrie-Blum* v. *Land Baden-Württemberg*

A worker is someone who performs services for and under the direction of another in return for remuneration during a certain period of time.

Deborah Lawrie-Blum, a UK national, was training to be a teacher in Germany. She passed the first exam but was not allowed to undertake probationary service required for the second exam as she was not a German national. The Court found that a trainee teacher giving lessons in return for remuneration under a period of supervised probationary service was a worker under Article 45(1).

The term 'worker' has been interpreted by the Court as including:

(a) A worker who had lost his job but was capable of finding another (Case 75/63 *Hoekstra* v. *BBDA*, arising from a claim for social assistance by a Dutch worker who fell ill and lost her job while visiting her parents in Germany).

(b) A part-time worker, provided the work was 'real' work of an economic nature and not nominal or minimal (Case 53/81 *Levin*).

(c) A part-time music teacher (from Germany) receiving supplementary benefit (in the Netherlands) to bring his income up to subsistence level (Case 139/85 *Kempf* v. *Staatssecretaris van Justitie*).

(d) A member of a religious community paid 'keep' and pocket-money but not formal wages where commercial activity was a genuine and inherent part of membership (Case 196/87 *Steymann* v. *Staatssecretaris van Justitie*).

(e) An EU national employed by an international organisation in another Member State, even if the rules of entry and residence are governed by an international agreement between the organisation and the host State (Cases 389 & 390/87 *GBC Echternach and A. Moritz*).

(f) A PhD student on a grant if undertaking paid work for a certain period of time under the direction of the supervising body (Case C-94/07 *Raccanelli* v. *Max-Planck-Gesellschaft zur Föffderung der Wissenschaften eV*, involving an Italian student working for a German research institute.)

To qualify as a 'worker', the activities performed must serve an economic purpose. In Case 344/87 *Bettray* v. *Staatssecretaris van Justitie* the Court held that paid activities within a drug rehabilitation scheme in Belgium were not, unlike *Steymann*, real and genuine economic activity. In Case C-456/02 *Trojani* a destitute individual performed tasks in return for keep in a hostel run by the Salvation Army to promote his reintegration into the community. The Court left the national court to determine whether he was in fact a worker. It followed a similar approach in Cases C-22 & 23/08 *Vatsouras and Koupatantze*, holding that professional activity for a short time may give an individual the status of 'worker' in principle, but it was for the national court to determine whether the work was real and genuine, giving rise to rights under Article 45.

A self-employed person who was previously a worker in another Member State, is not a 'worker' under Article 45, but is covered by Articles 49–56 (Case C-15/90 *Middleburgh* v. *Chief Adjudication Officer*, involving a British national who worked in Ireland where he entered into a relationship from which a child was born. The applicant later returned to the UK where he had periods of employment, unemployment and self-employment, but was refused unemployment benefit.) The Court held that a person working only in a self-employed capacity before being unemployed is not a worker.

A 'migrant worker' was defined in Case C-212/05 *Hartmann* as including a national of a Member State who worked in one Member State but lived in another and then worked as a frontier worker. In this case a German national resident in Austria had been refused child-rearing allowance because he did not live in Germany. The denial of the allowance infringed Article 7(2) of Regulation 1612/68 providing for workers in another Member State to enjoy the same tax advantages as national workers.

....**APPLICATION**

Imagine that three individuals want to find work in various EU Member States but are unsure of their rights. Paul, a French national, may work anywhere in the EU as a worker under Article 45 TFEU provided the work is paid. Helen, a UK national and a student, wants to work as a volunteer for a children's charity in Italy for two months over the summer. She would not be classed as a worker under Article 45 if unpaid, but could reside in Italy for up to three months as a Union citizen under Article 6 of Directive 2004/38. Martine, a Belgian national, has been working in Spain as a part-time waitress, supplementing her income with social assistance. She would be considered a worker under Article 45.

Jobseekers and the unemployed

Union citizens who were workers before losing their job are protected by Article 7(3) of Directive 2004/38. Under this Article, Union nationals who are unemployed due to illness or accident retain the status of workers, as do those who become involuntarily unemployed after being employed for more than one year and who have registered as jobseekers. Citizens employed for less than a year must register as jobseekers, retaining the status of worker for six months unless they embark on vocational training related to the previous employment. In Case C-413/01 *Ninni-Orasche* the Court held that a Union citizen whose fixed-term contract ended would not be regarded as voluntarily unemployed.

The Directive does not provide for rights in the event of voluntary unemployment, but jobseekers benefit from the ruling in Case C-292/89 *R* v. *Immigration Appeal Tribunal, ex p. Antonissen* (involving a Belgian national convicted of drugs offences whom the UK tried to deport after six months) that they are entitled to reside in the host State for a reasonable period of time to look for work. Six months was considered reasonable in this case, but the period of time will vary, depending on the circumstances. In Case C-138/02 *Collins* v. *Secretary of State for Work and Pensions* the Court held that jobseekers are also entitled to benefits intended to facilitate access to the labour market, but ruled that the status of worker is not indefinite. Collins, a dual Irish/US national looking for a job in the UK after working outside the EU, could not rely on having been a worker seventeen years earlier.

Workers from the accession states

Unlike previous enlargements, workers from most states joining the EU in 2004, 2007 and 2013 were subjected to transitional arrangements limiting access to the EU labour market.

The changed approach was largely due to the greater adaptation needed for states joining the EU in the twenty-first century after the collapse of Communism compared with previous enlargements such as Austria, Sweden and Finland in 1994 where there was no transitional period as adaptation to EU law took place before membership.

CONTEXT

The transitional period for workers from the 2004 accession states (including Poland and the Czech Republic) ended in April 2011 when the EU labour market opened up fully to their nationals. Romania and Bulgaria joined the EU in 2007. Workers from these countries were subjected to more restrictive transitional arrangements than in 2004, reflecting concern over the impact of the 2007 enlargement on the labour market. The transitional arrangements for Romania and Bulgaria ended on 31 December 2013.

Croatia is the newest Member State, having joined on 1 July 2013. The pattern for the seven-year transitional period under the Accession Agreement is similar to the 2007 accession. For the first two years Member States may apply restrictions to Croatian workers without reference to EU law (e.g. by requiring a work permit), before the arrangements are reviewed. For the next three years the Commission will be involved in deciding whether restrictions may be maintained where Member States claim there are serious disturbances to the labour market, with closer scrutiny in the final two years before restrictions are removed in 2020. Information on the current position may be found on the 'Europa' website.

The UK and the recent accession states

The UK did not impose restrictions on nationals from states joining the EU in 2004. However, numbers entering the UK to look for work were greater than anticipated, leading the UK to impose restrictions on nationals from Bulgaria and Romania, joining in 2007. These restrictions expired on 31 December 2013. Croatian nationals wanting to work in the UK are subject to similar transitional restrictions under the Accession of Croatia (Immigration and Workers Authorisation) Regulations 2013, and must obtain a worker authorisation document. Those qualifying for authorisation are mostly skilled workers such as plumbers satisfying the criteria under the UK's 'points-based' system by filling a gap in the work-force that cannot be filled by a settled worker. Highly skilled workers such as engineers may not require authorisation if they meet the UK's requirement for 'exceptional talent' with endorsement from a designated professional body, but still need to register. Self-employed Croatian nationals are not subject to restrictions in the UK if they can prove that they are genuinely self-employed. Croatian students may work twenty hours a week while studying and full-time in the vacations but require a registration certificate.

Employment in the public service

⊕ CORNERSTONE

Article 45(4) TFEU

Article 45(4) permits Member States to deny or restrict access to workers employed in the public service on the basis of nationality.

Some Member States tried unsuccessfully to rely on Article 45(4) to preserve jobs for their own nationals. Attempts to exclude public service jobs have usually been rejected as the Court has interpreted the exception narrowly. Case 152/73 *Sotgiu* v. *Deutsche Bundespost* concerned a claim for an allowance for post office workers living apart from their families in Germany. The Court accepted that the unavailability of the allowance discriminated against non-national workers resident abroad at the time of recruitment unless it was objectively justified. It held that Article 45(4) does not apply to *all* employment in the public service, only to certain activities connected with the exercise of official authority, and that it covers access to employment but not conditions of employment.

In Case C-473/93 *Commission* v. *Luxembourg* restrictions on jobs including teaching, health, telecommunications and electricity regardless of level of responsibility were found to be in breach of Article 45(4). A similar Belgian law reserving public service positions for its own nationals, including posts as nurses, plumbers and architects employed in central and local governmental so contravened Article 45. The Court held that the exception was intended to cover only the exercise of public authority to *safeguard the general interests of the state*, not at junior level (Case 149/79 *Commission* v. *Belgium (Re Public Employees)*).

While there is no secondary legislation on the exception, the Commission issued a Notice in 1988 announcing that certain sectors were only rarely to be regarded as covered. The list is indicative and unenforceable. It includes:

(a) public health services;

(b) teaching in state educational establishments;

(c) research for non-military purposes in public establishments;

(d) public bodies responsible for administering commercial services.

The Court found the following to be outside the exception:

(a) nurses in public hospitals (Case 307/84 *Commission* v. *France (Re French Nurses)*);

(b) teacher training scheme within the civil service (Case 66/85 *Lawrie-Blum*);

(c) lecturers at state universities (in Italy), as they do not exercise powers conferred by public law and are not responsible for safeguarding the interests of the state (Case 33/88 *Allué & Coonan* v. *Università degli studi di Venezia*);

(d) secondary school teachers (Case C-4/91 *Bleis* v. *Ministère de l'Education*).

The implication is that the exception only covers high-level posts in which the post-holder owes a particular allegiance to the state such as the armed forces, police, judiciary and high-ranking civil servants.

APPLICATION

Assume that Spain has advertised posts in three areas, all reserved for Spanish nationals. The first is a senior post in the Intelligence Service, the second for junior clerks in the police and the third for senior administrators in a large hospital. The Intelligence Service post clearly relates to the exercise of public authority to safeguard the interests of the state and would be within the exception. The post of junior clerk in the police would not be covered, as the Court in *Commission* v. *Belgium* held that exercising authority at junior level is outside the exception. A more senior police post might be included, depending on level of responsibility. The Commission's 1988 Guidance confirmed that posts in the health service are outside the exception. Thus a hospital administrator post would not be covered.

RIGHTS OF WORKERS AND THEIR FAMILIES

Regulation 492/2011 and Directive 2004/38

The rights of workers and their families are mainly set out in Regulation 492/2011 covering residence and Directive 2004/38 covering equality of treatment. These measures consolidated previous law, particularly Regulation 1612/68 on which most early decisions of the Court were based.

The rights of family members

The members of a worker's family, as defined by Article 2(2) of Directive 2004/38, are entitled under Article 7(1) of the directive to reside in another Member State for more than three months.

INTERSECTION

There is more extensive coverage of the residence rights of Union citizens and their families under Directive 2004/38 in Chapter 13.

As the rights of family members are 'parasitic' (i.e. dependent) on those of the worker, family members will benefit in the same way as the worker if he or she gains permanent residence rights under Article 16 through lawful residence for five or more years. Family members dependent on the Union citizen but outside the definition in Article 2(2) benefit from the host State's obligation to 'facilitate entry and residence' in Article 3(2). Similar considerations apply to individuals where there are serious health grounds requiring the personal care of the Union citizen.

Internal situations

There must be a cross-border element to rely on free movement and non-discrimination rights under Articles 45 and 18 TFEU. In Cases 35 & 36/82 *Morson* v. *the Netherlands* Surinamese parents were not permitted to join their son, a Dutch national living and working in the Netherlands who had not left the country. In Case C-370/90 *Surinder Singh* the Court held that Article 10(1) of Regulation 1612/68 (now Article 10 of Directive 2004/38) on residence rights of the spouse of an EU national covered family members where a worker who had worked outside his home State returned to establish a business there. Mr Singh, an Indian national who married a British national, after which the couple worked in Germany, returned to the UK to set up a business. The marriage failed and the couple got divorced. The UK sought to deport Mr Singh between the decrees nisi and absolute. Even though the marriage failed when there was no movement from one State to another, the situation was *not* regarded as purely internal.

A Union citizen who had never exercised free movement rights but remained in her home State cannot rely on Article 21 TFEU or Article 3(1) of Directive 2004/38 (Case C-434/09 *Macarthy* v. *Secretary of State for the Home Department*). In this case a dual Irish/UK national married to a Jamaican national had never worked or left the UK where she had been born. (Decisions on 'internal' situations are considered in more detail in Chapter 13.)

Regulation 492/2011

Article 45(2) of the Treaty provides for abolition of discrimination based on nationality between workers of Member States in employment, remuneration and other conditions of work and employment. Regulation 492/2011 implements Articles 45(2) (abolition of discrimination based on nationality as regards employment, etc.) and 3(a) and (b) (freedom to accept offers of employment and to move freely). The regulation requires equality of treatment in all matters relating to pursuit of activities of employed persons and elimination of obstacles to mobility, particularly the right to be joined by family members and integration of the family into the host country (Preamble, Sixth Recital).

> ## Take note
>
> Regulation 492/2011 has retained the same numbering as Regulation 1612/68 which it replaced, with the exception of Article 10, which was previously Article 12 of Regulation 1612/68.

Eligibility for employment (Articles 1–6)

Under Regulation 492/2011 EU nationals are guaranteed the right to take up and pursue employment in another Member State under the same conditions as nationals of that State (Article 1). Member States are prohibited from discriminating, overtly or covertly, against non-nationals by limiting applications and offers of employment under Article 3(1)(a), although they may impose on non-nationals conditions relating to linguistic knowledge required by the nature of the post. In Case 379/87 *Groener* v. *Minister for Education* the Irish government required teachers in vocational schools to be proficient in the Irish language. The Court held such a requirement permissible under Article 3(1) of Regulation 1612/68 in view of national policy to promote the Irish language.

Prescribing special recruitment procedures, limiting advertising or otherwise hindering recruitment of non-nationals is prohibited (Article 3(2)), as is restricting the number or percentage of foreign nationals employed in a particular activity (Article 4). In Case 167/73 *Commission* v. *France (Re French Merchant Seamen)* a ratio of three French to one non-French crew in the Code du Travail Maritime 1926 was held by the Court to contravene Article 4 of Regulation 1612/68 even though the French government had given oral instructions not to apply the ratio. Non-nationals must be offered the same assistance as nationals to seek employment (Article 5). Engagement or recruitment of non-nationals must not depend on discriminatory medical, vocational or other recruitment criteria (Article 6(1)). Vocational tests when expressly requested on making a job offer to a non-national are permitted (Article 6(2)).

Employment and equality of treatment (Articles 7–9)

CORNERSTONE

Conditions of employment

Article 7(1) of Regulation 492/2011 provides that a worker who is an EU national may not, in another Member State, be treated differently from national workers on account of nationality in relation to conditions of employment and work, particularly remuneration, dismissal and reinstatement or re-employment on becoming unemployed.

Examples of discriminatory treatment which is illegal under Article 7(1) includes:

(a) Legislation recognising national service in the home State but not in another Member State to calculate seniority (Case 15/69 *Ugliola*).

(b) A decision to increase separation allowances only for persons living away from home within the home State (Case 152/73 *Sotgiu* v. *Deutsche Bundespost*).

Entitlement to social and tax advantages

Under Article 7(2) non-national EU workers are entitled to 'the same social and tax advantages as national workers', a right interpreted liberally by the Court.

In Case 32/75 *Fiorini* v. *SNCF* a non-working Italian widow in France claimed the fare reduction card issued to parents of large families after her husband died in an industrial accident. The Court held that Article 7(2) covers all social and tax advantages, whether or not deriving from contracts of employment. Since the family had the right to remain in France, they were entitled to equal 'social advantage' under Article 7(2).

Fiorini was followed in Case 207/78 *Even*, where the Court held that Article 7(2) applies to any benefit whether or not linked to a contract of employment, payable by virtue of an individual's status as a worker or by virtue of residence on national territory. The ruling has been applied in later cases, with the following held to be a 'social advantage':

1. An old-age benefit for those not entitled to a pension under the national social security system (Case 157/84 *Frascogna*, an Italian widow living in France with her son).

2. A guaranteed minimum income for old persons, paid to an Italian widow living with her retired son in Belgium (Case 261/83 *Castelli* v. *ONPTS*).

3. A scholarship to study abroad under a reciprocal scheme (Case 235/87 *Matteucci* v. *Communauté Française de Belgique*, an Italian national resident in Belgium denied access to a scholarship to improve singing for teaching purposes).

Case C-386/02 *Baldinger* arose from the Austrian authorities' refusal to pay an allowance to an Austrian national who had served in the German Armed Forces during the Second World War and been a prisoner of war in the USSR. The Court found that an allowance paid to former prisoners of war who were Member State nationals was outside Article 7(2) as its purpose was to compensate nationals for hardships endured during the Second World War, not individuals such as workers.

Some cases under Article 7 have concerned financial assistance for higher education. In Case 197/86 *Brown* the applicant had a place at Cambridge to study engineering and in Case 39/86 *Lair*, languages at the University of Hanover. Brown, a dual UK/French national, sought a maintenance grant (then available from the UK government), having worked for a UK engineering company for eight months. Lair sought a similar grant from the German government after working for five years there with periods of involuntary unemployment. The Court held that, while neither course was vocational training, a grant for university education was a social advantage. The word 'worker' must have a Community (Union) meaning. Brown was a worker, but had acquired that status due to his university place. A migrant worker like Lair was entitled to equal treatment if involuntarily unemployed and legitimately resident. A worker who gave up a job to pursue further training in the host State was only eligible for a grant where there was a link between the work and the subject studied (Cases 197/86 *Brown* and 39/86 *Lair*).

INTERSECTION

Brown and *Lair* should be read subject to later developments as they preceded Union citizenship under Directive 2004/38 (considered in Chapter 13). While the directive does not provide for access to maintenance grants, *Bidar* supports the right of students who are Union citizens to claim financial support in another Member State where a sufficient degree of integration can be established.

Rights relative to sport and other activities

Professional and semi-professional sporting activities are regulated by EU Law where they constitute economic activity. Case 13/76 *Dona* v. *Mantero* arose from a dispute between two Italian nationals over costs associated with advertising for new players outside Italy. The Court found that excluding EU nationals from professional or semi-professional football matches on *economic grounds* (i.e. in relation to a contract of employment) infringed the Treaties, although exclusion on *non-economic grounds* such as injury or poor performance would not contravene Article 45.

The position of professional footballers was clarified in Case C-415/93 *Bosman* where the Court interpreted Article 45 and Article 4 of Regulation 1612/68 prohibiting quotas based on nationality in the context of football transfer rules.

Bosman, a Belgian national and professional footballer, wanted to move at the end of his contract from a Belgian to a French club, but was prevented from doing so by his club's refusal to accept a transfer fee, without which a move was impossible under UEFA rules including provision for nationality-based quotas. The Court held that such transfer rules infringed Article 45 and Article 4 of Regulation 1612/68 (Case C-415/93 *URBSFA* v. *Bosman*). The ruling opened up professional football and other sports, enabling players who were EU nationals to move freely between clubs across the EU. Restrictive national quotas were dropped and clubs such as Chelsea took on many players from other EU Member States. *Bosman* also recognised the right of 'free transfer', preventing clubs from requiring a transfer fee when EU players reached the end of their contract.

A further ruling on professional sport was made in Case C-176/96 *Lehtonen and ASBL Castors Canada Dry Namur-Braine* v. *ASBL Fédération Royale Belge des Sociétés de Basketball*. The referral arose from national rules prohibiting basketball clubs from fielding players from other Member States transferred after a certain date in national championships. The Court held that such a rule infringed Article 45 unless objectively justified.

In Case C-325/08 *Olympique Lyonnais SASP* v. *Bernard and Newcastle United Football Club* the Court held that a requirement for young footballers to pay damages if they signed to another club at the end of their training period infringed Article 45. Such a scheme was not necessary to achieve the objectives of the scheme and left trainee players liable for damages calculated without reference to training costs.

⋯⋯⋯⋯⋯⋯⋯⋯⋯⋯⋯⋯⋯⋯⋯⋯⋯ APPLICATION

Mario is a eighteen-year-old Italian professional footballer at a club in Belgium. He has just completed training and would like to move to a Spanish club, but has heard that they operate a quota system, requiring half the players to be Spanish nationals. He is also worried that the Italian club may require him to pay substantial damages if he moves, as they regard him as a potential 'star' player. Mario would benefit from *Bosman*, which made nationality-based quotas illegal. While the Italian club may recover some compensation for investment in his training, they are not entitled to damages out of proportion to actual loss (*Olympique Lyonnais*).

Migrant workers enjoy the same rights and benefits in *housing* including ownership as nationals of the host State (Article 9). Restrictions on the right to acquire land by non-nationals were held to be unlawful in Case 305/87 *Commission* v. *Greece*. Workers who are nationals of another Member State also are entitled to equal treatment in *trade union membership* (Article 8 of Regulation 492/2011).

Workers' families (Article 10)

Children's access to education and training

Article 10 of Regulation 492/2011 (previously Article 12 Regulation 1612/68) provides for children of migrant workers to be admitted to the host State's general educational, apprenticeship and vocational training courses under the same conditions as host nationals. In Case 76/72 *Michel S.* the mentally disabled son of an Italian employed in Belgium before his death was refused benefit from a fund set up to help people with employment prospects seriously affected by disability. The Court held that Article 12 entitled a child in such circumstances to benefit on the same basis as host State nationals.

In Case 9/74 *Casagrande* v. *Landeshauptstadt München*, where the son of a deceased Italian worker in Germany was refused an educational grant, Article 12 was held to entitle children of migrant workers to general measures of support (e.g. grants and loans). Such support included study abroad on the same basis as host State nationals in Case C-308/89 *Di Leo* v. *Land Berlin* where the daughter of an Italian migrant who had worked for twenty-five years in Germany was refused a grant by the German authorities to study medicine in Italy. The children of migrant workers including those who have retired or died in the State were entitled to equal treatment in access to vocational training in Case 42/87 *Commission* v. *Belgium*, where Belgium had denied access to finance for vocational training to applicants other than nationals of Luxembourg or Belgium.

In Cases 389 & 390/87 *GBC Echternach and A. Moritz* the child of a German migrant worker who had returned to Germany after working in the Netherlands sought an educational allowance from the Dutch authorities to study there when the German authorities refused to recognise his Dutch diploma. The Court held that a child did not cease to be a 'child of the family' under Regulation 1612/68 when his parent returned to the country of origin but was entitled to continue education in the host State if the educational systems were incompatible. In Case C-413/99 *Baumbast* the Court decided that Article 12 should not be interpreted so as to restrict entitlement of the children (here, of divorced parents, one of whom was an EU national) to complete their education in the host State to circumstances where they could not do so in their country of origin.

INTERSECTION

Article 12(3) of Directive 2004/38 embodies the right for children to stay on in the host State to complete their education if the parent who is the Union citizen leaves the host State or dies. It also protects the rights of parents with custody of their children, regardless of nationality, to stay on while the children are registered to study at an educational establishment. The *Baumbast* decision and rights under Article 12(3) are considered further in Chapter 13.

The Court of Justice made two further important rulings on rights under Article 12(3) in Case C-480/08 *Maria Texeira* v. *London Borough of Lambeth* and Case C-310/08 *London Borough of Harrow* v. *Ibrahim*. Both parents in *Texeira* were Portuguese nationals living in the UK where they worked and their daughter was born. They later separated but remained in the UK. Initially the daughter lived with her father, but later moved in with her mother while training in childcare. Ms Texeira was refused housing assistance. The Court held that Union citizens employed in another Member State where their child is in education may claim a residence right based solely on Article 12 as primary carers without satisfying the conditions in Directive 2004/38. It also ruled that the residence right in the host State of the primary carer does not depend on that parent having sufficient resources, nor on a parent having worked in the host State as a migrant worker. The parent's right ends when the child reaches majority unless he or she needs the parent to be present to follow or complete their education, for example, if the child were disabled.

The Court's ruling in *Ibrahim* was similar. The father, Yusuf, a Danish national married to a Somali, entered the UK in 2002, working for seven months before claiming incapacity benefit. His wife and their three children came to the UK in 2003 where she gave birth to a fourth child before the couple separated in 2004. The two oldest children attended schools in the UK. Yusuf left the UK after being declared fit for work in 2004, returning in 2006. His wife did not work and depended on social assistance. Her application for housing assistance was rejected as she was not considered to have residence rights. The Court held that the children of an EU national working in the host State and their parent and primary carer can claim a residence right in the host State solely on the basis of Article 12 without having sufficient resources or comprehensive sickness insurance.

SOCIAL SECURITY

It is important to appreciate that there is *no EU-wide system of social security*. The Council is required under Article 48 TFEU (ex 42 TEC) to adopt measures to ensure the implementation of two principles:

1. *aggregation*, to acquire and retain the right to benefit and calculate the amount, taking account of all periods of contribution under the laws of several Member States;
2. *payment of benefit to persons resident in the territories of Member States*.

The purpose of social security is to enable EU nationals to be treated equally when working in other Member States and retain their entitlements in the home State. These entitlements are governed by Regulation 1408/71 and Regulation 883/2004.

Regulation 883/2004

Regulation 883/2004 (adopted in 2004 but in force only from May 2010 under implementing Regulation 987/2009) repealed and replaced Regulation 1408/71 under which most case law of the Court of Justice was decided, while Regulation 987/2009 repealed and replaced Regulation 574/72. Regulation 883/2004 is intended to simplify, modernise and coordinate rules governing social security systems in accordance with the principles in Article 48 TFEU, making it easier for workers and their families to move around the EU without loss of entitlement. Healthcare benefits are aligned. Jobseekers can extend the period of looking for work from three to six months. The rights of the economically inactive are included and cooperation between Member States improved to make it easier for individuals to receive benefits.

Article 2(1) provides that the Regulation applies to nationals of a Member State, stateless persons and refugees residing in a Member State subject to its legislation, as well as their family members and survivors, whereas Regulation 1408/71 applied to the employed, the self-employed and their families, and was interpreted by the Court by reference to whether a person belonged to a national social security scheme for employed or self-employed persons in Case 75/63 *Hoekstra*. The Court held that national authorities could not impose stricter conditions for benefits in the case of temporary residence in another Member State.

Regulation 883/2004 embodies the five *general principles* of social security:

1. *equality of treatment* with the nationals of the host State (Article 4);
2. *payment regardless of residence* – the competent State provides benefits in relation to insured persons and family members resident in a State other than the competent State (Article 17) and to insured and family members staying temporarily in a State other than the competent State) (Article 18);
3. *no entitlement to double benefits* (Article 10);
4. *the single state principle* (Article 11) by which a worker is subject to the legislation of a single Member State only;
5. *aggregation* (Article 6) takes account of periods of contribution in all Member States where the worker has worked in order to determine eligibility to benefit.

Article 3(1) provides that the Regulation applies to legislation on sickness and maternity benefits, invalidity benefits, old-age benefits, survivors' benefits, benefits in relation to accidents at work and occupational diseases, death grants, unemployment benefits, pre-retirement benefits and family bene-fits. It covers all general and special social security schemes, both contributory and non-contributory (Article 3(2)(a)).

Social assistance

Article 3(5) provides that Regulation 883/2004 does *not* apply to social and medical assistance, benefit schemes for the victims of war or its consequences. The term 'social assistance' is not defined but has been narrowly interpreted by the Court. It tends to be based on need and is discretionary whereas social security benefits are available as of right. Some benefits have elements of both, in which case they have been treated by the Court as social security, applying a 'double function' test whereby a benefit is treated as both social assistance and social security, so it can be exported to another Member State as in Case 1/72 *Frilli* v. *Belgian State* (claim for old-age pension from an Italian living in Belgium involving a non-contributory minimum income based on need, but treated as social security and assimilated into the old-age pension).

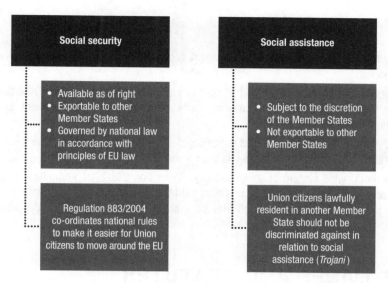

Figure 14.1 Social security and social assistance

Social advantages

During the 1980s the Court moved from finding most benefits to be social security under Regulation 1408/71 to regarding them as a 'social advantage' under Regulation 1612/68, the scope of 'social advantage' having been extended in cases such as Case 207/78 *Even* (French national living in Belgium claimed early pension under scheme to reward people who had fought for the country during the Second World War) and Case 65/81 *Reina* (interest free loan to German nationals as incentive to increase the population). Claims which might previously have failed as social security stood more chance of success as a social advantage.

Union citizenship and social advantages

The restrictive approach to social security and social advantage underlying the Regulations, particularly exclusion of social and medical assistance, seems out of step with the rights of Union citizens even though these rights are subject to 'limitations and conditions' under Article 21(1) TFEU. Member States remain preoccupied with preventing 'benefits tourism', i.e. discouraging individuals from taking up residence in their territory and claiming benefits. However, the position of the non-working Union citizen is increasingly acknowledged by the Court. In Case C-456/02 *Trojani* the Court found that the economically inactive may claim social assistance by applying the principle of non-discrimination provided they are lawfully resident.

KEY POINTS

- The free movement of workers is an important economic right, and an essential element of the single market.

- EU nationals who are workers have the right to work throughout the EU under Article 45 TFEU, although workers from recent accession states such as Croatia are subject to transitional restrictions.

- Workers and their families are entitled under Regulation 493/2011 equal treatment in employment, remuneration and other conditions of work, on a par with nationals of the host State.

- There is no EU-wide system of social security. Regulation 883/2004 embodies the principles of social security including equality of treatment with the nationals of the host State. Social security benefits are available as of right and may be exported to other Member States whereas social assistance (or social advantage) is discretionary and cannot be exported.

CORE CASES AND STATUTES

Case	About	Importance
Case 53/81 *Levin* v. *Staatssecretaris van Justitie*	UK national working part-time as waitress in Netherlands was denied residence permit.	Concept of 'worker' is based on EU not national law and includes part-time workers, provided work is 'real', not nominal or minimal.
Case 66/85 *Lawrie-Blum* v. *Land Baden-Württemberg*	Status of probationary teacher.	Defines essential characteristics of worker as performance of services for and under direction of another in return for remuneration during a certain period of time.
Case 196/87 *Steymann* v. *Staatssecretaris van Justitie*	Member of religious community performed services in return for keep and pocket money.	Individual could be worker where work had economic value and was part of ethos of community (unlike *Bettray* where work was undertaken for rehabilitation and did not have economic value).
Case C-456/02 *Trojani* v. *Centre public d'aide Sociale de Bruxelles*	Whether someone performing tasks in return for keep in hostel was a worker.	CJEU left national court to determine whether applicant was worker.
Case C-292/89R *R* v. *Immigration Appeal Tribunal ex p. Antonissen*	Jobseeker has reasonable period of time to look for work, before risking deportation.	Six months was considered to be reasonable in this case.

Case	About	Importance
Case 149/79 *Commission* v. *Belgium*	Belgium had reserved list of posts such as nurses and plumbers for Belgian nationals, relying on public service exception under Article 45(4) TFEU.	Only high-level posts where there is special allegiance to the state are covered.
Case C-415/93 *URBSFA* v. *Bosman*	Belgian professional footballer was refused permission to move to French club at end of contract without payment of transfer fee under UEAFA rules which also imposed national quotas.	Such restrictions on professional sportsmen infringed their rights as workers under Article 45 TFEU and Article 4 of Regulation 1612/68. Decision enabled professional sports players who are EU nationals to move without payment of transfer fee at end of contract period and outlawed national quotas.

Statute	About	Importance
Article 18 TFEU (ex 12 TEC)	Principle of non-discrimination on grounds of nationality.	Underlies free movement of persons.
Article 45(1) TFEU (ex 39 TEC)	Provides that freedom of movement for workers shall be secured within Union.	Central to single market as one of 'four freedoms'. It is directly effective.
Article 45(2) TFEU (ex 39(2) TEC)	Requires abolition of nationality-based discrimination between workers of Member States in relation to employment, remuneration and other conditions of employment.	Gives effect to principle of non-discrimination in employment.
Article 45(3) TFEU (ex 39(3) TEC)	Freedom of movement covers right to accept offers of employment, move freely, stay in another Member State on same terms as its own nationals and remain after work, subject to limitations on grounds of public policy, health and security.	Detailed provision is contained in Regulation 492/2011 (previously Regulation 1612/68) and Article 27 of Directive 2004/38 (limitation of freedom).

→

Statute	About	Importance
Article 45(4) TFEU (ex 39(4) TEC)	Permits Member States to restrict access to employment on basis of nationality.	Strictly interpreted by CJEU to cover only certain activities connected with exercise of state authority.
Article 7(3) Directive 2004/38	Union citizens who become unemployed due to illness or accident.	Such individuals retain status as workers, as do involuntarily unemployed, if employed for year or more and registered as jobseekers.
Article 1 Regulation 492/2011	Right of EU nationals to take up and pursue employment in another Member State on same terms as nationals of host State.	Regulation 492/2011 repealed and replaced Regulation 1612/68, retaining same numbering and basic provision for Articles 1–9.
Article 4 Regulation 492/2011	Prohibition on restricting number or percentage of foreign nationals employed in particular activity.	Quotas based on nationality found to be illegal in *Bosman* under Article 4, Regulation 1612/68.
Article 7(1) Regulation 492/2011	Requires workers from other Member States not to be treated differently from national workers on grounds of nationality in conditions of employment.	Has formed basis of case law (under Regulation 1612/68), particularly on remuneration.
Art. 7(2) Regulation 492/2011	Workers from other Member States are entitled to same social and tax advantages as national workers.	Case law of CJEU (under Regulation 1612/68) has provided for liberal interpretation of scope of 'social advantage'.
Article 10 Regulation 492/2011 (formerly Art. 12 Reg. 1612/68)	Children of migrant workers shall be admitted to host State's general educational, apprenticeship and vocational courses on same terms as nationals of host State.	Article 12, Regulation 1612/68 has given rise to extensive case law (e.g. *Baumbast*).

FURTHER READING

Carrera, S. (2005) 'What does free movement mean in theory and in practice in an enlarged EU?' (2005) 11 *European Law Journal* 699
Examines free movement rights, particularly in relation to the 2004 enlargement.

Kranz, A. 'The *Bosman* Case: The relationship between European law and the transfer system in European law' (1999) 5 *Cambridge Law Journal* 431
Analyses significance of *Bosman* for professional football.

O'Brien, C. 'Social blind spots and monocular policy making: the ECJ's migrant worker model' (2009) 46 *Common Market Law Review* 1107
Comprehensive comparison of workers' rights in EU law relative to Union citizens.

Tryfonidou, A. 'In search of the aim of the EC free movement of persons provisions: Has the Court of Justice missed the point?' (2009) 46 *Common Market Law Review* 1591
Examines development of case law on market access, particularly over differences in treatment of workers and Union citizens.

CHAPTER 15

The right of establishment and the freedom to provide services

BLUEPRINT

The right of establishment and the freedom to provide services

LEGISLATION

- Article 49 TFEU
- Article 56 TFEU
- Directive 2005/36

CONTEXT

- Completion of the single market
- Capital and payments

CONCEPTS

- Right of establishment,
- Provision and receipt of services
- Recognition of qualifications
- Regulated professions

- Will social concerns and protection of fundamental rights take on greater importance in relation to the provision and receipt of services?

- Should companies be free to locate in the Member State with the lowest regulation?
- How far should Member States be able to restrict the provision of services?

CASES

- *Luisi* and *Carbone*
- *Gebhard*
- *Carpenter*

SPECIAL CHARACTERISTICS

- Role of Court of Justice in developing law in absence of secondary legislation.
- Objective justification of restrictions.

REFORM

- Developments are likely to come through the Court of Justice rather than legislation

CRITICAL ISSUES

Setting the scene

The single market can only function effectively if businesses can operate across national borders within the EU. Imagine a builder based in Italy wants to work in France. If he moves there as an employee, he is covered by Articles 45–48 TFEU on workers. This is how most Union citizens exercise their economic rights within the single market. If he wants to set up another business in France by opening an office there, he is exercising the right of establishment under Articles 49–55 TFEU. The builder may decide to direct his workforce on a French building project from his base in Italy, in which case he is exercising the freedom to provide services under 56–62 TFEU.

THE RIGHT OF ESTABLISHMENT AND PROVISION OF SERVICES

This chapter covers the right of establishment (freedom to set up a business) in Articles 49–55 TFEU (ex 43–48 and 294 TEC) and provision of services in Articles 56–62 (ex 49–55 TEC), as well as the case law of the Court of Justice.

Definition of services

'Services' are defined in Article 57(1) TFEU as 'normally provided for remuneration, in so far as they are not governed by the provisions relating to the freedom of movement of goods, capital and persons'. They include commercial services and the activities of professionals (e.g. architects) and craftsmen (e.g. plasterers), but not areas separately covered in the Treaties (e.g. transport).

CORNERSTONE

Article 49(1) TFEU (ex 43(1) TEC) prohibits restrictions on freedom of establishment of nationals of a Member State in the territory of another Member State.

Article 49(2) TFEU entitles self-employed persons to pursue their activities and to set up and manage undertakings on the same conditions as nationals of the host State. The right of establishment benefits both companies and individuals as Article 54(1) provides for companies or firms based in the EU to be treated in the same way as natural persons (individuals). As different national requirements may obstruct the registration of companies from other Member States, the right of establishment has provided an important basis for harmonising company law.

Establishment or services?

The right of establishment is supplemented by the freedom to provide services. It is important to identify whether the provisions on establishment or services apply as the rights differ. While the right to establish a business is a *permanent* right, the provision of services is *temporary*, for the duration of the services. It may be a question of degree rather than principle which determines this question. In

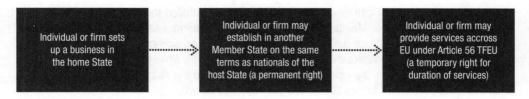

Figure 15.1 Establishment and services

Case 205/84 *Commission* v. *Germany* the Commission brought proceedings against Germany, Ireland, France and Denmark over national requirements for insurance undertakings to conduct their business through persons already established and authorised to practise there. The Court found such a requirement unjustified and held that an insurance undertaking *maintaining a permanent presence* in another Member State was covered by provisions on establishment rather than services, even where there was *no branch or agency but only an office* managed by the undertaking's own staff or authorised independent person.

In Case C-55/94 *Gebhard*, arising from disciplinary proceedings against a German lawyer for using the term 'avvocato' ('advocate') contrary to Italian law, the Court found the activities covered by the services provisions, holding that the *temporary* nature of services should be determined in view 'not only of the duration . . . of the services but also of its regularity, periodicity or continuity'. In Case C-215/01 *Bruno Schnitzler* the Court held that a business established in one Member State supplying similar services in another is not established in the host State where it lacks an infrastructure such as an office to pursue its activities on a stable and continuous basis.

Who benefits from establishment?

Self-employed persons such as advocates who are nationals of a Member State, as well as companies and other businesses established there, may rely on the right of establishment before the national courts following Case 2/74 *Reyners* v. *Belgian State*. A Dutch national born, educated and resident in Belgium with a doctorate in Belgian law was refused admission to the Belgian bar because he was not a Belgian national. The Court found that Article 49 was directly effective. While the exercise of state authority is excluded from the right of establishment under Article 51 TFEU (ex 45 TEC), the profession of advocate was not covered.

It is possible to exercise the right of establishment by relocating a business to another Member State or by retaining the main base in one State and setting up a branch or subsidiary in another. In Case 107/83 *Klopp* the Court considered establishment in relation to a prohibition of the Paris Bar on practising law without a main office in Paris which prevented registration of a German lawyer wishing to maintain his office in Germany. The Court held that establishment includes the right for members of the liberal professions to set up and maintain more than one place of business in the EU subject to observance of professional rules of conduct.

Can a company transfer its place of business to another Member State?

Case 81/87 *R* v. *HM Treasury, ex p. Daily Mail and General Trust plc* arose from UK rules requiring Treasury consent before a company could transfer its head office to another Member State. The Court held that although freedom of establishment is a fundamental right, it does *not* confer on a company incorporated in a Member State where its registered office is situated the right to transfer management and control to another Member State in the absence of harmonisation. However, a company registered in one Member State but operating entirely through an agency in another Member State could establish in the State where it operated (Case 79/85 *Segers*). While the Court developed a more liberal line of case law over the next twenty years, it confirmed the strict approach in *Daily Mail* in Case C-210/06 *Cartesio Oktató és Szolgáltató Bt* (discussed below).

While many businesses relocate or set up a branch or subsidiary in another Member State for commercial reasons, others do so to benefit from a more liberal regime, as Case C-212/97 *Centros Ltd* v. *Erhvervs- og Selskabsstyrelsen* illustrates. Centros was incorporated in the UK which did not require a minimum share capital. The company did not trade there but conducted its business in Denmark which operated stricter rules on company formation. Centros's application to establish a branch in Denmark was refused by the Danish Board of Trade which claimed that the company was trying to circumvent Danish rules. The Court nevertheless found that such a refusal infringed the right of establishment.

> *Centros* was a surprising decision. It meant that a company's choice to establish in a Member State with less demanding requirements than the State where services were provided was not an abuse but the exercise of a legitimate right in the absence of harmonisation. While the decision was welcomed by some (Cabral and Cunha, 2000), others were more critical. Deakin (1999) considered it a form of 'competitive federalism' undermining national diversity unless balanced by EU measures providing for a basic minimum protection of rights and supplemented by further Member State action.

REFLECTION

For many years the Court stayed firm to the *Centros* approach. In Case C-208/00 *Überseering* v. *NCC* it held that a company legitimately incorporated in one Member State moving its administration to another Member State could not be denied legal personality by the State to which it moves. It followed a similar line over Dutch legislation imposing minimum share capital and other requirements on a company registered in the UK which was held to be disproportionate and unnecessary in Case C-167/01 *Kamer van Koophandel en Fabrieken voor Amsterdam* v. *Inspire Art Ltd*.

Case C-196/04 *Cadbury Schweppes* concerned Schweppes's establishment of a subsidiary in Ireland where the tax regime was more favourable than the UK. The Court found that it was not an abuse to take advantage of such a regime by establishing a subsidiary in another Member State, although a restriction may be justified to prevent wholly artificial arrangements not reflecting economic reality to escape paying tax on profits. The Court employed similar reasoning in Case C-446/03 *Marks & Spencer* v. *Halsey*, finding that a Member State may treat non-resident companies differently from resident companies in direct taxation in appropriate circumstances (here, deduction of a subsidiary's losses in another Member State), subject to the principle of proportionality.

Although the Court has not overruled its post-*Centros* case law, the return to the strict *Daily Mail* approach in *Cartesio* makes it clear that Member States can decide on the basic requirements for incorporation in the absence of harmonisation although they must not impose unnecessary restrictions on setting up of branches or subsidiaries. *Cartesio* concerned a business seeking to transfer its seat of operations from Hungary to Italy while retaining its status as a company under Hungarian law by remaining on the commercial register, a request refused by the Hungarian authorities. The Court applied *Daily Mail*, finding that in the absence of harmonisation, the exercise of the right of establishment was determined by national law. It held that a prohibition on transferring a company's seat to another Member State from the State of incorporation did not infringe Article 49 or Article 54TFEU. The Member

State should define the 'connecting factor' governing incorporation to decide whether moving the seat to another Member State broke the connection.

Article 49 TFEU and collective action

The Court of Justice made two controversial rulings on collective action. In Case C-438/05 *International Transport Workers' Federation and Finnish Seamen's Union* v. *Viking Line ABP*, a company incorporated in Finland operated a ferry between Estonia and Finland under a collective agreement requiring the crew to be paid at the rate applied in Finland. The company could not compete with Estonian vessels paying lower wages and decided to 'reflag' the vessel under Estonian law but was prevented by the Finnish Seamen's Union and the International Transport Workers' Federation. The Court found that the unions' collective action restricted Viking's exercise of the right of establishment, but that the national court should decide whether it was necessary and proportionate to defend workers' rights.

Case C-341/05 *Laval* v. *Svenska Byggnadsarbetareförbundet* arose in relation to posted workers on building sites in Sweden employed by Laval, a company incorporated in Latvia on lower terms and conditions than Swedish workers under a collective agreement between Laval and the building workers' trades union. Industrial action in Sweden followed, including boycotts of supplies to try to make the company accept the terms of the collective agreement. This time the Court did not leave proportionality to the national court. It interpreted Directive 96/71 on posted workers, ruling that collective action was *unjustified* as Laval should not be forced to agree to terms.

> *Viking* and *Laval* demonstrate how far the Court has been drawn into identifying the boundaries of social and political rights on the provision of services in controversial areas such as the right to strike. This is not surprising, given the burgeoning EU social dimension, particularly in relation to Union citizens. Nevertheless, despite the Court's acknowledgement of the need to balance the free movement provisions with the objectives of social policy, both decisions favoured economic over social arguments. As Syrpis and Novitz (2008) observe, '[T]he choices which the Court has made in the *Viking* and *Laval* cases represent a tipping of the delicate balance between economic and social rights in favour of the former.' The Lisbon Treaty gave the Social Charter (recognising the right to strike) the same legal status as the Treaties. Although the Court acknowledged in *Viking* that the right to strike is a fundamental right, it also held it is for the national courts to determine whether strike action is a proportionate form of action in a particular dispute, leaving scope for uncertainty over the legality of strike action.

REFLECTION

Non-discrimination and the right of establishment

In the absence of secondary legislation comparable to Regulation 492/2011 (previously Regulation 1612/68), the principle of non-discrimination under Article 18 TFEU has been particularly important in the Court's case law. It has interpreted 'discrimination' liberally to cover taking up and pursuing a particular activity. The following cases provide examples of discriminatory practices:

(a) A restriction on renting premises to nationals of the host State preventing a German artist exhibiting his pictures (Case 197/84 *Steinhauser* v. *City of Biarritz*).

(b) A cheap mortgage facility available only to Italian nationals (Case 63/86 *Commission* v. *Italy (Re Housing Aid)*).

(c) A prohibition under Greek law against ownership of land by non-Greek nationals (Case 305/87 *Commission* v. *Greece*).

Objective justification

Discriminatory restrictions may be upheld but only where they are objectively justified. Several cases have arisen over healthcare provision where Member States have a particular duty to safeguard the public, such as Case C-169/07 *Hartlauer Handelsgesellschaft mbH* v. *Wiener Landesregierung* concerning an Austrian requirement for authorisation before independent outpatient clinics could set up in business. The legislation prevented Hartlauer, a company based in Germany, from establishing two private dental outpatient clinics in Austria where the authorities considered they were not needed. The Court held that a requirement for authorisation taking account of health needs was incompatible with the right of establishment as it applied to independent private dental clinics but not group practices and was not based on a condition which could reasonably limit national authorities' discretion.

The Court reached a different conclusion in Cases C-171 & 172/07 *Apothekerkammer des Saarlandes*, a referral from actions by the Saarland Pharmacists' Association in Germany against the Ministry of Justice over challenges to a national requirement permitting only qualified pharmacists to own and operate pharmacies. The proceedings were joined by DocMorris NV, a Netherlands company selling medicinal products by mail order which had been granted a licence to operate a pharmacy provided it recruited a qualified pharmacist to manage the pharmacy personally. The restriction on establishment was held to be proportionate and justified to protect public health and ensure that the public was provided with reliable, good quality medical products. Enforcement proceedings by the Commission from a similar prohibition in Italy were dismissed in Case C-531/06 *Commission* v. *Italy*.

APPLICATION

Imagine Spain adopts a law requiring all self-employed persons to pay their taxes in person on a specific day annually. The stated objective is to combat crime as the authorities wish to identify individuals face-to-face since businesses have been set up as 'shams' to launder money. Such a law would infringe the right of establishment as the requirement to be present on a particular day would be more difficult for nationals of other Member States to fulfil than for local Italian residents. However, it may be objectively justified if it is the most appropriate way to address the problem.

FREEDOM TO PROVIDE SERVICES

CORNERSTONE

Article 56 TFEU

Restrictions on freedom to provide services within the EU are prohibited in respect of nationals of Member States established in a Member State other than that of the person for whom the services are intended (Article 56 TFEU (ex 49TEC)).

Unlike the right of establishment which is a permanent right, the provision of services is *temporary* (Article 57(3) TFEU (ex 50(3) TEC)), enabling a service provider to pursue his activity in the State where the service is provided under the same conditions as the state's own nationals for the duration of the services. The right only applies to persons established in the EU. In Case C-452/04 *Fidium Finanz* the Court held that a company established outside the EU (here, Switzerland) was not entitled to provide services within it.

Restrictions on establishment and the provision of services

Articles 51 TFEU (ex 45 TEC) provides for the right of establishment to be subject to the exercise of state authority, while Article 52 TFEU (ex 46 TEC) covers the exceptions of public policy, security and health. Article 27 of Directive 2004/38 also applies to establishment and services.

INTERSECTION

Article 27 of Directive 2004/38 applies to *all* categories of Union citizen including the self-employed. Restrictions under the Article are considered in Chapter 13.

While both rights are subject to the same conditions as host State nationals, Article 49(2) TFEU covers establishment and Article 57(3) TFEU, services. The conditions laid down by law or by trade or professional bodies for education or training as well as rules of professional conduct may provide a barrier if they are harder for nationals of other states to satisfy than for home State nationals. The EU institutions have been trying to abolish restrictions on establishment and services since 1961 when the Council first adopted non-binding programmes. The Commission has also had responsibilities under Article 53 TFEU (ex 47 TEC) to draft directives harmonising professional qualifications.

Professional rules of conduct as a barrier to free movement

Professional rules of conduct may restrict the free movement of professionals, particularly where a residential qualification is required. The Court ruled in Case 33/74 *Van Binsbergen* that a residential qualification in a properly qualified person is not a legitimate condition of exercising a profession unless necessary to ensure observance of professional rules of conduct. It also held that the right to provide services under what is now Article 56 TFEU was directly effective. The case arose from proceedings in the Netherlands where the client was represented by a legal adviser who moved to Belgium. He was then told he could no longer represent his client as he was not resident in the Netherlands. The Court held that a residence requirement infringed the right of establishment unless objectively justified.

Later case law follows a similar approach. In Case 292/86 *Gulling* v. *Conseils des Ordres des Barreaux et de Savene* a registration requirement by the German Bar for barristers wishing to establish in Germany applying equally to host State nationals was held to be permissible. Case C-340/89 *Vlassopoulou* v. *Ministerium für Justiz* arose over German rules on qualification which excluded a Greek lawyer from practising. The Court held that the right of establishment in Article 43 TEC (now 49 TFEU) entitles national authorities to examine qualifications of non-nationals for equivalence.

CORNERSTONE

Restrictions

National measures restricting one of the fundamental freedoms under the Treaties infringe EU law unless they are non-discriminatory, justified, suitable and proportionate (Case C-55/94 *Gebhard* v. *Consiglio dell'Ordine Degli Avvocati Procuratori di Milano*).

The reference in *Gebhard* arose from disciplinary proceedings by the Milan Bar against a German member of the Stuttgart Bar for using the term 'avvocato' contrary to Italian law. The Court held that fundamental freedoms under the Treaties may only be upheld if applied in a non-discriminatory manner, justified by imperative requirements in the general interest, suitable to attain the objective, and proportionate.

APPLICATION

Imagine the UK adopts a law requiring coach drivers and tour party guides from other Member States to pass a diploma covering road safety (coach drivers) and knowledge of monuments, museums and art galleries (guides). The measure has been introduced after statistics showed that most coach accidents involved drivers from outside the UK. Such a law would clearly restrict the provision of services under Article 56 TFEU, but might be justifiable for coach drivers if it could be shown that this was the only way to reduce coach accidents. It would be unjustifiable for guides as it would be likely to have a disproportionate effect by reducing the number of available tourist guides, as the Court held in Case C-198/89 *Commission* v. *Greece*.

Eliminating barriers to the free movement of professionals: the early years

Before adoption of directives on recognition of qualifications there were two distinct approaches: sectoral harmonisation of professional qualifications under Article 53 TFEU and application of the principle of non-discrimination under Article 18 TFEU. The harmonisation directives adopted covered specific sectors or professions, particularly in areas such as health where skills were readily transferable, covering the qualifications of doctors, nurses, dentists, pharmacists and veterinary surgeons who were entitled to establish and practise throughout the EU.

Lawyers and the harmonisation of qualifications

It has been difficult to harmonise professional qualifications where training required detailed knowledge specific to Member States. Two directives on lawyers were adopted but with limited scope. Directive 77/249 enables lawyers to provide services but not to establish in other Member States. Directive 98/5 seeks to facilitate practising as a lawyer in a State other than the State which awarded the professional qualification. The Commission brought proceedings against Luxembourg under the directive over its requirement for lawyers to satisfy a proficiency test in the three national languages before being permitted to practise (Case C-193/05 *Commission* v. *Luxembourg*). The proceedings were heard in conjunction with a preliminary reference on the same point (Case C-506/04 *Graham Wilson* v. *Ordre des Avocats du barreau de Luxembourg*). The Court ruled that Luxembourg had infringed the Directive by making registration subject to a prior language test.

Professional qualifications and the Court of Justice

The Court has played an important role in developing the law on recognition, particularly in individual cases before harmonisation. Case 71/76 *Thieffry* v. *Conseil de l'Ordre des Avocats à la Cour de Paris*) a Belgian national with a Belgian law degree, challenged the decision of the French Bar Council denying him access to practical training for the French Bar. His law degree had been recognised by the University of Paris and he held a further certificate for practising as an 'avocat' in France. The Court held that when a national of one Member State wishes to practise a profession such as advocate in another, holding a qualification in his own country recognised as equivalent by the other Member State, it contravenes the right of establishment and freedom to provide services to demand the national diploma as well as the special qualifying examination. The Court made a similar ruling in Case 11/77 *Patrick* v. *Ministre des Affaires Culturelles*, where a UK-trained architect was prevented from practising in France although his qualifications had been recognised as equivalent under a French ministerial decree. The Court held that recognition enabled the individual to practise in that State.

Where a directive has been issued for a particular profession, it may no longer insist on compliance with its own requirements from persons qualified in another Member State, even where the individual in question is a national of the Member State where he seeks to practise (Case 246/80 *Broekmeulen*, concerning a Dutch national qualified as a doctor in Belgium but refused permission to practise as a GP in the Netherlands because he had not undertaken a further GP three-year training, not required under Directive 75/362 on the training of GPs).

A fresh initiative on qualifications

It became clear to the Commission that the sectoral approach to harmonisation was too slow. A new approach was needed.

To complete the single market programme and remove barriers to free movement by December 1992 the Commission applied the *Cassis de Dijon* principle under which goods made in one Member State must be recognised as fit for circulation throughout the internal market. Directive 89/48 was introduced to create a single system of mutual recognition of higher education qualifications, covering both workers and the self-employed.

Directive 89/48

The central element of Directive 89/48 (which did not apply to professions already harmonised such as doctors, nurses and pharmacists) was mutual recognition throughout the EU of higher education diplomas requiring professional education or training of three or more years' duration. 'Diplomas' were defined as qualifications awarded by a competent authority in a Member State establishing that the holder had successfully completed a post-secondary period of education and training of at least three years' duration at a university or higher education establishment and had the professional qualifications required to take up a regulated profession in that Member State. Directive 89/48 was followed by Directive 92/51 extending recognition to programmes under three years and Directive 99/42 replacing various sectoral directives in industrial and professional areas. As a result all post-secondary education and training was covered.

Directive 2005/36 on the recognition of professional qualifications

Directive 2005/36 consolidated the directives of 1989, 1992 and 1999 as well as twelve sectoral directives on health professionals but left untouched Directives 77/249 and 98/5 on lawyers' rights to practise. It distinguishes between the right of establishment and provision of services, depending on duration, frequency and regularity.

CORNERSTONE

Mutual recognition

The principle of mutual recognition applies to any EU nationals wishing to pursue a regulated profession in a self-employed or employed capacity, including those belonging to the liberal professions, in a Member State other than the State where they obtained their qualifications (Article 2 Directive 2005/36).

A 'regulated profession'

A 'regulated profession' is defined in Article 1(a) of Directive 2005/36 as covering any professional activity where possession of a diploma is required in the Member State, either directly or indirectly. The definition is a matter of EU not national law, as the Court ruled in Case C-285/01 *Burbaud*, holding that hospital public service requiring a diploma was a regulated profession. A lay health practitioner known as a '*heilpraktiker*', was not covered and so outside Directive 92/51, as the Court held in Case C-294/00 *Gräbner*, a decision arising from an Austrian prohibition on persons offering medical services unless they were qualified as doctors. The Court's decisions on the earlier directives remain relevant as Directive 2005/36 consolidated previous case law and directives.

Recognition of qualifications in another Member State cannot be used as a 'backdoor' route to circumvent home state requirements. In Case C-311/06 *Consiglio degli Ingegneri* v. *Ministero della Giustizia Cavallera* the Court held that approval by one Member State of a qualification awarded by another does not constitute a 'diploma' giving access to a regulated profession in the host State. The case arose over an Italian national who successfully applied in Spain for recognition of his qualification as a mechanical engineer after three years study at an Italian university. The applicant had enrolled on the register of the engineers in Spain, but had never worked outside Italy where a further examination (which he had not taken) was needed to enter the profession. Member States are entitled under the directive to fix the minimum level of qualification to guarantee quality of service. The Court held that it would contravene that right if access to a regulated profession resulted from recognition in another Member State without evidence of an additional qualification or professional experience.

Lawyers and legal academics

University law lecturers are not regarded as members of a regulated profession. In Case C-586/08 *Rubino* v. *Ministero dell'Università e della Ricerca* an Italian national qualified in Germany, enabling him to teach at a university there as a full professor. He applied unsuccessfully to have his qualifications recognised in Italy for entry on the register of holders of the National Academic Qualification, required for academic posts at Italian universities. The Court held that a requirement restricting access to university lecturing to those who were successful in a selection procedure did not mean that the profession was regulated under Directive 2005/36.

The legal profession, however, is regarded as regulated. Case C-345/08 *Krzysztof Peśla* v. *Justizministerium Mecklenburg-Vorpommern* arose due to the German authorities' refusal to recognise the academic legal qualifications of a Polish national denied access to a legal traineeship in Germany. The Court held that while Member States can lay down knowledge and qualifications required in the absence of harmonisation, they must assess equivalence in view of academic and professional experience as a whole and cannot be restricted to comparing intellectual level, time and effort.

Regulated profession where access requires specific qualifications (Article 13(1))	• Host state will allow access to and pursuit of profession on same terms as own national, subject to attestation of competence of formal qualifications • Host state may require aptitude test or period of adaptation where there are substantial differences in training
Activites requiring only general or commercial knowledge (Article 13(1))	• Host state will recognise previous pursuit of activity as sufficient proof of knowledge and aptitude • Applies to activities listed in Annex IV
Professionals covered by previous sectoral directives (Article 21)	• Applies to health professionals such as doctors, nurses, pharmacists and dentists, as well as architects • Covered by the principle of automatic recognition requiring Member States to recognise evidence of formal qualifications of reaching minimum standards

Figure 15.2 Recognition of qualifications under Directive 2005/36

Recognition of professional qualifications enables the beneficiary to practise his or her profession in another Member State on the same terms as the national of the host State under Article 4(1) of Directive 2005/36.

Routes to recognition under Directive 2005/36

There are three categories of persons with different routes to recognition:

1. persons covered by the general system for the recognition of qualifications
2. persons whose activities require only general or commercial knowledge
3. professionals covered by previous sectoral directives.

Persons covered by the general system for the recognition of qualifications

Under Article 13(1) of the directive, where access to a regulated profession requires specific qualifications, the host State will allow access to and pursuit of that profession on the same terms as its own nationals where the applicant has attestation of competence or evidence of formal qualifications. Access will also be granted to persons who have pursued the profession on a full-time basis for two of the previous ten years, with attestations of competence issued by the competent authority of a Member State. Member States may require applicants to take an aptitude test or complete an adaptation period of less than three years where:

(a) training is substantially different from the host State;

(b) the regulated profession in the host State comprises one or more regulated activities which do not exist in the corresponding home State;

(c) the difference consists of specific training required by the host State which is substantially unlike anything covered by the applicant's home State.

Under Article 14 the applicant may choose whether to take an aptitude test or undergo an adaptation period unless the activity requires a precise knowledge of national law, in which case the host State may choose.

Activities requiring only general or commercial knowledge

Under Article 16 the host State will recognise previous pursuit of the activity in another Member State as proof of knowledge and aptitude for activities requiring only general or commercial knowledge listed in Annex IV, such as electrical engineering. Articles 17 and 18 provide rules on how long the activity must have been pursued.

Professionals covered by previous sectoral directives

Under Article 21 of Directive 2005/36 professionals such as doctors, nurses, pharmacists, architects and dentists are covered by the principle of *automatic recognition* requiring Member States to recognise evidence of formal qualifications that the applicant has satisfied minimum training requirements.

Cases outside the legislation

Where qualifications are not covered by a specific directive and are outside Directive 2005/36 Member States may specify the knowledge and qualifications required, as in Case C-104/91 *Colegio Oficial de Agentes de la Propiedad Inmobiliara* v. *Aguirre*, where a UK national was prosecuted for practising as an estate agent in Spain without a Spanish qualification although he was a member of the Royal Institute of Chartered Surveyors in the UK. As the facts arose before implementation of Directive 89/48, Spain could specify its own qualifications.

APPLICATION

Imagine that three individuals, all self-employed Union citizens, seek advice on whether their qualifications will be recognised in other Member States:

1. Amélie, a French national, runs a business as a personal trainer from her home in France. She wants to offer her services in Belgium but has been told she can only do so if she undertakes a one-year diploma in fitness training. Amélie has no formal qualifications but has many years of experience as a personal trainer.

2. Ben is a GP with his own practice in London, having qualified as a doctor in the UK. He wants to move his practice to Italy but has been told that he must retrain.

3. Sally is a chartered accountant in the UK. She wants to know how far her qualification would be recognised in Spain where she would like to open an office.

Amélie's occupation as a personal trainer is not regulated, so it is outside the scope of Directive 2005/36. France may thus impose its requirement for a one-year diploma (*Colegio Oficial de Agentes*). Ben is covered by the specific provisions for doctors under Article 21 of the directive. Italy cannot impose a requirement to retrain but must recognise his UK qualification. Accountancy is a regulated profession. Sally's professional qualification is covered by a general system of recognition under the directive. As access to accountancy requires specific professional qualifications, Spain should grant her access on the same conditions as its own nationals under Article 13. An aptitude test or adaptation period may be required under Article 14 where the training Sally has received is substantially different from an accountant in Spain (which it would be). As a precise knowledge of Spanish law would be required, Spain may stipulate that Sally undertakes an aptitude test.

Human rights and the provision of services

CORNERSTONE

Carpenter

Any measure restricting freedom of movement under the Treaties, including Article 56 TFEU on the provision of services, must respect fundamental human rights (Case C-60/00 *Mary Carpenter* v. *Secretary of State for the Home Department*).

The Court of Justice adopted an innovative approach to services in *Carpenter*. Instead of viewing services as an essentially economic right, it read Article 49 TEC (now 56 TFEU) subject to Article 8 of the ECHR (respect for family life). The case arose in the context of a marriage between a third-country national and a UK national. Mrs Carpenter, a national of the Philippines, had entered the UK on a six-month visa. She stayed on after her visa expired without permission and married Mr Carpenter, a UK national, looking after the children from his first marriage. When the UK sought to deport her, she appealed to the Immigration Appeals Tribunal which referred to the Court. The services dimension derived from Mr Carpenter's business in the UK involving cross-border activity selling advertising space and providing publishing services to medical and scientific journals. He claimed that the business would be affected if his wife were deported to the Philippines as he would have to choose to accompany her there or remain in the UK, separating the family. The Court read the provisions of services as subject to Article 8 ECHR, holding that a decision to deport would infringe Article 8 and was therefore incompatible with Article 49.

INTERSECTION

While the Court's thinking on fundamental rights in *Carpenter* is novel in relation to services, this dimension has been very significant in its case law on citizenship (considered in Chapter 13). It is likely to become increasingly important as the Treaty of Lisbon gave the Charter of Fundamental Rights full legal status.

Justifications for restrictions on the provision of services

The Court has developed its case law on Article 52 TFEU, applied to services by Article 62 TFEU (ex 55 TEC), in relation to justifications for restricting services in the public interest on grounds of public policy, security or health. Directive 2004/38 makes detailed provision in Article 27 on these grounds for all categories of persons including service providers. Areas in which restrictions have been accepted by the Court include betting and gambling, illegal services associated with drugs, consumer protection and fundamental rights.

Betting and gambling

Most Member States are concerned about risks associated with betting and gambling, although the degree of regulation varies. Case C-275/92 *HM Customs and Excise* v. *Schindler* arose after agents in the Netherlands acting on behalf of administrators of the German state lottery wrote to individuals in the UK and Netherlands inviting them to buy tickets. The letters were seized by the UK Customs and Excise authorities for infringement of UK law on gambling and lotteries. The Court ruled that sending the letters amounted to providing a service under Article 49 TEC (now 56 TFEU). While the seizure restricted this right, it was justified by social policy concerns and fraud prevention. The Court adopted a similar approach in Case C-124/97 *Läärä* v. *Finland*, holding that the grant of exclusive rights to a single public body to operate slot machines was justified by public interest objectives, including control of gambling.

In Case C-42/07 *Liga Portuguesa de Futebol Profissional and Bwin International* v. *Department de Jogos da Santa Casa da Misericórdia de Lisboa* the Court found that a measure such as a law granting a non-profit-making body the exclusive right to regulate lotteries and other sporting bets via the internet restricted provision of services under Article 49 TEC. However, it was justified by overriding considerations relating to the public interest (combatting fraud and crime) in view of the special risks associated with betting and gambling on the internet. Since *Liga Portuguesa* the Court has consistently allowed Member States to restrict betting and gambling provided the action is proportionate and not discriminatory.

Illegal services

Throughout the EU, Member States impose prohibitions on drugs. Although the Netherlands retains a general prohibition on cannabis, its use is tolerated in licensed coffee shops. Case C-137/09 *Josemans* v. *Burgemeester van Maastricht* arose in relation to a restriction on access to coffee shops preventing non-residents from using them, imposed to reduce drug tourism and public nuisance. Josemans, the coffee shop owner, sought to rely on the principles of free movement and non-discrimination over the marketing of cannabis. The Court held that the owner could rely on the right to provide services under Article 56 TFEU over provision of food and non-alcoholic drinks as the rules indirectly discriminated against nationals from other Member States, but not in relation to the sale of cannabis, an illegal activity. Thus it found the restriction justifiable in view of the legitimate aim to combat drug tourism. It was also appropriate and proportionate, as other methods to combat drug tourism had failed and the restriction only applied to premises selling cannabis.

··· APPLICATION

Imagine the UK adopts the Control of Websites Act requiring yearly licensing of websites for internet dating as a link has been found between such websites and prostitution. Amour SA, a (fictitious) online dating company in France, objects to the licensing procedure claiming that the requirement makes it more difficult to offer its services in the UK. The directors say that the company merely provides introductions between its carefully screened adult customers, and that it has no links with prostitution. The Act restricts provision of services under Article 56 TFEU. However, the UK may argue that it is justified by an overriding consideration, to combat the nuisance of prostitution, provided the link between online dating agencies and prostitution can be established. Subject to that provision, the measure appears proportionate (see e.g. *Liga Portuguesa*) and appropriate, so should be seen as justifiable.

Consumer protection

In Case C-384/93 *Alpine Investments BV* v. *Minster van Financiën* a ban in the Netherlands on 'cold calling' in principle infringed Article 49 TEC (now 56 TFEU) by denying the applicant, a UK financial services company, access to the market in the Netherlands. While such a restriction operated against the internal market principles, the Court found it was necessary to protect consumers and the Dutch securities market and was not disproportionate.

Fundamental human rights

In Case C-36/02 *Omega* a company based in Germany operated a laser installation inspired by the film *Star Wars*, featuring laser targeting devices and tags fixed in the firing corridors or on jackets worn by players. The German authorities prohibited the company from operating on human targets, on the basis that entertainment games featuring simulated killings were contrary to human dignity and constituted a threat to public policy. The company argued that the ban infringed the freedom to provide services as the installation used equipment and technology supplied by a British company. The Court held that such a measure restricted the provision of services but was justified to protect fundamental rights provided the prohibition was necessary and proportionate.

DIRECTIVE 2006/123 – THE SERVICES DIRECTIVE

Directive 2006/123 on services in the internal market was adopted in 2007, coming into force in 2009 after prolonged negotiation and compromises. It aims to remove remaining barriers to establishing a business and providing services anywhere in the EU. Despite its short title the directive covers both establishment and services. Although intended to simplify the law, prolonged negotiations resulted in complexities.

Summary of the main provisions of Directive 2006/123

Article	Provision	Significance
1–3	Provides a series of exclusions.	Specifies important exceptions e.g social services and criminal law.
5–8	Simplifies procedure over creation of 'single point of contact' under Article 6 to facilitate access to service activities	This should make it easier for service providers to obtain all the information they need from one place.
9–15	Covers authorisation in relation to freedom of establishment, i.e.: • authorisation schemes • conditions for granting of authorisations • duration of procedures • requirements which are prohibited or must be evaluated • selection and authorisation procedures.	• Schemes must be proportionate and not discriminatory. • Service providers under Article 16(2)(a) can no longer be required to be established in the host State (previously unclear).
17–18	Provide complex derogations, including 'case-by-case' derogations under Article 18	Subject to requirements of non-discrimination, necessity and proportionality.
21	Covers rights of recipients of services such as assistance on service activities.	Particularly relevant to consumer protection.

Article	Provision	Significance
22–27	Provides for the quality of services, including information on providers and their services (Art. 22), professional liability insurance and guarantees (Art. 23), commercial communications (Art. 24), policy on quality of services (Art. 26) and settlement of disputes (Art. 27)	Case C-119/09 *Société fiduciaire nationale d'expertise comptable* v. *Ministre du Budget* clarifies obligation in Article 24 (see below).
28–36	Provides for administrative cooperation.	For example mutual assistance and alert mechanisms.

The only Court of Justice decision so far on the directive is Case C-119/09 *Société fiduciaire nationale d'expertise comptable* v. *Ministre du Budget* arising from a French prohibition on canvassing by a regulated profession (accountants). Such a prohibition was found to be incompatible with Article 24 of the directive requiring Member States to remove all total prohibitions on communications by regulated professions.

FREEDOM TO RECEIVE SERVICES

Articles 56 and 57 TFEU are worded in terms of the freedom to *provide* services, with no mention of receipt of services. However, the Court has extended the freedom to include the freedom to *receive* services.

CORNERSTONE

The freedom to receive services is the essential corollary to the freedom to provide services (Joined Cases 286/82 & 26/83 *Luisi and Carbone* v. *Ministero del Tesoro*).

Luisi and Carbone arose from criminal prosecutions for taking more money out of Italy for tourism and medical services than currency regulations permitted. (Before completion of the single market programme in 1992, free movement of capital was subject to exceptions enabling Member States to restrict capital movement as part of national economic policy.) The Court found that the money was not capital but payment for services, holding that freedom to provide services included the freedom to *receive* services, with no limit on how much money could be exported.

Non-discrimination and receipt of services

Tourists

The Court applied the principle of non-discrimination in Case 186/87 *Cowan* v. *French Treasury* over receipt of tourist services. Cowan had been attacked and robbed on the Paris Metro while on holiday. The French Criminal Injuries Compensation Board refused to pay compensation as French law only provided for compensation to French nationals. The Court held that the recipient of services was entitled to equal protection from, and compensation for, the risks of assault as a corollary of the right to receive services.

Medical treatment, the right to travel and the receipt of services

The right to travel to receive medical services

The right to life is protected under the Irish constitution, preventing women from obtaining an abortion there. Case C-159/90 *SPUC* v. *Grogan* arose from an action by a pro-life group against a student union in Ireland to stop it distributing information on abortion services in other Member States. The Court held that the case could not be treated as involving receipt of services as there was no economic activity. (The position of the Irish government on right to life was recognised in a protocol to the Maastricht Treaty.)

In the UK the Court of Appeal considered Article 43 TEC (now 49 TFEU) in *R* v. *Human Fertilisation and Embryology Authority, ex p. Diane Blood* in relation to receipt of services without referring to the Court of Justice. A British woman refused fertility treatment using her dead husband's sperm sought an order allowing her to travel to another EU State for treatment. The Court of Appeal granted the order on the basis that refusal would have been an unreasonable restriction on her right to travel to receive medical services.

Reimbursement for medical treatment

It was clear from *Luisi and Carbone* that the freedom to receive services covers private healthcare where there is an obvious economic element. Most cases have arisen in the context of national systems based on health insurance. The Court made several decisions on the scope for travel to another Member State for treatment and reimbursement of the cost. Case C-157/99 *Geraets-Smits* v. *Stichting Ziekenfonds VGZ; HTM Peerbooms* v. *Stichting CZ Groep Zorgverzekeringen* concerned two Dutch citizens treated in other Member States. In the Netherlands citizens could be treated abroad if treatment was approved in advance by a sickness insurance fund and seen as 'normal' and 'necessary'. Geraets-Smits had sought treatment in Germany for Parkinson's disease. Treatment in Austria was sought on behalf of Peerbooms after he fell into a coma. In both cases applications to the sickness fund were rejected as the applicants did not meet the criteria. The Court found that the requirement for prior authorisation did not breach EU law provided it was objectively justifiable and proportionate, holding that the criterion for treatment to be 'normal' should be interpreted with reference to international medical standards. The requirement for 'necessity' could be justified where authorisation would be refused only where the same or equally effective treatment could be obtained without undue delay from an establishment with which sickness fund has arrangements. In Case C-385/99 *Müller Fauré* the Court distinguished between hospital and non-hospital care, finding that requirements for prior authorisation did not infringe EU law if necessary and proportionate, whereas restrictions on non-hospital care could not be objectively justified. In Case C-368/98 *Vanbraekel and others* v. *Alliance Nationale des Mutualités Chrétiennes* the applicant sought reimbursement of expenses for an operation outside her home State. The Court held that reimbursement should be on no less favourable terms than in the home State.

Health services 'free at the point of delivery'

All services including public services such as state-funded healthcare services are covered by Articles 56–57 TFEU where they are 'provided for remuneration'. In Case C-372/04 *Watts* v. *Bedford*

Primary Health Care Trust the applicant had sought approval from her primary healthcare trust in the UK for hip replacement surgery abroad under an EU scheme. Under national rules authorisation could not be refused where treatment in the home State involved undue delay. The Health Care Trust rejected her application, stating that as treatment could be provided within the government's target period (the waiting list was a year), it did not involve 'undue delay'. In the meantime Mrs Watts's condition worsened and her waiting period was reduced to three months although refusal of authorisation was maintained. Having applied unsuccessfully for judicial review, she appealed to the Court of Appeal which referred to the Court of Justice. While the ruling was awaited she travelled to France where the operation was undertaken.

The Court held that Article 56 TFEU covers receipt of medical services in a hospital in a Member State other than the state of residence regardless as to type of national system, holding there was no need to determine whether hospital treatment in a national health service like the NHS was a service under Article 56 TFEU. *Watts* treats all services including public services as within Articles 56–57 TFEU provided they are paid services. State-funded healthcare services are thus included as 'provided for remuneration'. Union citizens consume services for which national healthcare providers may seek reimbursement from the citizen's home provided there is a cross-border element. However, it remains risky to seek treatment abroad without prior authorisation.

APPLICATION

Assume that Elsa, an Estonian national, has a rare heart problem which cannot be treated in Estonia. The health authority rejects her application for treatment in Italy which has pioneered a new operation for the condition as it considers the operation unnecessary and unproven. Elsa travels to Italy anyway and has the operation, but the Estonian authority refuses to refund the cost of treatment. Applying *Smits and Peerbooms*, a requirement for prior authorisation does not contravene EU law if exercised in accordance with proportionality. In the absence of treatment at home, the rejection of Elsa's application for treatment in Italy is disproportionate. The same is true of her request for reimbursement after having the operation without authorisation. She should be reimbursed on the same terms as if the operation had been done at home (*Vanbraekel*).

The case law of the Court was consolidated in Directive 2011/24 on patients' rights in cross-border healthcare.

Education and vocational training

Access to education and vocational training was considered in Case 293/83 *Gravier* v. *City of Liège*. Gravier, a French national, had been accepted on a course at the Liège Académie des Beaux-Arts in the art of the strip cartoon, but was required to pay the *minerval*, a special fee not payable by Belgian nationals. The Court held that 'vocational training' covered all forms of teaching leading to a particular profession, trade or employment or providing the necessary skills for such a profession, even if it involves an element of general education and that such training was covered by the principle of non-discrimination. The reasoning derived from an imaginative interpretation of Article 166 TFEU (ex 150 TEC) empowering the Council to lay down general principles implementing a common vocational training programme. The Court held that this general provision brought vocational training within the scope of EU law, making the training subject to the principle of non-discrimination. Article 166 was thus treated as directly effective.

Education and training after *Gravier*

The scope of 'vocational training' was clarified by further decisions of the Court. After *Gravier* a number of veterinary students claimed reimbursement of the *minerval*. In Case 24/86 *Blaizot* v. *University of Liège* the Court found that a university course such as veterinary medicine was 'vocational training' where it provided specific training in the form of knowledge necessary to practise a trade or profession. Union citizens thus have access to university courses on equivalent terms to host State nationals provided the courses are 'vocational'. Degree courses like medicine and veterinary studies with both an academic and vocational stage are considered as a single 'vocational' stage (*Gravier, Blaizot*).

In Case 263/86 *Belgian State* v. *Humbel* the Belgian authorities claimed payment of the *minerval* for a one-year vocational course in Belgium forming part of general secondary education for the son of a French national living in Luxembourg. The Court held that such a course is 'vocational' if it forms an integral part of an overall programme of education. In Case 42/87 *Commission* v. *Belgium* the Court held that the rules limiting access to higher education to two per cent of non-nationals contravened the principle of non-discrimination as far as they applied to vocational training.

INTERSECTION

The introduction of Union citizenship under the Maastricht Treaty has had a profound effect on the position of students undertaking degree courses outside their home State, particularly in relation to financial support. In Case C-209/03 *Bidar* the Court held that Union citizens studying in another Member State may be entitled to financial support if they are sufficiently integrated into the society of the host State (see Chapter 13).

KEY POINTS

- Article 49 TFEU prohibits restrictions on freedom of establishment of EU nationals in another Member State, entitling EU nationals to set up and manage businesses, pursuing their activities on the same terms as host State nationals.
- The Court of Justice has confirmed its strict approach in *Daily Mail* to the transfer of companies to other Member States.
- The principle of non-discrimination has been important in the Court's case law on establishment and services in the absence of secondary legislation.
- Restrictions on establishment infringe Article 49 TFEU unless objectively justified.
- Article 56 TFEU prohibits restrictions on providing services in another Member State where the individual is established.
- Establishment and services are subject to the exercise of state authority under Article 51 TFEU and restrictions on grounds of public policy, security and health and in the public interest.
- Directive 2005/36 provides for recognition of qualifications for persons pursuing a regulated profession.
- Directive 2006/123 seeks to remove remaining barriers to provision of services.
- The freedom to provide services covers receipt of services, including medical treatment, tourism and education.

CORE CASES AND STATUTES

Case	About	Importance
Case 2/74 *Reyners* v. *Belgian State*	Dutch national with doctorate in Belgian law refused admission to Belgian bar as not Belgian national.	Right of establishment is directly effective.
Cases 286/82 and 26/83 *Luisi and Carbone* v. *Ministero del Tesoro*	Luisi and Carbone were prosecuted for taking money out of Italy to pay for services in other Member States.	Money was held to be for payments, so outside exceptions to free movement on capital. Freedom to provide services includes freedom to receive services.
Case 293/83 *Gravier* v. *City of Liège*	French national was charged overseas students fee for degree studies in Belgium. CJEU found 'vocational training' was covered by Article 166 TFEU.	Students from one EU Member State undertaking degree courses in another must be charged at same rate as home students.
Case 81/87 *R* v. *HM Treasury ex p. Daily Mail and General Trust plc*	UK rules required Treasury consent for company to transfer head office to another Member State.	Right of establishment does not confer on company with registered office in one Member State the right to transfer management and control to another.
Case 186/87 *Cowan* v. *French Treasury*	Cowan was attacked and robbed on Paris Metro but denied compensation.	Person receiving services as tourist was entitled to compensation on same basis as host State national.
Case C-275/92 HM *Customs and Excise* v. *Schindler*	Administrators of state lottery in Germany wrote to individuals in UK and Netherlands inviting them to buy lottery tickets. Letters were seized by UK Customs and Excise for infringement of UK gambling and lotteries law.	Seizure was restriction of services, but justified by social policy considerations and fraud prevention.
Case C-219/97 *Centros Ltd*	Centros was incorporated in UK with no requirement for minimum share capital, but conducted business in Denmark where rules on company formation were stricter. Danish Board of Trade refused to allow Centros to establish branch or subsidiary to avoid restrictions.	Refusal to register was breach of right of establishment, enabling companies to choose to establish in Member State with less demanding requirements in absence of harmonisation.

Case	About	Importance
Case C-60/00 *Mary Carpenter* v. *Secretary of State for the Home Department*	Union citizen married TCN who had entered UK on six-month visa, then stayed on, and looked after his children. She resisted deportation on basis that husband's provision of services would be affected as he would have to stay in UK without her or accompany her to Philippines, separating family.	Right to provide services read as subject to Article 8 ECHR (right to family life).
Case C-36/02 *Omega Spielhallen*	German authorities banned German-based company with laser installation game from operating on human targets as contrary to human dignity and threat to public policy.	Measure restricted provision of services but was justified under Article 52 to protect fundamental rights provided it was necessary and proportionate.
Case C-372/04 *Watts* v. *Bedford Primary Health Care Trust*	UK national denied approval for hip replacement surgery in another Member State had operation in France and sought reimbursement from UK authorities which refused to pay.	Article 56 covers receipt of medical services in another Member State. There was no need to determine whether health service free at point of delivery is covered by Article 56. Such service is covered as receipt of services involves payment by state rather than EU citizen.
Case C-438/05 *International Transport Workers' Federation and Finnish Seamen's Union* v. *Viking Line*	Ferry operator based in Finland paid employees at Finnish rates under collective agreement. As it could not compete with Estonian operators paying less, company decided to 'reflag' vessel as Estonian, but was prevented by collective action.	Collective action restricted freedom of establishment but left national courts to determine whether it was necessary or proportionate to defend workers.
Case C-210/06 *Cartesio Oktato es Szolgato bt*	Company was prevented from keeping name on Commercial Register in Hungary when it sought to transfer seat of operations to Italy.	CJEU moved away from liberal approach of *Centros* back to strict approach in *Daily Mail*, holding that in absence of harmonisation Member State may determine whether company can exercise right of establishment.

Statute	About	Importance
Article 18 TFEU (ex 12 TEC)	Non-discrimination on grounds of nationality.	Important for services in the absence of secondary legislation.
Article 49(1) TFEU (ex 43 TEC)	Prohibits restrictions on establishment in another Member State.	Applies to individuals and to setting up agencies, branches or subsidiaries in another Member State.
Article 49(2) TFEU (ex 43(2) TEC)	Freedom of establishment includes right to take up and pursue activities as self-employed persons and set up and manage companies in another Member State.	Has provided basis for company law harmonisation.
Article 52 TFEU (ex 46 TEC)	Exception on grounds of public policy, health or security.	Also covers services (Art. 62 TFEU).
Article 54 TFEU (ex 48 TEC)	Companies and firms to be treated on par with nationals of host state.	Applies principle of non-discrimination.
Article 56 TFEU (ex 49 TEC)	Prohibits restrictions on services for nationals of Member States established in Member State other than where services are intended.	May be extended by EU to cover TCNs established in Union and providing services.
Article 62 TFEU (ex 55 TEC)	Arts. 51–54 TFEU apply to services as well as establishment.	Particularly important to Article 52, for measures based on public policy, security and health not otherwise covered for services.
Directive 2005/36	Art. 4(1) Recognition of qualifications of nationals of Member States pursuing regulated profession in another Member State.	Provides three routes to recognition: 1. persons covered by general system for recognition; 2. persons whose activities only require general/commercial knowledge; 3. professionals covered by previous sectoral directives.
Directive 2006/123	Aims to remove remaining restrictions on setting up business and providing services in EU.	Arguable whether directive achieves objectives due to complexity and compromise.

FURTHER READING

Cabral, P. and Cunha, P. ' "Presumed innocent": Companies and the exercise of the right of establishment under Community law' (2000) 25 *European Law Review* 157
A comment on *Centros*.

Deakin, S. 'Two types of regulatory competition: competitive federalism versus reflexive harmonisation, a law and economics perspective on *Centros*' (1999) 2 *Cambridge Yearbook of European Legal Studies* 231
Explores need for balance in relation to 'competitive federalism' (by which companies establish in the least demanding regime) after *Centros* by ensuring that EU provides minimum level of rights supported by institutions at local and national level to meet social needs.

Hatzopoulos, V. and Do, T. 'The case law of the ECJ concerning the Free Provision of Services 2000–2005' (2006) 43 *Common Market Law Review* 923
Analysis of important period in case law on services.

Roth, W-H. 'From *Centros* to *Überseering*: free movement of companies, private international law and Community law' (2003) 52 *International and Comparative Law Quarterly* 126
Frequently cited analysis of *Centros* and related case law.

Spaventa, E. 'From *Gebhard* to *Carpenter*: towards (non)-economic European constitution' (2004) 41 *Common Market Law Review* 743
Examines the social dimension in services.

Syrpis, P. and Novitz, T. 'Economic and social rights in conflict: political and judicial approaches to their reconciliation' (2008) 33 *Common Market Law Review* 411
Analyses how the Court determined the right to strike in *Viking* and *Laval*.

Van Nuffel, P. (2005) 'Patients' free movement rights and cross-border access to healthcare' (2005) 12 *Maastricht Journal* 253
Analyses case law on cross-border healthcare.

Glossary

Accession The act of a new Member State joining the EU.

Acte clair Where the meaning is clear, national courts need not refer a question for interpretation to Court of Justice (CJEU) under Article 267 TFEU.

Acte éclairé When CJEU has already pronounced on a materially identical point, there is no need to refer under Article 267 TFEU.

Acts of the EU institutions Acts adopted under Article 288(1) TFEU to exercise the Union's competences, i.e. regulations, directives and decisions.

Advocate-General Official of CJEU making non-binding submissions to assist the Court in reaching its judgment.

Approximation (or harmonisation) Process of adopting common standards through directives.

Area of freedom, security and justice (AFSJ) Requires EU to remove border controls between Member States and frame common policy on asylum, immigration and external border controls under Articles 67–89 TFEU.

Acquis Body of EU law and rules.

Association Agreement Agreement between EU and non-Member State, e.g. for preferential trading terms.

Cassis de Dijon principle Principle of mutual recognition by which goods lawfully produced and marketed in one Member State may be marketed in another without need to satisfy further requirements. Underpinned the single market programme in 1992. The CJEU in *Cassis* also recognised certain mandatory requirements enabling some national restrictions to be imposed where necessary (i.e. proportionate).

Charge having equivalent effect (CEE) Pecuniary charge imposed on domestic or foreign goods crossing a frontier and which is not a customs duty in the strict sense. CEEs are prohibited under Article 30 TFEU.

Charter of Fundamental Rights Annexed to Treaty of Nice as Declaration but given same legal value as Treaties by Treaty of Lisbon, so it can be invoked before national courts.

Comitology Process of delegation of legislative powers to committees, reformed by Treaty of Lisbon which introduced new legislative categories (legislative and non-legislative acts, delegated and implementing acts).

Committee of Permanent Representatives (COREPER) Examines and sifts Commission proposals before final decision is made by Council.

Committee of the Regions (CoR) Advisory committee providing opinion in matters of local or regional interest within the EU.

Common market Area in which goods, persons, services and capital circulate freely.

Competence Capacity to act. EU can only act where Treaties confer capacity (principle of 'conferral') to attain objectives of the Treaties under Article 5(2) TEU. May be 'exclusive' (conferred on EU alone – only EU may act) or 'concurrent' (shared with Member States – both EU and Member States may act).

Conciliation Committee Committee of Council and European Parliament whose function is to reach agreement on legislation under ordinary legislative procedure.

Constitutional Treaty (CT) Adopted under the Convention process to cover areas requiring further action after Treaty of Nice. Signed in 2004 but not fully ratified.

Copenhagen criteria Criteria for EU membership agreed at 1993 Copenhagen summit:

- stable institutions which guarantee democracy, rule of law, human rights, etc.
- a functioning market economy
- ability to take on obligations of membership, including EU *acquis*.

Customs duty Charge payable when goods cross a border, prohibited between Member States by Article 30 TFEU.

Customs union Area in which goods circulate freely with no tariffs (customs duties) on crossing border within the union, and a common external tariff on goods entering from outside the union.

Decision Act of Council or Commission binding those to whom it is addressed (Article 288(4) TFEU).

Delegated acts Acts of general application, amending or supplementing a legislative act.

Democratic deficit Lack of democracy in EU decision-making, as European Parliament (the only directly elected EU institution) can only adopt legislation jointly with unelected Council.

Derogation Exception. NB Meaning differs from general UK usage.

Direct action Proceedings beginning in CJEU or General Court (e.g. annulment under Article 263), unlike preliminary references under Article 267 which begin in national courts.

Direct applicability EU law taking effect in national law without the need for further action.

Direct effect EU law creating rights and duties which may be enforced before national courts. Treaty provisions may be horizontally effective against individuals, whereas directives are only vertically effective against the State or a public body.

Directive EU act binding Member States to which it is addressed as to result to be achieved but leaving national authorities 'choice of form and method' (Article 288(3) TFEU).

Economic and Social Committee (ESC) Provides non-binding advice to EU institutions on impact of proposals where it is consulted.

Economic and monetary union (EMU) Introduced the euro as a single currency under control of European Central Bank for participating states under Treaty of Maastricht in 1999.

Equality (or non-discrimination) General principle requiring persons in similar situations to be treated in the same way unless different treatment is objectively justified.

European Arrest Warrant (EAW) Enables Member State to pursue suspect who has left the country and moved into another Member State. Surrender under EAW replaced extradition as mechanism to retrieve suspects.

European Central Bank (ECB) Central bank responsible for monetary policy for states participating in EMU, based in Frankfurt.

European Community (EC) The first pillar under Maastricht Treaty, subsumed into EU under Treaty of Lisbon in 2009. The EC was previously known as the European Economic Community (EEC).

European Convention on Human Rights and Fundamental Freedoms (ECHR) ECHR, opened for signature 1950, in effect from 1953. International treaty setting minimum standards to protect individual human rights, e.g. right to liberty (Article 5), procedural fairness (Article 6) and freedom of expression (Article 10).

European Court of Human Rights (ECtHR) Hears cases under ECHR in Strasbourg. Should not be confused with Court of Justice (CJEU) in Luxembourg.

Enlargement The process by which EU grows to take in more Member States.

Europe Agreements Agreements between EU and former Communist states providing for structured relationship with EU prior to accession.

European Council Heads of state or government and President of Commission, meeting at least twice a year to provide EU with strategic direction.

European Union (EU) Created by Maastricht Treaty as overarching body made up of three pillars subsumed into one (the EU) under Treaty of Lisbon.

Federalism Relationship between states where each has conceded some independence to share in decision-making in defined areas.

Framework decision Adopted to harmonise law under third pillar before Treaty of Lisbon.

Free trade area Tariff barriers, e.g. customs duties are removed on goods between Member States but with no common external tariff.

Freedom to provide services Right under Articles 56–62 TFEU to provide services in Member States other than the one in which Union national is established.

General principles Identified in Article 6(3) TEU as:

- the Charter of Fundamental Rights
- fundamental rights under the ECHR and resulting from constitutional traditions common to Member States, constituting general principles of EU law (e.g. proportionality, equality, legal certainty).

Implementing act Give effect to a legislative act without amending or supplementing it.

Intergovernmental conference (IGC) Discussion between Member States preceding Treaty reform.

Internal market Area without internal frontiers in which free movement of goods, persons, services and capital is ensured under the Treaties (Article 26 TFEU).

Kompetenz-Kompetenz Capability of body to determine extent of its own powers (according to German Constitutional Court).

Legal certainty Principle subdivided into:

- non-retroactivity: EU legislation is presumed not to be retroactive in absence of clear evidence to the contrary;
- legitimate expectations: EU legislation should not infringe what is within reasonable contemplation of a prudent person acting within the course of business.

Legislative act Legal act 'adopted by legislative procedure', i.e. under ordinary procedure (Article 289(1) TFEU) or a special procedure (Article 289(4) TFEU).

Measure having equivalent effect (MEQR) 'All trading rules enacted by Member States . . . capable of hindering directly or indirectly, actually or potentially, intra-Community trade' (*Dassonville*), prohibited under Article 34 (imports) and 35 (exports). May be distinctly applicable (targeting imports, only justifiable under Article 36 TFEU) or indistinctly applicable (applying to both imports and domestic goods, justifiable under *Cassis*).

Ombudsman Receives complaints about maladministration but with no powers of enforcement.

Opinion Form of non-binding 'soft law' under Article 288(5) TFEU.

Ordinary legislative procedure Introduced as co-decision procedure under Treaty of Maastricht and renamed by Treaty of Lisbon. Provides for European Parliament and Council to adopt laws jointly under Article 289 TFEU.

Passerelle (or 'ratchet') clauses Areas requiring unanimous vote which may be moved to QMV by unanimous vote of the European Council with consent of Parliament but without formal amendment of the Treaties. European Union Act (EUA) 2011 provides for increased control by UK parliament.

Political union (EPU) Commitment to cooperate to achieve closer integration introduced under the Maastricht Treaty.

Preliminary reference procedure Enables national court to ask CJEU to clarify meaning of EU law or rule on validity of secondary legislation under Article 267 TFEU, providing uniform interpretation of EU law throughout EU.

Primacy of Union law Declaration annexed to the Treaties provides for Treaties and secondary legislation to have primacy (supremacy) over law of Member States under conditions laid down by CJEU.

Product requirement Specific national requirement in relation to product. Invalid unless covered by mandatory requirement under *Cassis de Dijon*.

Proportionality EU action should not exceed what is necessary to achieve objective in question (Article 5(4) TEU).

Public body (or emanation of the state) A body responsible for providing a public service under state control, with special powers exceeding those normally applicable in relations between individuals (Case C-188/89 *Foster* v. *British Gas*).

Purposive interpretation Interpretation of legislation in accordance with the purpose and context in which it was adopted.

Qualified majority voting (QMV) System of weighted voting in the Council.

Quantitative restriction Measure restricting import of product by amount, number, volume or value, prohibited on imports between EU Member States under Article 34 TFEU and exports under Article 35.

Ratification National procedure to incorporate Treaties, usually either by national parliament or referendum.

Recommendation Non-binding 'soft law' under Article 288(5) TFEU.

Referendum lock Transfer of further powers from UK to EU requiring consent of UK voters in a referendum under the European Union Act 2011.

Regulation EU act of general application, binding all Member States in its entirety and directly applicable (Article 288(2) TFEU).

Regulatory act Act of general application apart from legislative act (Case C-583/11P *Inuit and others*).

Right of establishment Freedom to set up in business in another Member State under Articles 49–55 TFEU. Applies to companies and individuals.

Selling arrangement National rule restricting the way goods are sold – outside Article 34 TFEU if it does not discriminate against imports (Cases C-267 & 8/91 *Keck and Mithouard*).

Single market programme Required removal of barriers to free movement by end of 1992.

Sovereignty Capability of States to enact laws independently.

Special legislative procedure Enables Council to adopt legislation after consultation with Parliament where Treaties provide.

Standing (or *locus standi*) Entitlement to bring action before CJEU or General Court (e.g. Article 263 TFEU challenge)

State liability Member State is liable for breach of EU law where:

- rule of law breached is intended to confer rights on individuals;
- breach is sufficiently serious;
- there is a direct causal link between breach and damage suffered by injured party (Cases C-46 & 48/93 *Brasserie du Pêcheur and R* v. *Secretary of State for Transport ex p. Factortame (No. 3)*).

Subsidiarity Where EU does not have exclusive competence, it will act only where objectives of proposed action cannot be sufficiently achieved by Member States at central or regional level, but can be better achieved at EU level (Article 5(3) TEU).

Supranationalism Decision-making above level of Member States, but binding States concerned.

Supremacy See 'primacy'.

Three-pillar structure Introduced under Maastricht Treaty but collapsed into single pillar (EU) by Treaty of Lisbon. Pillar one covered the EC, regulated by law; pillar two covered Common Foreign and Security Policy; and pillar three, police and judicial cooperation in criminal matters. Pillars two and three were regulated by intergovernmental cooperation.

Transposition (or implementation) Process by which Member State gives effect to EU obligation under national law.

Treaty International agreement between sovereign states.

Trilogues Preparatory meetings during the legislative process, usually between a Council representative, a senior Commission official and several MEPs.

Union Citizenship Operates in parallel to national citizenship to provide residence and political rights in EU for Member State nationals under Article 20 TFEU.

Index